W9-COV-104

Arata
THE LEGEND

19

We are Man, born of Heaven and Earth,
Moon and Sun and everything under them.

Eyes, Ears, Nose, Tongue, Body, Mind...

Purity will pierce evil and
open up the world of darkness.

All life will be reborn and invigorated.

Appear now.

STORY & ART BY
Yuu Watase

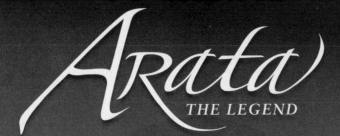

Arata
THE LEGEND

CHARACTERS

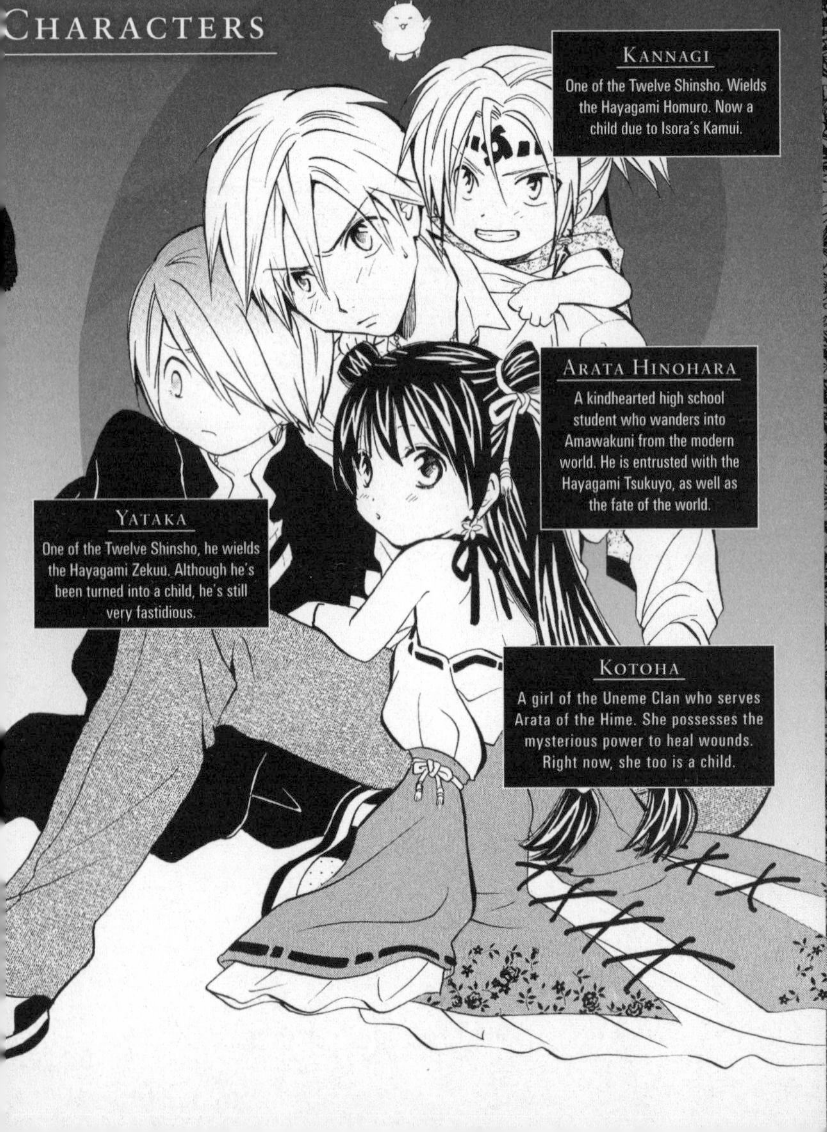

KANNAGI
One of the Twelve Shinsho. Wields the Hayagami Homuro. Now a child due to Isora's Kamui.

ARATA HINOHARA
A kindhearted high school student who wanders into Amawakuni from the modern world. He is entrusted with the Hayagami Tsukuyo, as well as the fate of the world.

YATAKA
One of the Twelve Shinsho, he wields the Hayagami Zekuu. Although he's been turned into a child, he's still very fastidious.

KOTOHA
A girl of the Uneme Clan who serves Arata of the Hime. She possesses the mysterious power to heal wounds. Right now, she too is a child.

MIKUSA
Swordswoman of the Hime Clan. Although she is an Uneme, she cannot use the power of the Amatsuriki. Is this because she, like Hinohara, came from the modern world...?!

KADOWAKI
Arata Hinohara's one-time friend and now archenemy, summoned into the other world and made a Sho in order to force Arata to submit to the Hayagami called Orochi.

ISORA
One of the Six Sho. Wields the Hayagami Kohaku, which controls words. He kidnaps Mikusa and waits for Arata at his palace.

THE STORY THUS FAR

Arata Hinohara, a modern Japanese high school student, finds himself in Amawakuni, a land in another dimension. There he is chosen as the new wielder of the legendary Hayagami Tsukuyo and embarks on a quest to save Princess Hime, who has kept the powers of the various Hayagami in check but now hovers precariously near death.

Arata and his companions have defeated Kikutsune, one of the Six Sho, and have entered the territory of his erstwhile ally, Isora, who possesses a Hayagami with the ability to unleash the power of the written word. Isora is ready for them and deals first with Arata's friends, abducting Mikusa and turning Kannagi, Yataka and Kotoha into children.

Arata and his infantalized comrades head for Isora's palace in order to rescue Mikusa, but fiendish traps have been laid by Isora to test and ultimately break the bonds of trust and loyalty that bind Arata and his friends together. Arata loses the ability to speak and must rely on the written word to take the fight to his latest deadly adversary!

19
Arata
THE LEGEND

CONTENTS

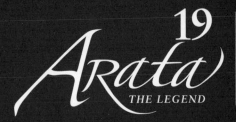

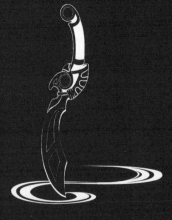

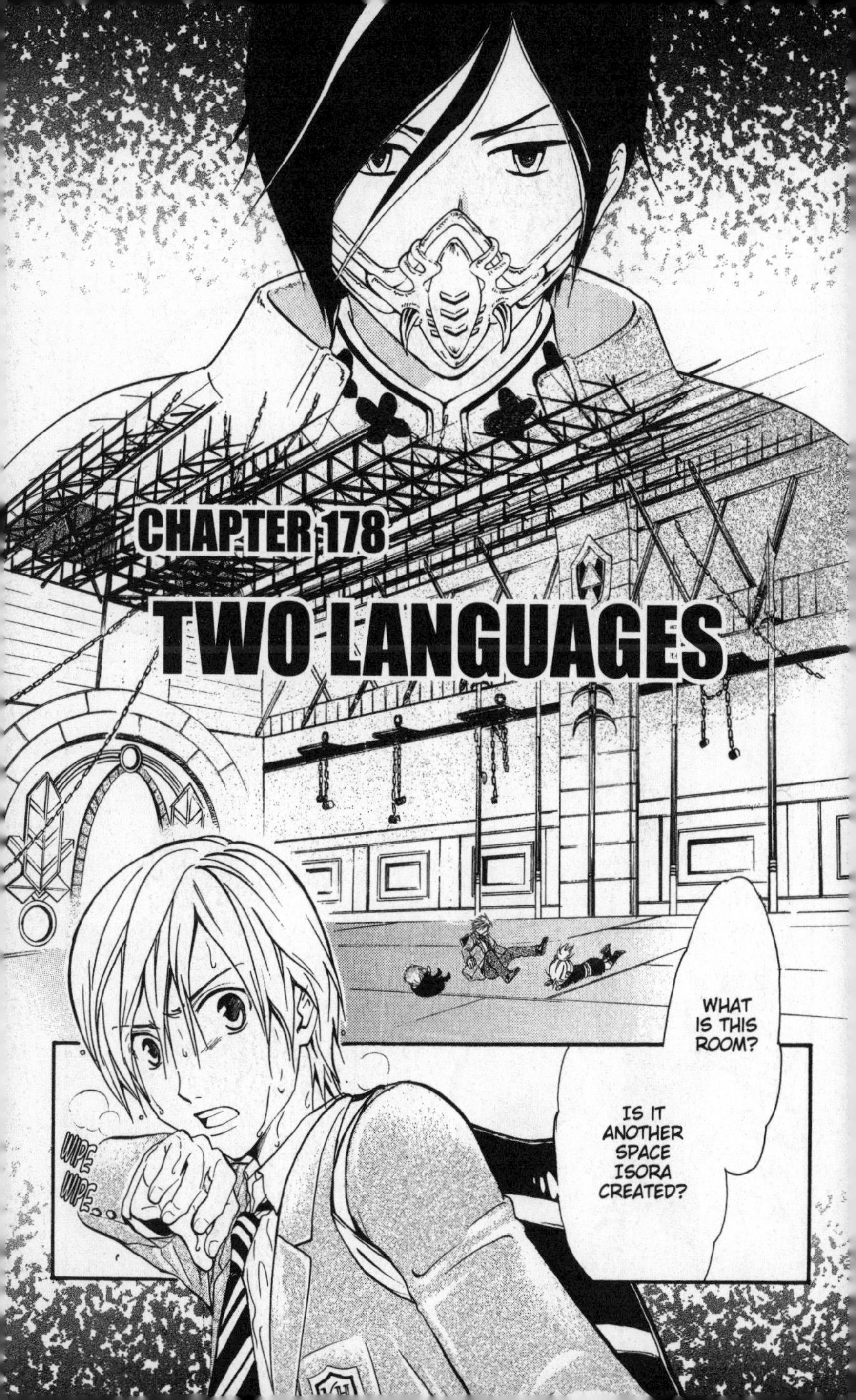
CHAPTER 178
TWO LANGUAGES
WHAT IS THIS ROOM?
IS IT ANOTHER SPACE ISORA CREATED?
WIPE WIPE...

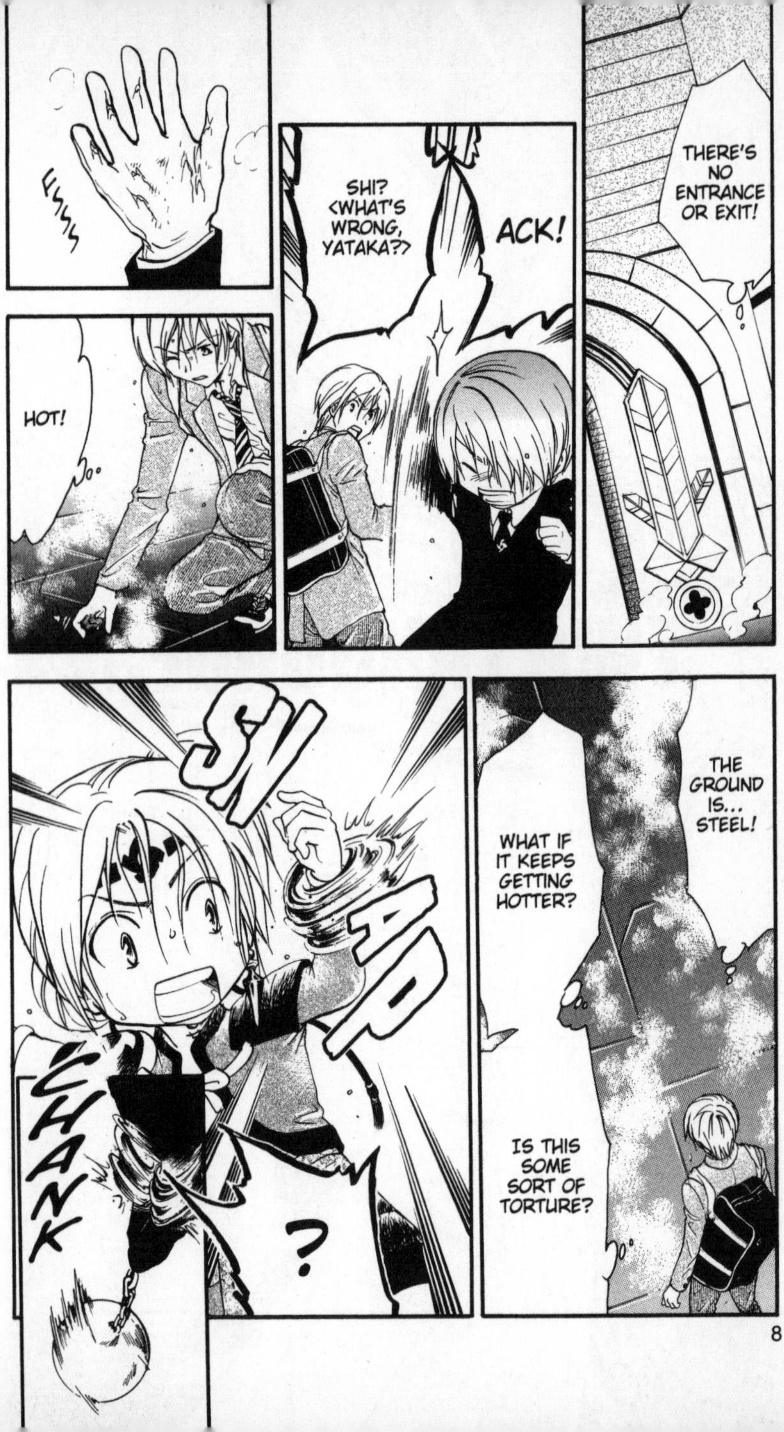
THERE'S NO ENTRANCE OR EXIT!
ACK!
SHI? <WHAT'S WRONG, YATAKA?>
HOT!
THE GROUND IS... STEEL!
WHAT IF IT KEEPS GETTING HOTTER?
IS THIS SOME SORT OF TORTURE?
SNAP
CHANK
?

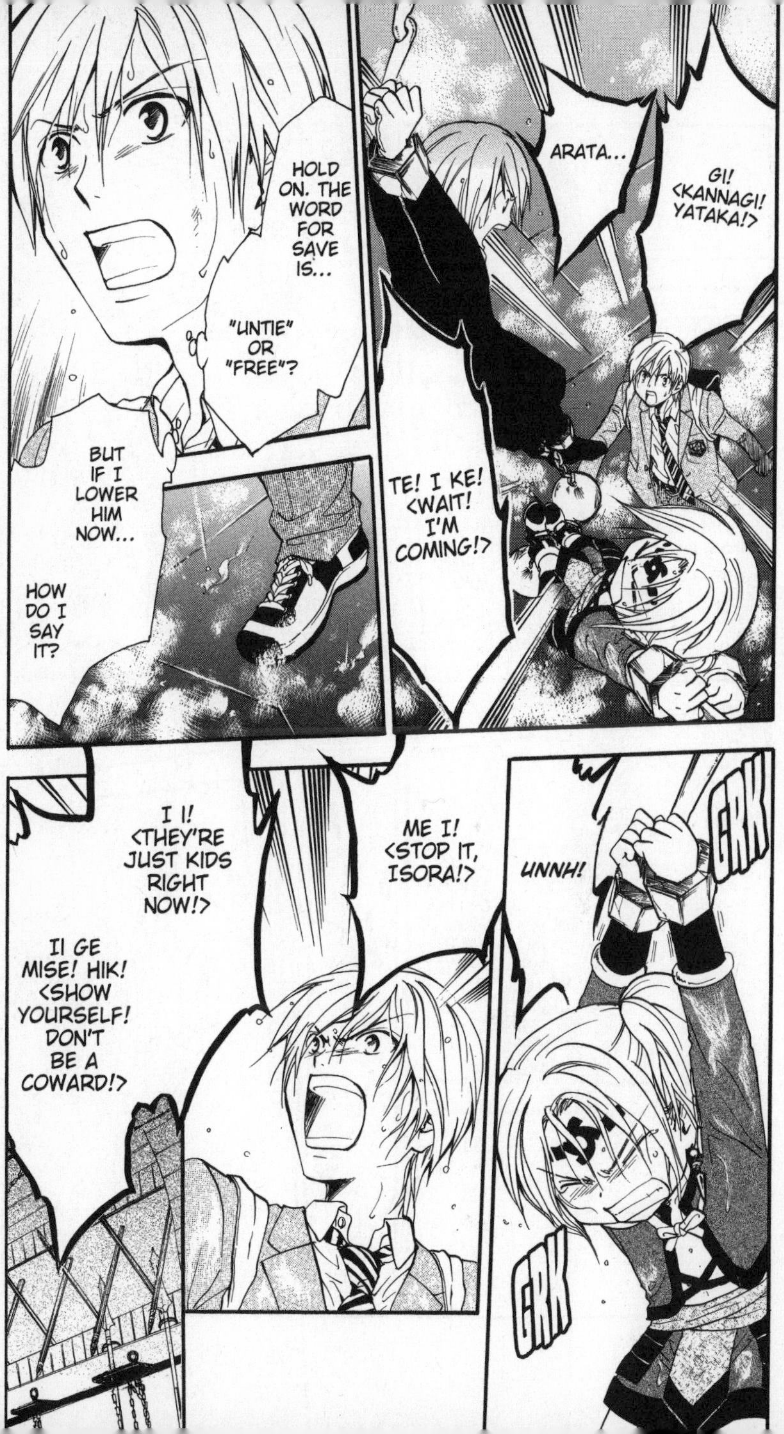
GI! <KANNAGI! YATAKA!>
ARATA...
TE! I KE! <WAIT! I'M COMING!>
HOLD ON. THE WORD FOR SAVE IS...
"UNTIE" OR "FREE"?
BUT IF I LOWER HIM NOW...
HOW DO I SAY IT?
GRK
UNNH!
GRK
ME I! <STOP IT, ISORA!>
I I! <THEY'RE JUST KIDS RIGHT NOW!>
II GE MISE! HIK! <SHOW YOURSELF! DON'T BE A COWARD!>

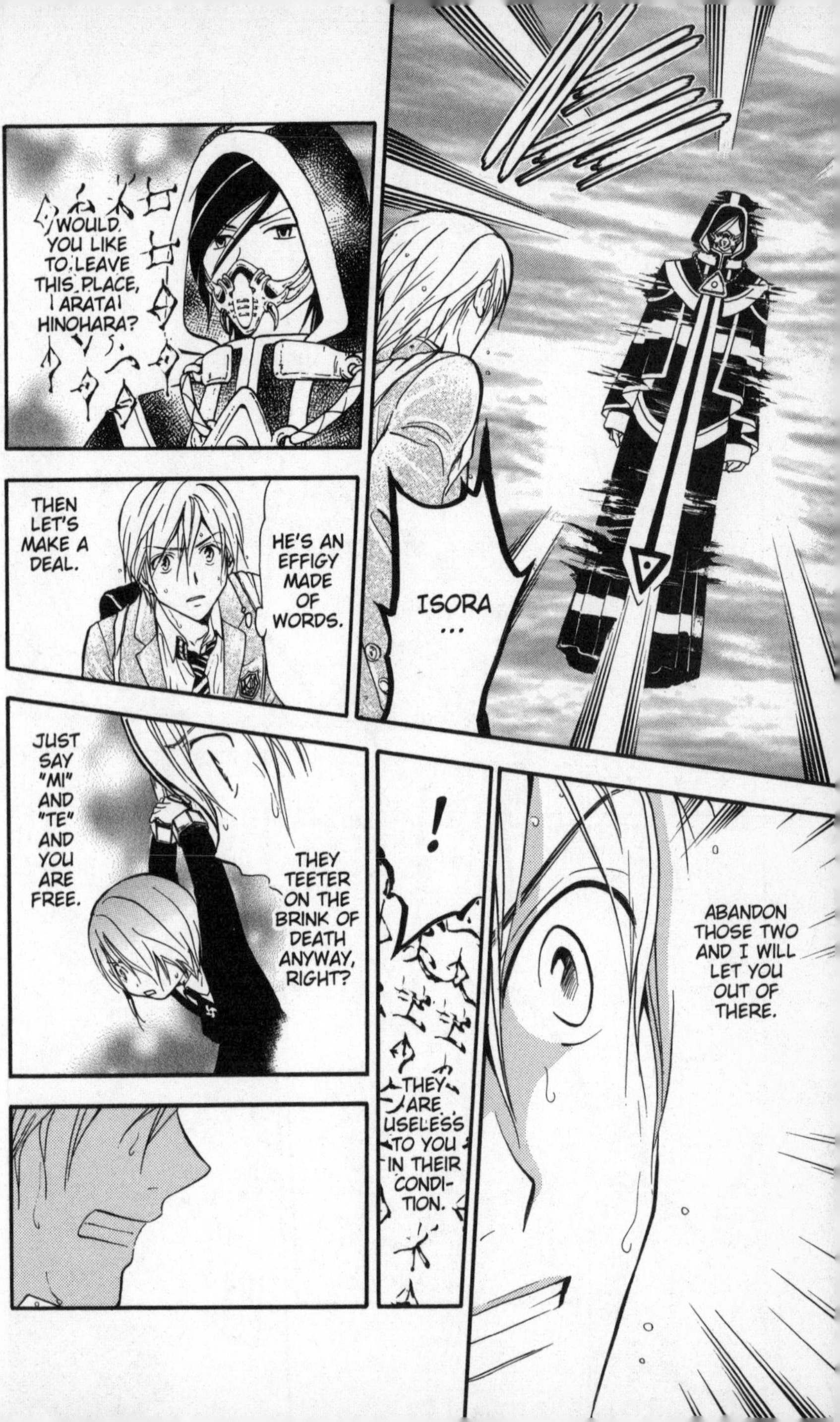
ISORA ...
WOULD YOU LIKE TO LEAVE THIS PLACE, ARATA HINOHARA?
HE'S AN EFFIGY MADE OF WORDS.
THEN LET'S MAKE A DEAL.
ABANDON THOSE TWO AND I WILL LET YOU OUT OF THERE.
!
THEY ARE USELESS TO YOU IN THEIR CONDI-TION.
THEY TEETER ON THE BRINK OF DEATH ANYWAY, RIGHT?
JUST SAY "MI" AND "TE" AND YOU ARE FREE.

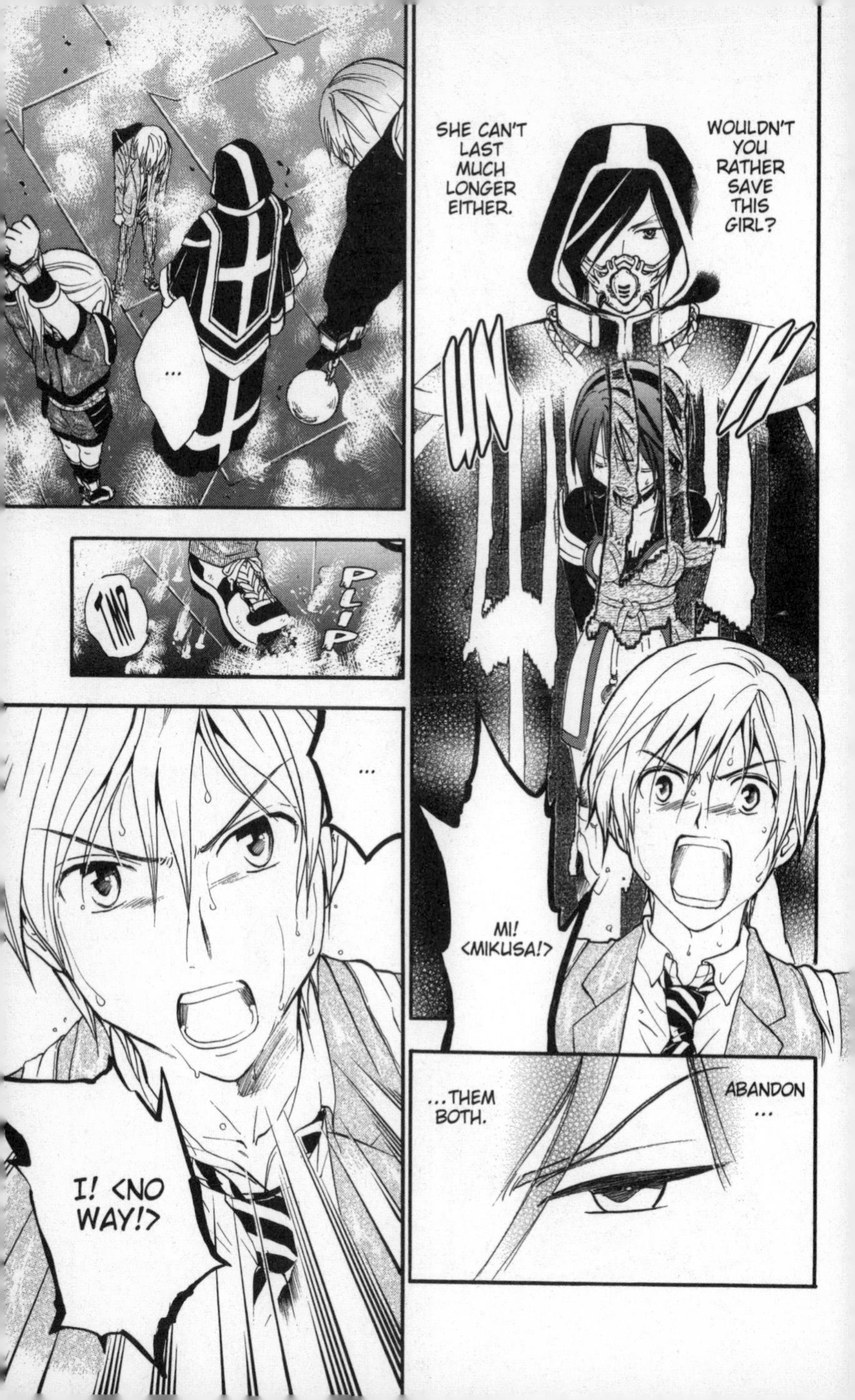
WOULDN'T YOU RATHER SAVE THIS GIRL?
SHE CAN'T LAST MUCH LONGER EITHER.
UNH
MI! <MIKUSA!>
ABANDON ...
...THEM BOTH.
...
TMP
PLIP
...
I! <NO WAY!>

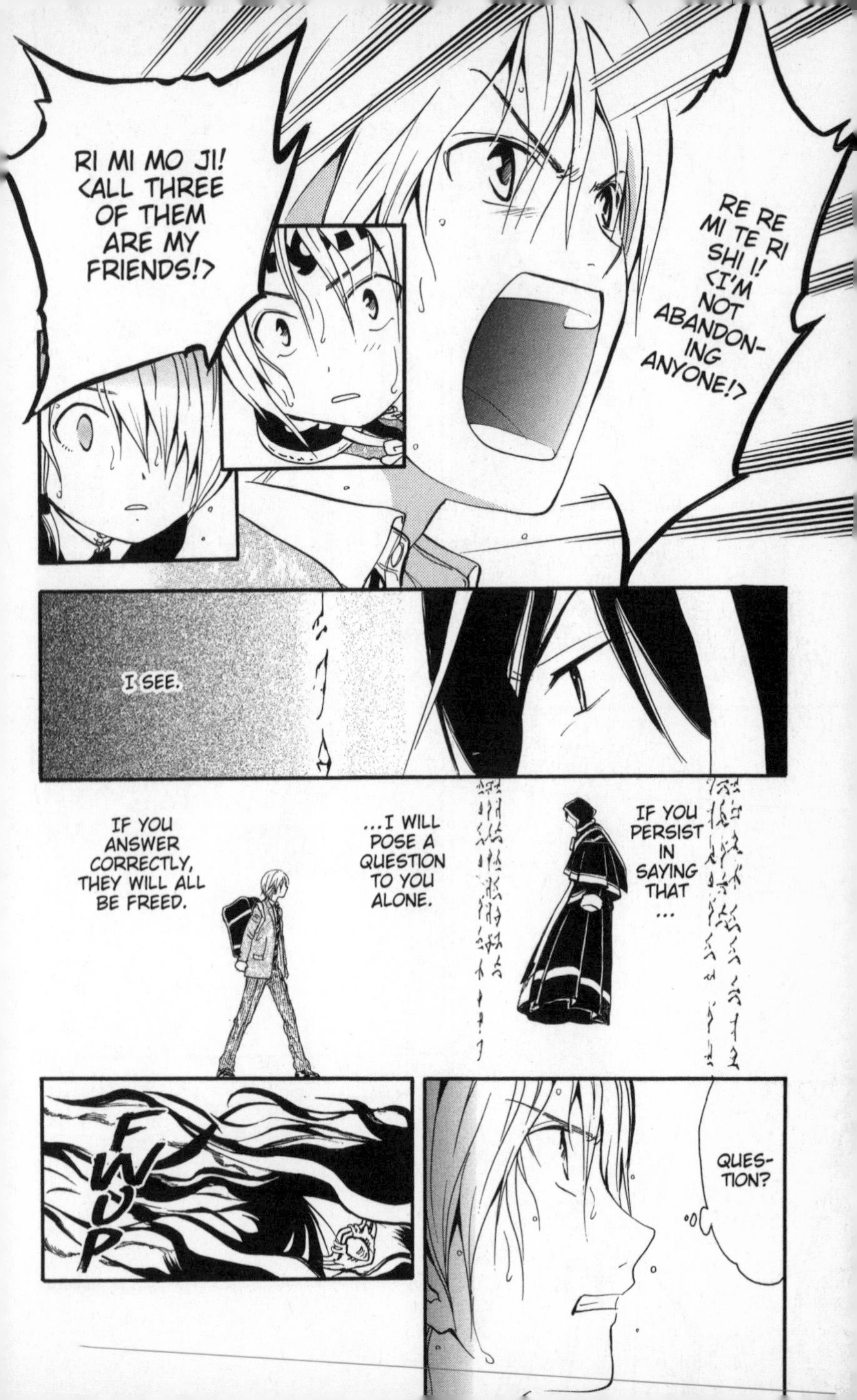
RE RE MI TE RI SHI I! <I'M NOT ABANDONING ANYONE!>
RI MI MO JI! <ALL THREE OF THEM ARE MY FRIENDS!>
I SEE.
IF YOU PERSIST IN SAYING THAT ...
...I WILL POSE A QUESTION TO YOU ALONE.
IF YOU ANSWER CORRECTLY, THEY WILL ALL BE FREED.
QUESTION?
FWOP

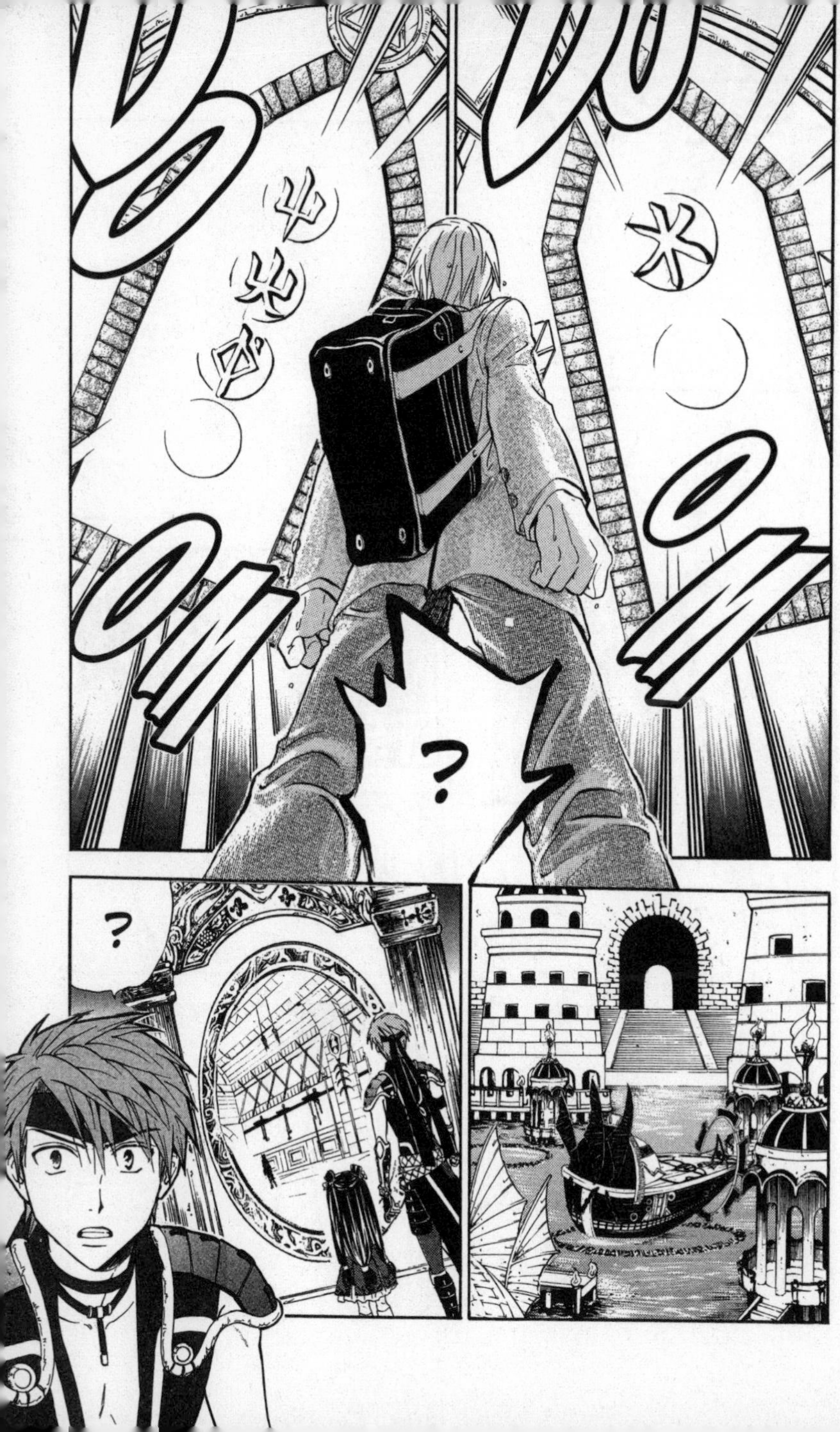
?
?

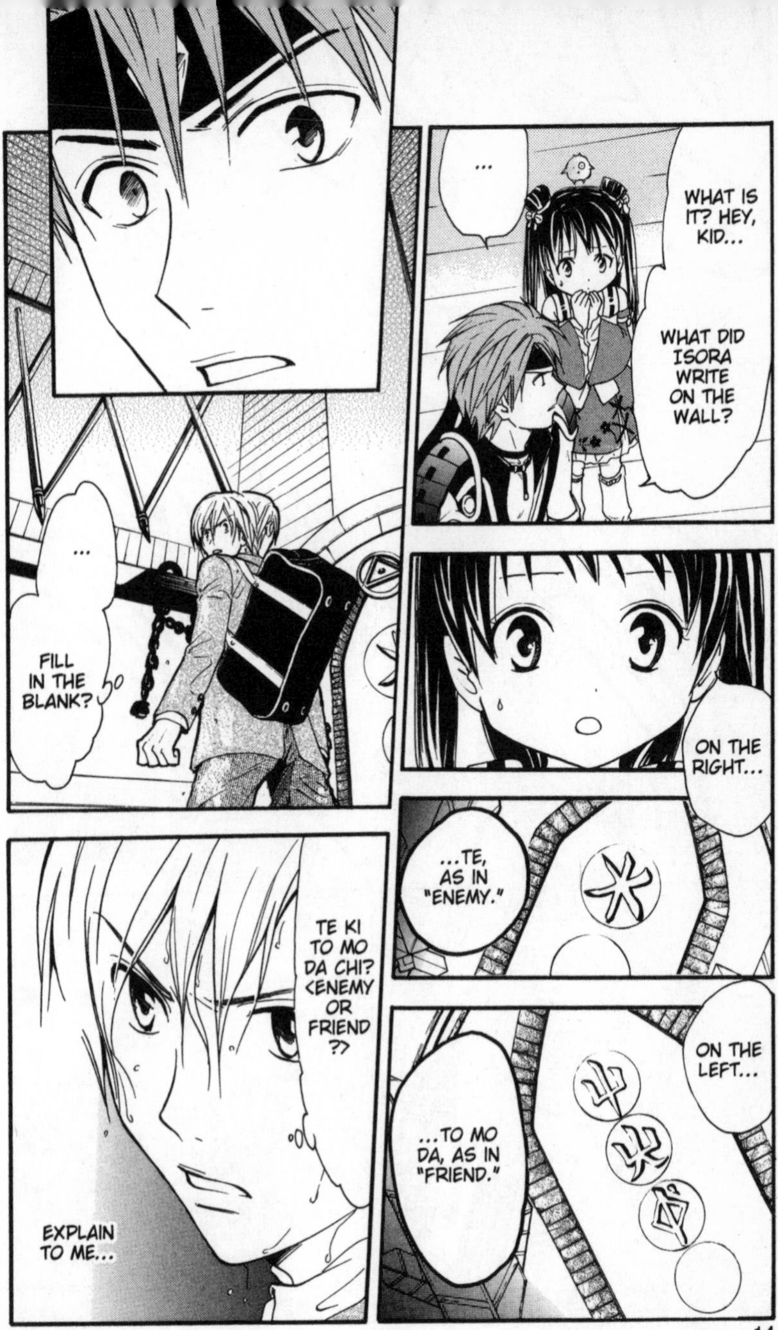
WHAT IS IT? HEY, KID...
WHAT DID ISORA WRITE ON THE WALL?
...
ON THE RIGHT...
...
FILL IN THE BLANK?
...TE, AS IN "ENEMY."
ON THE LEFT...
...TO MO DA, AS IN "FRIEND."
TE KI TO MO DA CHI? <ENEMY OR FRIEND?>
EXPLAIN TO ME...

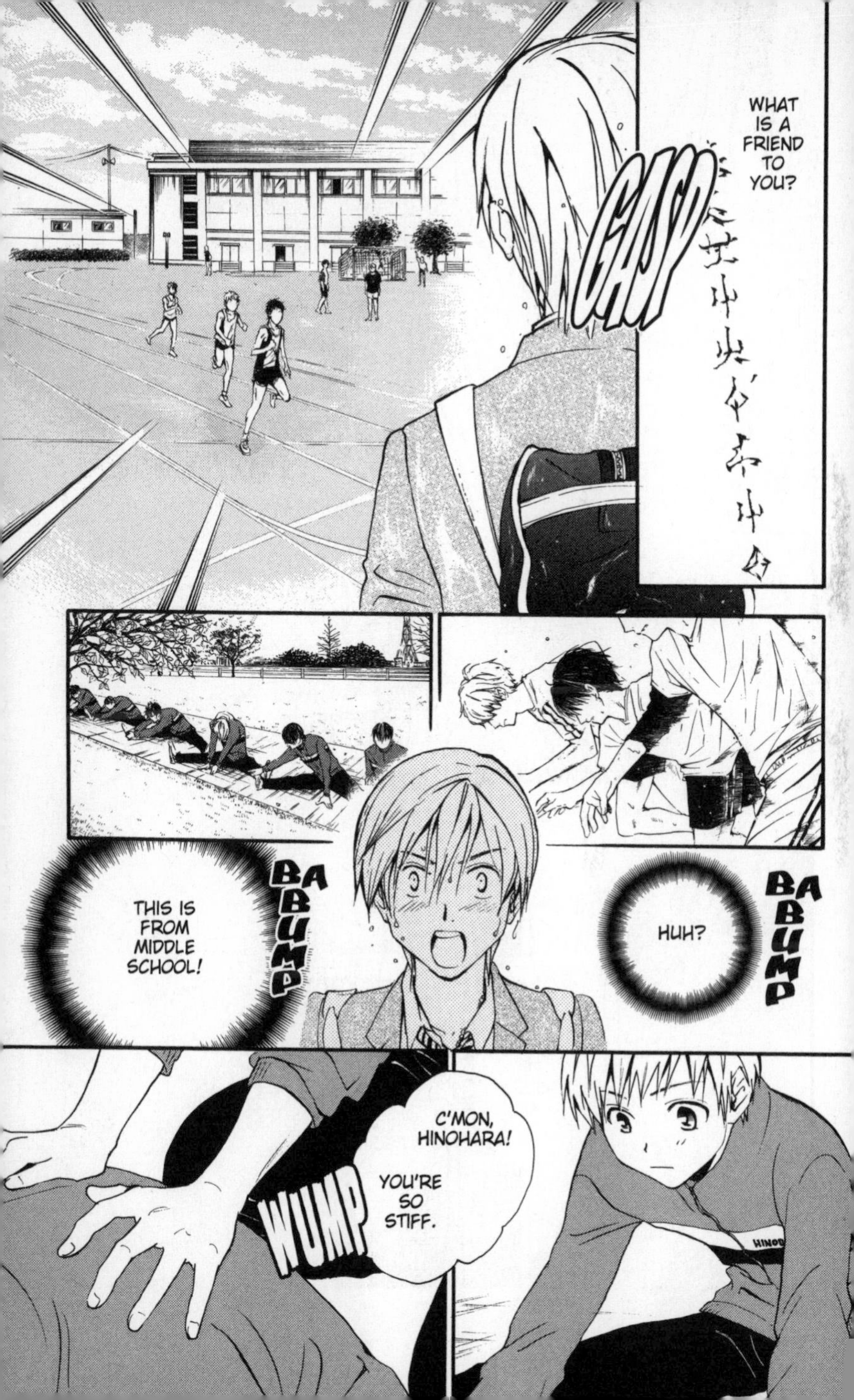
WHAT IS A FRIEND TO YOU?
GASP
BABUMP
HUH?
THIS IS FROM MIDDLE SCHOOL!
BABUMP
C'MON, HINOHARA!
YOU'RE SO STIFF.
WUMP

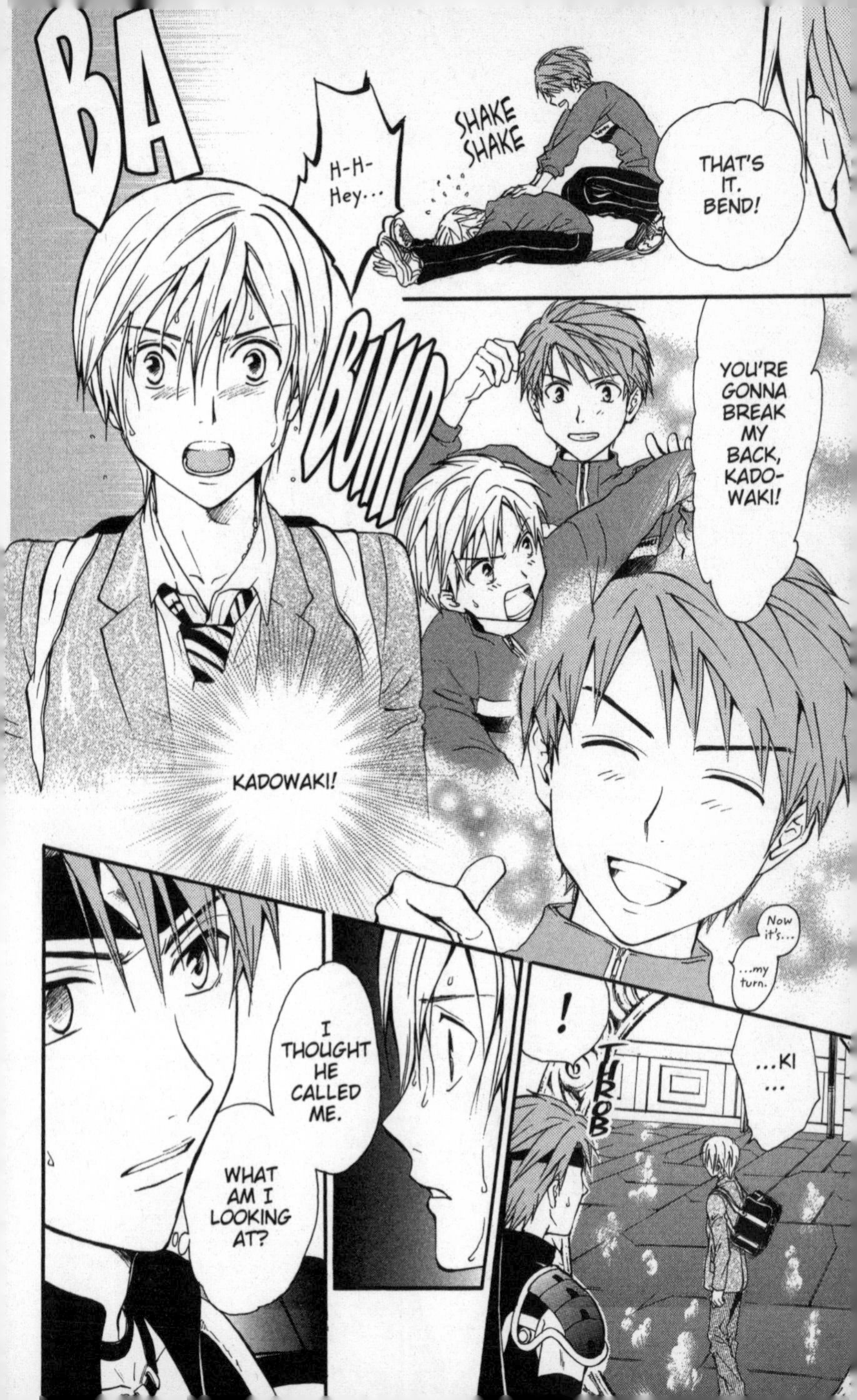
THAT'S IT. BEND!
SHAKE SHAKE
H-H- Hey...
YOU'RE GONNA BREAK MY BACK, KADO-WAKI!
Now it's...
...my turn.
BUMP
BA
KADOWAKI!
...KI ...
THROB
!
I THOUGHT HE CALLED ME.
WHAT AM I LOOKING AT?

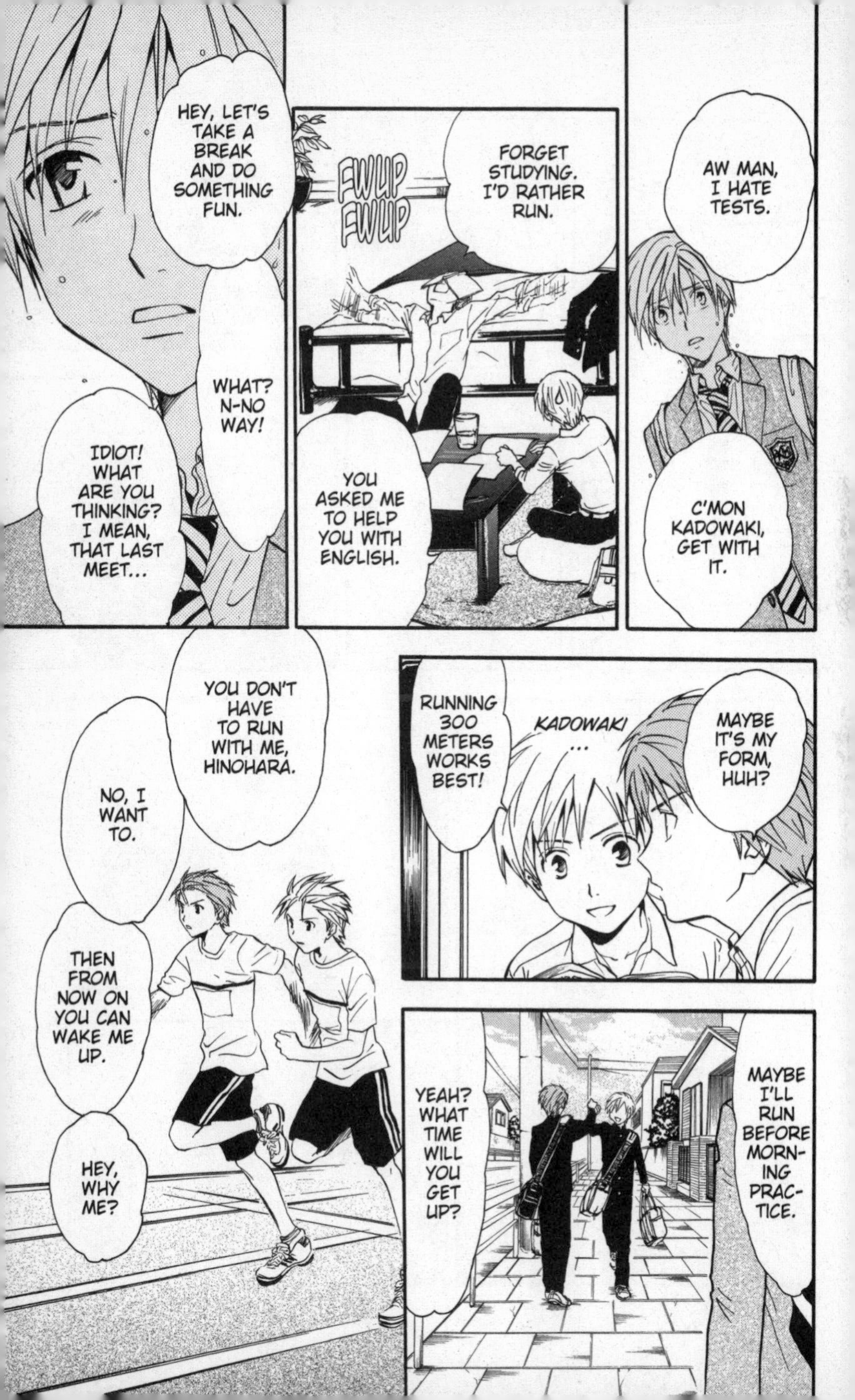
AW MAN, I HATE TESTS.
C'MON KADOWAKI, GET WITH IT.
FORGET STUDYING. I'D RATHER RUN.
FWUP FWUP
YOU ASKED ME TO HELP YOU WITH ENGLISH.
HEY, LET'S TAKE A BREAK AND DO SOMETHING FUN.
WHAT? N-NO WAY!
IDIOT! WHAT ARE YOU THINKING? I MEAN, THAT LAST MEET...
MAYBE IT'S MY FORM, HUH?
KADOWAKI...
RUNNING 300 METERS WORKS BEST!
MAYBE I'LL RUN BEFORE MORNING PRACTICE.
YEAH? WHAT TIME WILL YOU GET UP?
YOU DON'T HAVE TO RUN WITH ME, HINOHARA.
NO, I WANT TO.
THEN FROM NOW ON YOU CAN WAKE ME UP.
HEY, WHY ME?

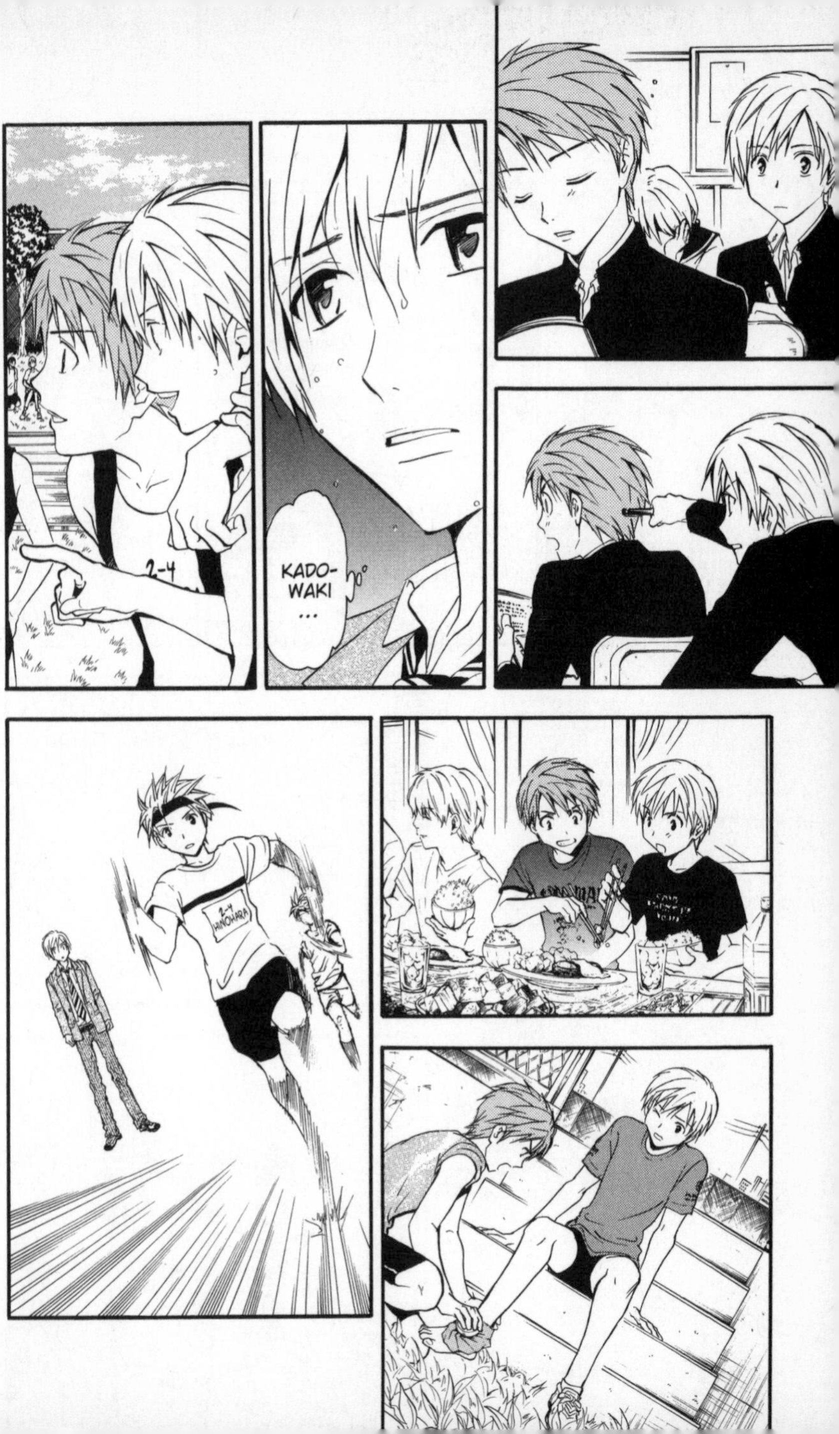
KADO-WAKI ...
2-4
2-4 HINOHARA

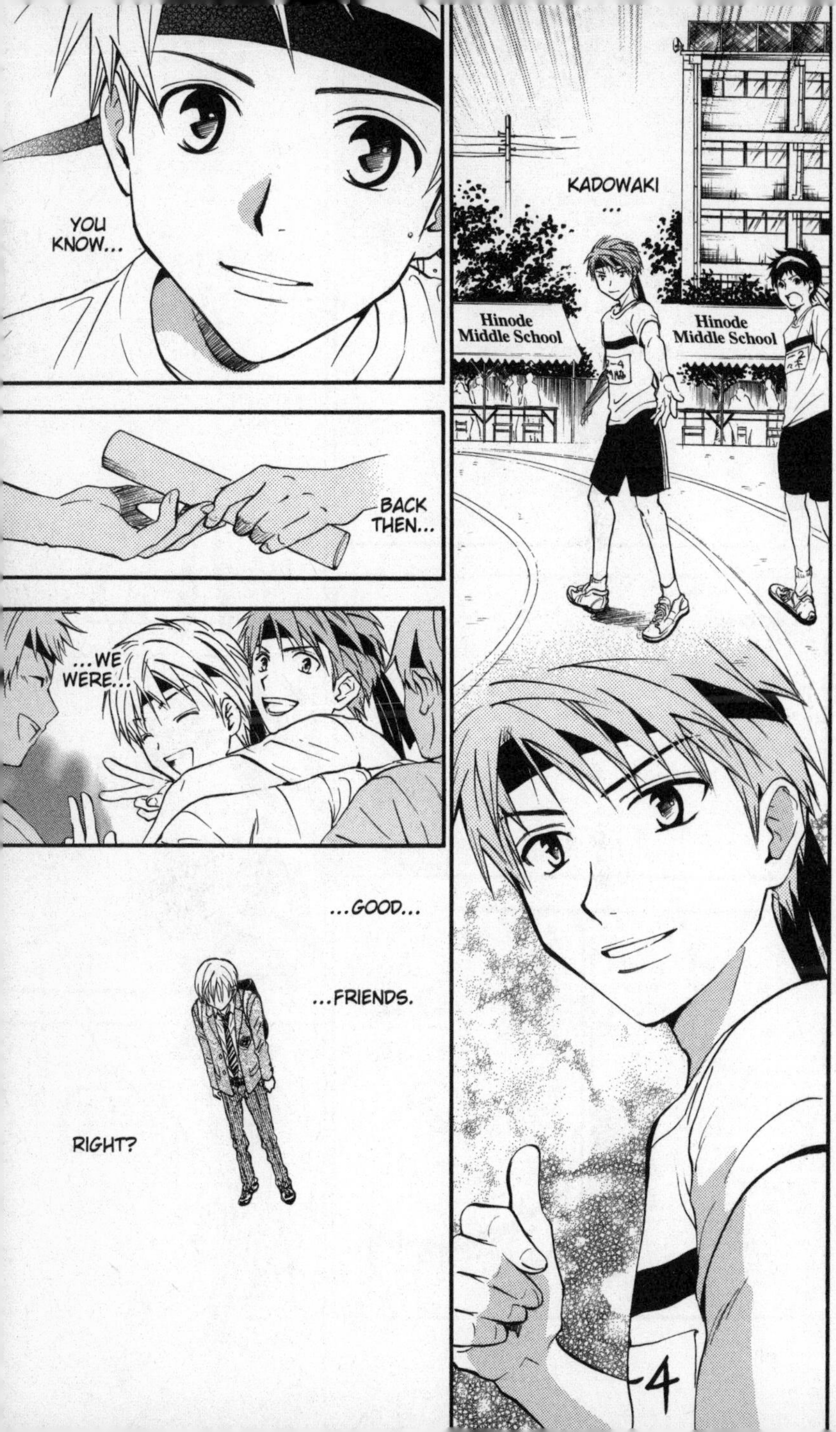
KADOWAKI ...
Hinode Middle School
Hinode Middle School
4
YOU KNOW...
BACK THEN...
...WE WERE...
...GOOD...
...FRIENDS.
RIGHT?

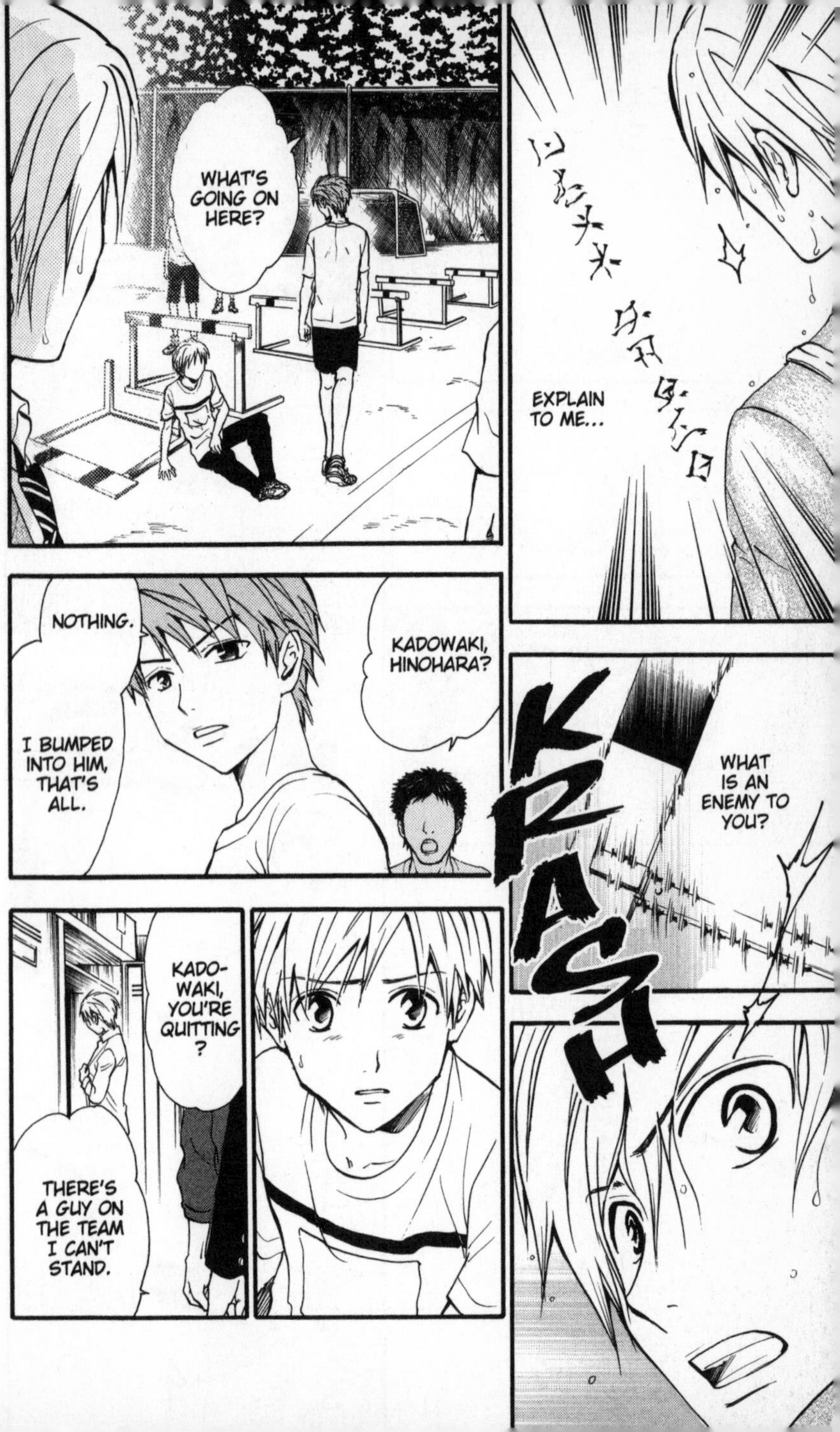
EXPLAIN TO ME...
KRASH
WHAT IS AN ENEMY TO YOU?
WHAT'S GOING ON HERE?
KADOWAKI, HINOHARA?
NOTHING.
I BUMPED INTO HIM, THAT'S ALL.
KADO-WAKI, YOU'RE QUITTING?
THERE'S A GUY ON THE TEAM I CAN'T STAND.

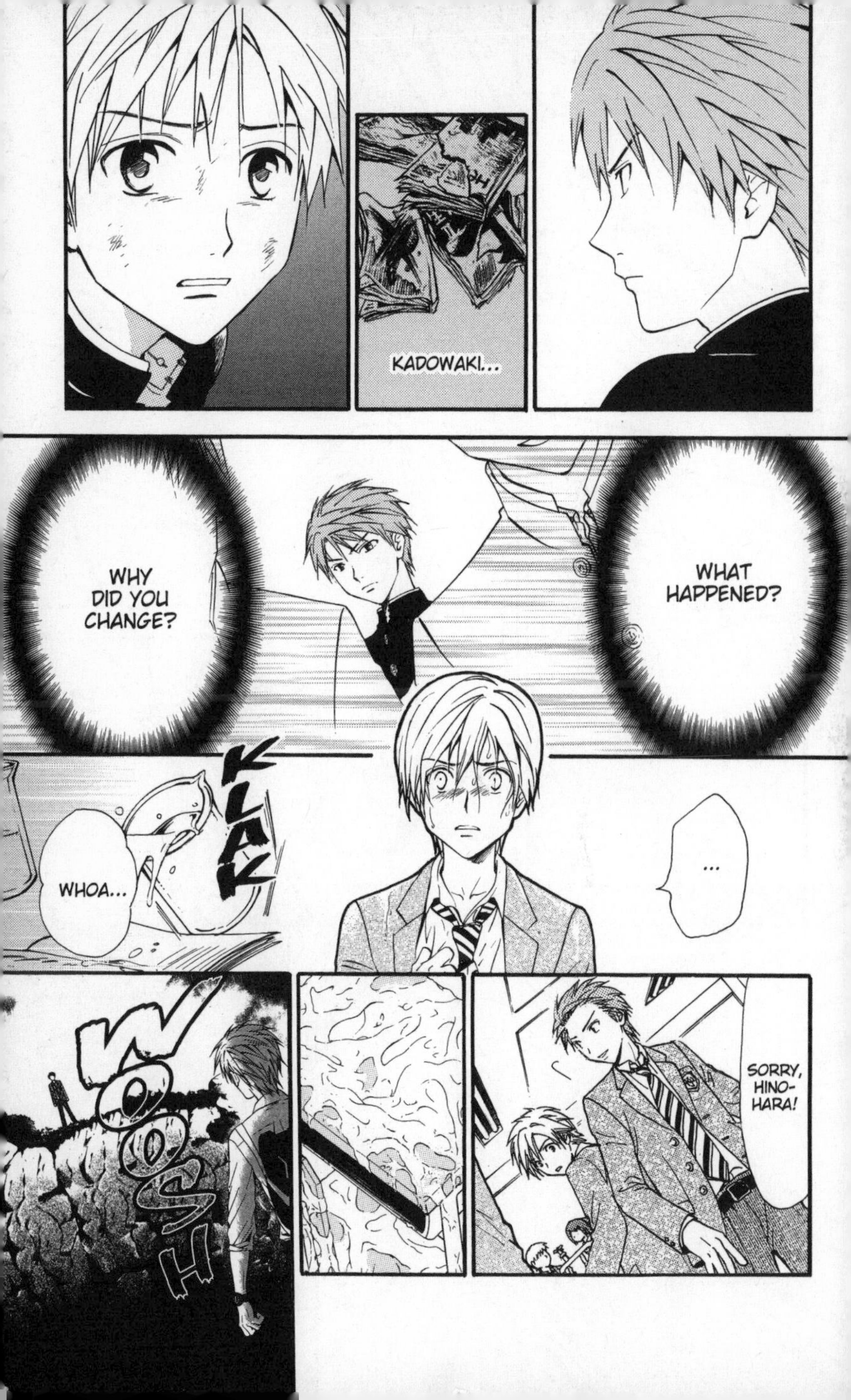
KADOWAKI...
WHAT HAPPENED?
WHY DID YOU CHANGE?
...
KLAK
WHOA...
SORRY, HINO-HARA!
WOOSH

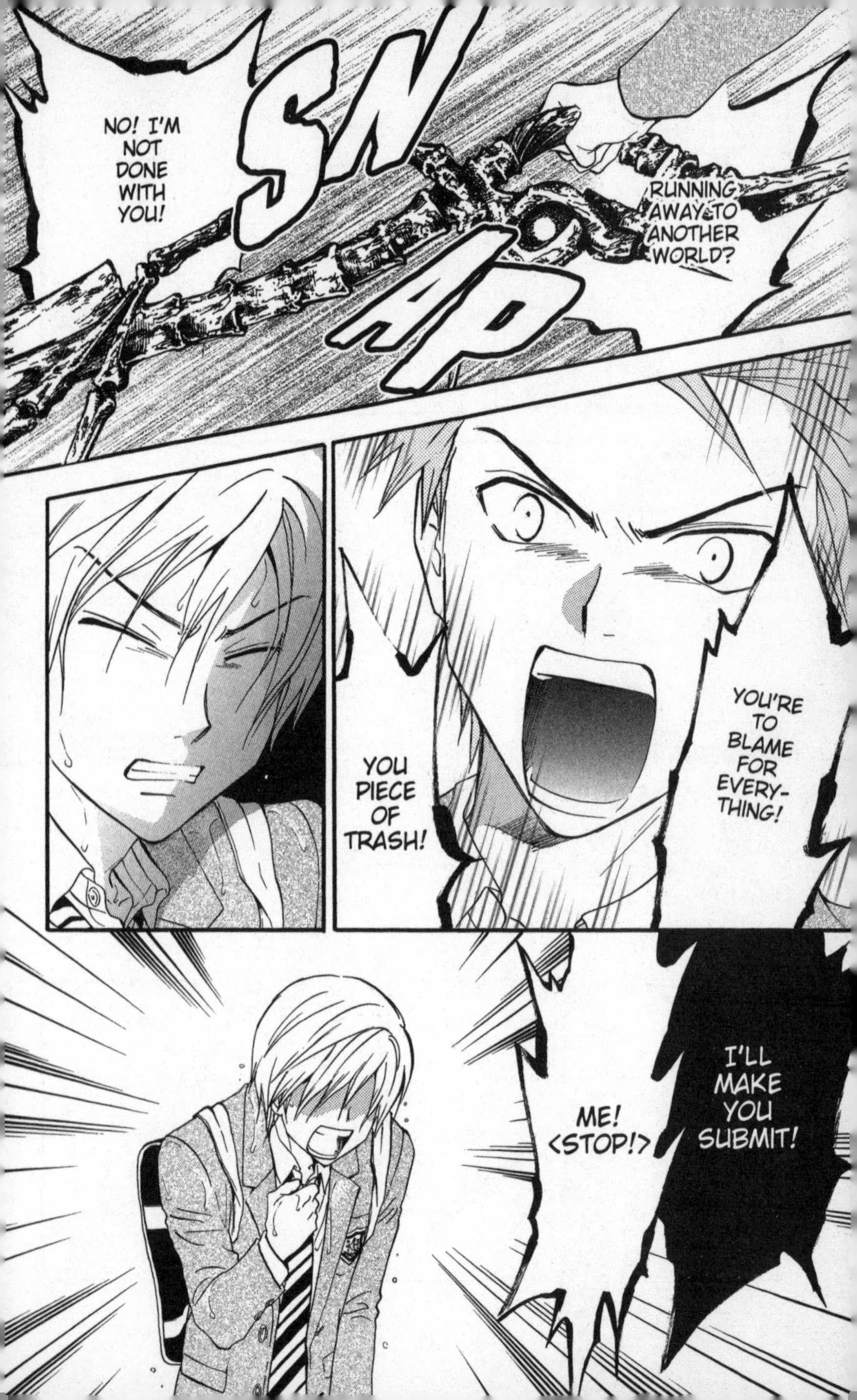
RUNNING AWAY TO ANOTHER WORLD?
SNAP
NO! I'M NOT DONE WITH YOU!
YOU'RE TO BLAME FOR EVERY-THING!
YOU PIECE OF TRASH!
I'LL MAKE YOU SUBMIT!
ME! <STOP!>

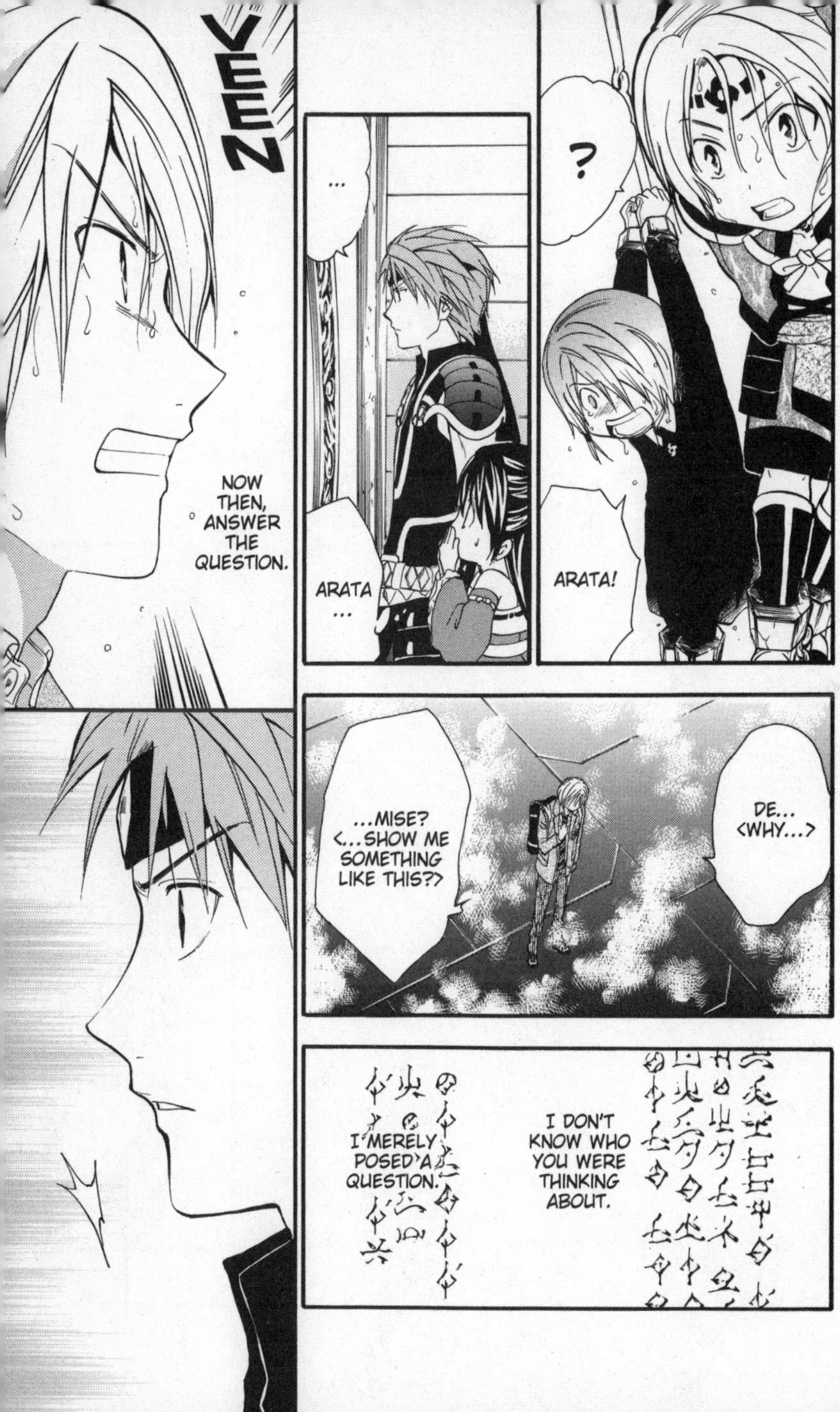
?
ARATA!
...
ARATA ...
VEEN
NOW THEN, ANSWER THE QUESTION.
DE... <WHY...>
...MISE? <...SHOW ME SOMETHING LIKE THIS?>
I DON'T KNOW WHO YOU WERE THINKING ABOUT.
I MERELY POSED A QUESTION.

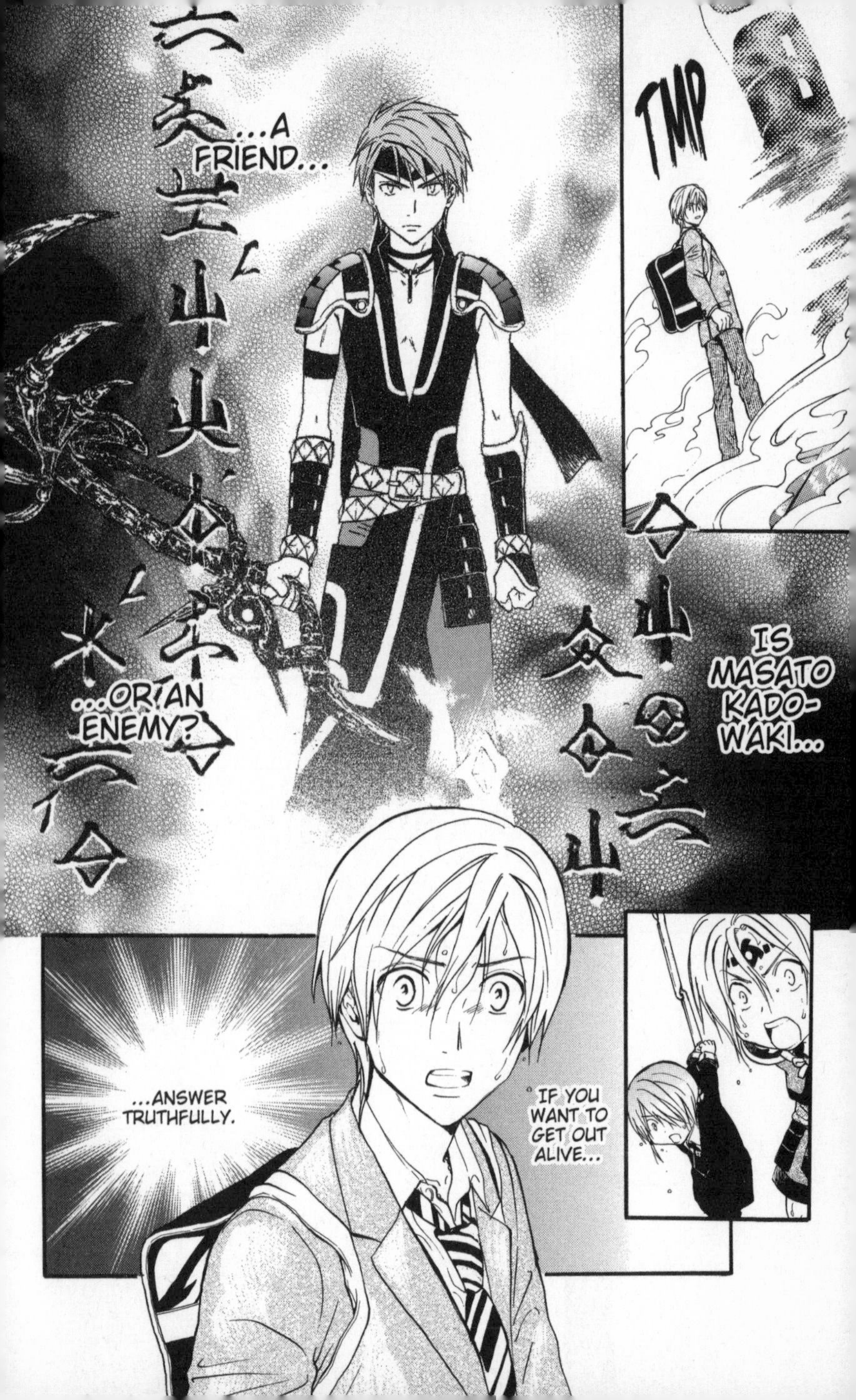
TMP
IS MASATO KADO-WAKI...
...A FRIEND...
...OR AN ENEMY?
IF YOU WANT TO GET OUT ALIVE...
...ANSWER TRUTHFULLY.

CHAPTER 179
INTERROGATION

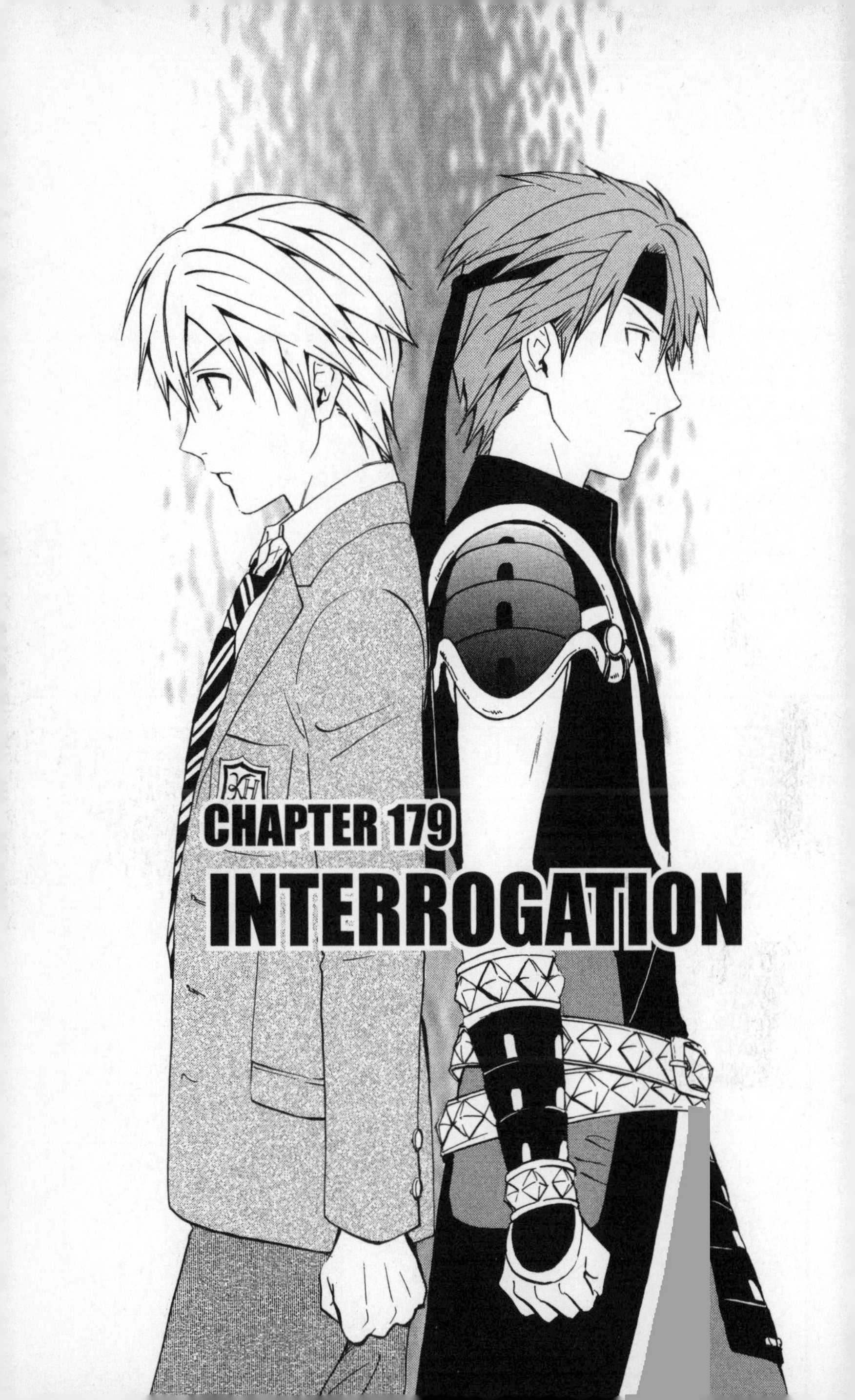

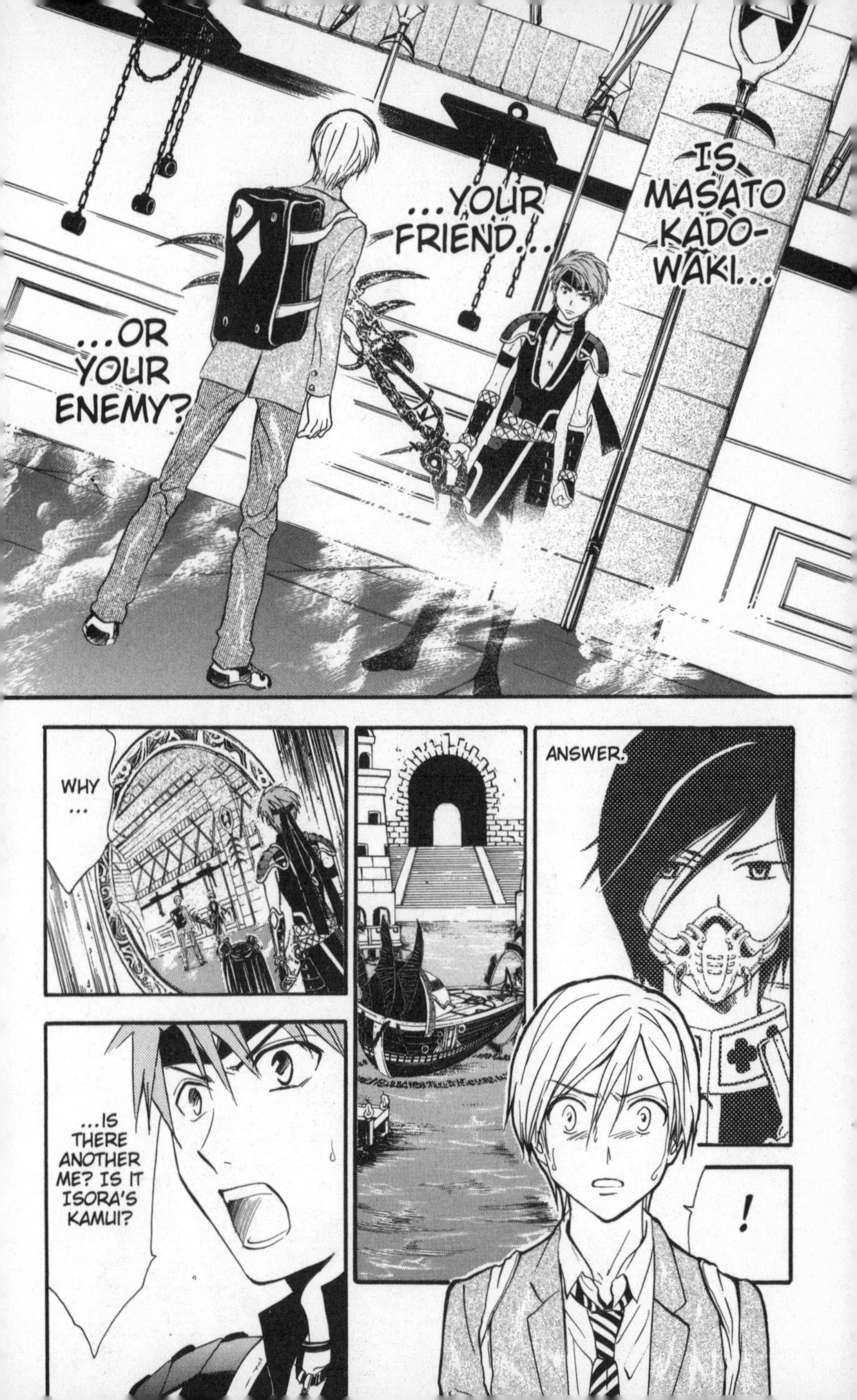
IS MASATO KADOWAKI...
...YOUR FRIEND...
...OR YOUR ENEMY?
ANSWER.
!
WHY ...
...IS THERE ANOTHER ME? IS IT ISORA'S KAMUI?

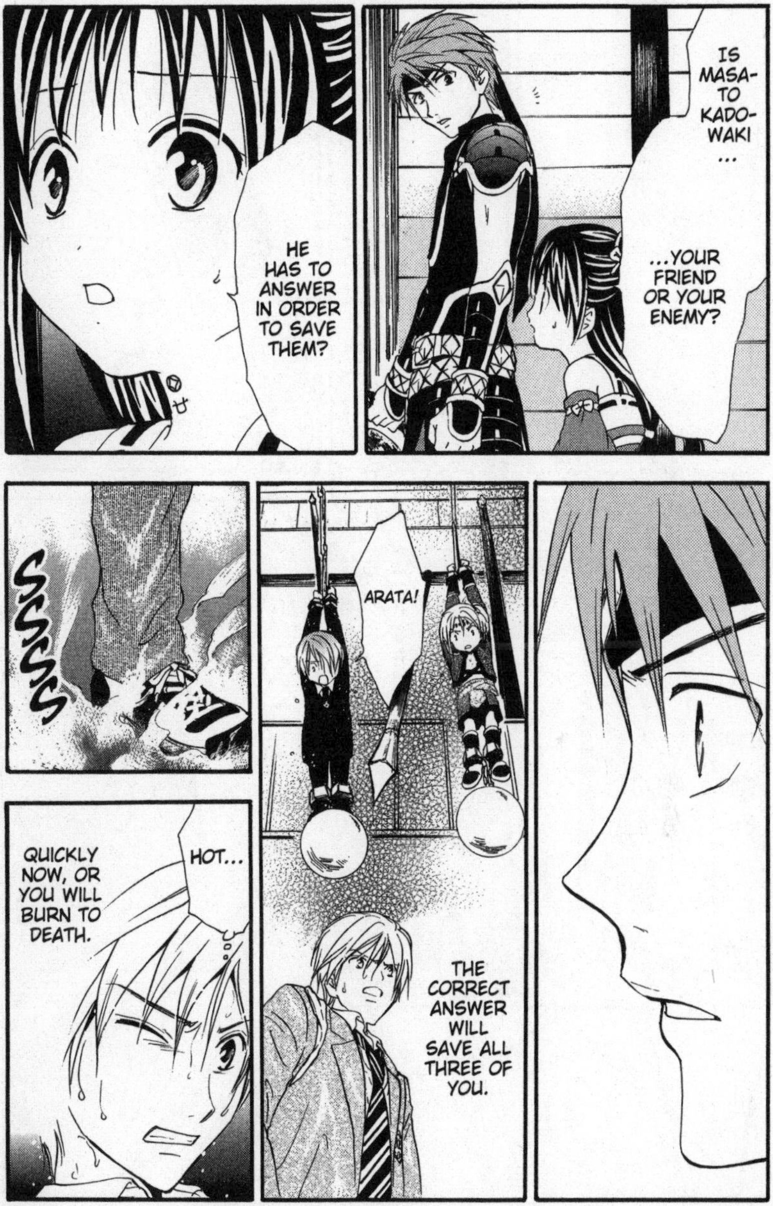
IS MASA-TO KADO-WAKI ...
...YOUR FRIEND OR YOUR ENEMY?
HE HAS TO ANSWER IN ORDER TO SAVE THEM?
ARATA!
THE CORRECT ANSWER WILL SAVE ALL THREE OF YOU.
SSSSS
HOT...
QUICKLY NOW, OR YOU WILL BURN TO DEATH.

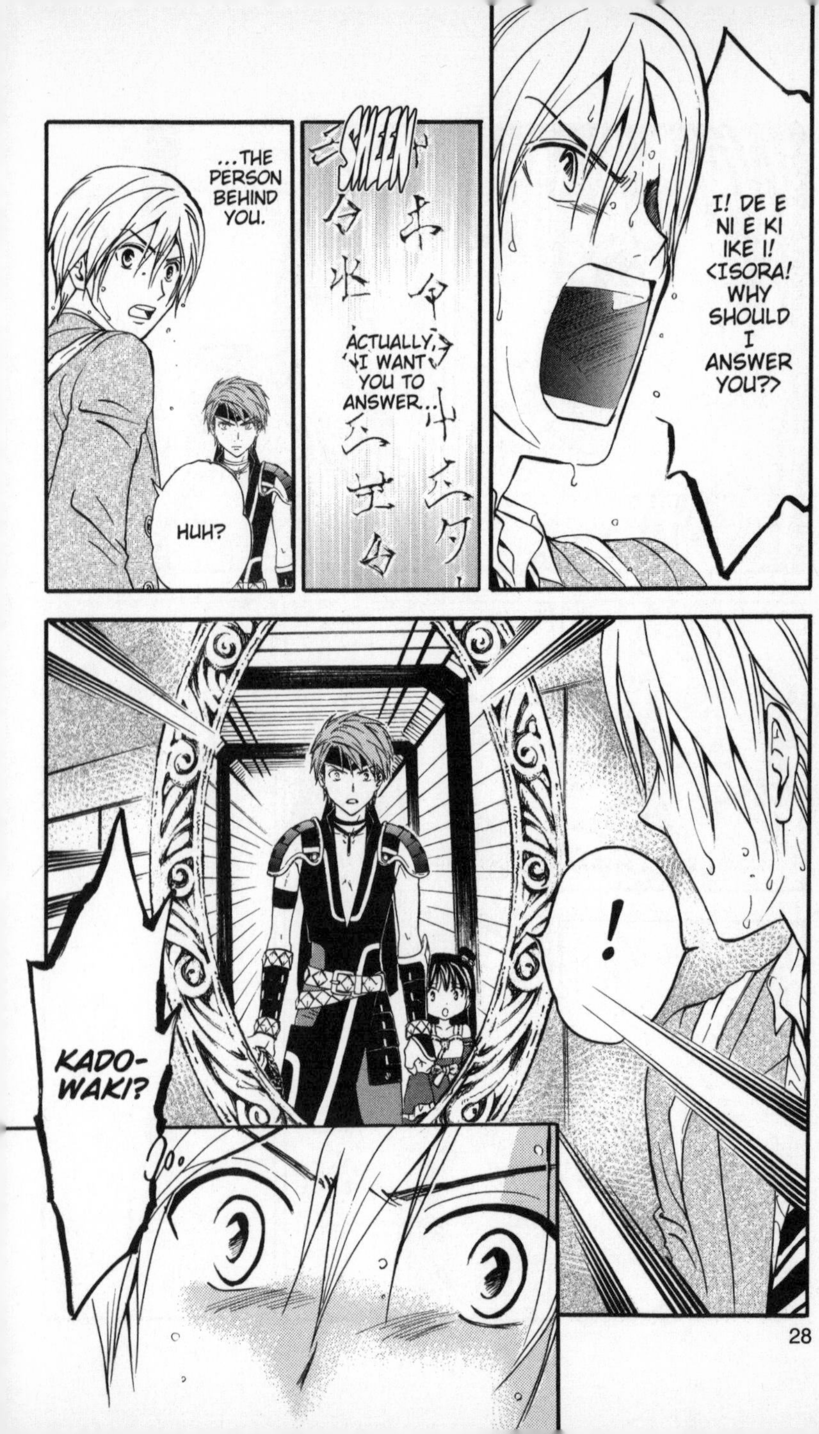
I! DE E NI E KI IKE I!
<ISORA! WHY SHOULD I ANSWER YOU?>
SHEEN
ACTUALLY, I WANT YOU TO ANSWER...
...THE PERSON BEHIND YOU.
HUH?
!
KADO-WAKI?

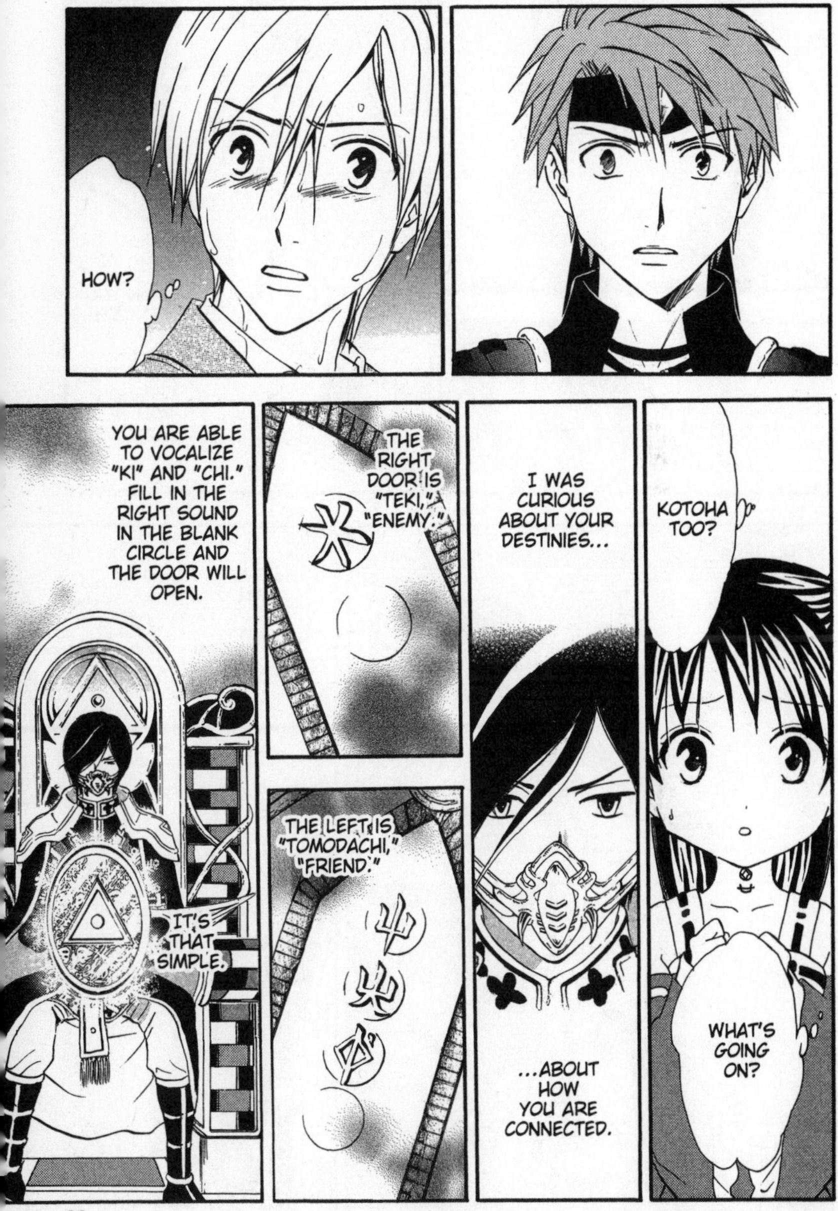
HOW?
KOTOHA TOO?
WHAT'S GOING ON?
I WAS CURIOUS ABOUT YOUR DESTINIES...
...ABOUT HOW YOU ARE CONNECTED.
THE RIGHT DOOR IS "TEKI," "ENEMY."
THE LEFT IS "TOMODACHI," "FRIEND."
YOU ARE ABLE TO VOCALIZE "KI" AND "CHI." FILL IN THE RIGHT SOUND IN THE BLANK CIRCLE AND THE DOOR WILL OPEN.
IT'S THAT SIMPLE.

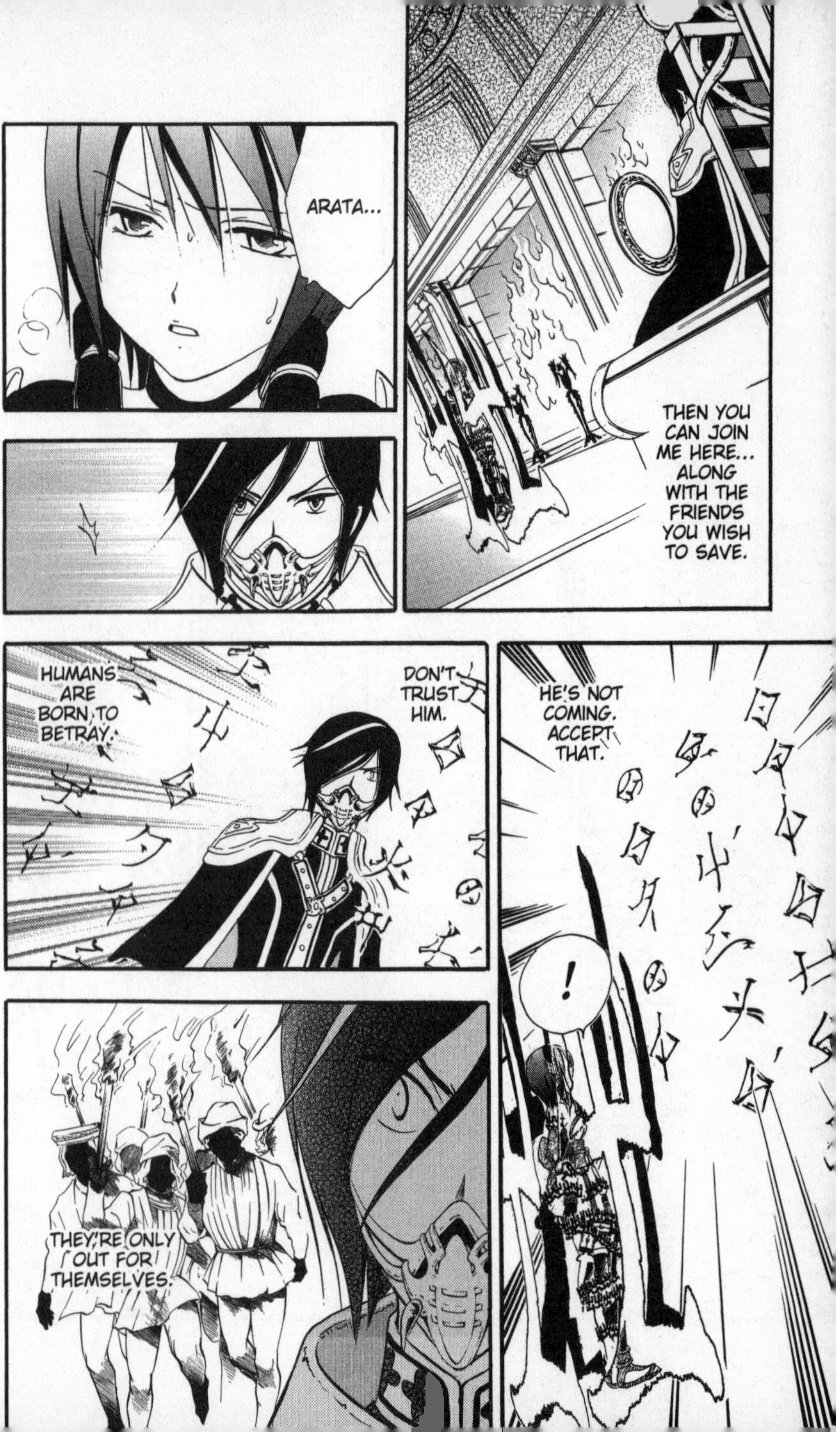
THEN YOU CAN JOIN ME HERE... ALONG WITH THE FRIENDS YOU WISH TO SAVE.
ARATA...
HE'S NOT COMING. ACCEPT THAT.
!
DON'T TRUST HIM.
HUMANS ARE BORN TO BETRAY.
THEY'RE ONLY OUT FOR THEMSELVES.

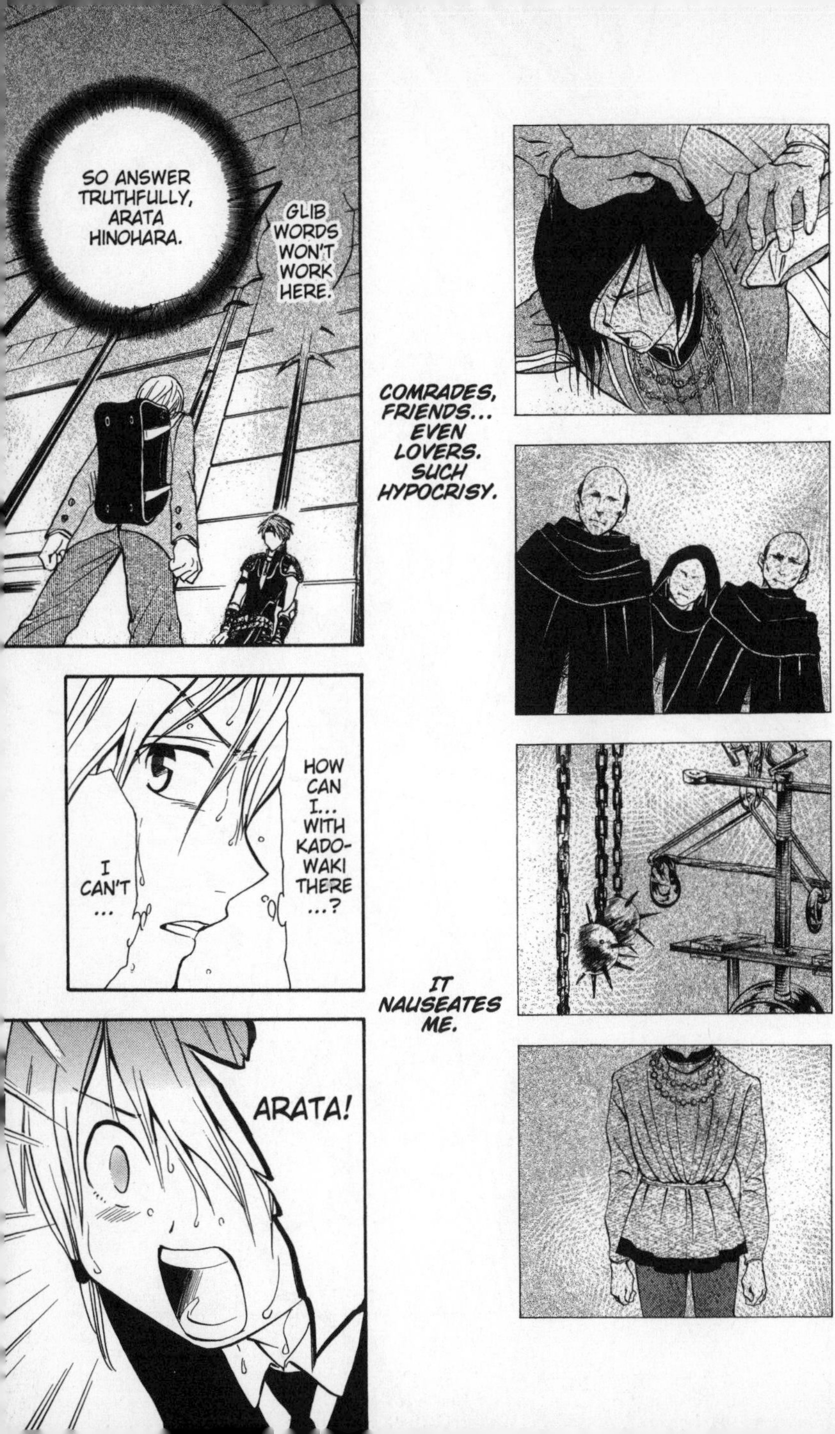
COMRADES, FRIENDS... EVEN LOVERS. SUCH HYPOCRISY.
IT NAUSEATES ME.
GLIB WORDS WON'T WORK HERE.
SO ANSWER TRUTHFULLY, ARATA HINOHARA.
HOW CAN I... WITH KADO-WAKI THERE ...?
I CAN'T ...
ARATA!

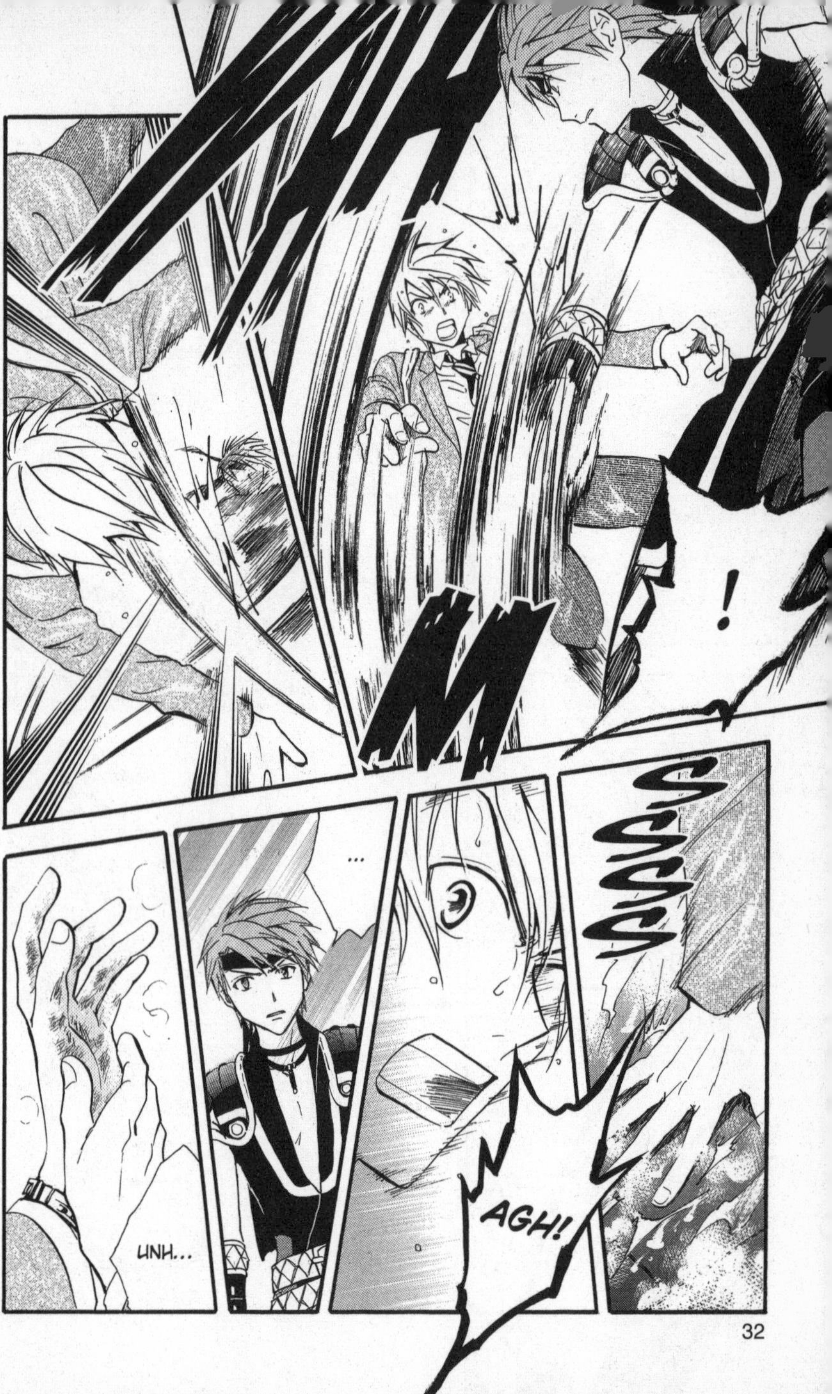
!
AGH!
...
UNH...

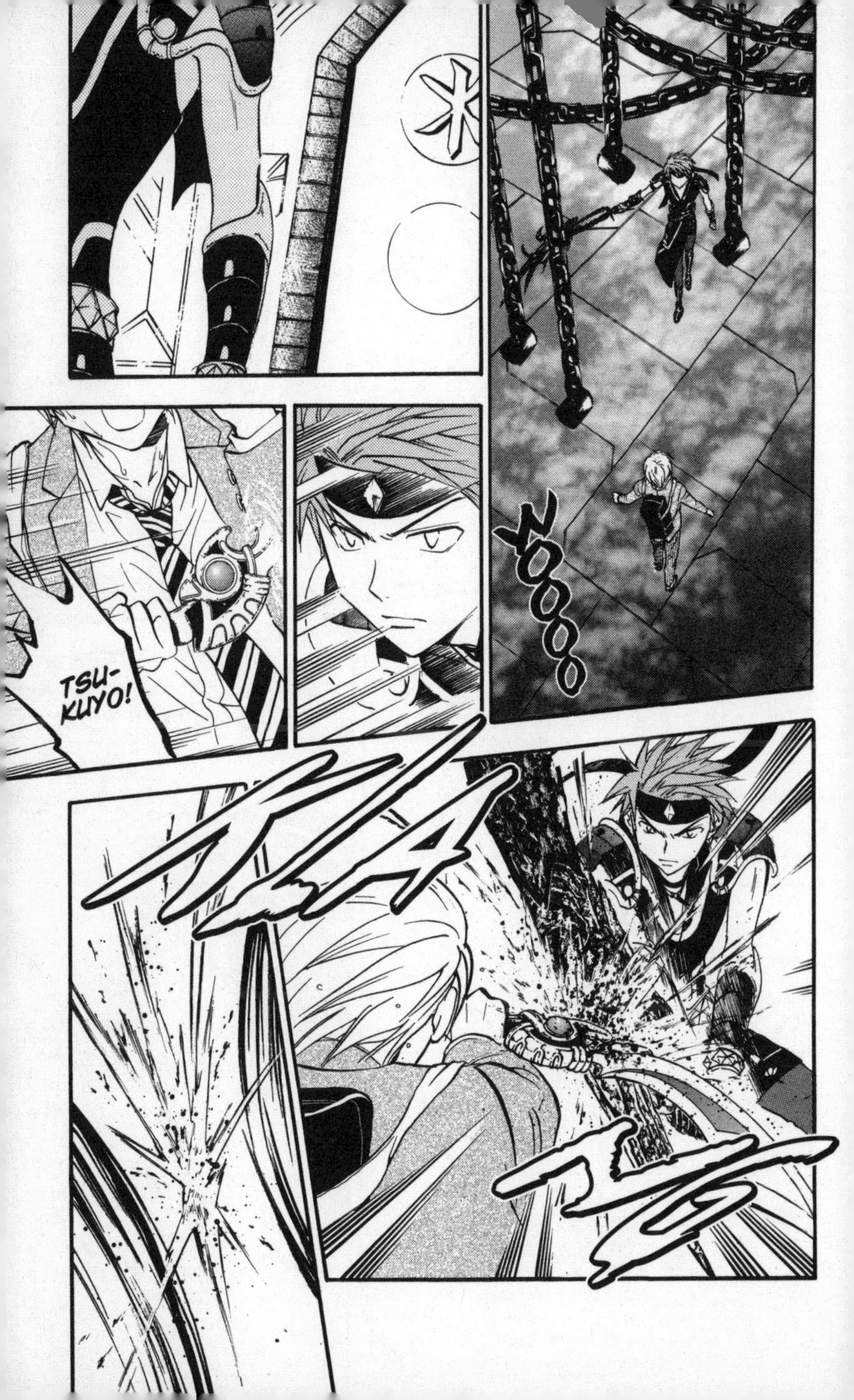
ZOOOO
TSU-
KUYO!

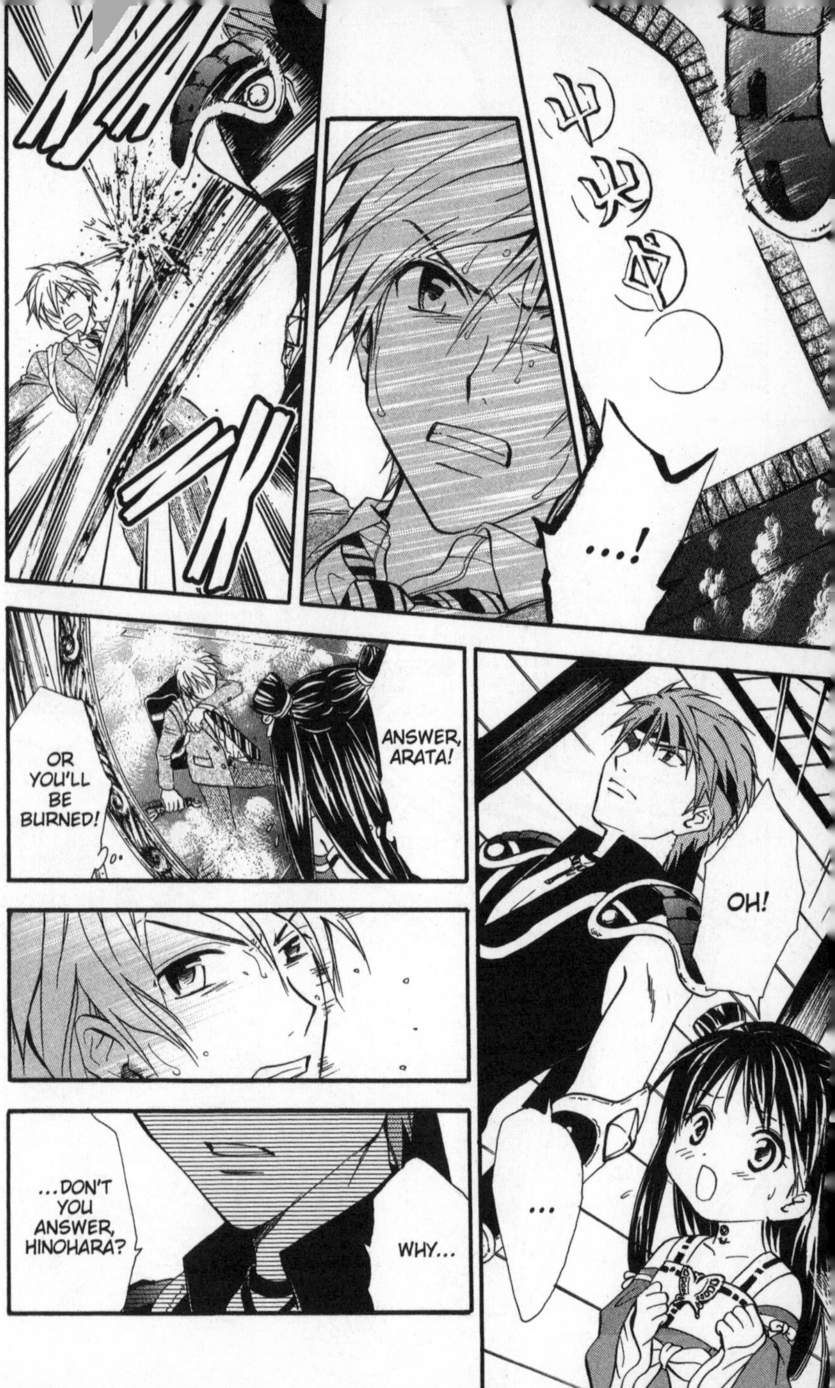

...!
OH!
...
ANSWER, ARATA!
OR YOU'LL BE BURNED!
WHY...
...DON'T YOU ANSWER, HINOHARA?

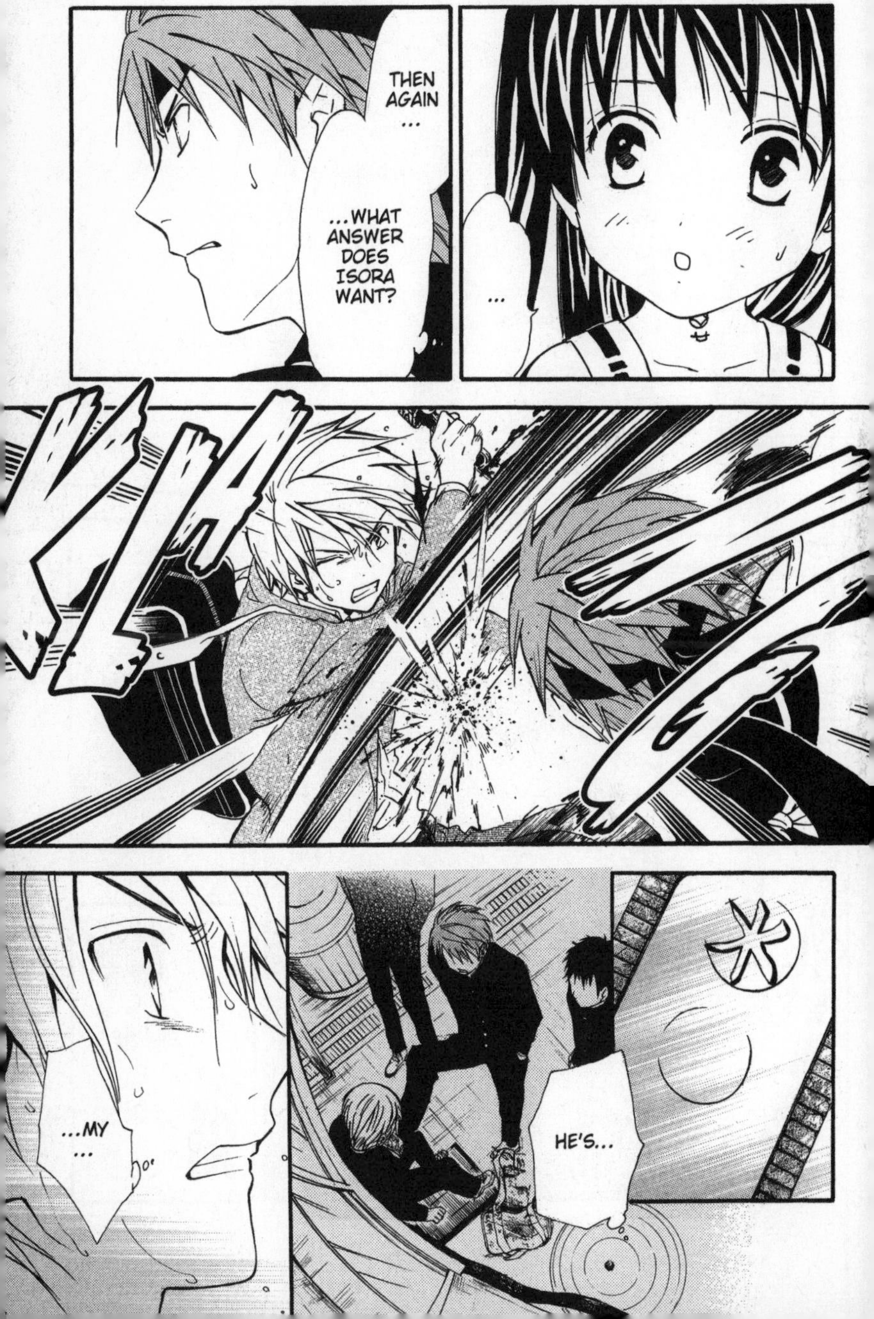
...
THEN AGAIN ...
...WHAT ANSWER DOES ISORA WANT?
HE'S...
...MY ...

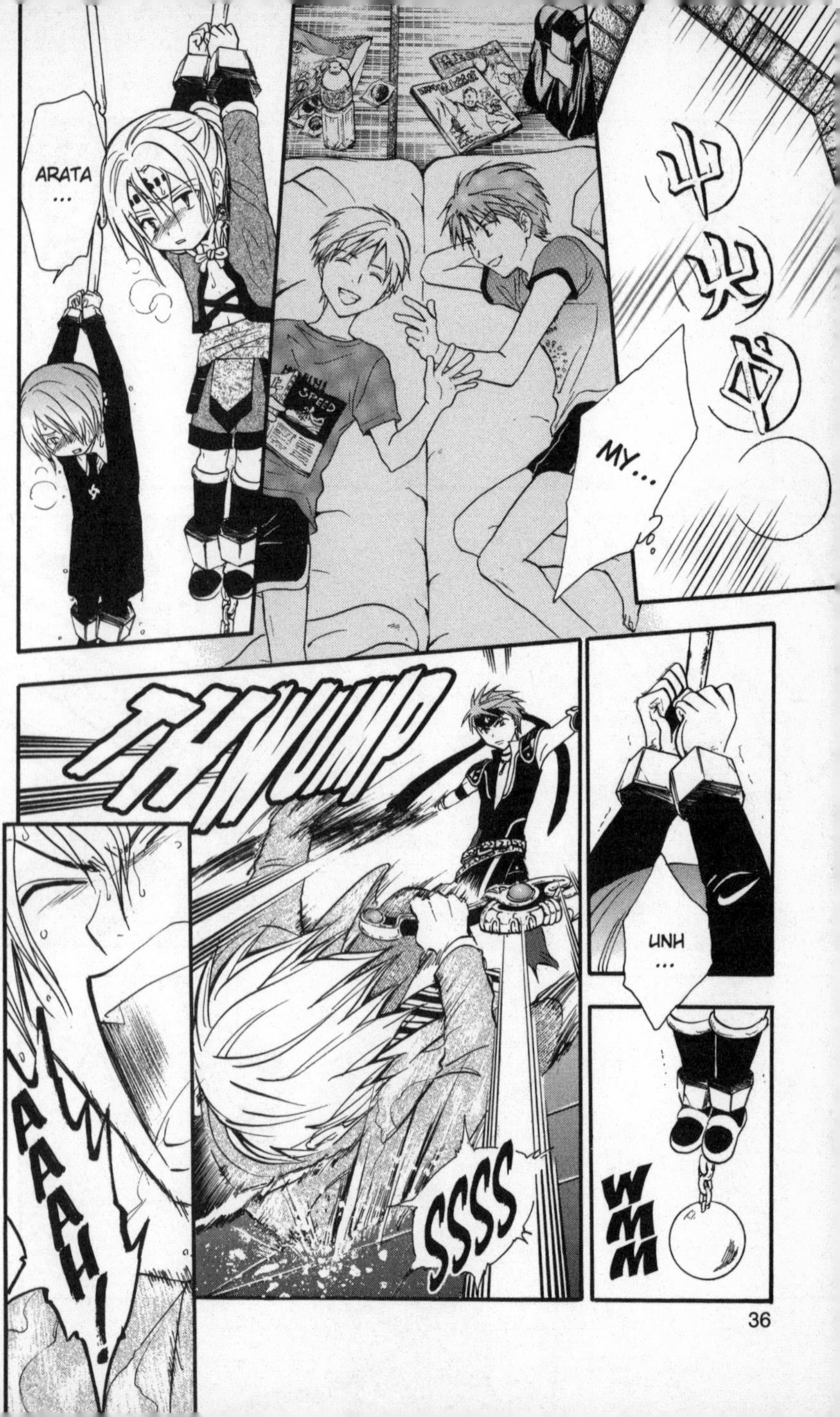
MY...
ARATA ...
UNH ...
WMM
THWUMP
SSSS
AAAAH!

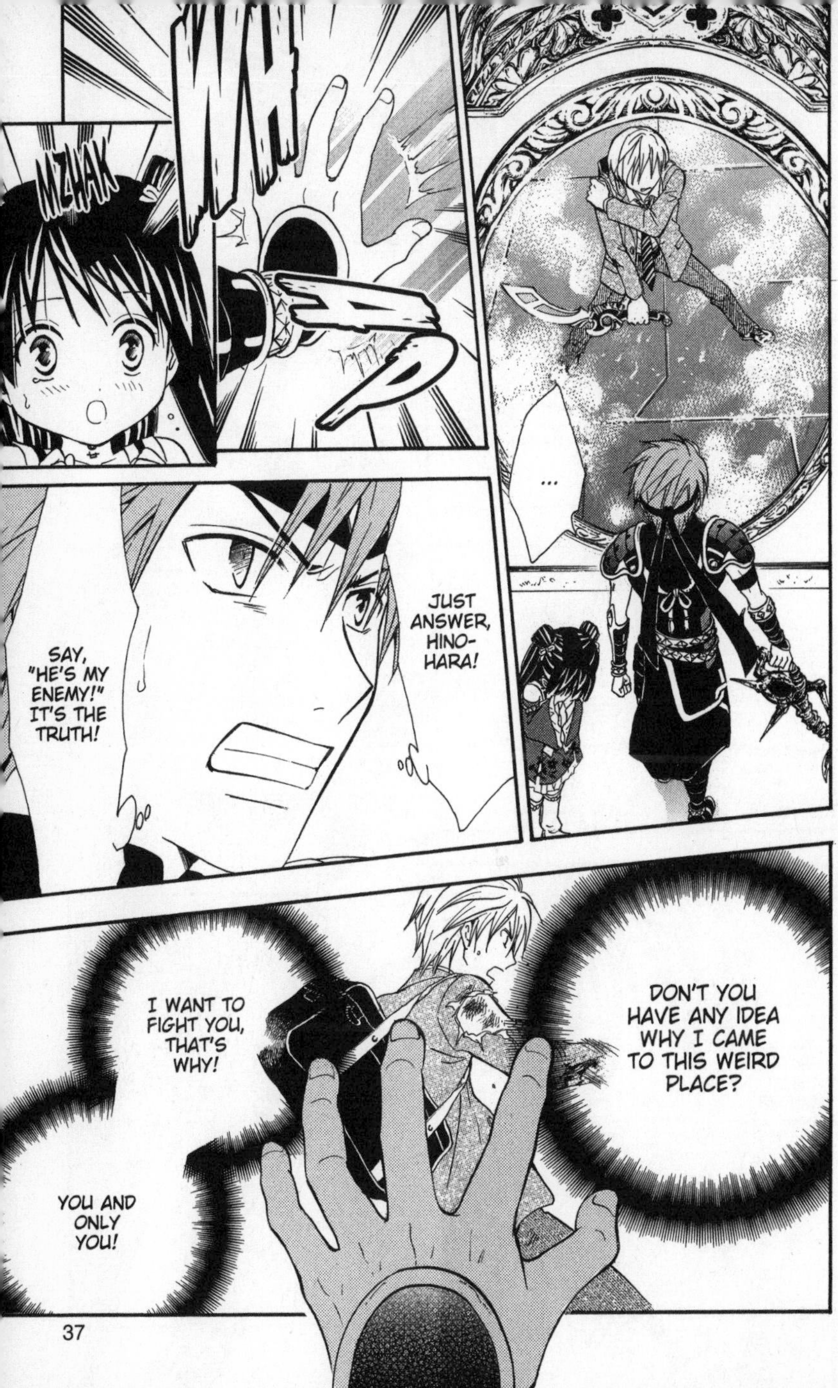
...
MZHAK
WHAP
JUST ANSWER, HINO-HARA!
SAY, "HE'S MY ENEMY!" IT'S THE TRUTH!
DON'T YOU HAVE ANY IDEA WHY I CAME TO THIS WEIRD PLACE?
I WANT TO FIGHT YOU, THAT'S WHY!
YOU AND ONLY YOU!

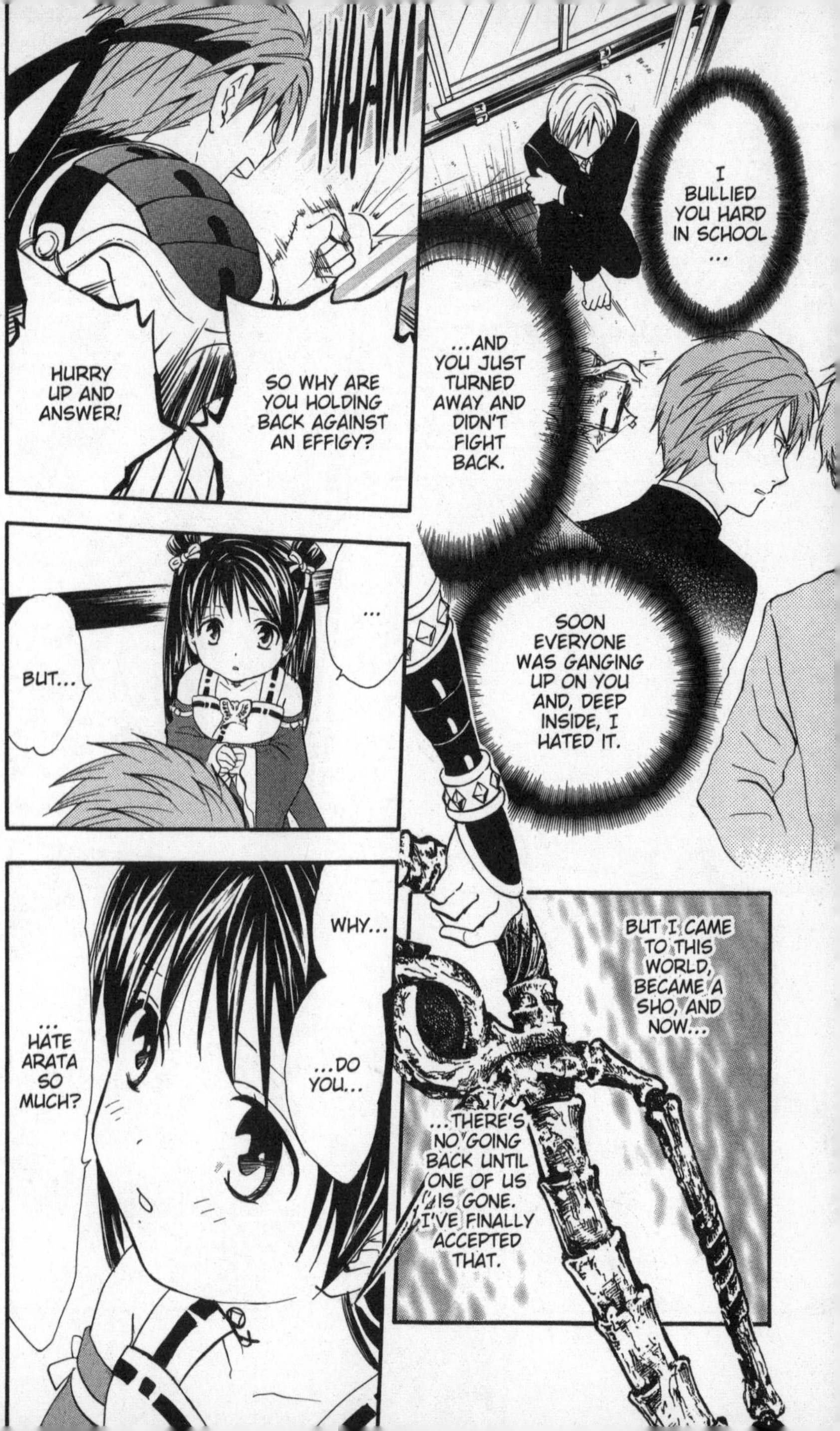
I BULLIED YOU HARD IN SCHOOL...
...AND YOU JUST TURNED AWAY AND DIDN'T FIGHT BACK.
SOON EVERYONE WAS GANGING UP ON YOU AND, DEEP INSIDE, I HATED IT.
WHAM
SO WHY ARE YOU HOLDING BACK AGAINST AN EFFIGY?
HURRY UP AND ANSWER!
...
BUT...
BUT I CAME TO THIS WORLD, BECAME A SHO, AND NOW...
...THERE'S NO GOING BACK UNTIL ONE OF US IS GONE. I'VE FINALLY ACCEPTED THAT.
WHY...
...DO YOU...
...HATE ARATA SO MUCH?

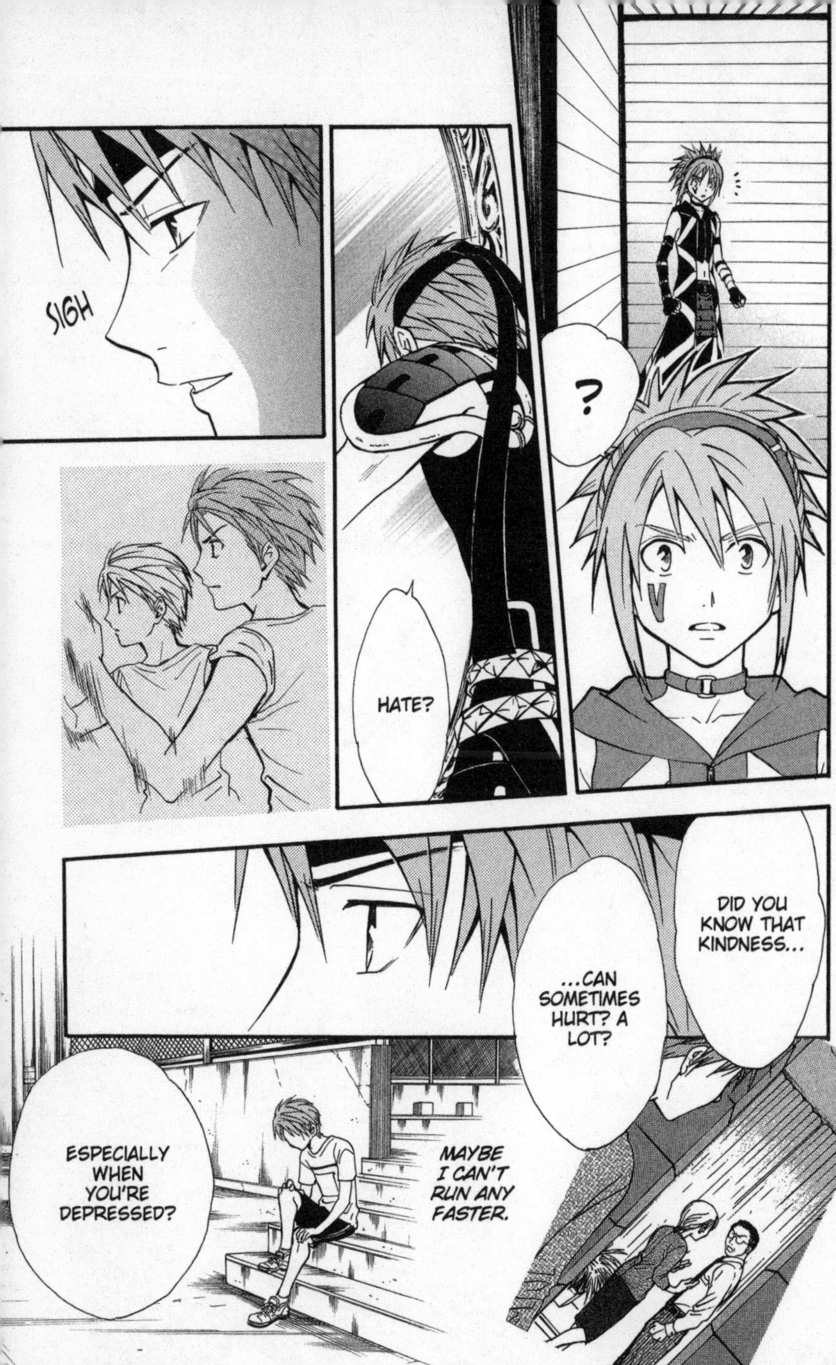
?
HATE?
SIGH
DID YOU KNOW THAT KINDNESS...
...CAN SOMETIMES HURT? A LOT?
MAYBE I CAN'T RUN ANY FASTER.
ESPECIALLY WHEN YOU'RE DEPRESSED?

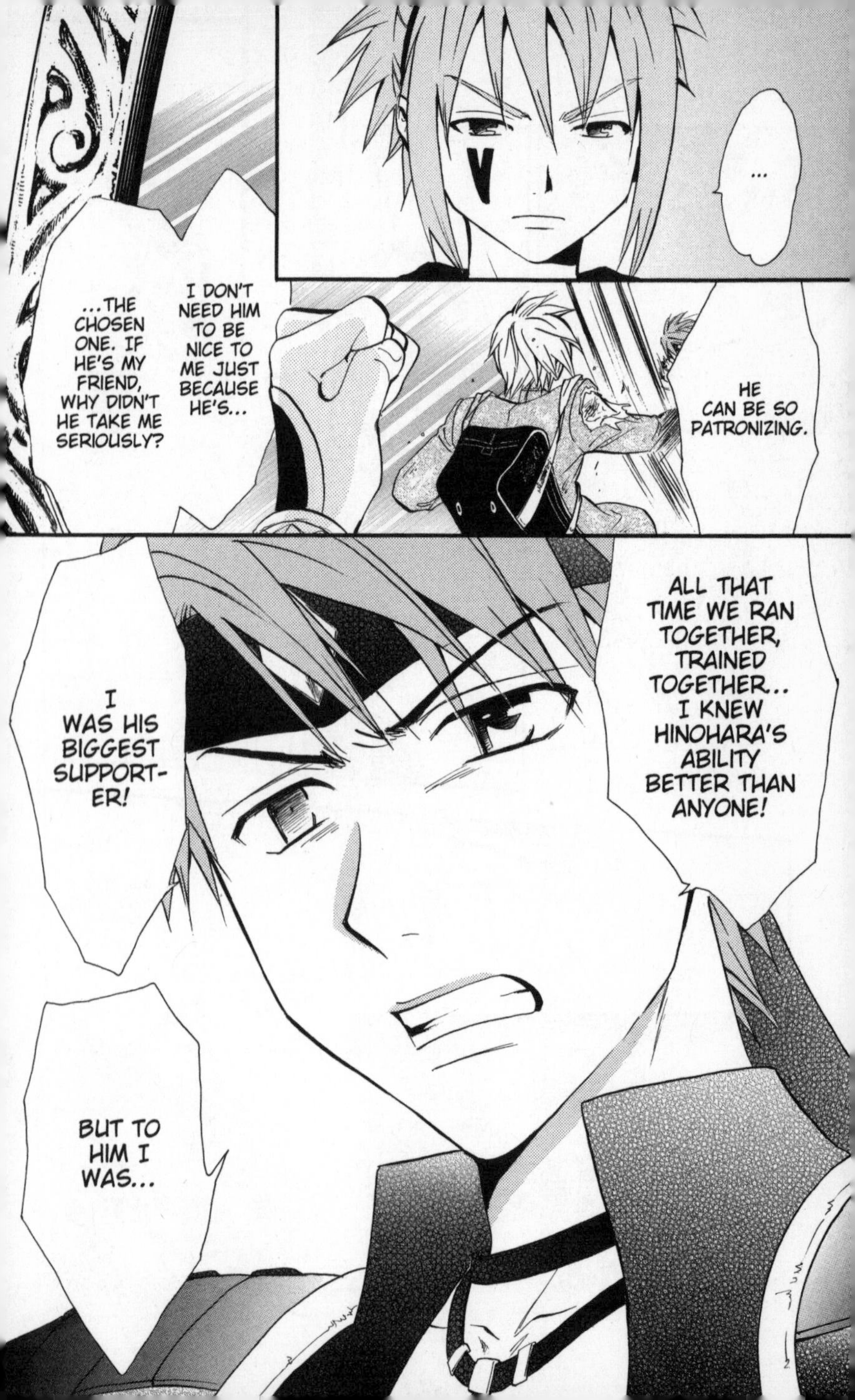
...
HE CAN BE SO PATRONIZING.
I DON'T NEED HIM TO BE NICE TO ME JUST BECAUSE HE'S...
...THE CHOSEN ONE. IF HE'S MY FRIEND, WHY DIDN'T HE TAKE ME SERIOUSLY?
ALL THAT TIME WE RAN TOGETHER, TRAINED TOGETHER... I KNEW HINOHARA'S ABILITY BETTER THAN ANYONE!
I WAS HIS BIGGEST SUPPORT-ER!
BUT TO HIM I WAS...

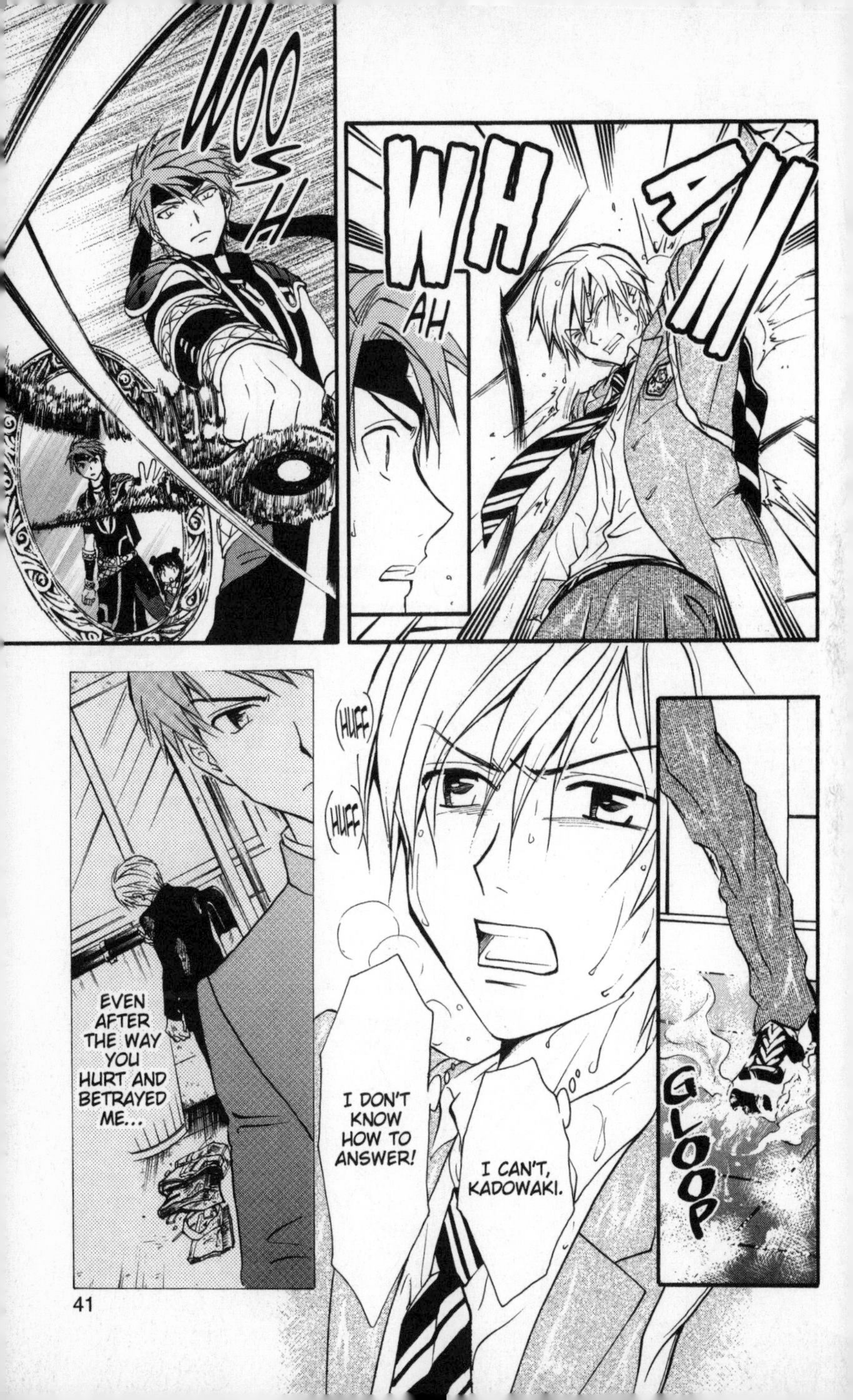
WH
AH
AH
WOOSH
GLOOP
HUFF
HUFF
I CAN'T, KADOWAKI.
I DON'T KNOW HOW TO ANSWER!
EVEN AFTER THE WAY YOU HURT AND BETRAYED ME...

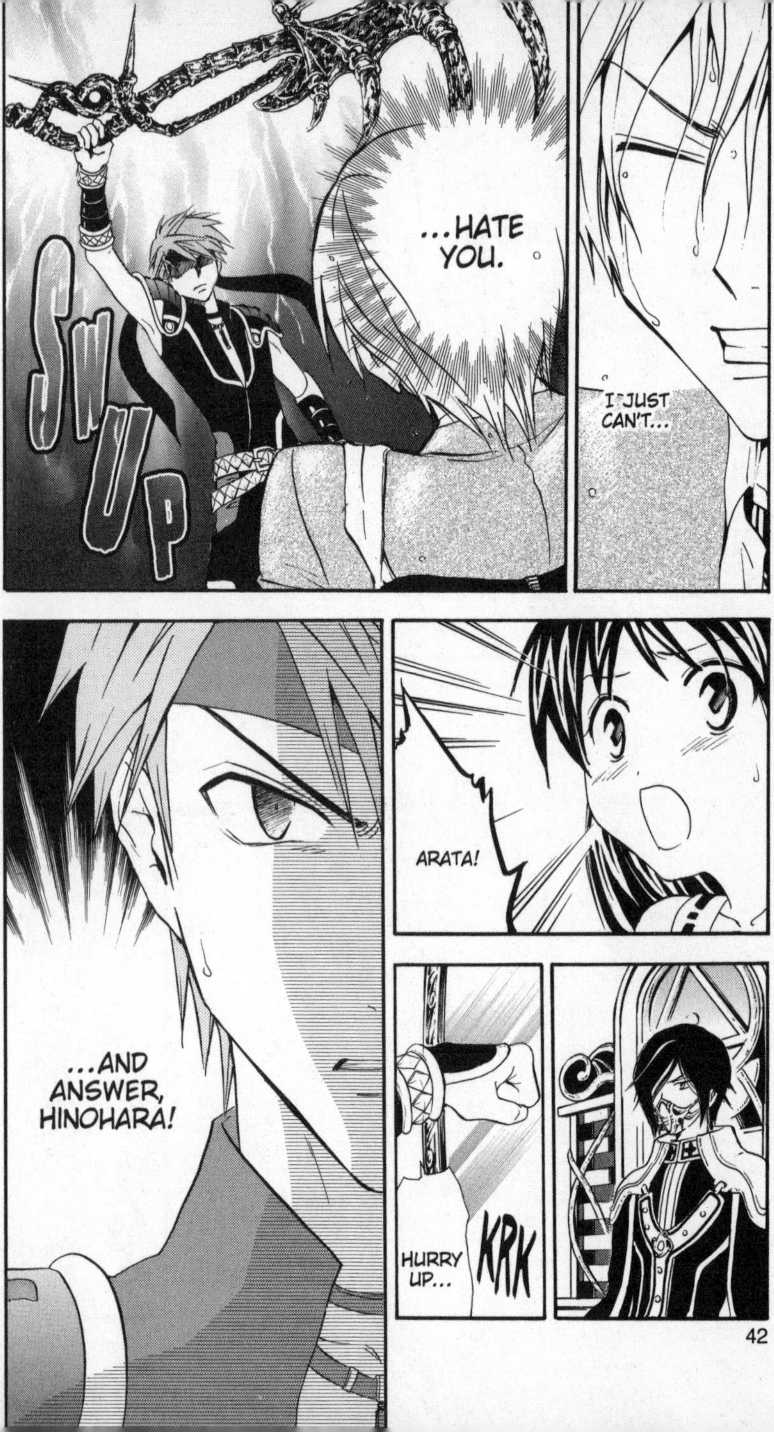
I JUST CAN'T...
...HATE YOU.
SWUP
ARATA!
KRK
HURRY UP...
...AND ANSWER, HINOHARA!

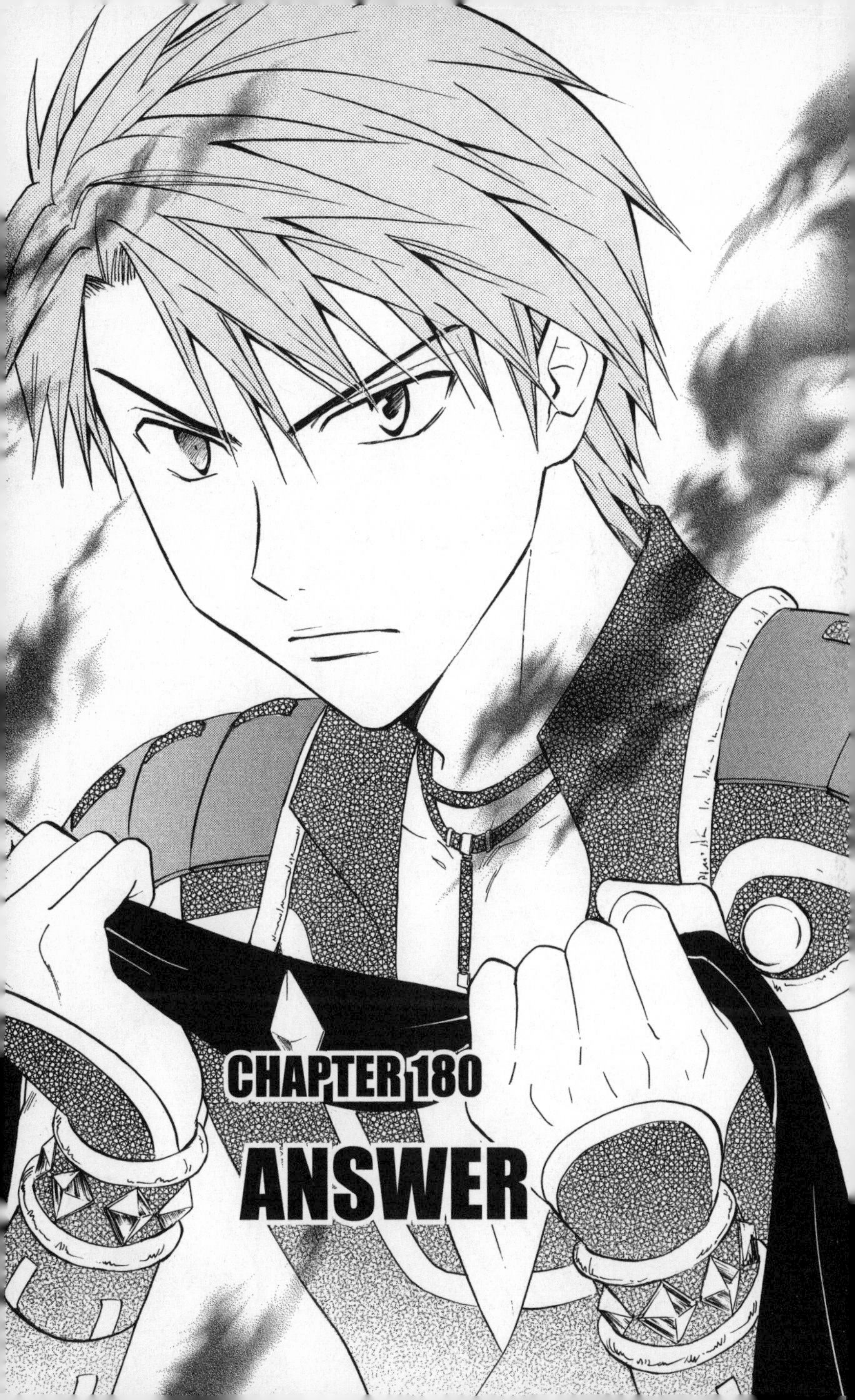
CHAPTER 180
ANSWER

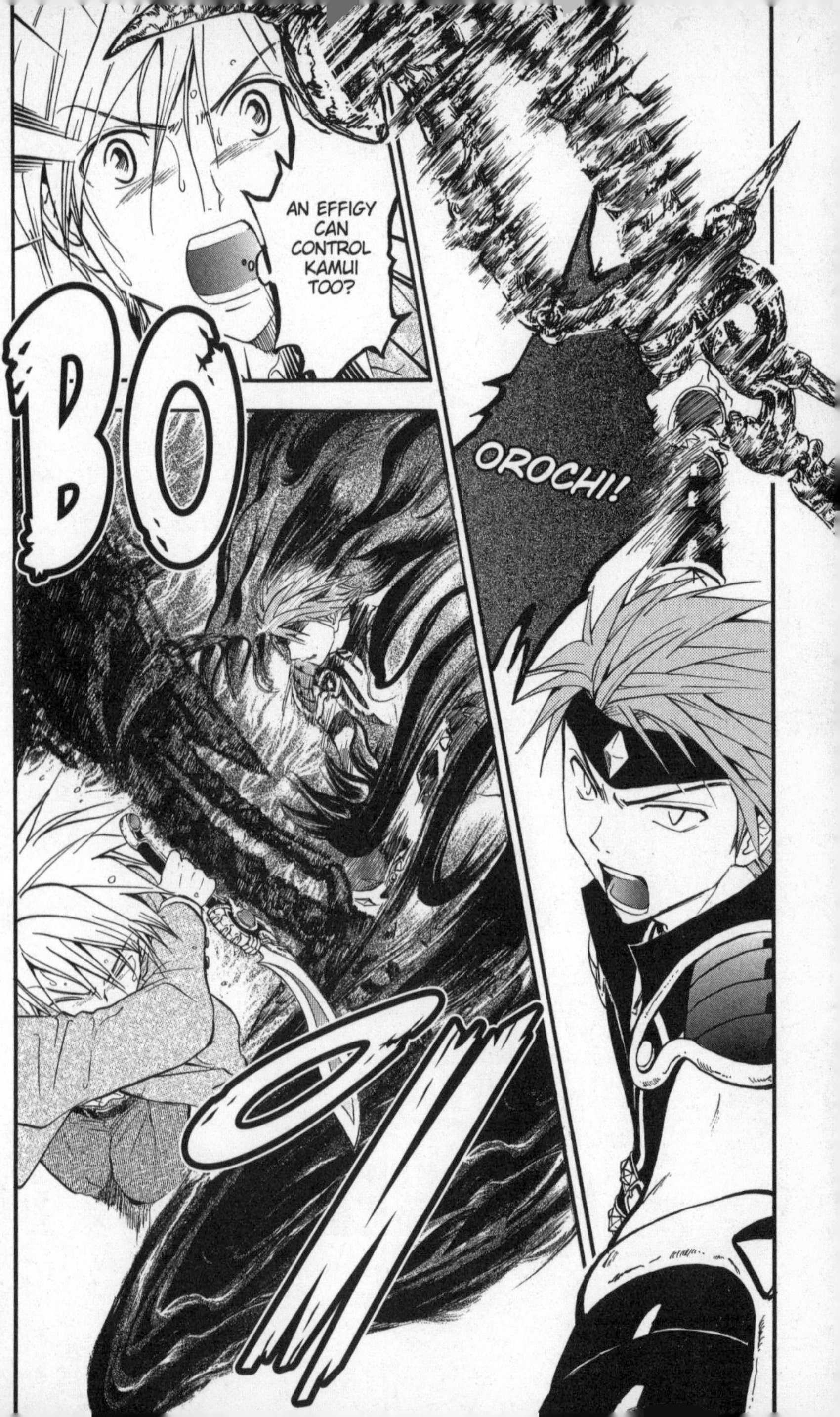
OROCHI!
AN EFFIGY CAN CONTROL KAMUI TOO?
BO
OM

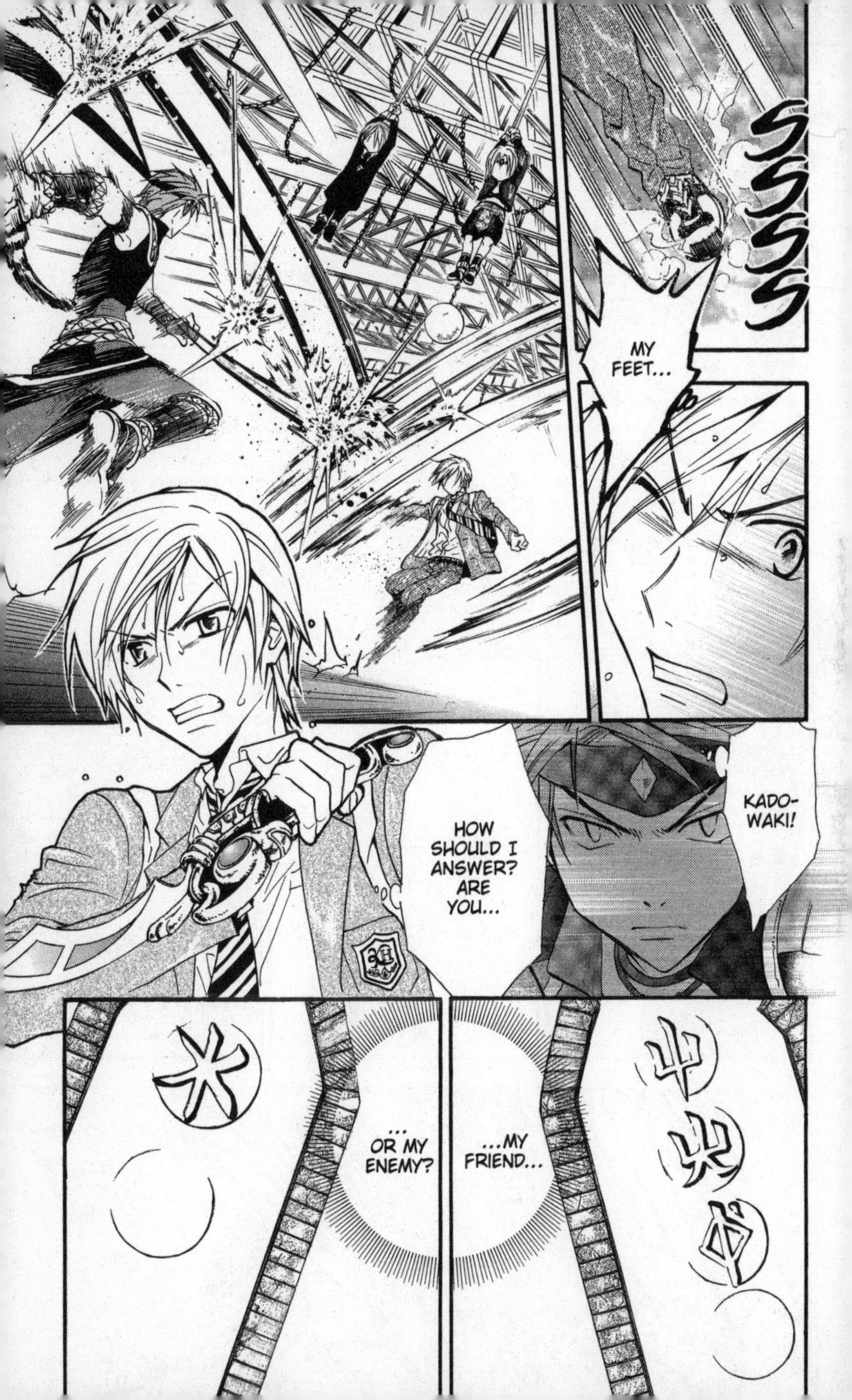
SSSS
MY FEET...
KADO-WAKI!
HOW SHOULD I ANSWER? ARE YOU...
...MY FRIEND...
...OR MY ENEMY?

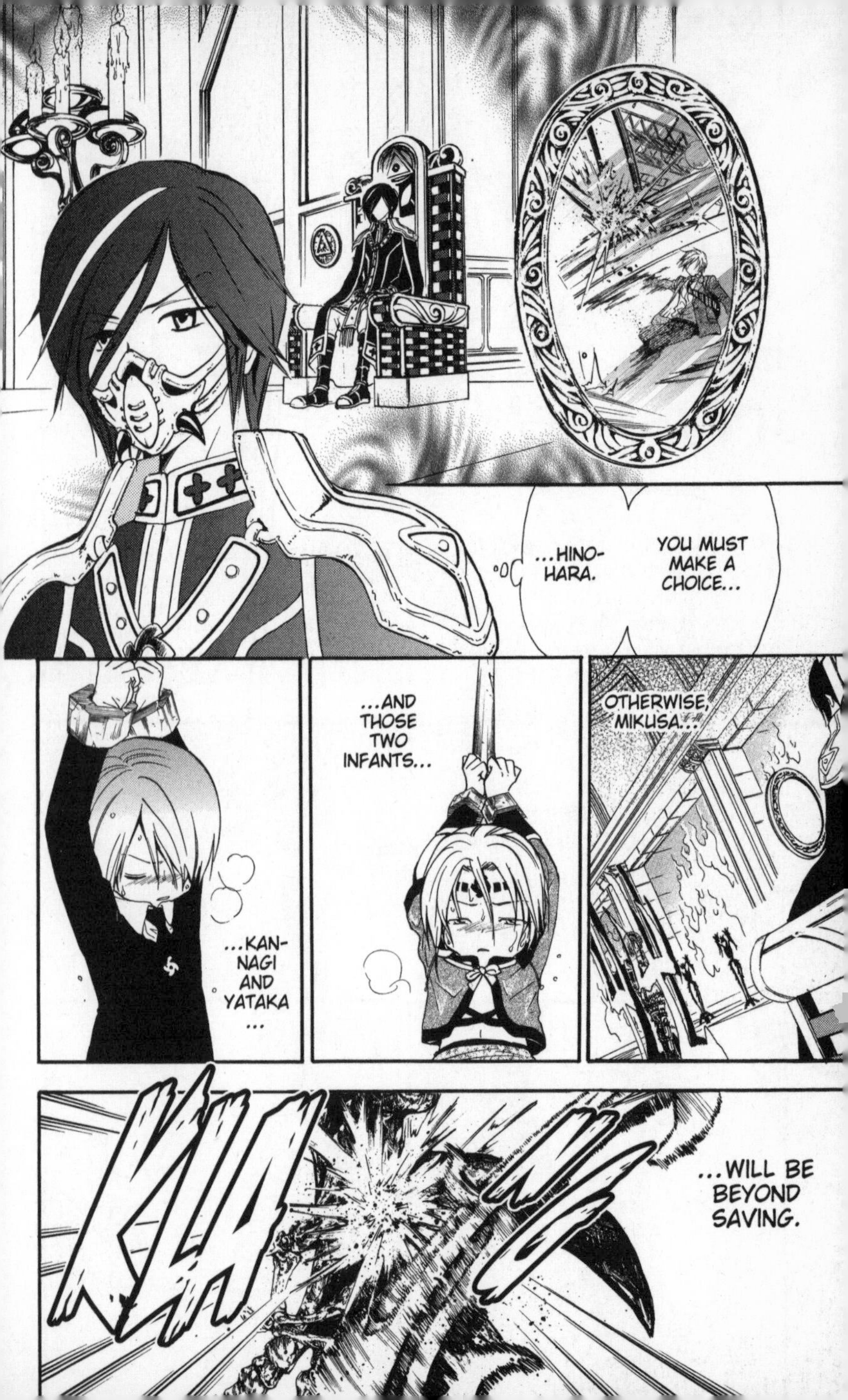
...HINO-HARA.
YOU MUST MAKE A CHOICE...
OTHERWISE, MIKUSA...
...AND THOSE TWO INFANTS...
...KAN-NAGI AND YATAKA...
...WILL BE BEYOND SAVING.

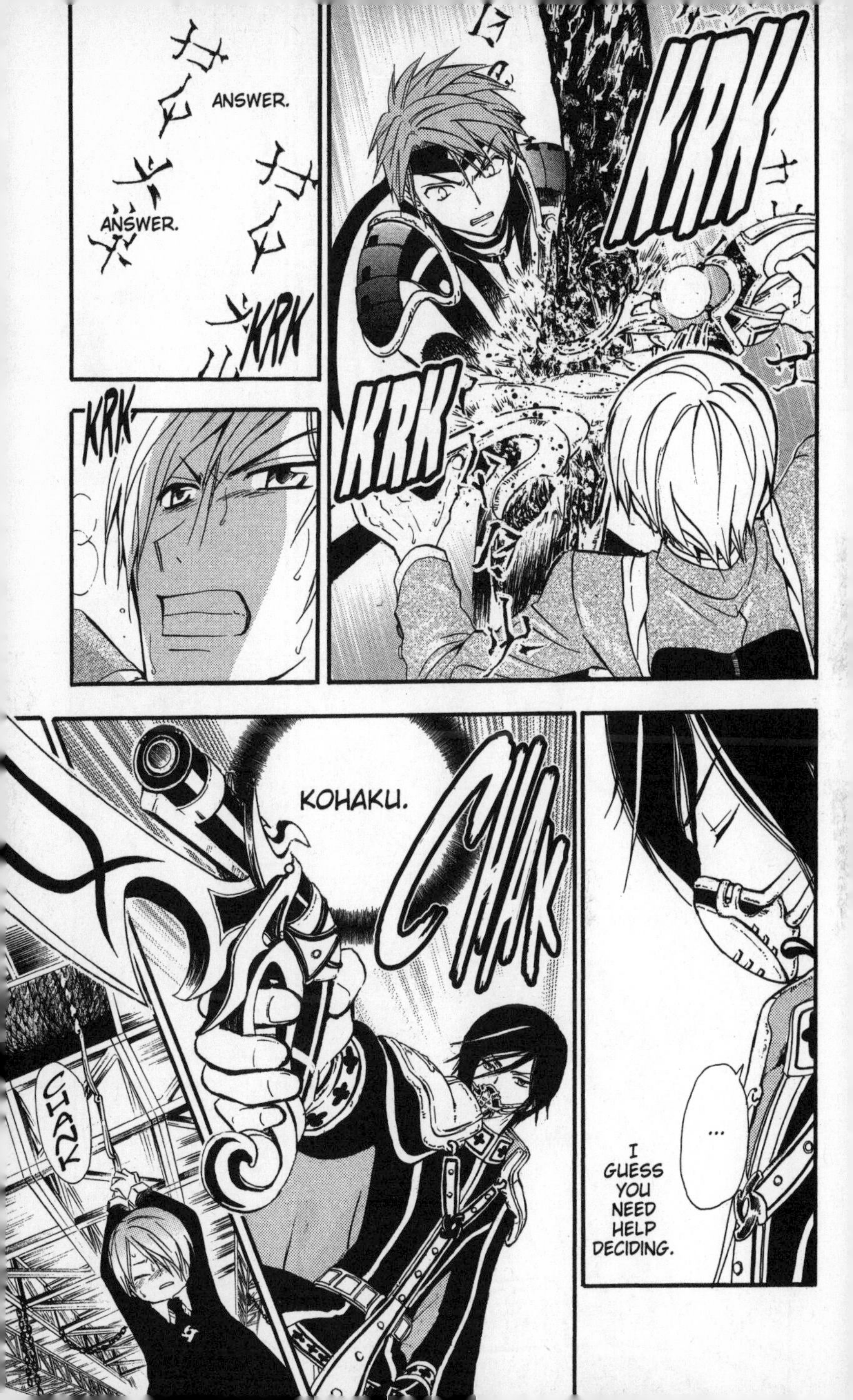
KRK
KRK
ANSWER.
ANSWER.
KRK
KRK
...
I GUESS YOU NEED HELP DECIDING.
KOHAKU.
CHAK
CHAK

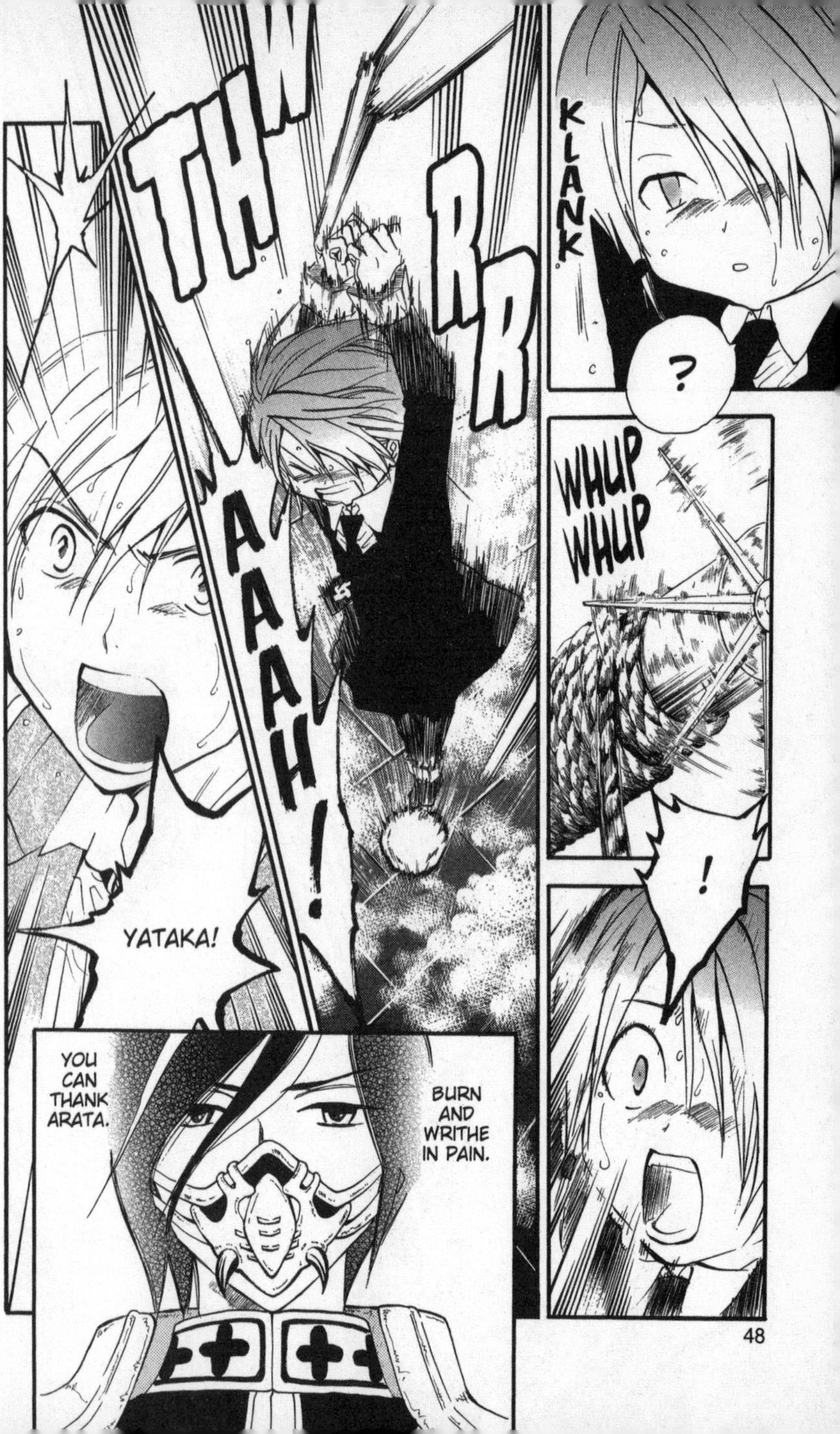
KLANK
?
WHUP WHUP
WHUP WHUP
!
THRR
AAAAH!
YATAKA!
BURN AND WRITHE IN PAIN.
YOU CAN THANK ARATA.

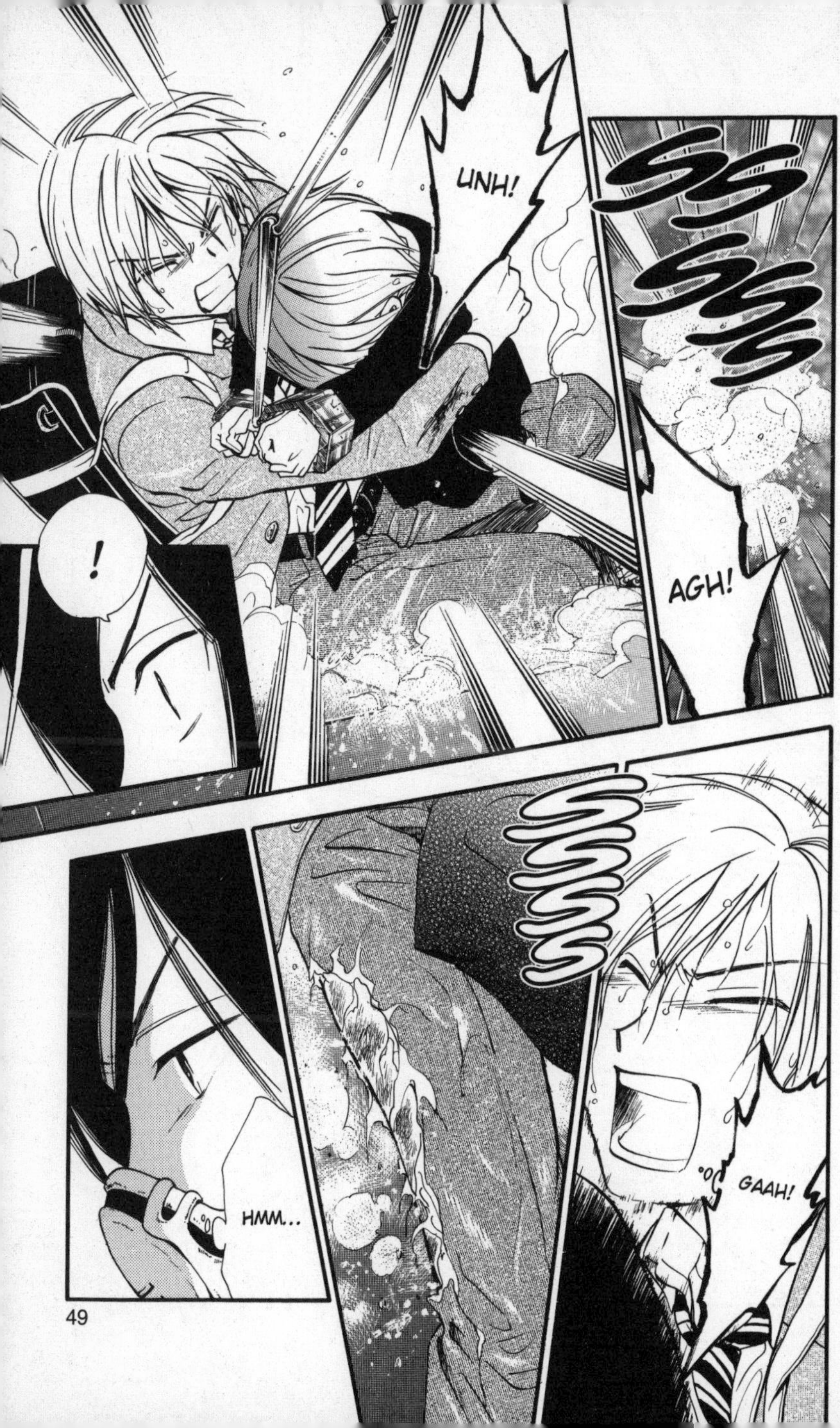
SSSSSS
AGH!
UNH!
!
SSSSS
GAAH!
HMM..

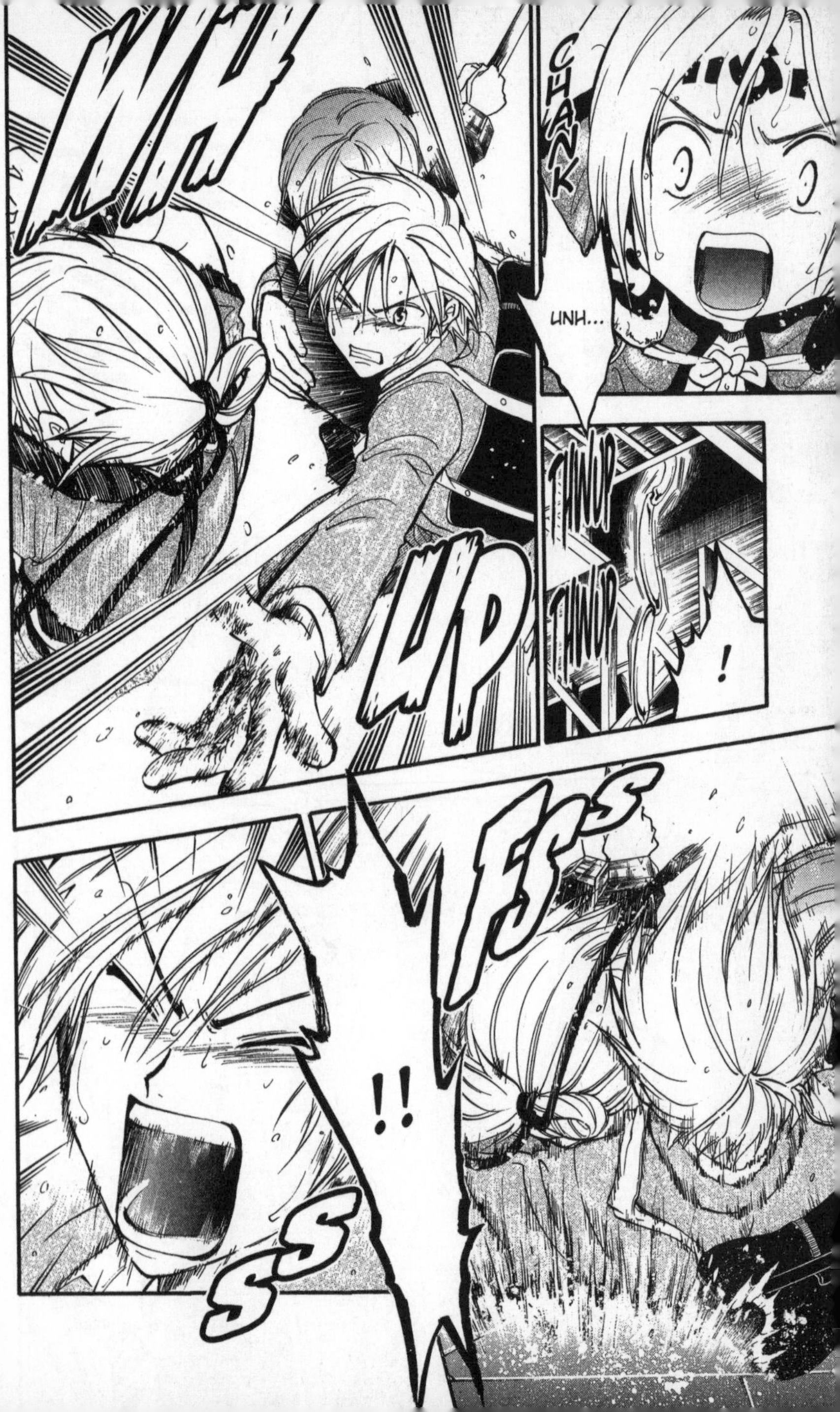
CHANK
UNH...
THWUP
THWUP
!
WHUP
FSS
!!
SSS

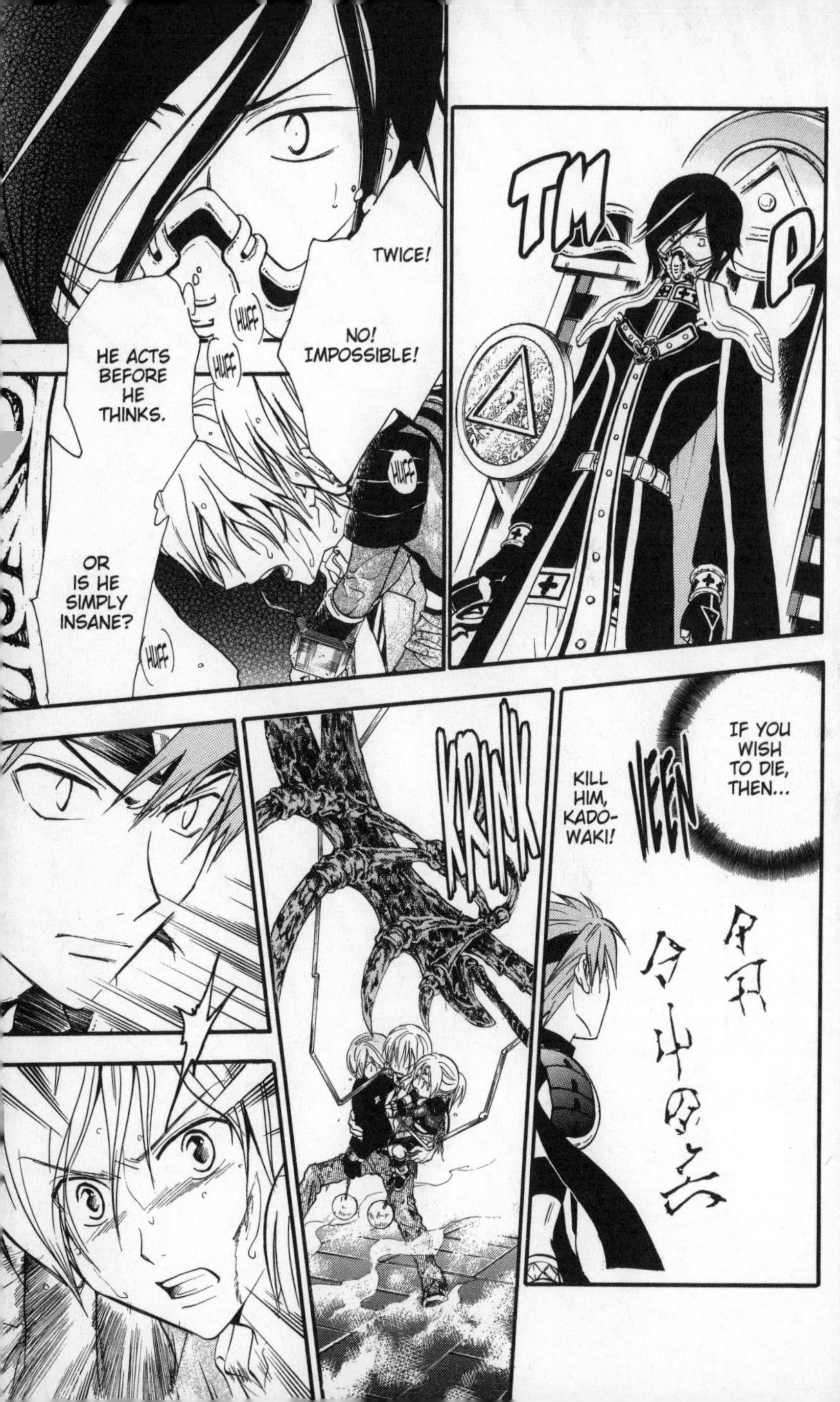
TM
P
TWICE!
HUFF
NO! IMPOSSIBLE!
HUFF
HE ACTS BEFORE HE THINKS.
HUFF
OR IS HE SIMPLY INSANE?
HUFF
IF YOU WISH TO DIE, THEN...
VEEN
KILL HIM, KADO-WAKI!
KRINK

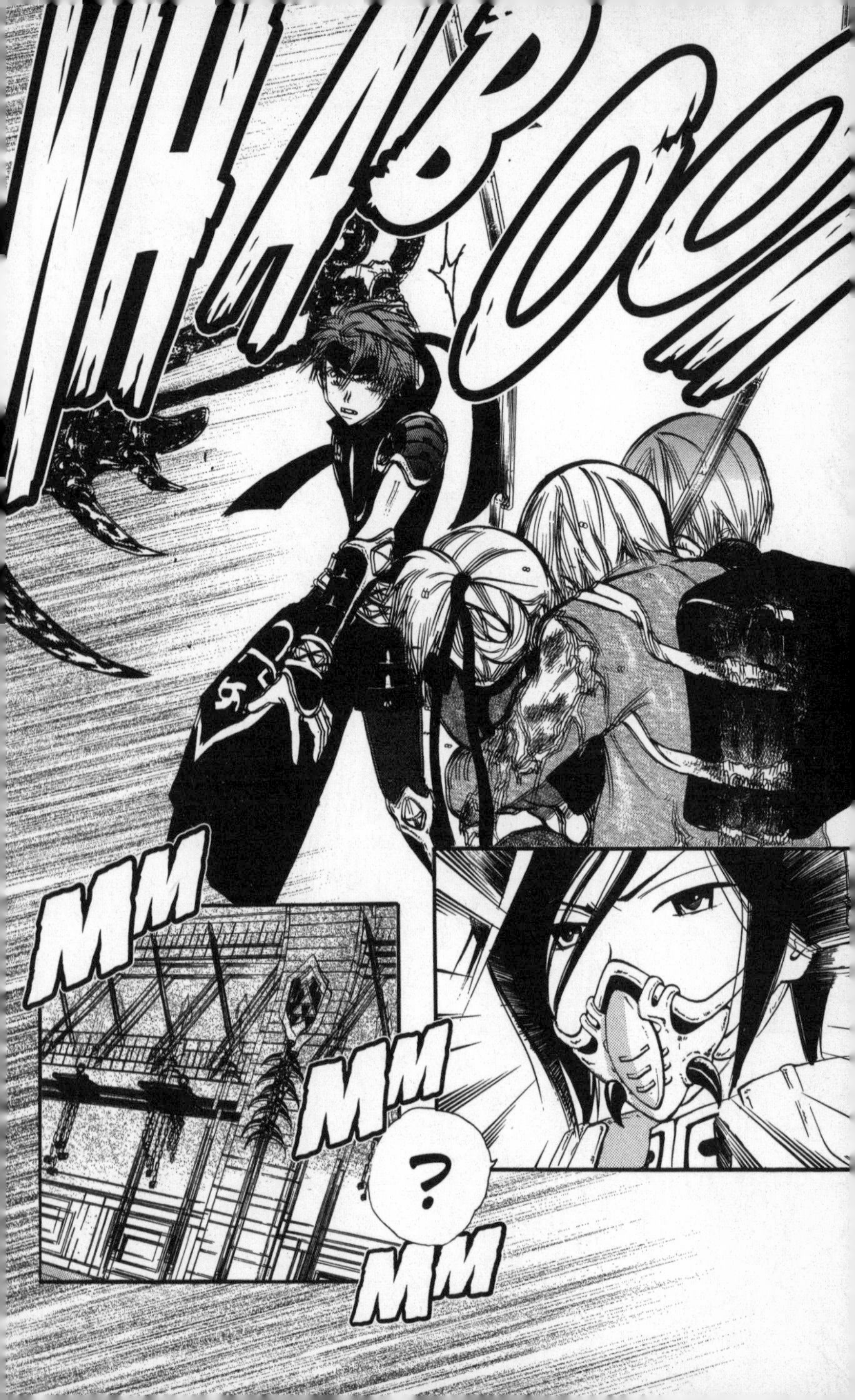
WHABOOM
MM
MM
?
MM

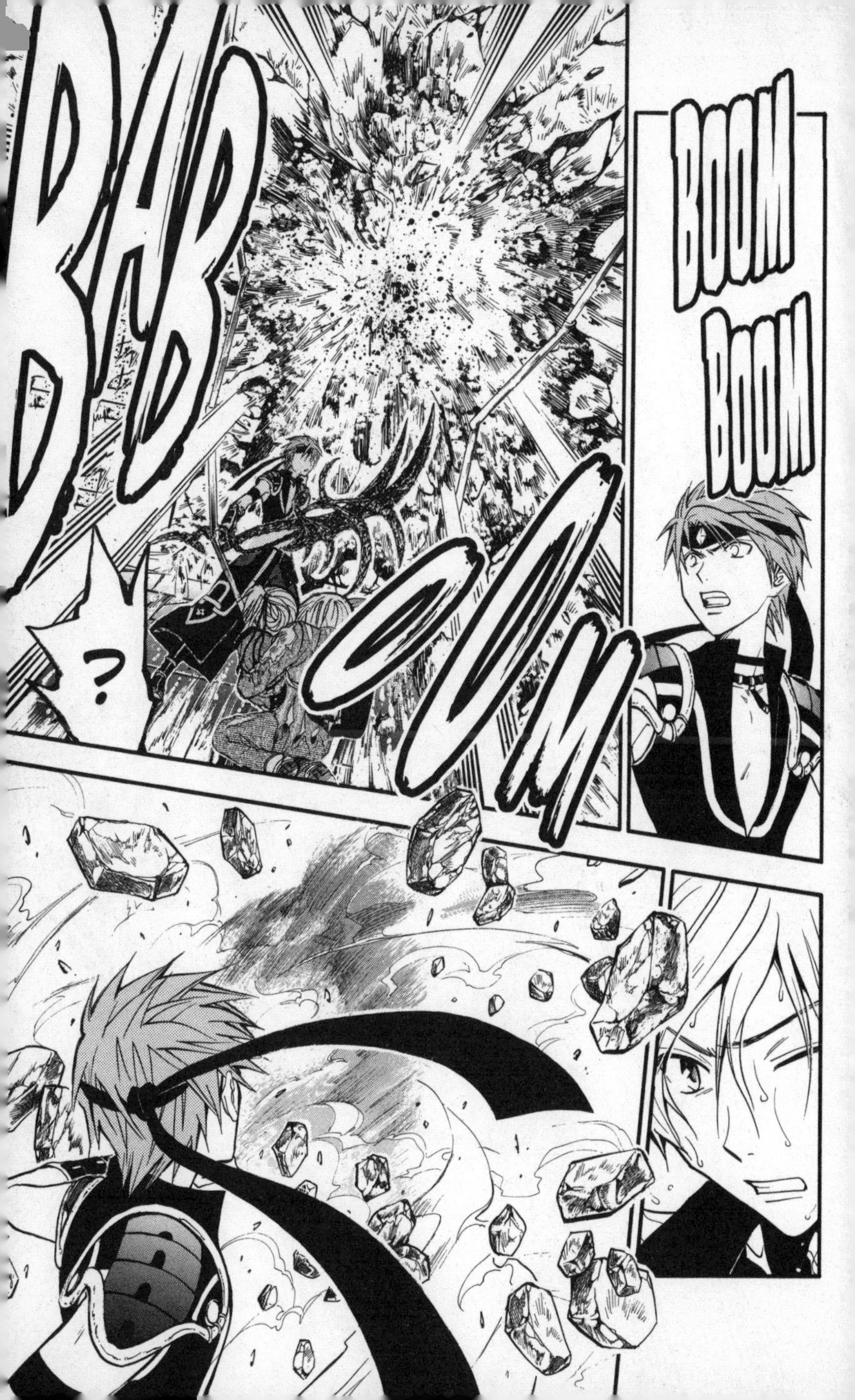
BOOM
BOOM
?

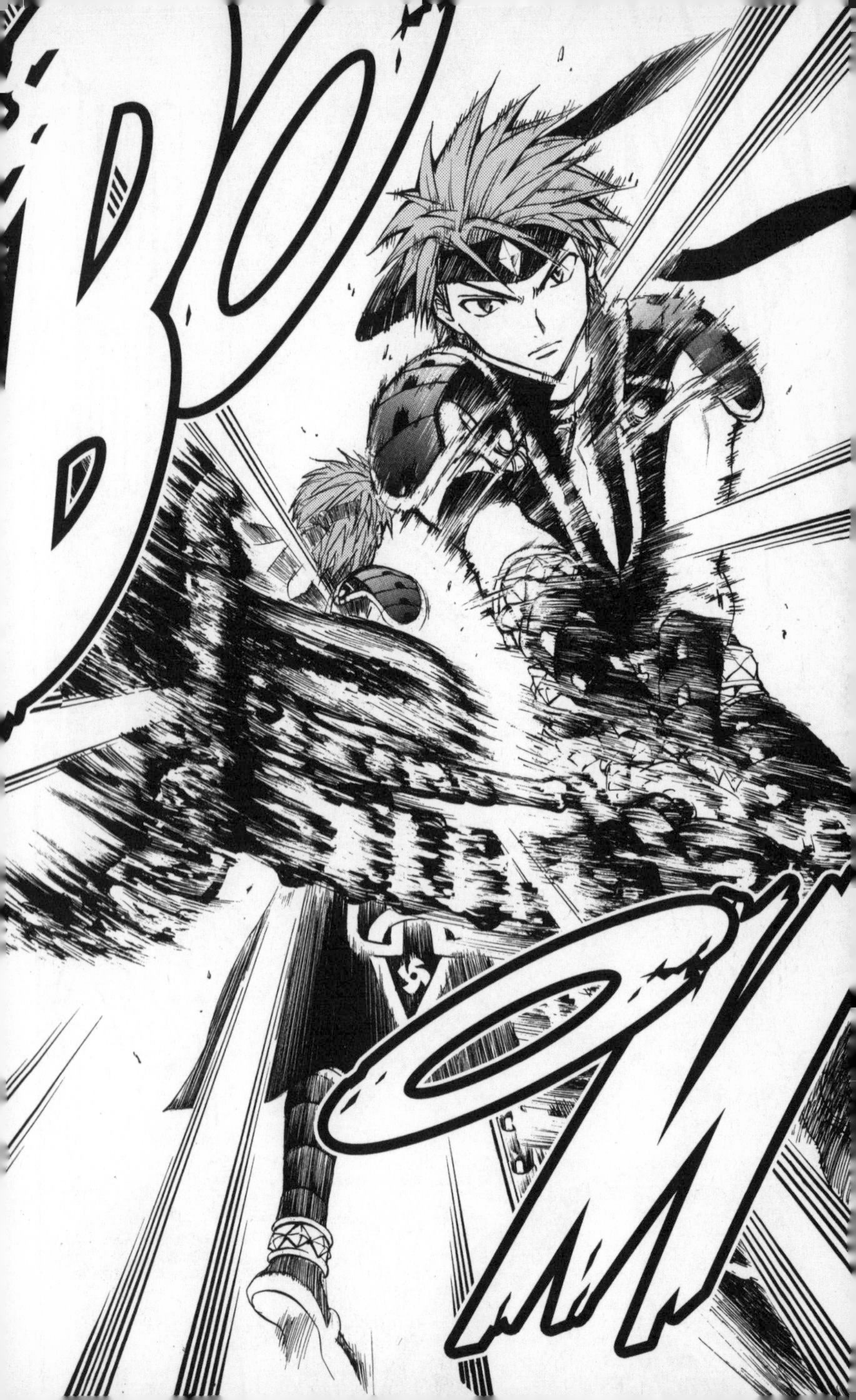
DOOM

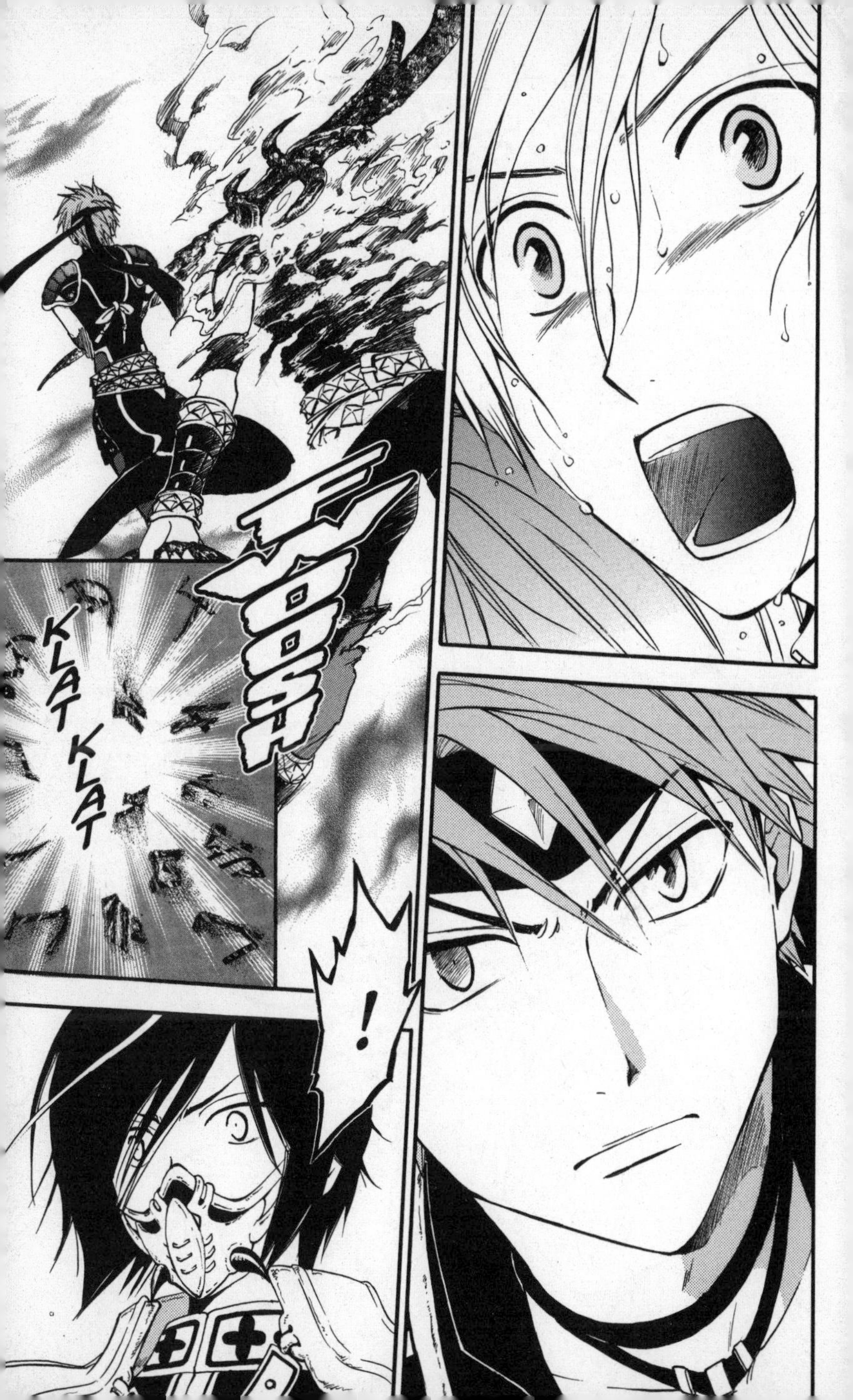
FOOSH
KLAT KLAT
!

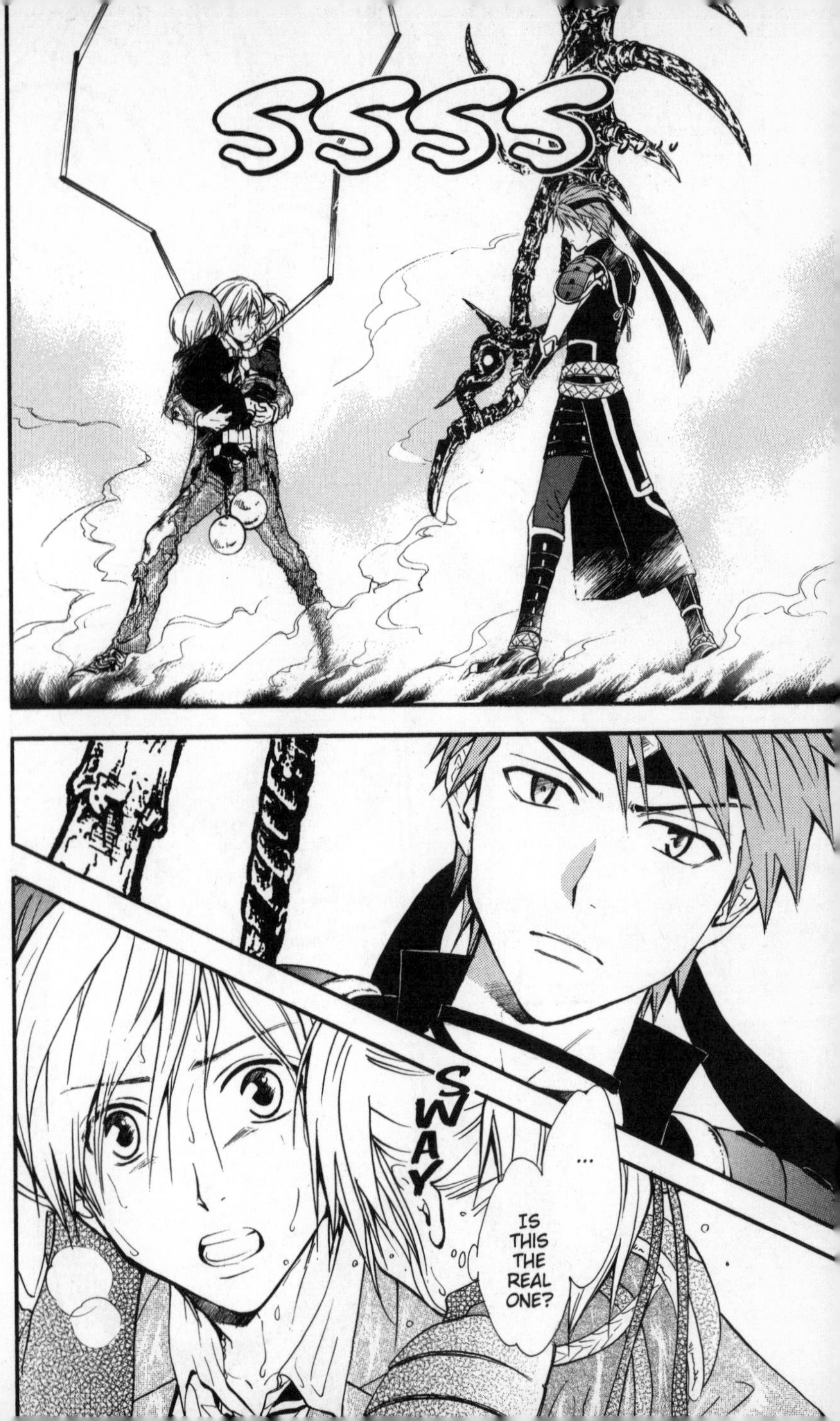
SSSS
SWAY
...
IS THIS THE REAL ONE?

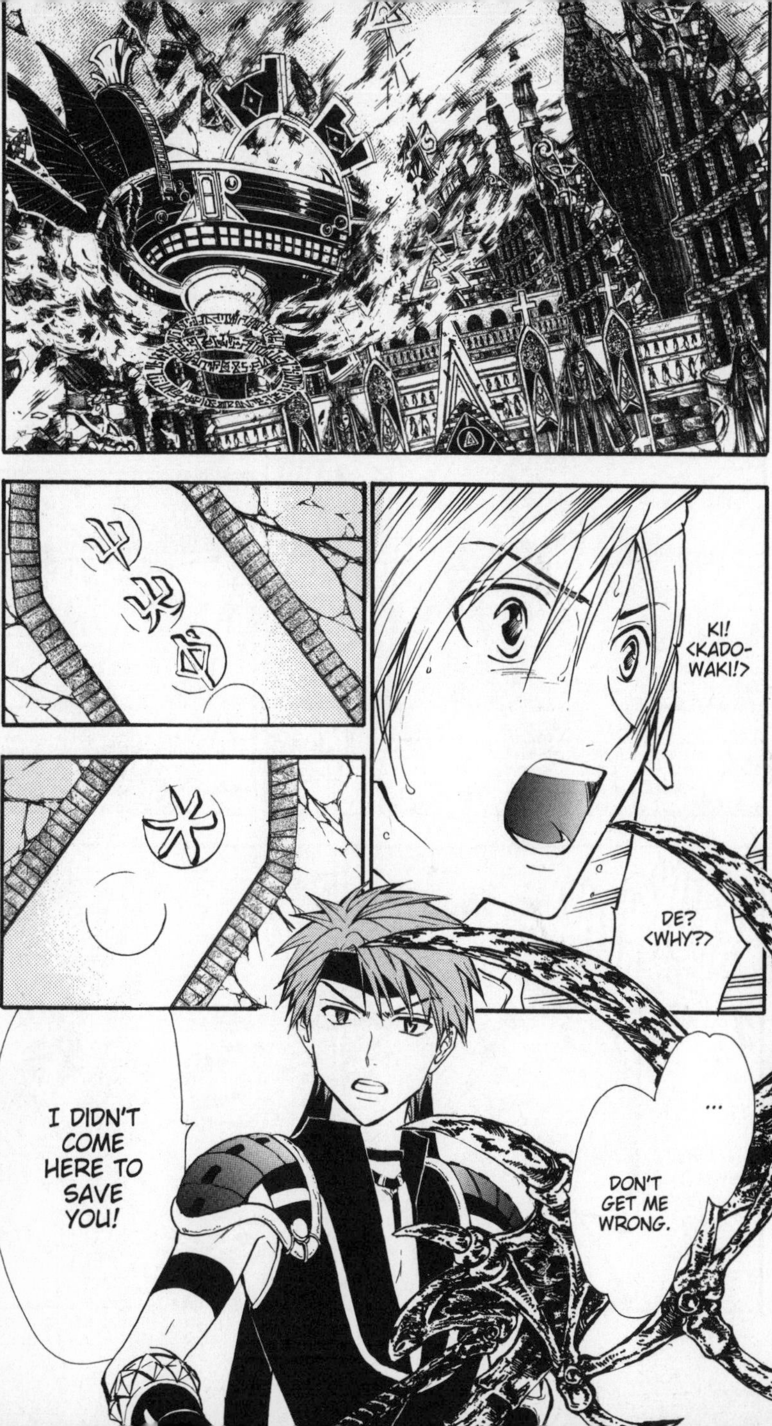
KI! <KADO-WAKI!>
DE? <WHY?>
... DON'T GET ME WRONG.
I DIDN'T COME HERE TO SAVE YOU!

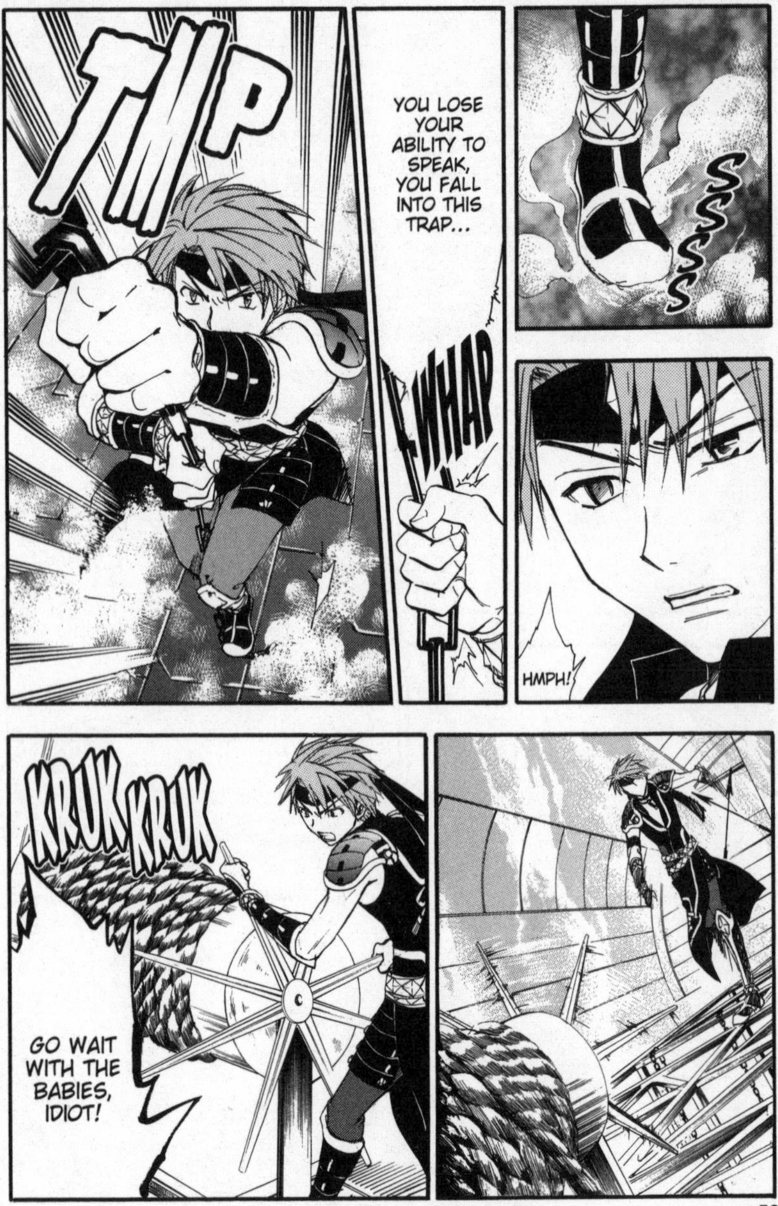
SSSSS
HMPH!
YOU LOSE YOUR ABILITY TO SPEAK, YOU FALL INTO THIS TRAP...
WHAP
TWIP
KRUK KRUK
GO WAIT WITH THE BABIES, IDIOT!

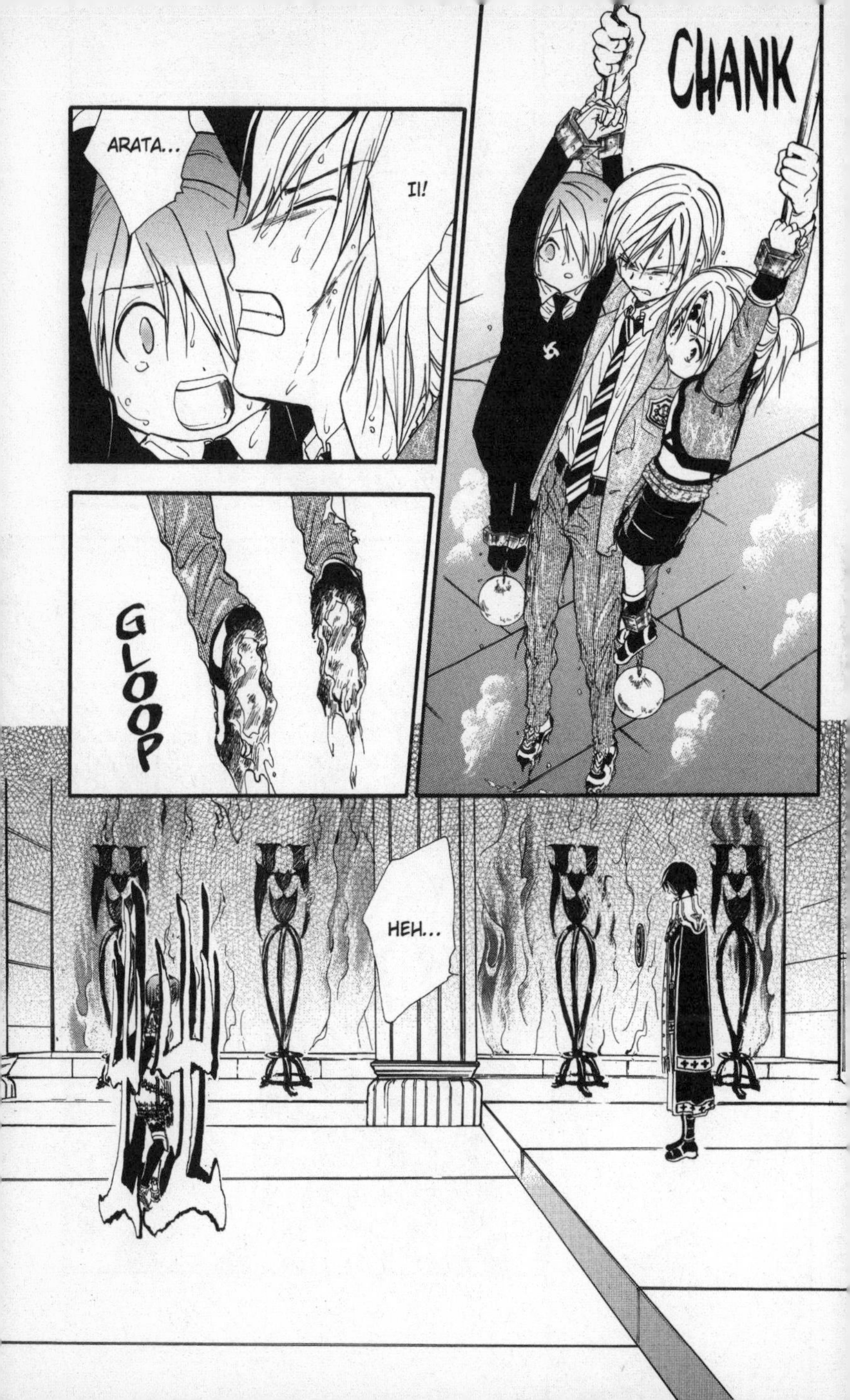
CHANK
ARATA...
II!
GLOOP
HEH...

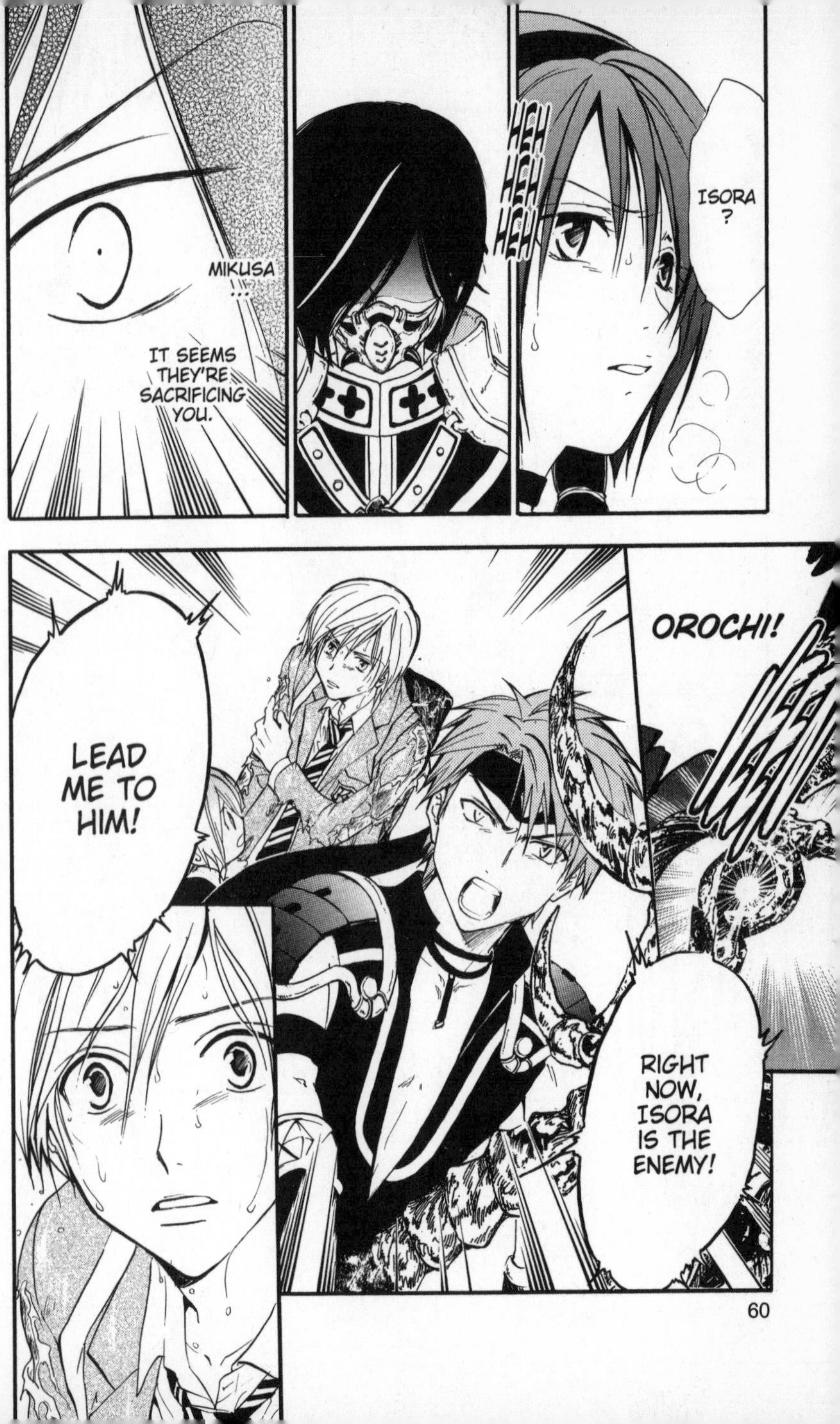
HEH HEH HEH
ISORA ?
MIKUSA !...
IT SEEMS THEY'RE SACRIFICING YOU.
OROCHI!
RIGHT NOW, ISORA IS THE ENEMY!
LEAD ME TO HIM!

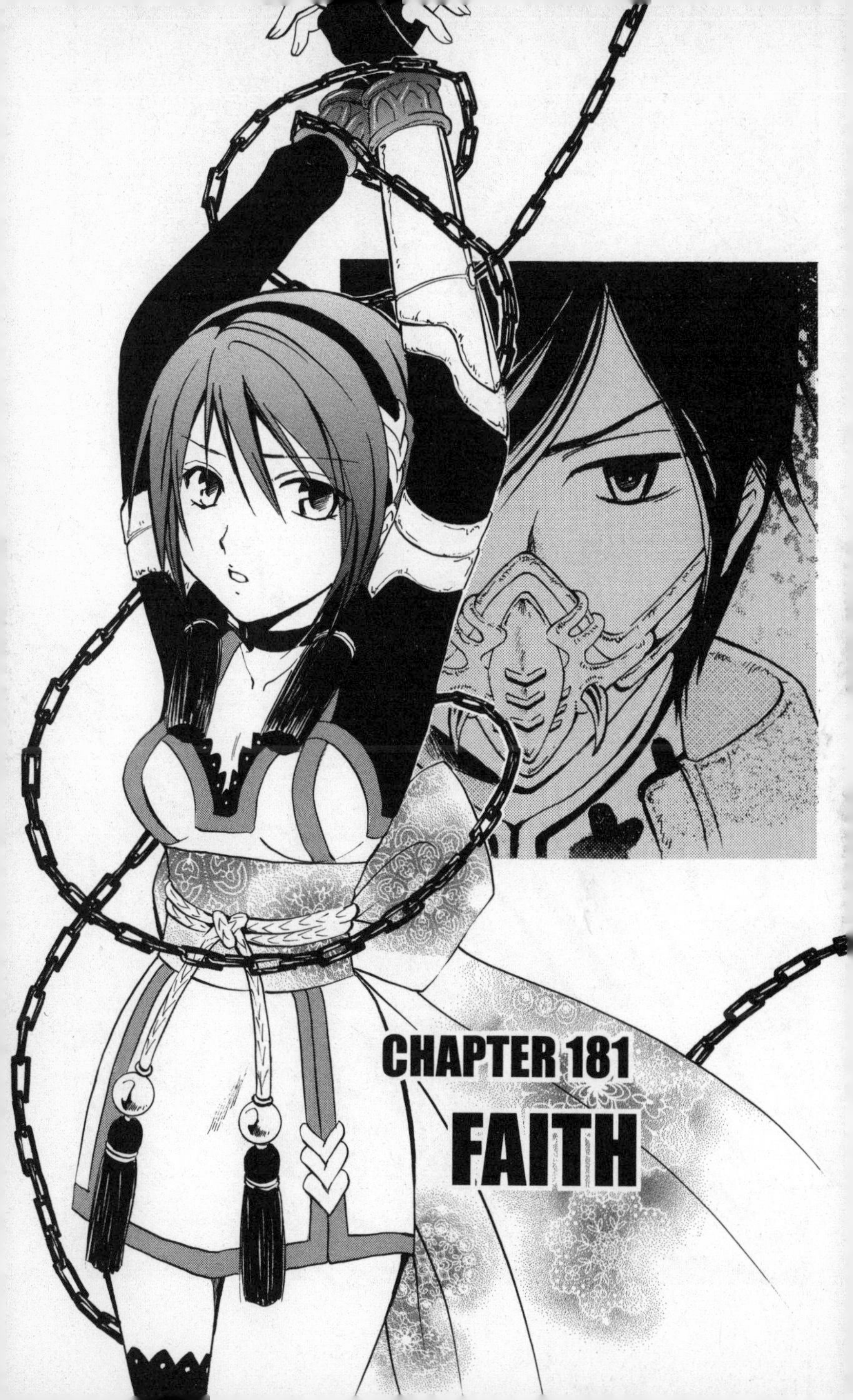
CHAPTER 181
FAITH

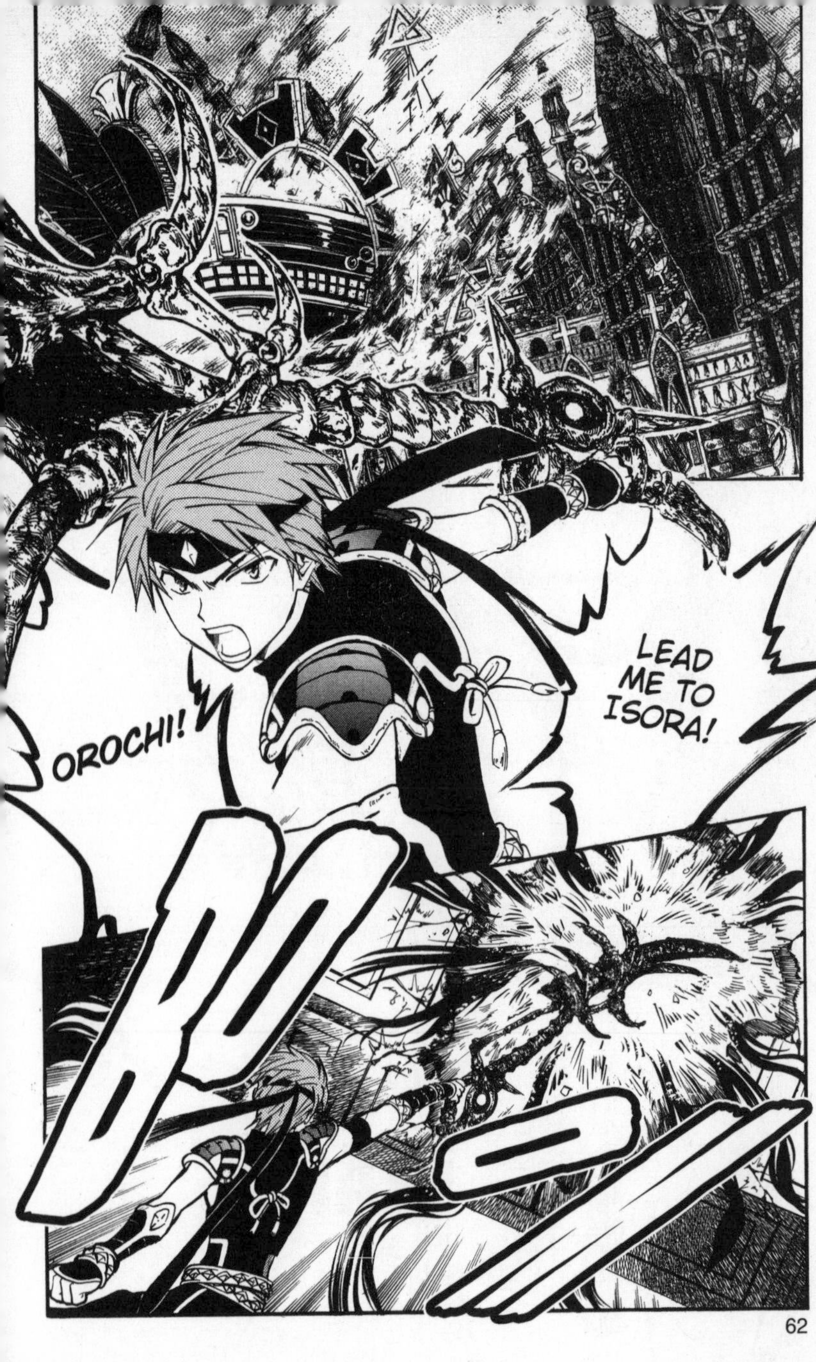
LEAD ME TO ISORA!
OROCHI!

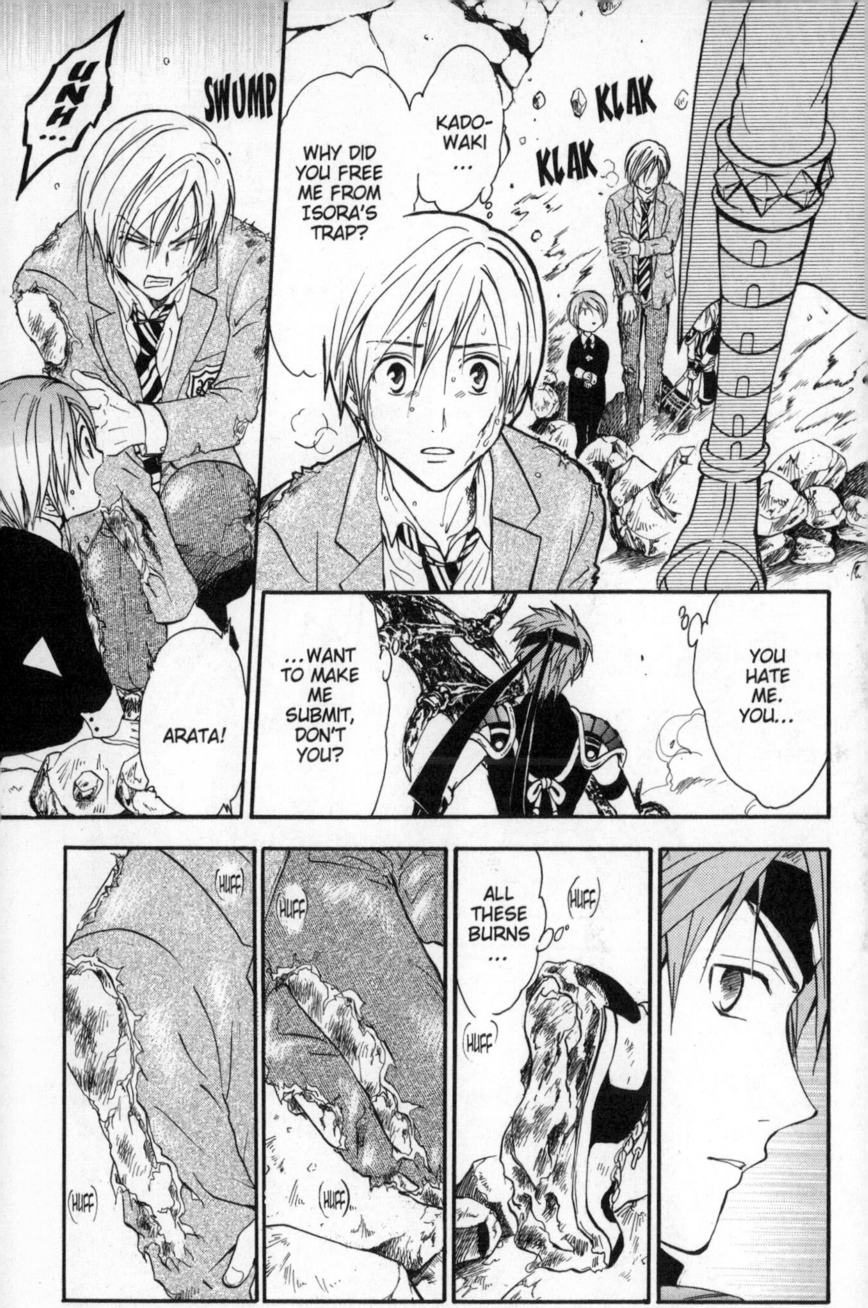
KLAK
KLAK
KADO-WAKI...
WHY DID YOU FREE ME FROM ISORA'S TRAP?
YOU HATE ME. YOU...
...WANT TO MAKE ME SUBMIT, DON'T YOU?
SWUMP
UNH...
ARATA!
(HUFF)
ALL THESE BURNS...
(HUFF)
(HUFF)
(HUFF)
(HUFF)
(HUFF)

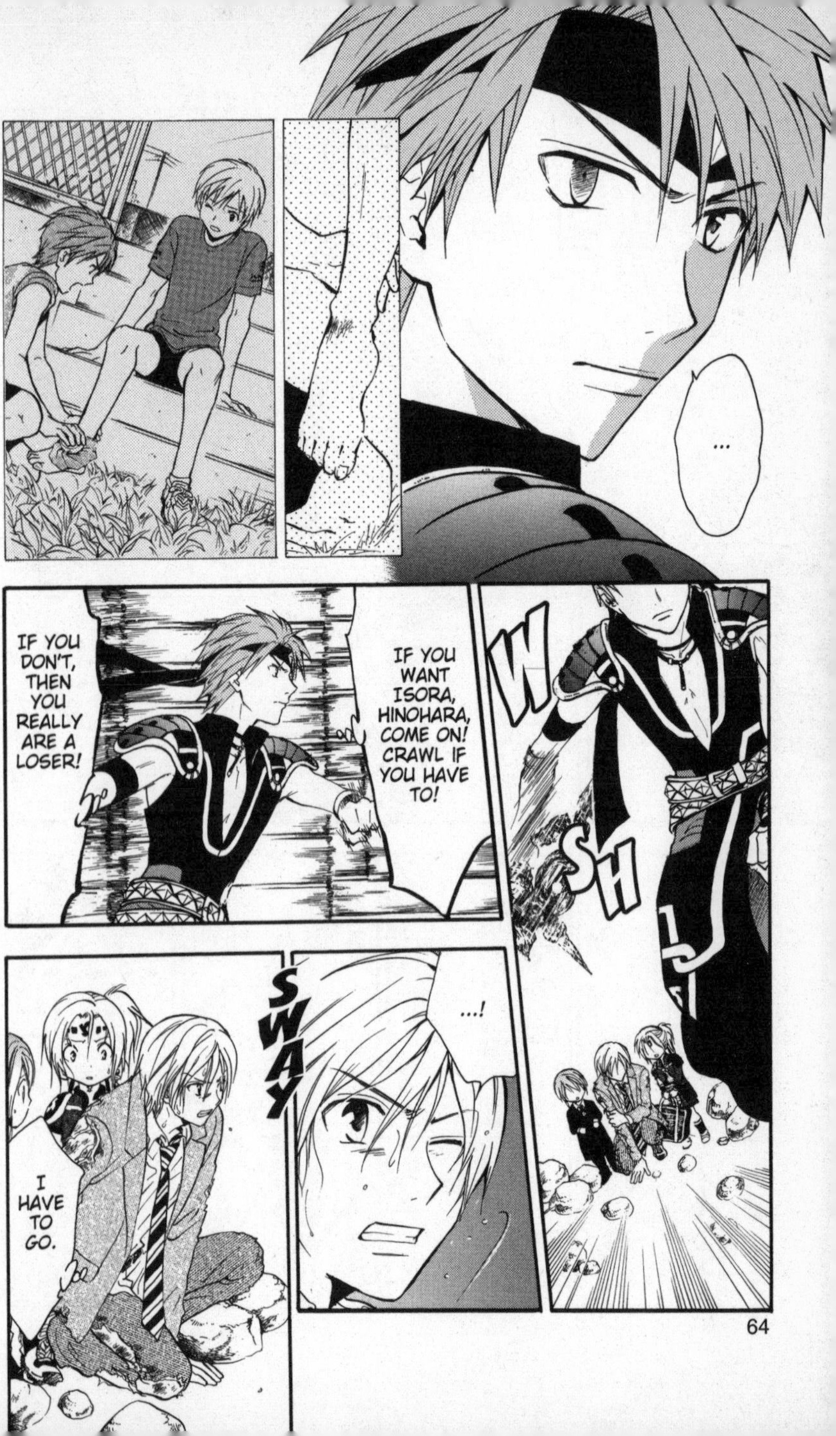
...
WHSH
IF YOU WANT ISORA, HINOHARA, COME ON! CRAWL IF YOU HAVE TO!
IF YOU DON'T, THEN YOU REALLY ARE A LOSER!
SWAY
...!
I HAVE TO GO.

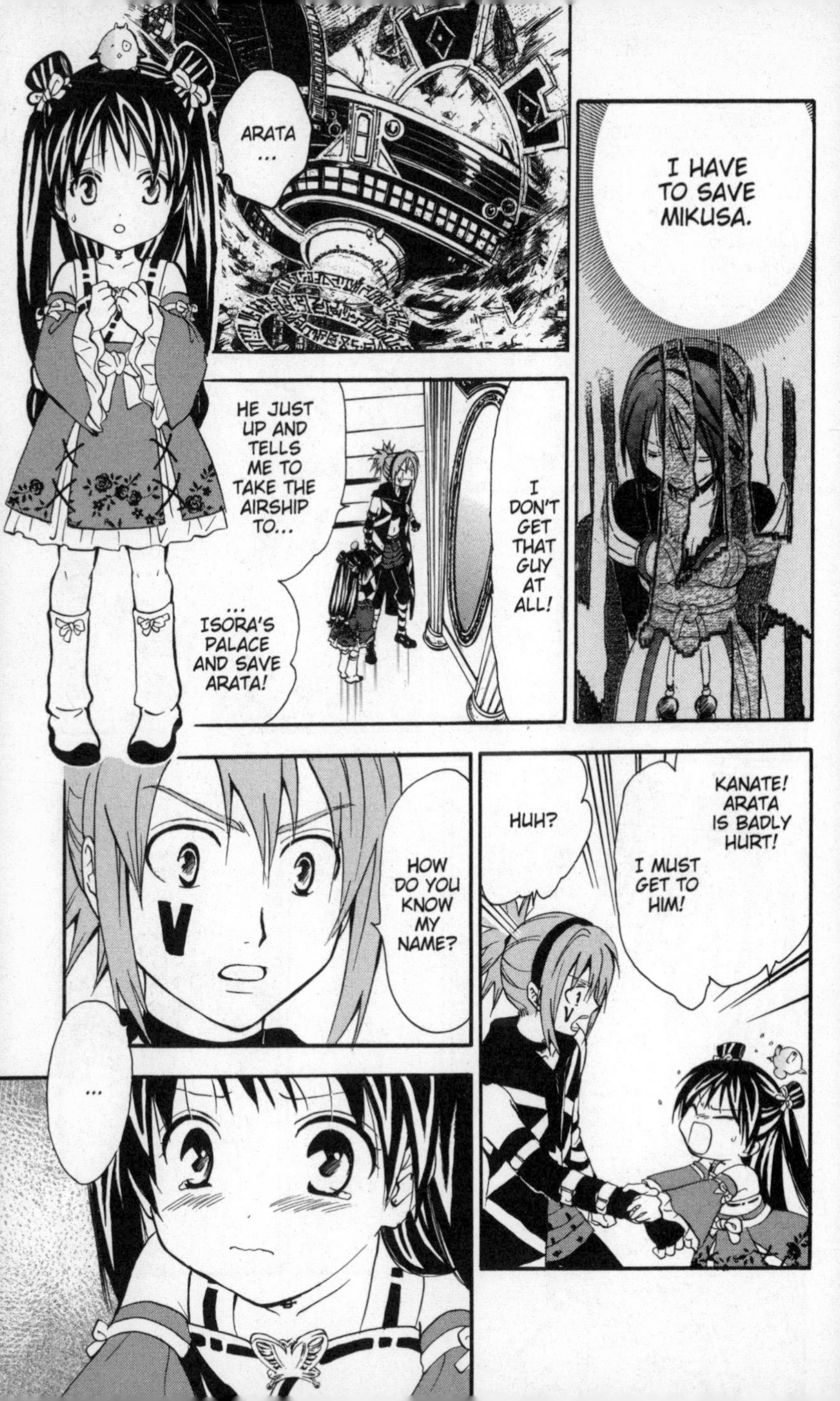
I HAVE TO SAVE MIKUSA.
ARATA ...
I DON'T GET THAT GUY AT ALL!
HE JUST UP AND TELLS ME TO TAKE THE AIRSHIP TO...
... ISORA'S PALACE AND SAVE ARATA!
KANATE! ARATA IS BADLY HURT!
I MUST GET TO HIM!
HUH?
HOW DO YOU KNOW MY NAME?
...

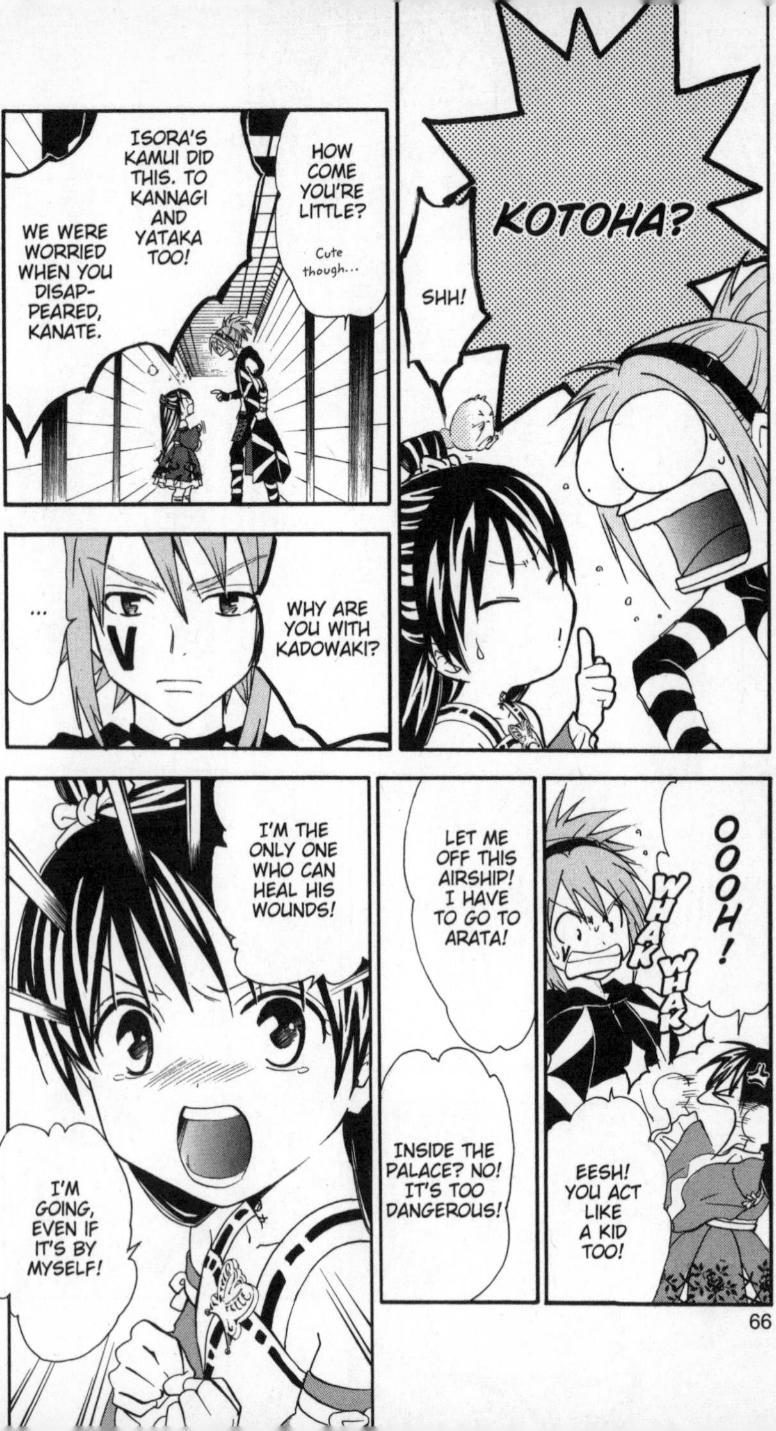
KOTOHA?
SHH!
HOW COME YOU'RE LITTLE?
Cute though...
ISORA'S KAMUI DID THIS. TO KANNAGI AND YATAKA TOO!
WE WERE WORRIED WHEN YOU DISAPPEARED, KANATE.
WHY ARE YOU WITH KADOWAKI?
...
OOOOH!
WHAK WHAK
EESH! YOU ACT LIKE A KID TOO!
LET ME OFF THIS AIRSHIP! I HAVE TO GO TO ARATA!
INSIDE THE PALACE? NO! IT'S TOO DANGEROUS!
I'M THE ONLY ONE WHO CAN HEAL HIS WOUNDS!
I'M GOING, EVEN IF IT'S BY MYSELF!

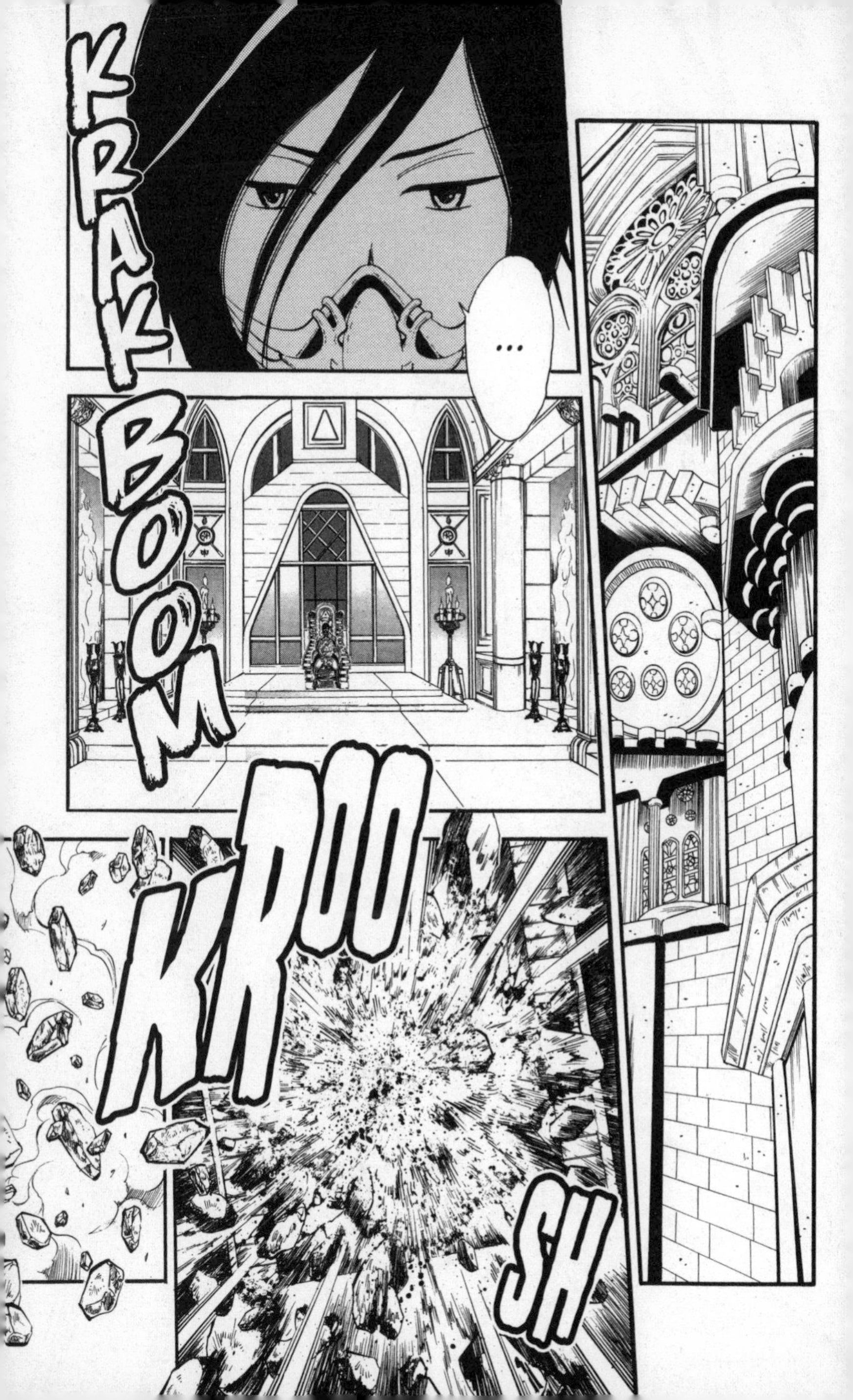
...
KRAKBOOM
KRDOOSH

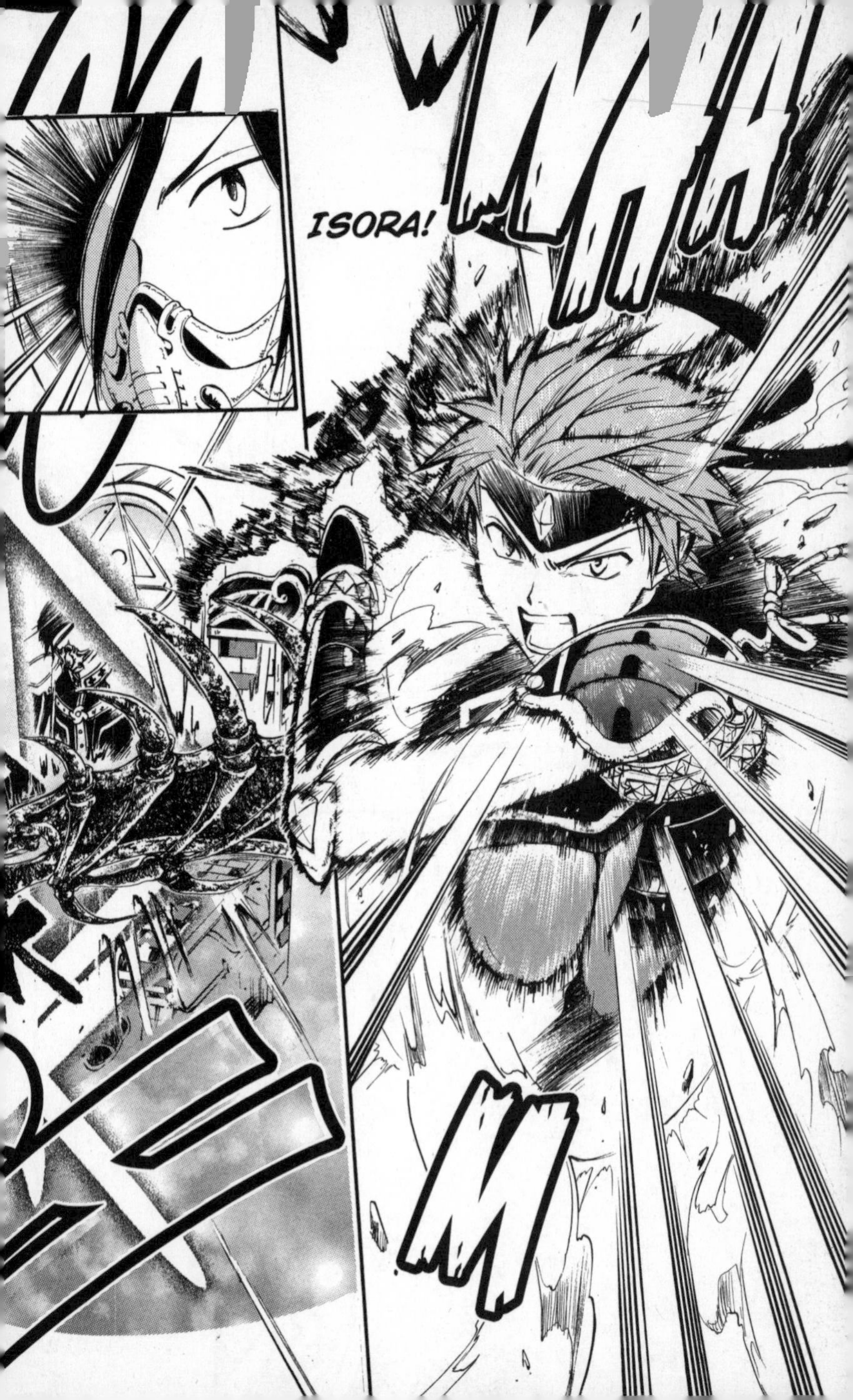
ISORA!

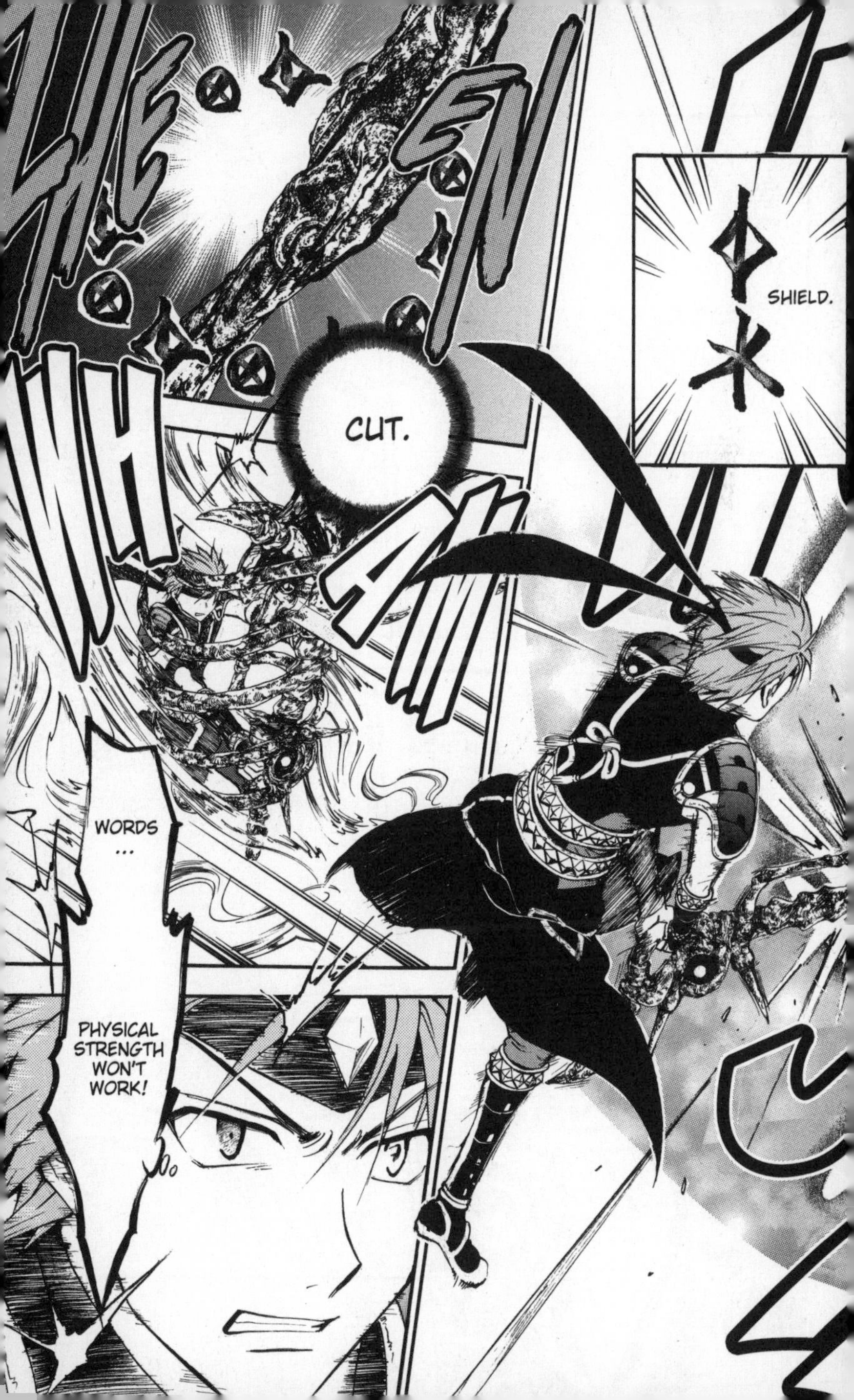
SHIELD.
CUT.
WORDS ...
PHYSICAL STRENGTH WON'T WORK!

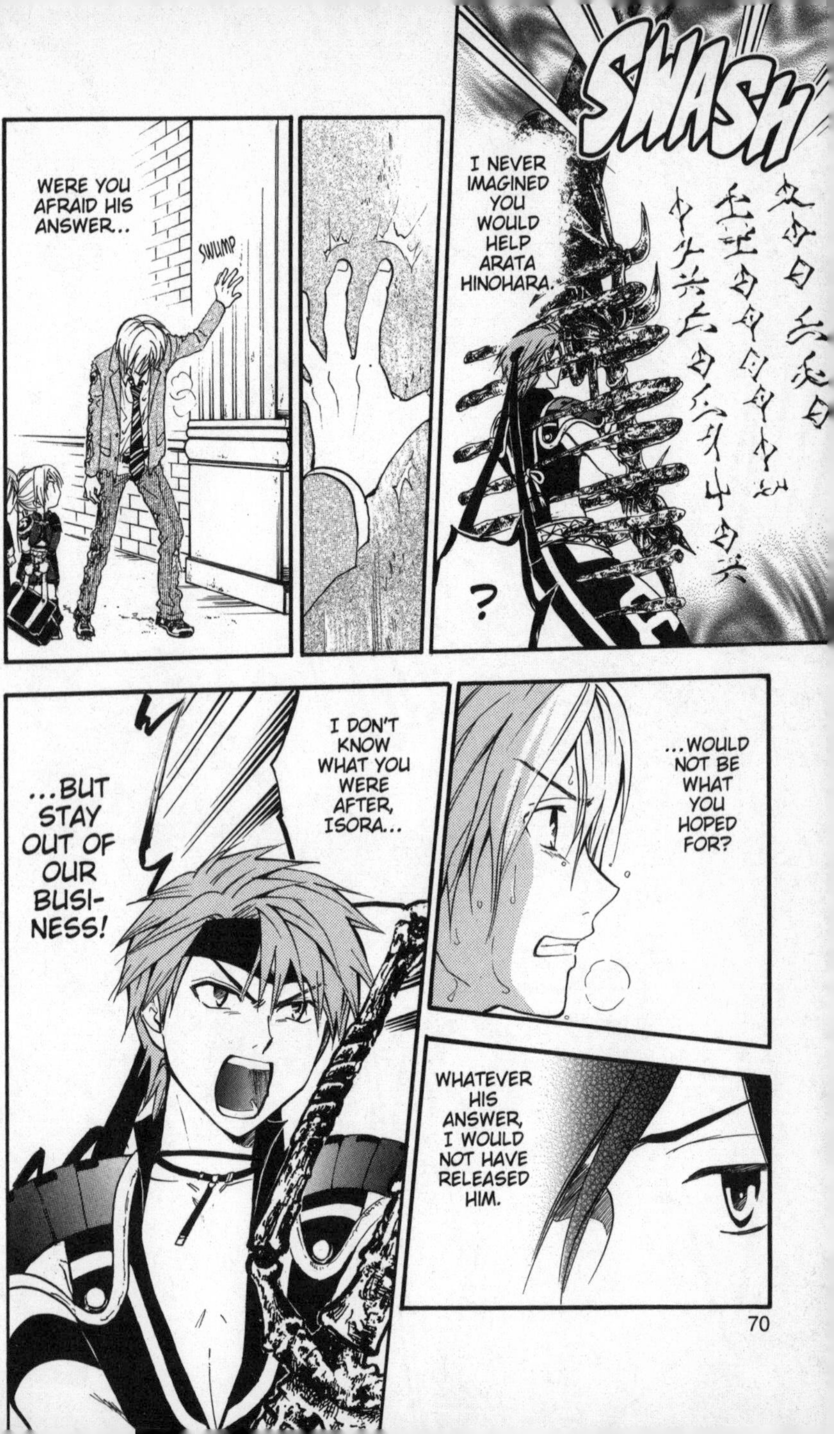
SHASH
I NEVER IMAGINED YOU WOULD HELP ARATA HINOHARA.
?
WERE YOU AFRAID HIS ANSWER...
SWUMP
...WOULD NOT BE WHAT YOU HOPED FOR?
WHATEVER HIS ANSWER, I WOULD NOT HAVE RELEASED HIM.
I DON'T KNOW WHAT YOU WERE AFTER, ISORA...
...BUT STAY OUT OF OUR BUSINESS!

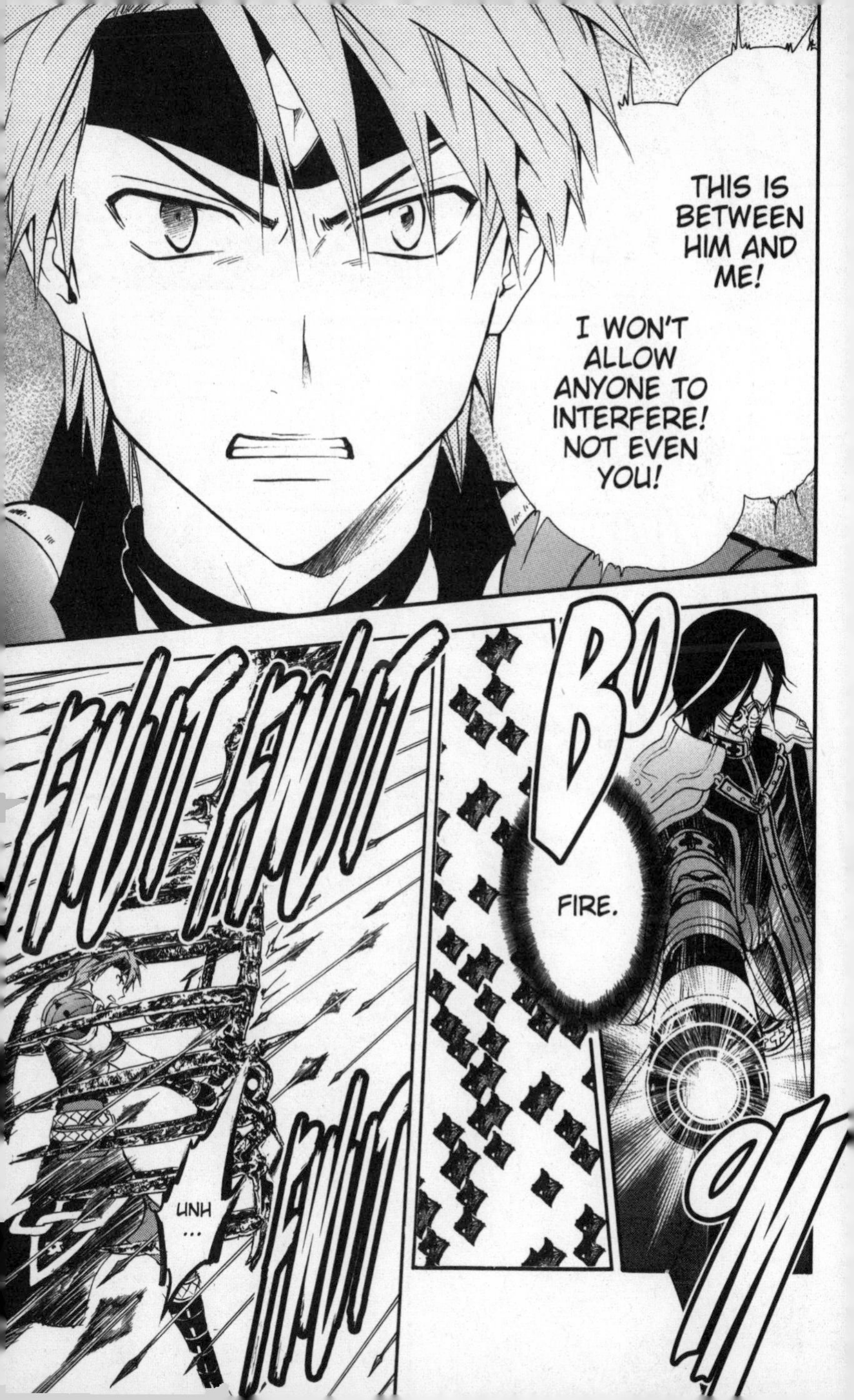
THIS IS BETWEEN HIM AND ME!
I WON'T ALLOW ANYONE TO INTERFERE! NOT EVEN YOU!
BO
FIRE.
UNH ...

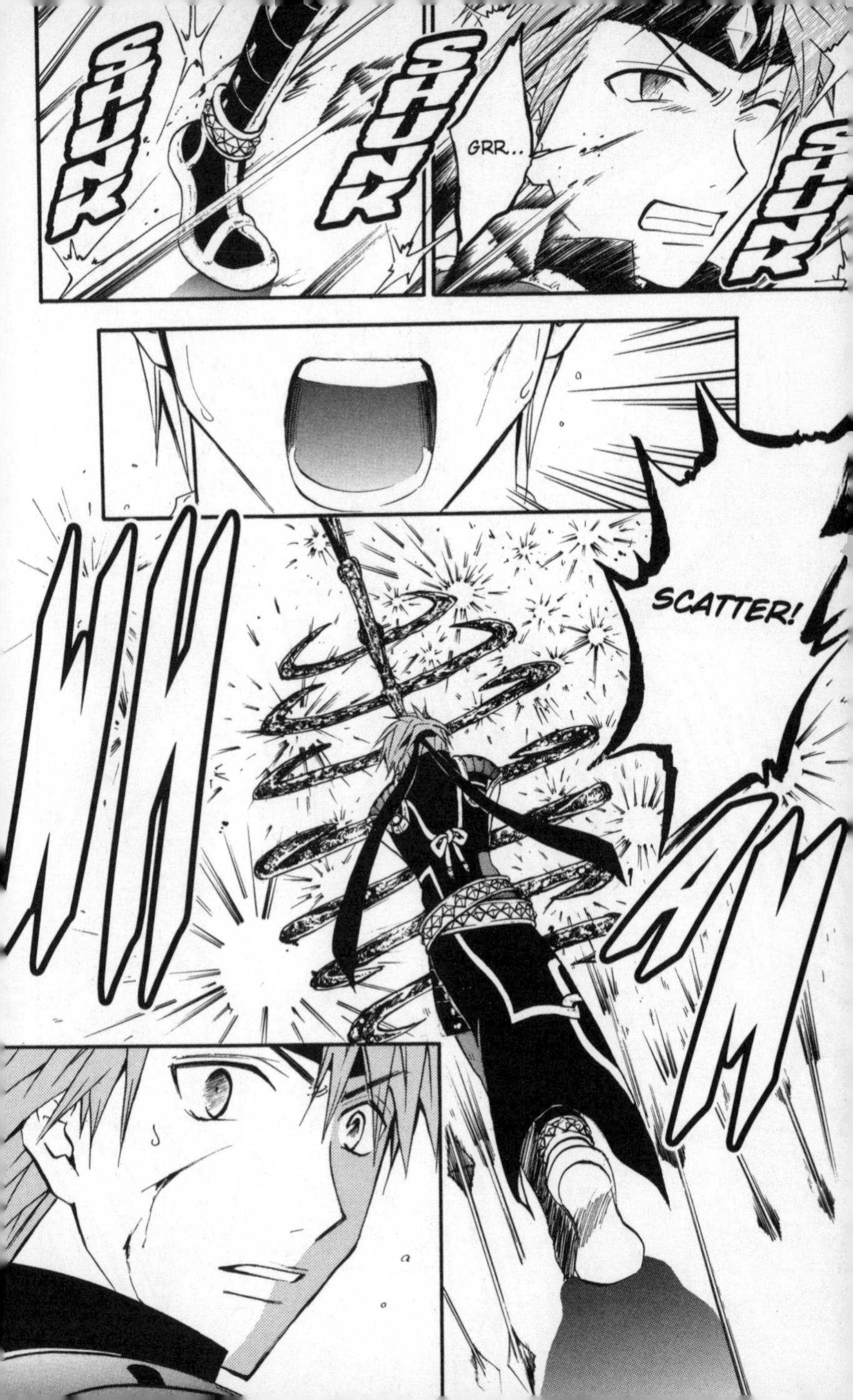
SHUNK
GRR...
SHUNK
SHUNK
SCATTER!

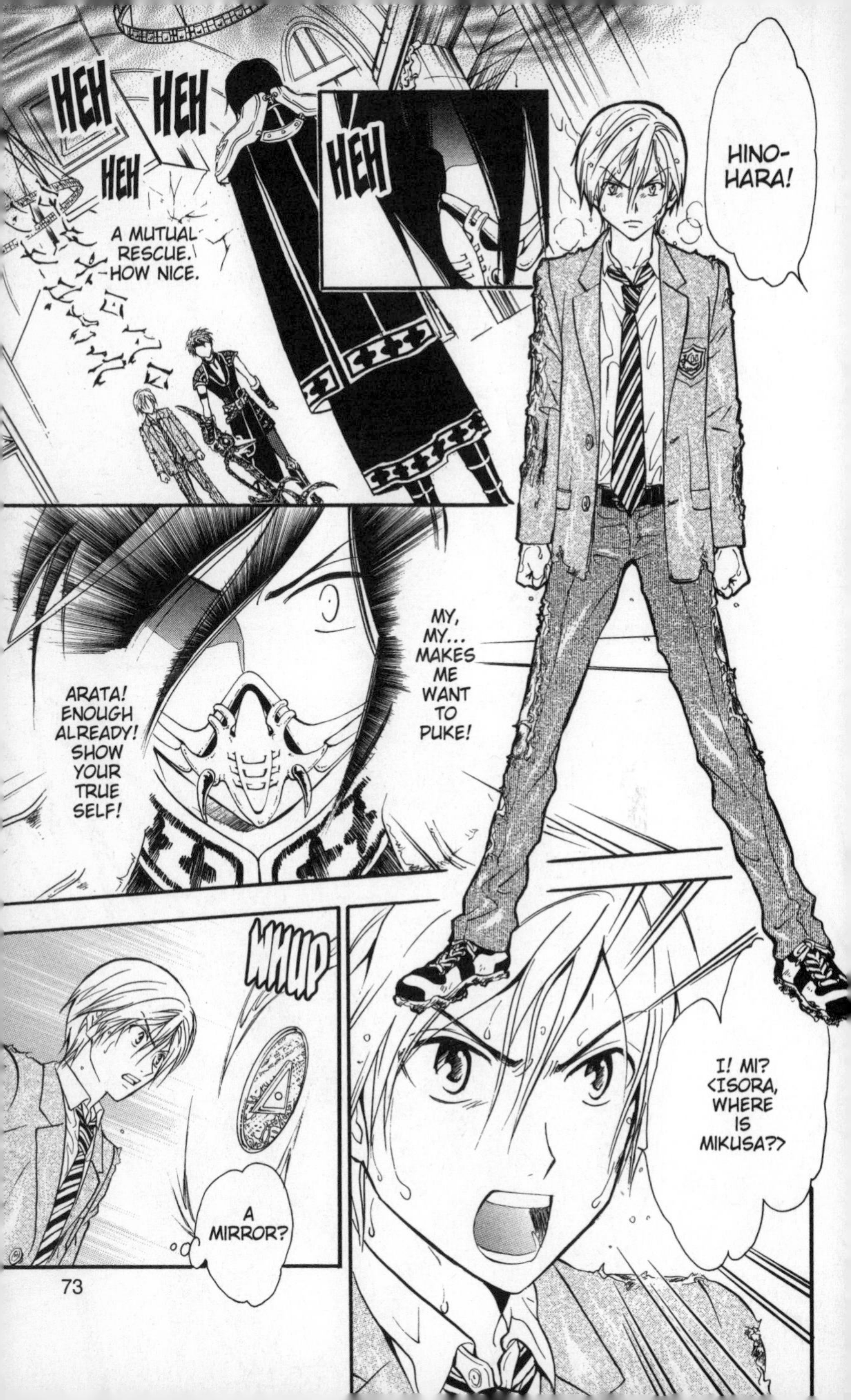

HINO-HARA!
HEH
HEH HEH HEH
A MUTUAL RESCUE. HOW NICE.
MY, MY... MAKES ME WANT TO PUKE!
ARATA! ENOUGH ALREADY! SHOW YOUR TRUE SELF!
I! MI? <ISORA, WHERE IS MIKUSA?>
WHUP
A MIRROR?

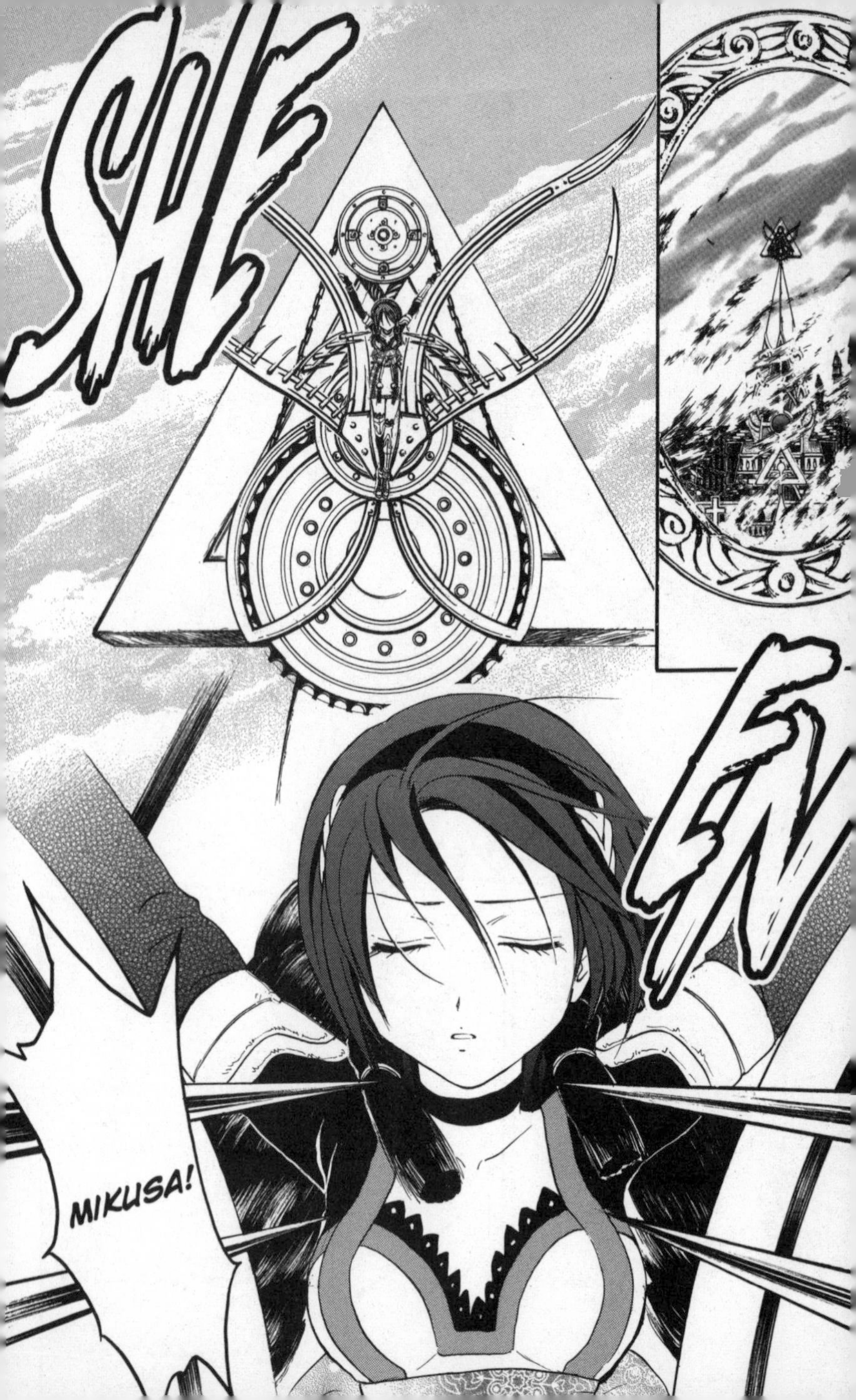
SHEN
MIKUSA!

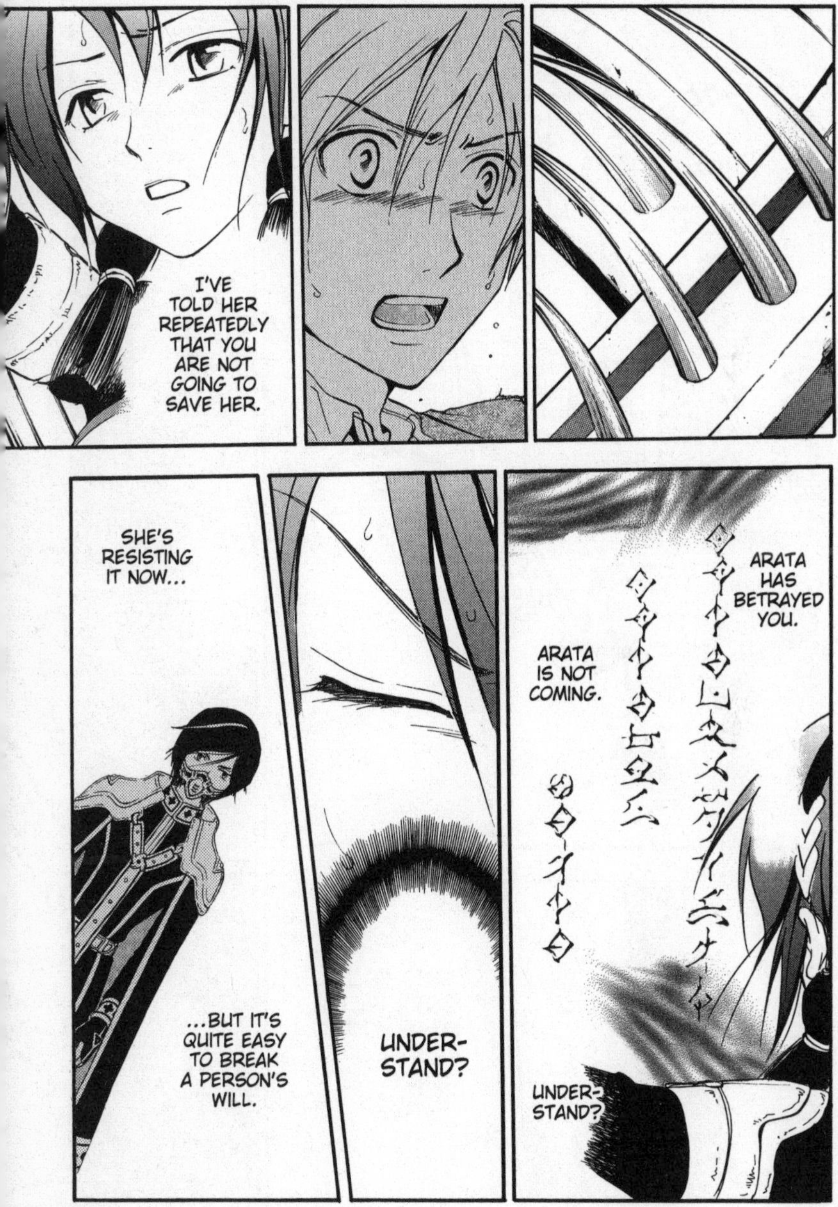
I'VE TOLD HER REPEATEDLY THAT YOU ARE NOT GOING TO SAVE HER.
ARATA HAS BETRAYED YOU.
ARATA IS NOT COMING.
UNDER-STAND?
UNDER-STAND?
SHE'S RESISTING IT NOW...
...BUT IT'S QUITE EASY TO BREAK A PERSON'S WILL.

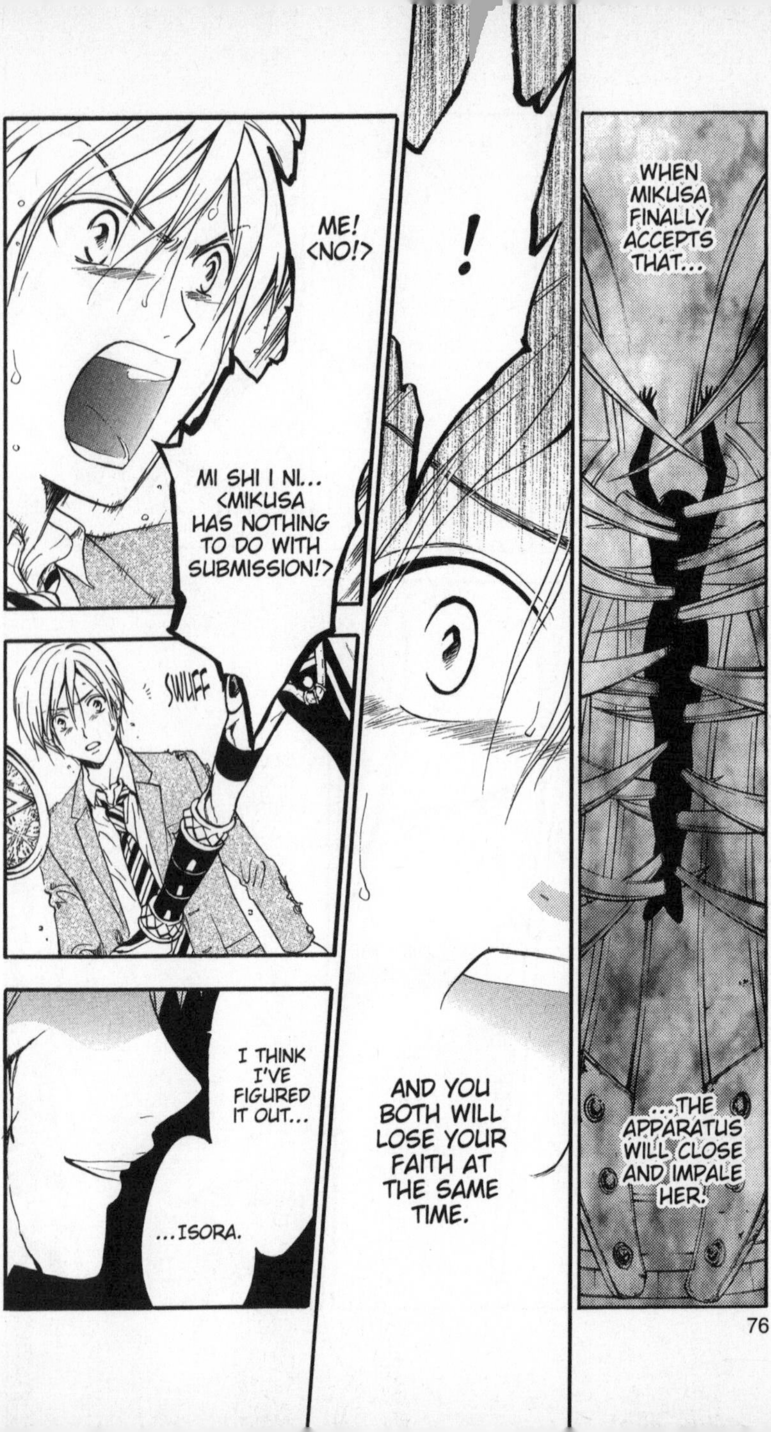
WHEN MIKUSA FINALLY ACCEPTS THAT...
...THE APPARATUS WILL CLOSE AND IMPALE HER.
!
AND YOU BOTH WILL LOSE YOUR FAITH AT THE SAME TIME.
ME! <NO!>
MI SHI I NI... <MIKUSA HAS NOTHING TO DO WITH SUBMISSION!>
SWUFF
I THINK I'VE FIGURED IT OUT...
...ISORA.

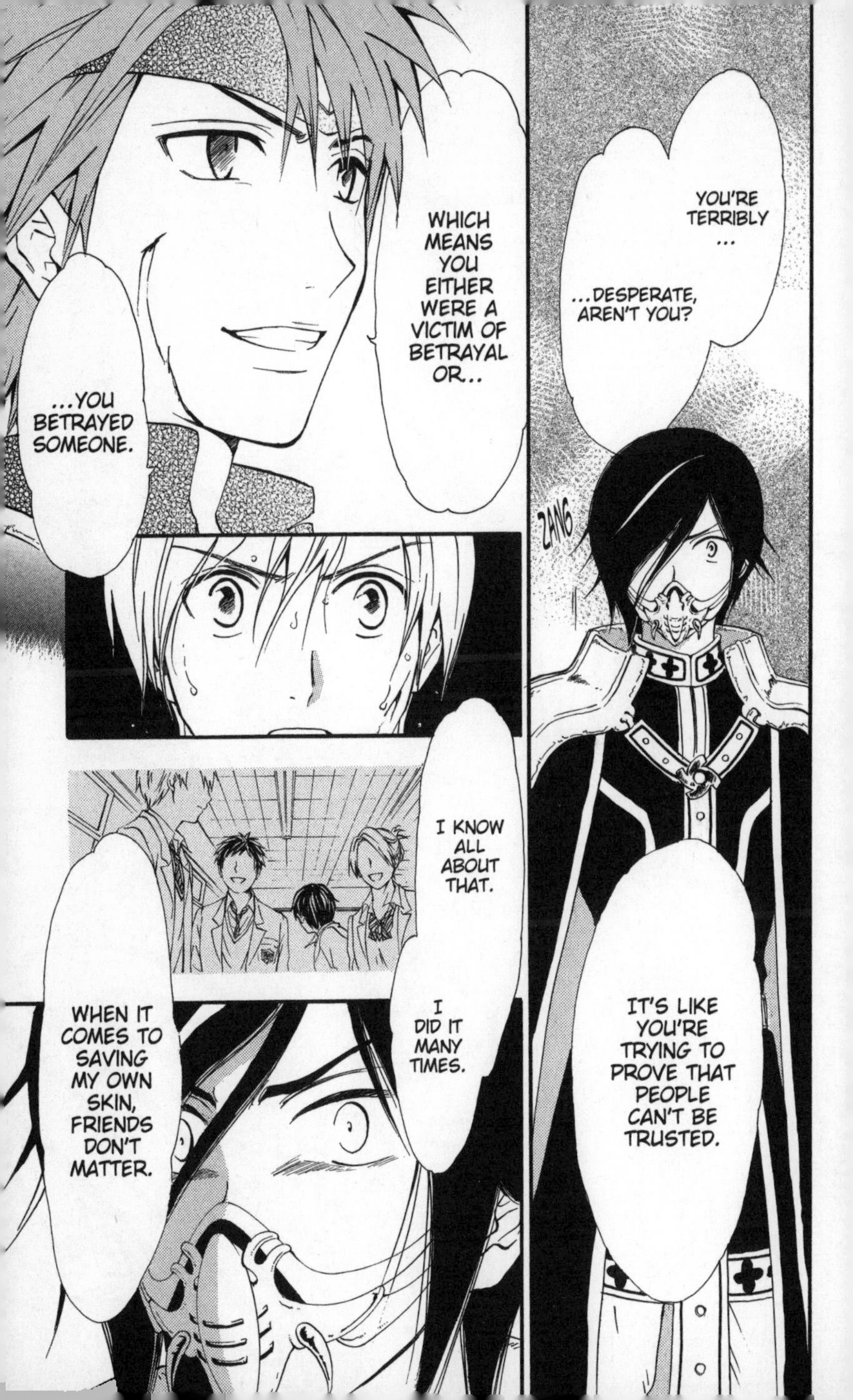
YOU'RE TERRIBLY ...
...DESPERATE, AREN'T YOU?
ZANG
IT'S LIKE YOU'RE TRYING TO PROVE THAT PEOPLE CAN'T BE TRUSTED.
WHICH MEANS YOU EITHER WERE A VICTIM OF BETRAYAL OR...
...YOU BETRAYED SOMEONE.
I KNOW ALL ABOUT THAT.
I DID IT MANY TIMES.
WHEN IT COMES TO SAVING MY OWN SKIN, FRIENDS DON'T MATTER.

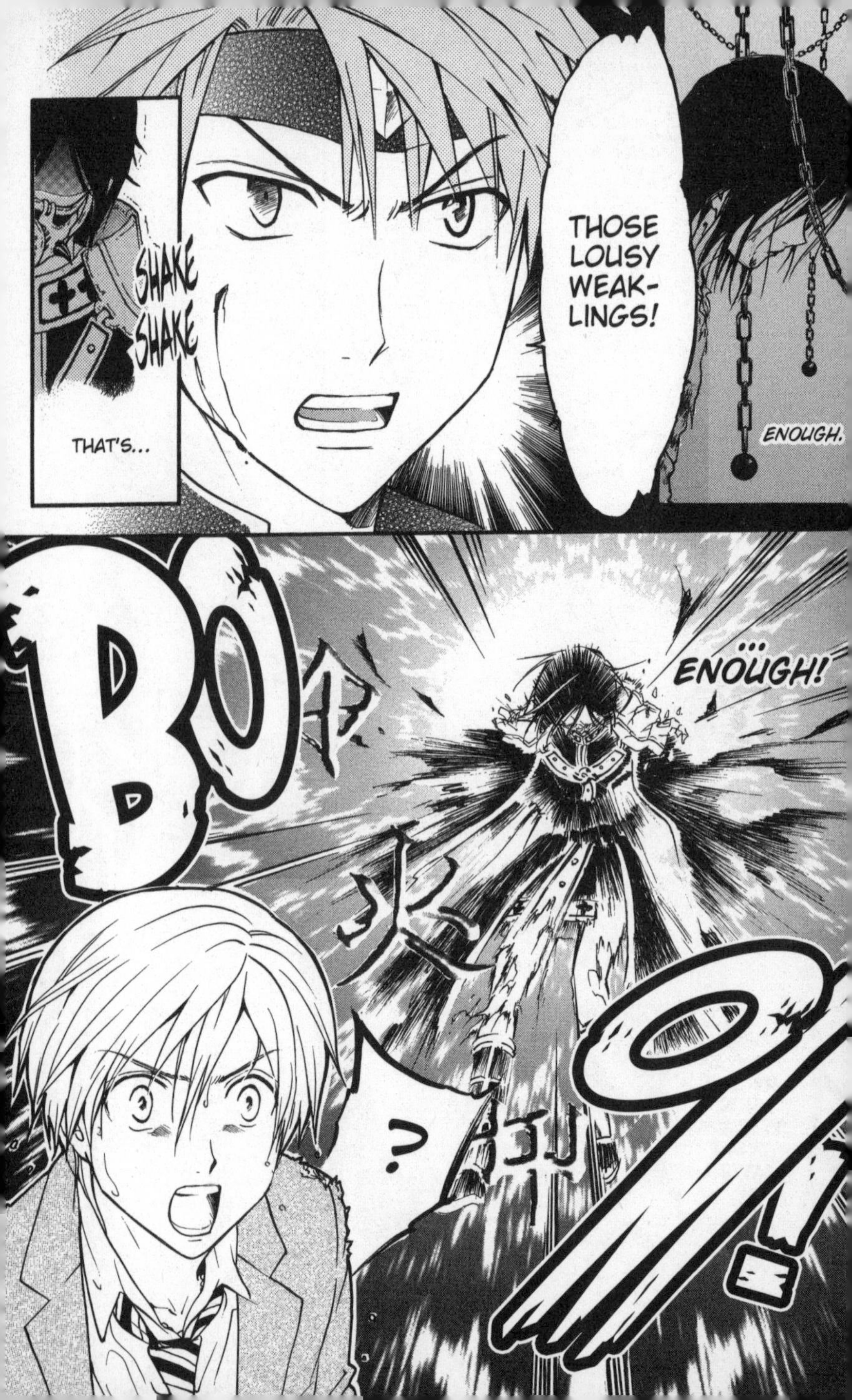
ENOUGH.
THOSE LOUSY WEAK-LINGS!
SHAKE SHAKE
THAT'S...
...ENOUGH!
?

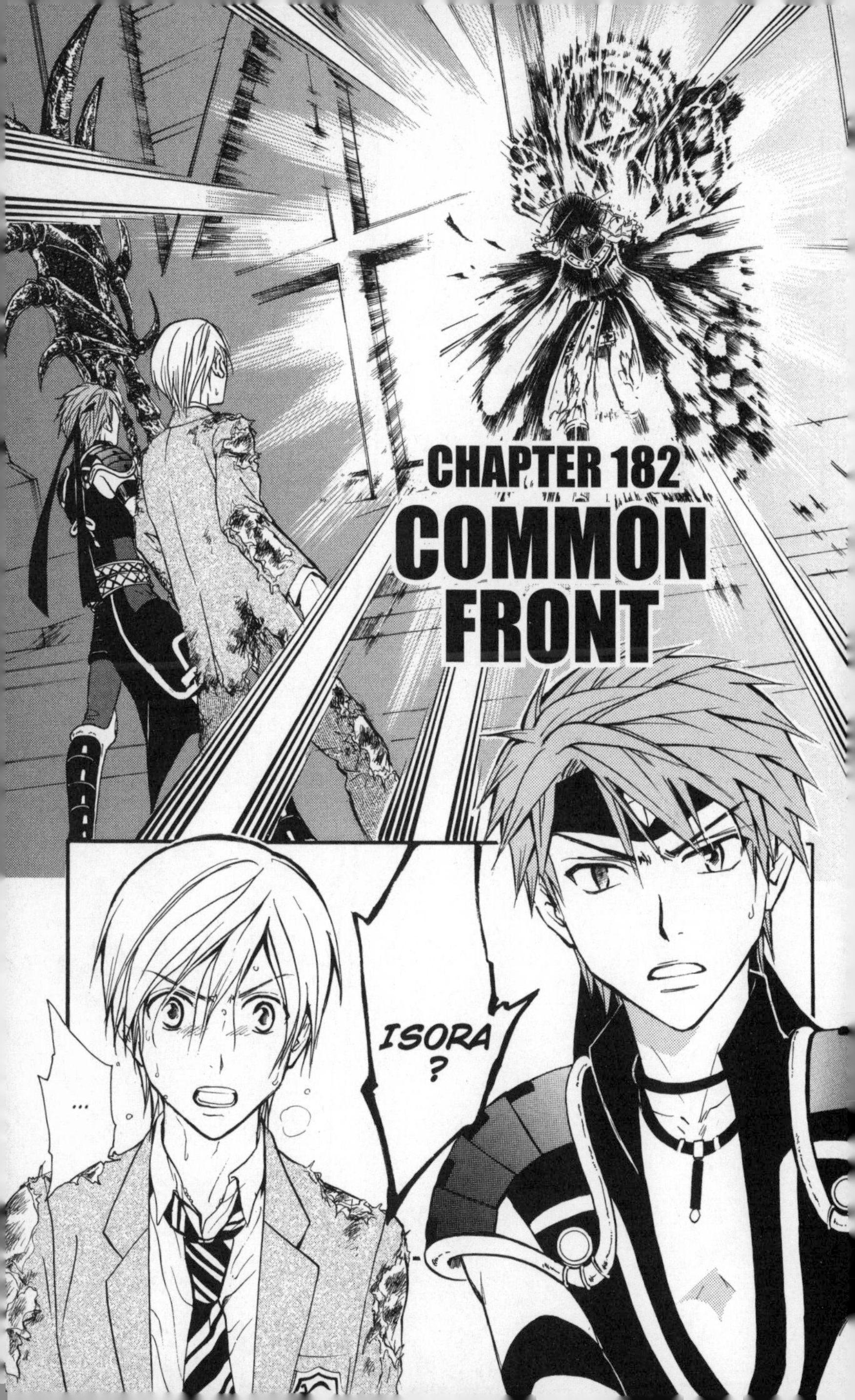
CHAPTER 182
COMMON FRONT
ISORA ?
...

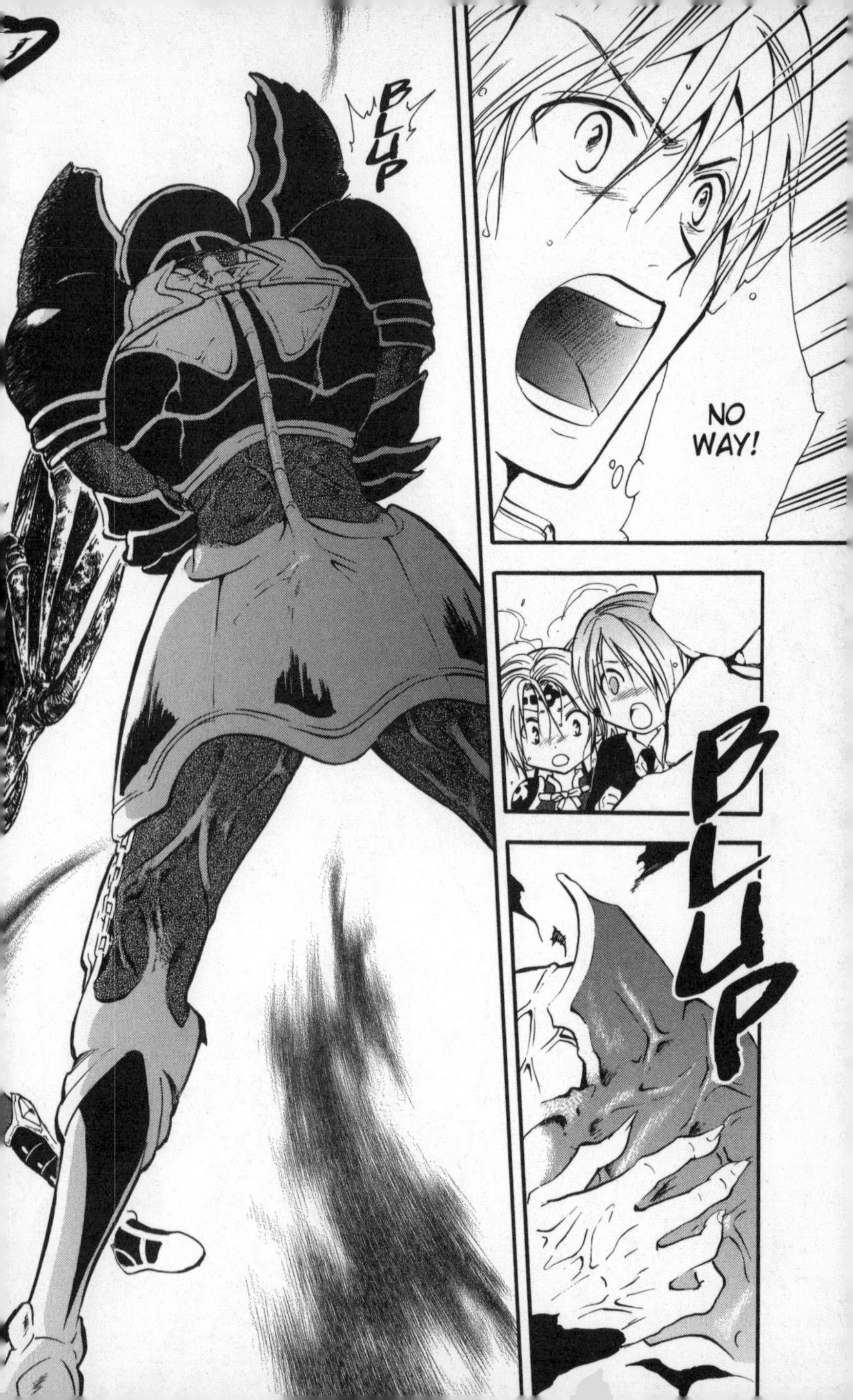
NO WAY!
BLUP
BLUP

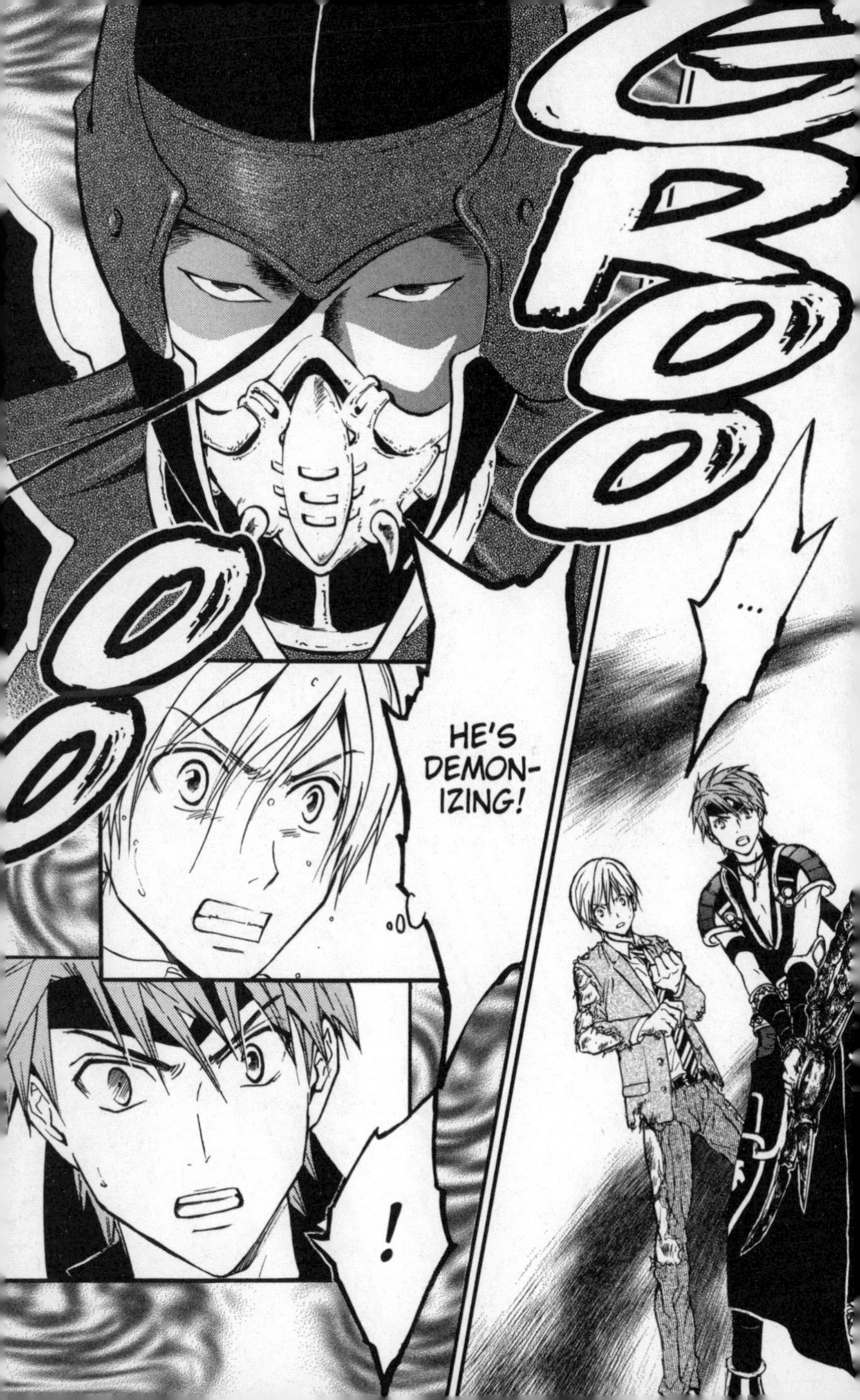
GROOOOOO
...
HE'S DEMON-IZING!
!

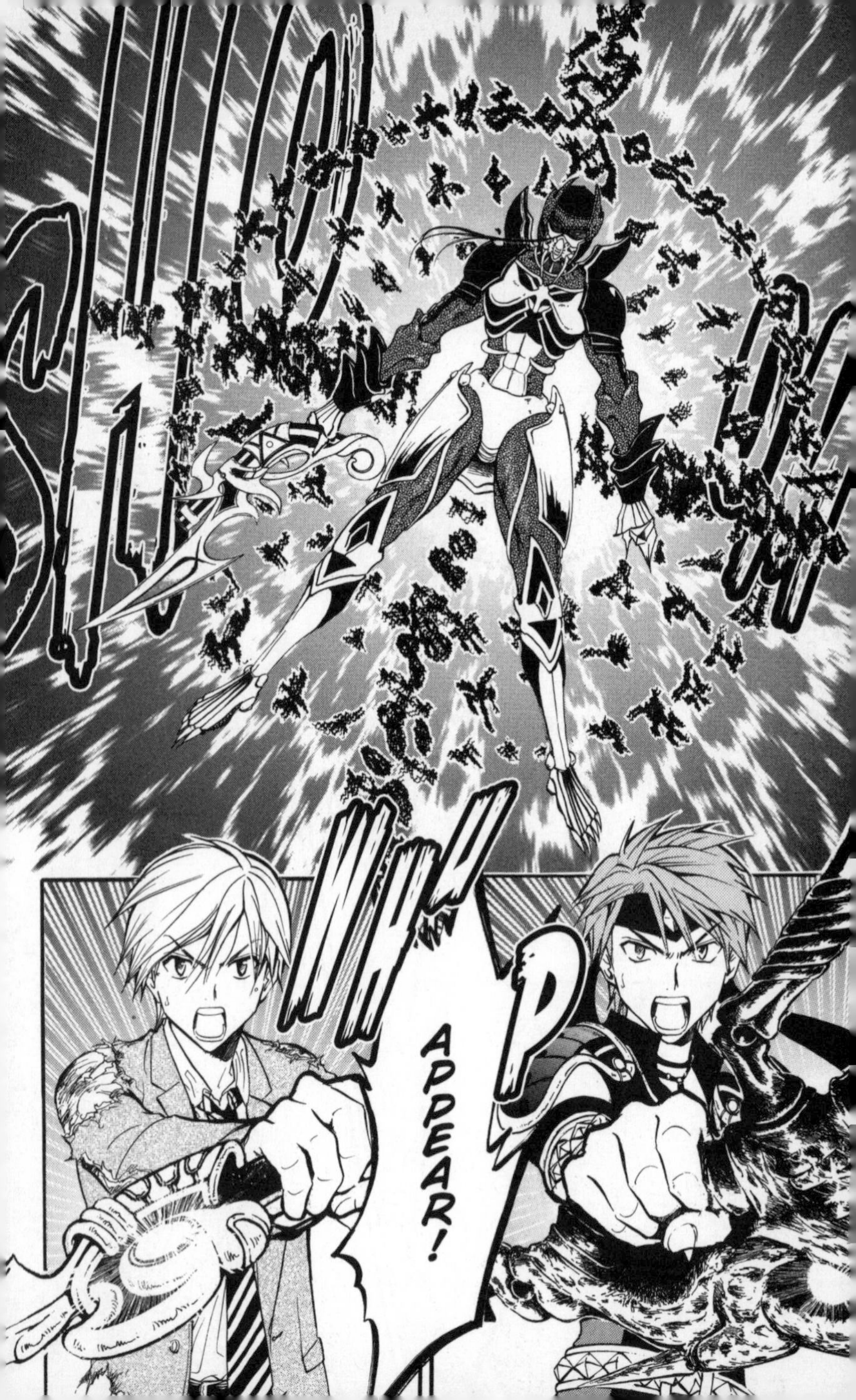
APPEAR!

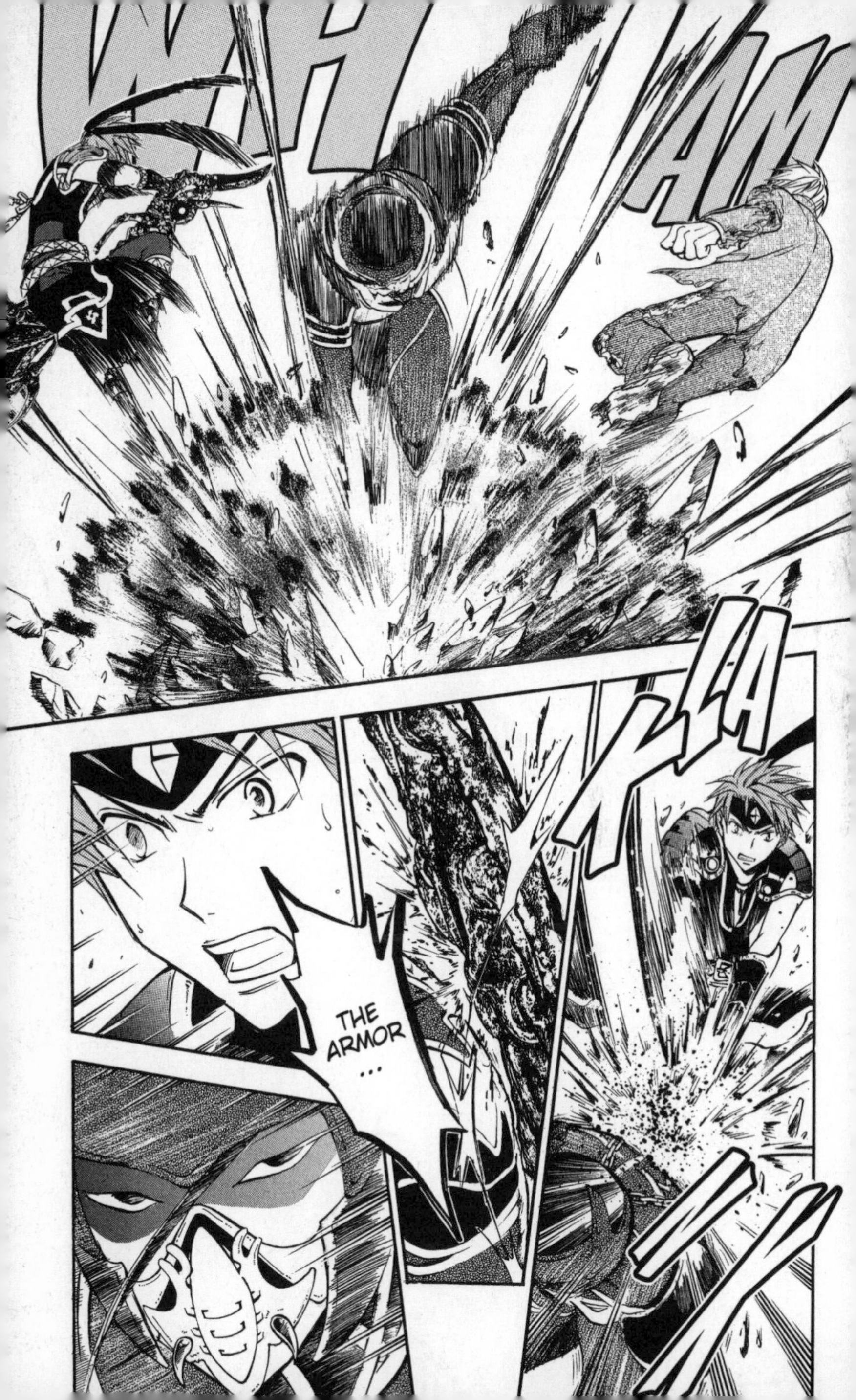
WHAM
THE ARMOR ...

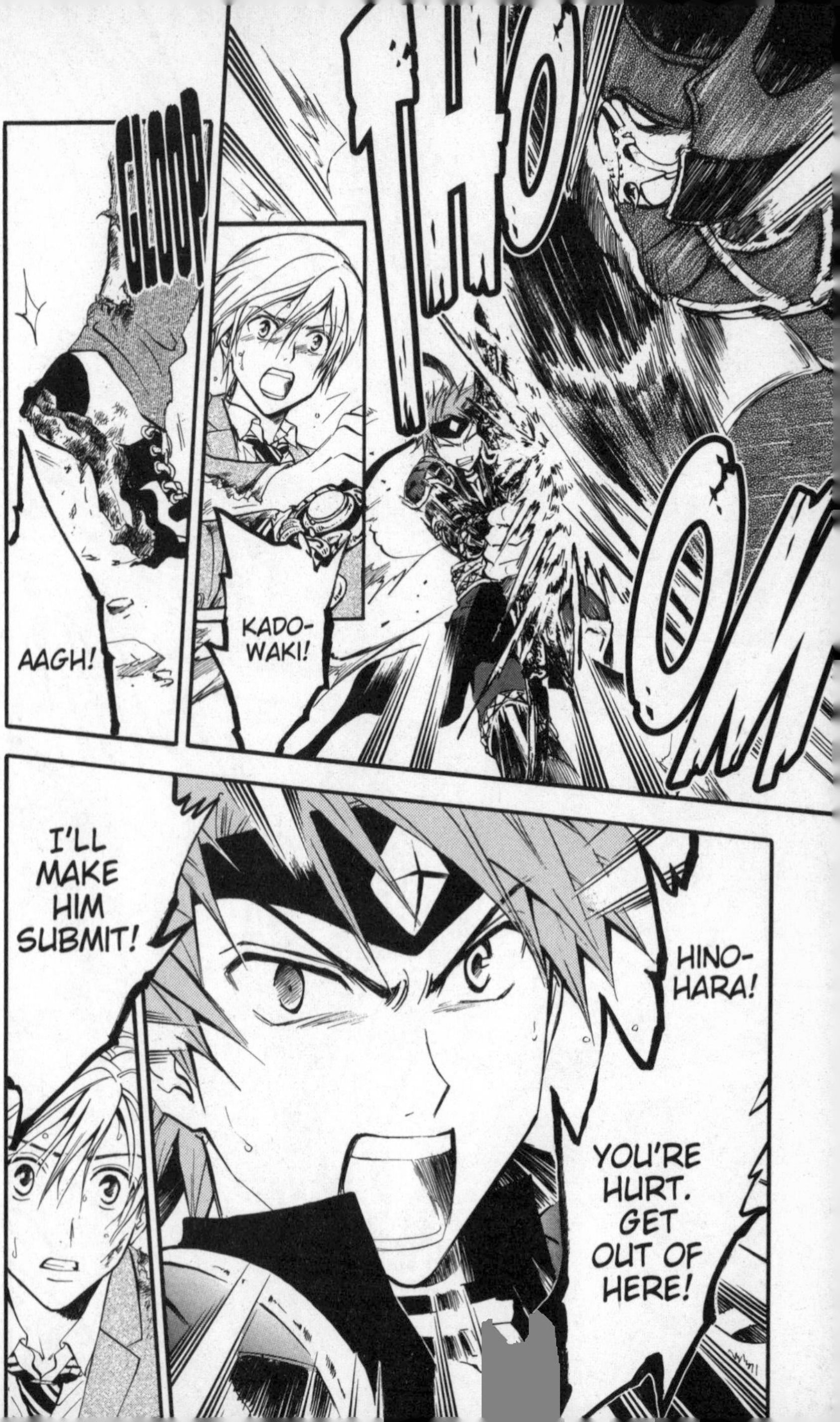
THOOM
KADO-WAKI!
GLOOP
AAGH!
HINO-HARA!
YOU'RE HURT. GET OUT OF HERE!
I'LL MAKE HIM SUBMIT!

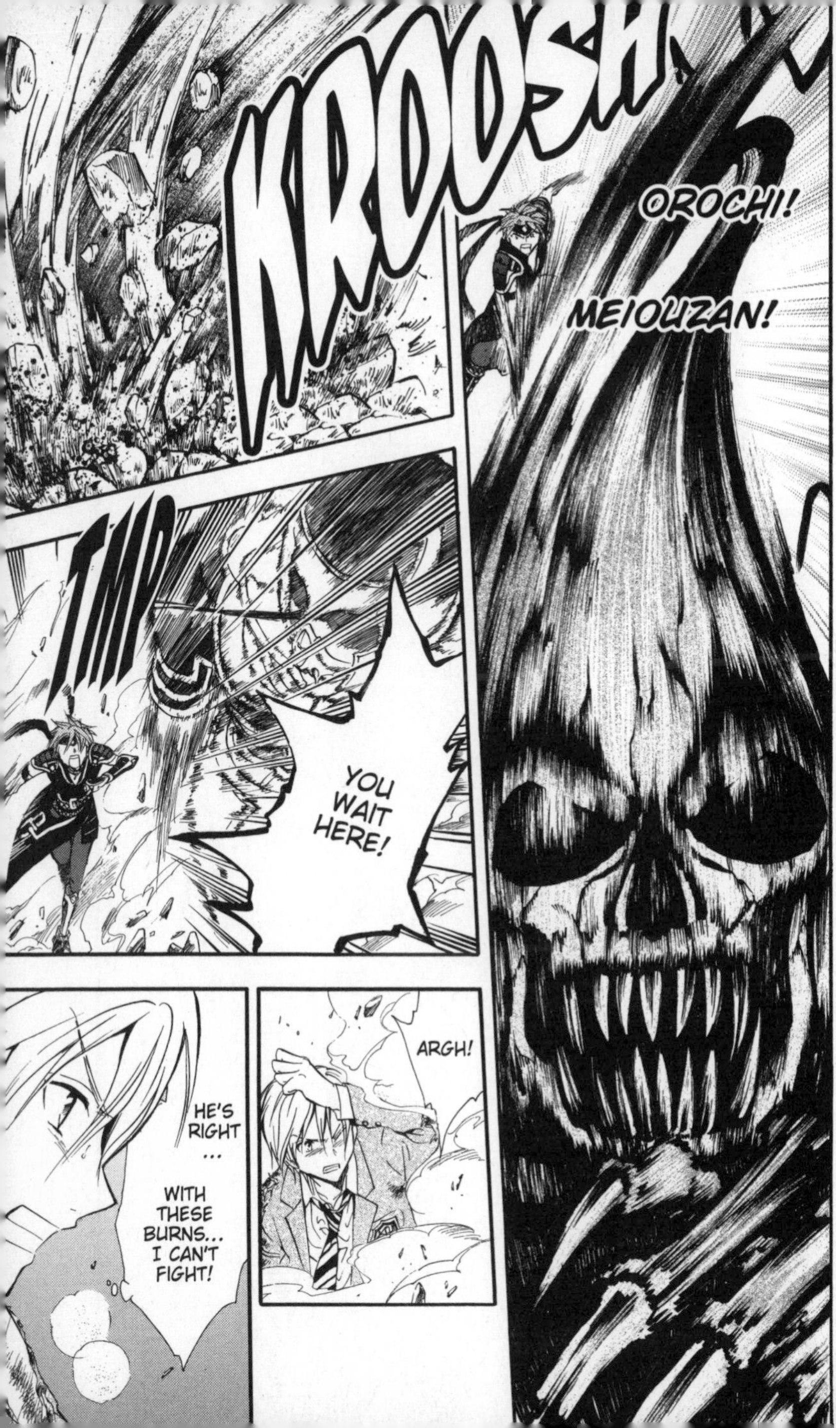
OROCHI!
MEIOUZAN!
KROOSH
TMP
YOU WAIT HERE!
ARGH!
HE'S RIGHT...
WITH THESE BURNS... I CAN'T FIGHT!

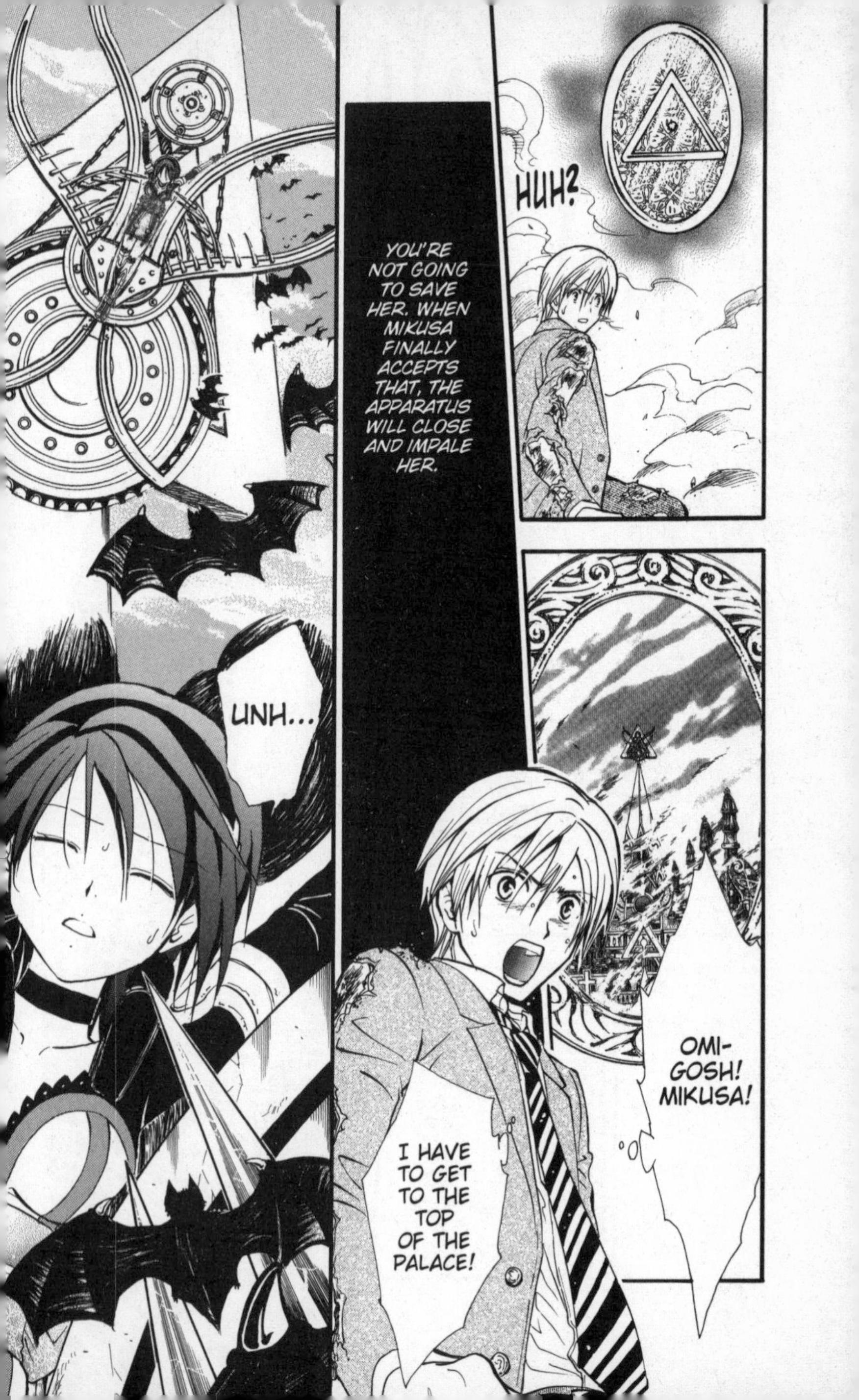
HUH?
OMI-GOSH! MIKUSA!
I HAVE TO GET TO THE TOP OF THE PALACE!
YOU'RE NOT GOING TO SAVE HER. WHEN MIKUSA FINALLY ACCEPTS THAT, THE APPARATUS WILL CLOSE AND IMPALE HER.
UNH...

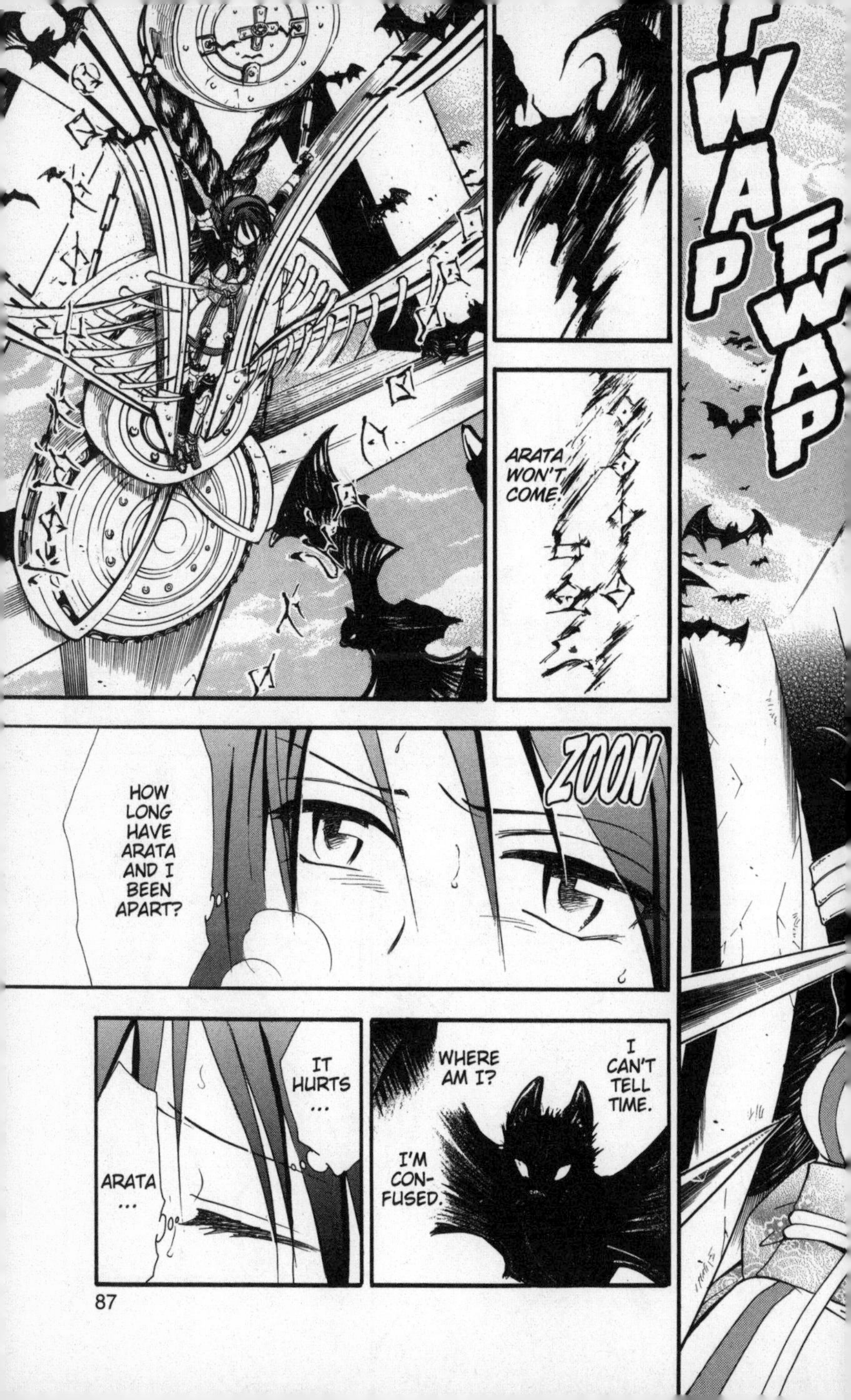
TWAP
FWAP
ARATA WON'T COME.
ZOON
HOW LONG HAVE ARATA AND I BEEN APART?
I CAN'T TELL TIME.
WHERE AM I?
I'M CON-FUSED.
IT HURTS...
ARATA...

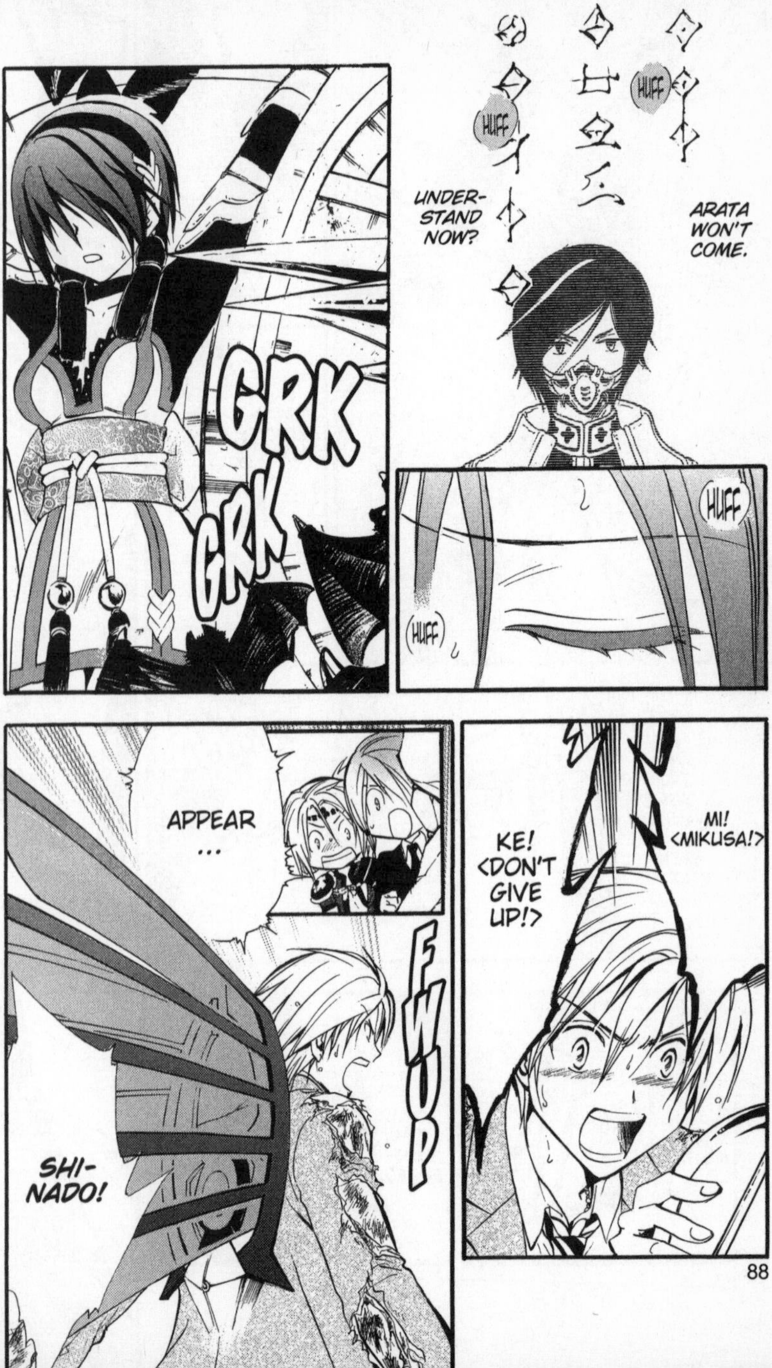
ARATA WON'T COME.
HUFF
HUFF
UNDER-STAND NOW?
HUFF
HUFF
GRK GRK
MI! <MIKUSA!>
KE! <DON'T GIVE UP!>
APPEAR ...
FWUP
SHI-NADO!

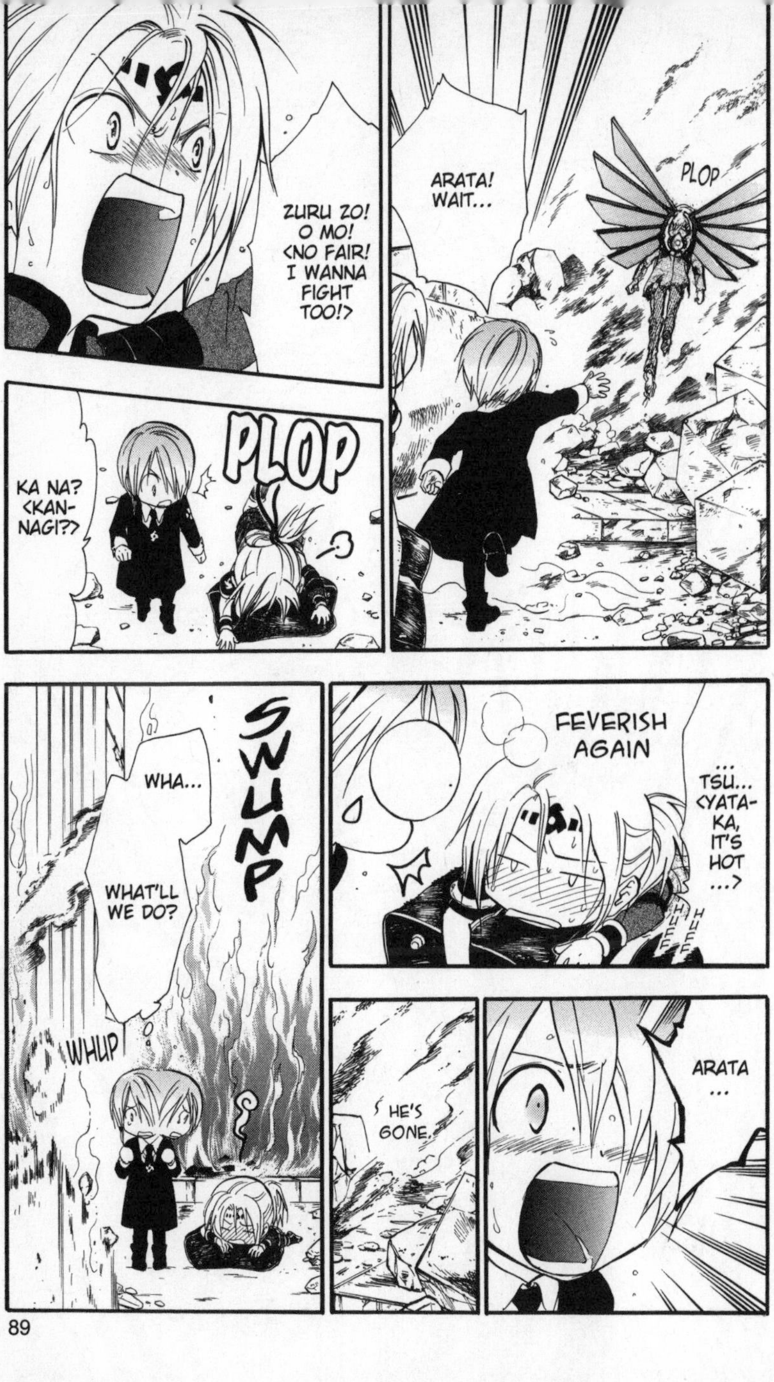
PLOP
ARATA! WAIT...
ZURU ZO! O MO! <NO FAIR! I WANNA FIGHT TOO!>
PLOP
KA NA? <KAN-NAGI?>
FEVERISH AGAIN
... TSU... <YATA-KA, IT'S HOT ...>
HUFF HUFF
ARATA ...
HE'S GONE.
SWUMP
WHA...
WHAT'LL WE DO?
WHUP

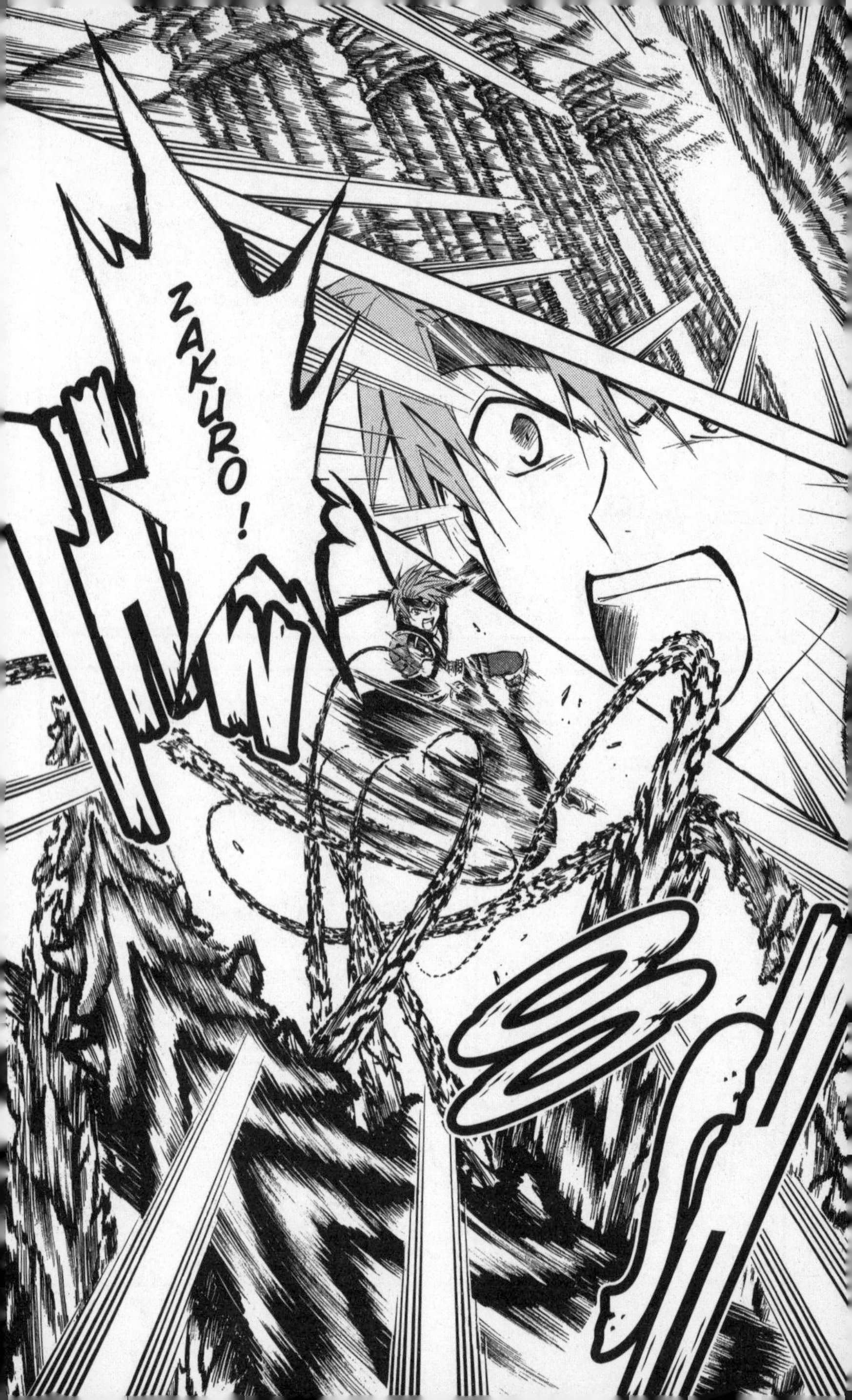
ZAKURO!

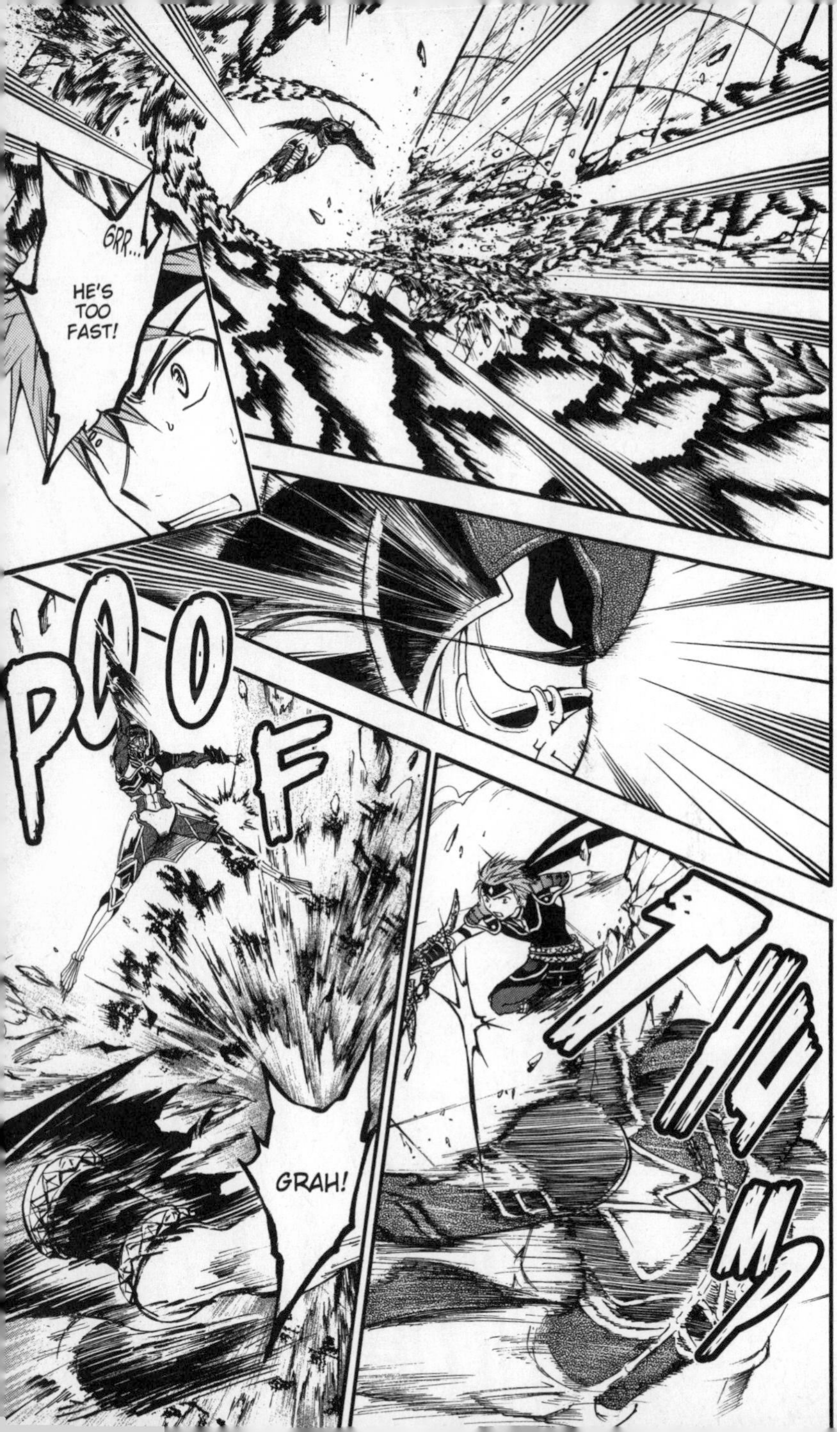
GRR...
HE'S TOO FAST!
THUMP
POOF
GRAH!

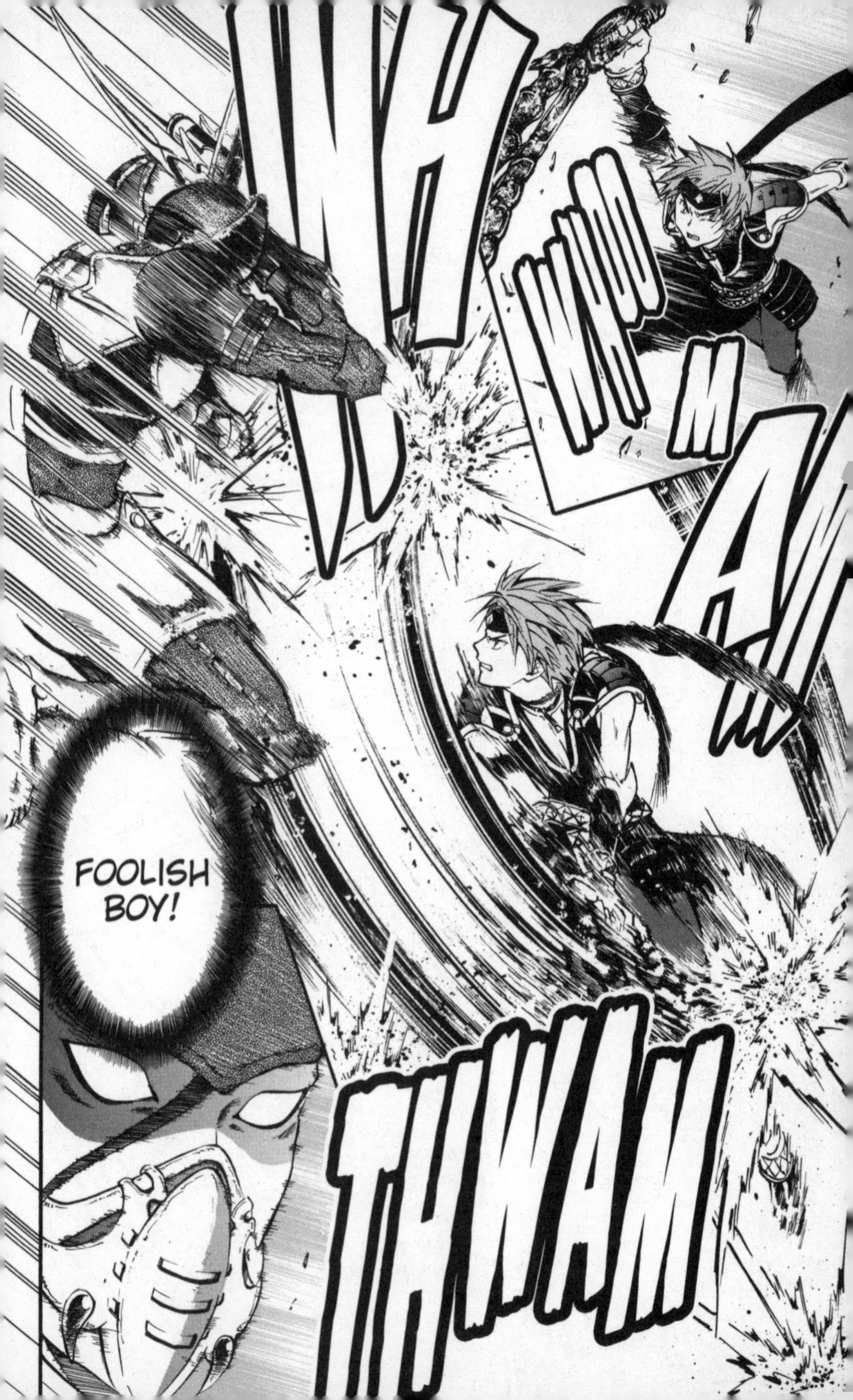
FOOLISH BOY!
THWAM

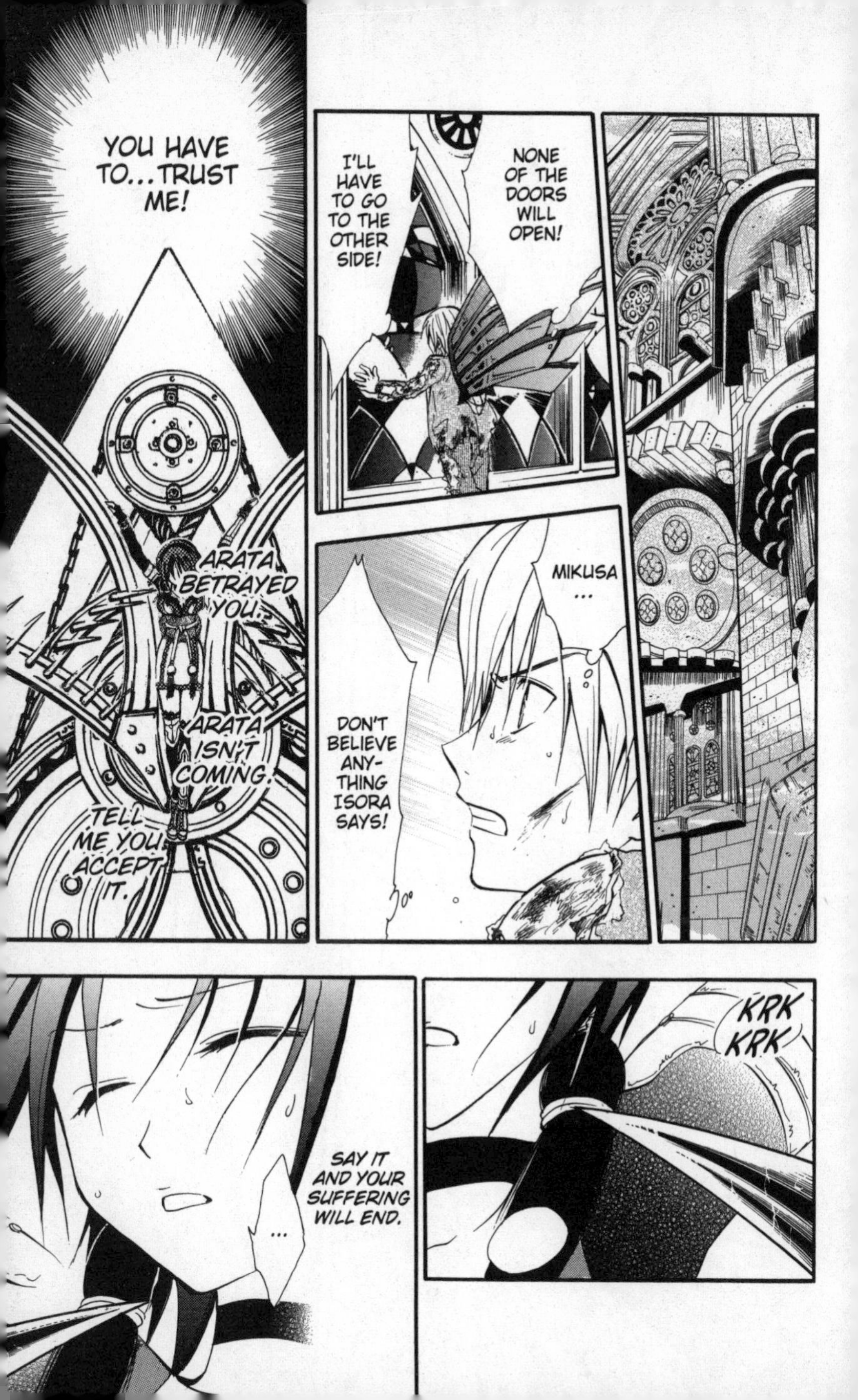
NONE OF THE DOORS WILL OPEN!
I'LL HAVE TO GO TO THE OTHER SIDE!
MIKUSA...
DON'T BELIEVE ANYTHING ISORA SAYS!
YOU HAVE TO...TRUST ME!
ARATA BETRAYED YOU.
ARATA ISN'T COMING.
TELL ME YOU ACCEPT IT.
KRK KRK
SAY IT AND YOUR SUFFERING WILL END.
...

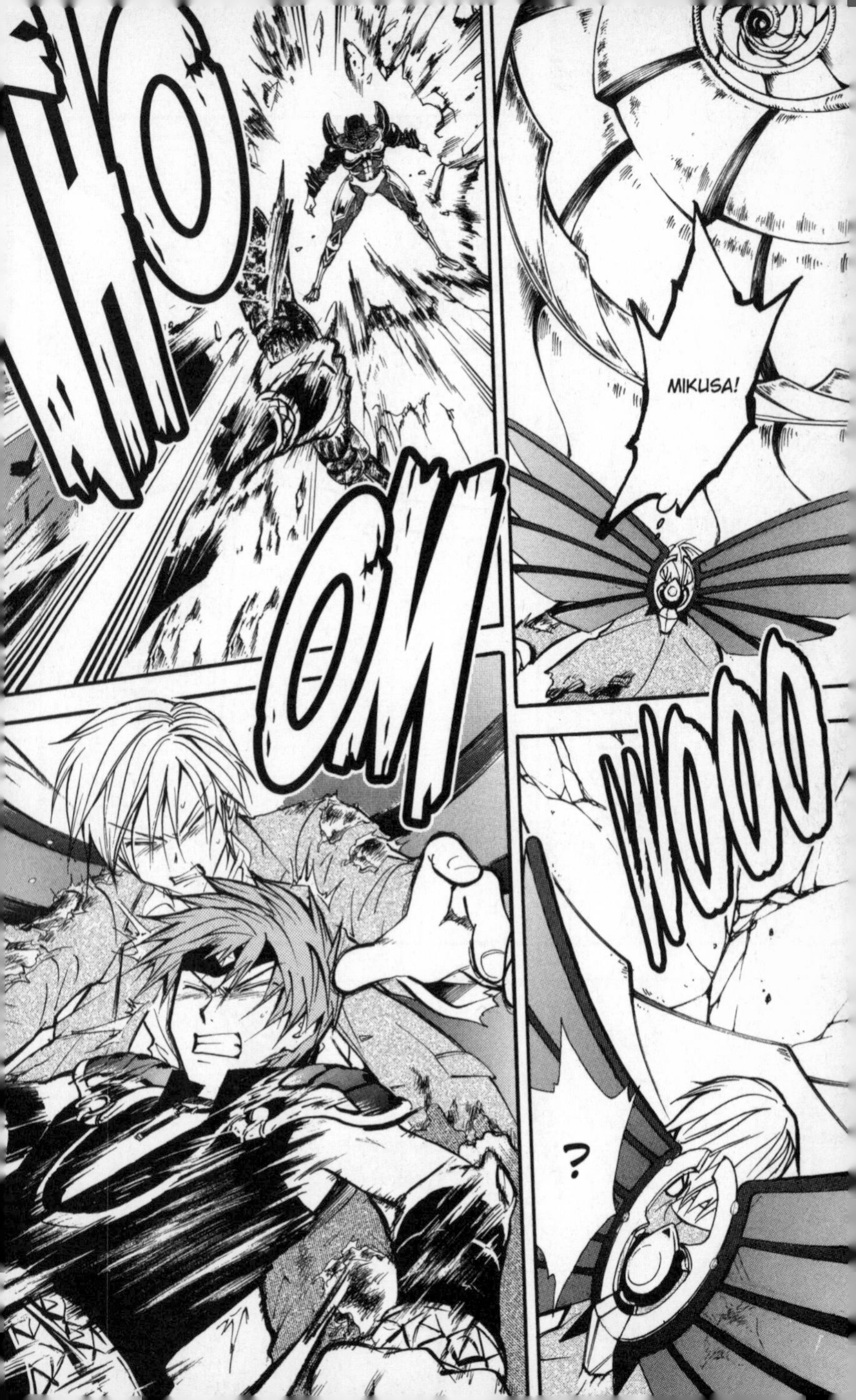
MIKUSA!
WOOO
?
WHO
OM

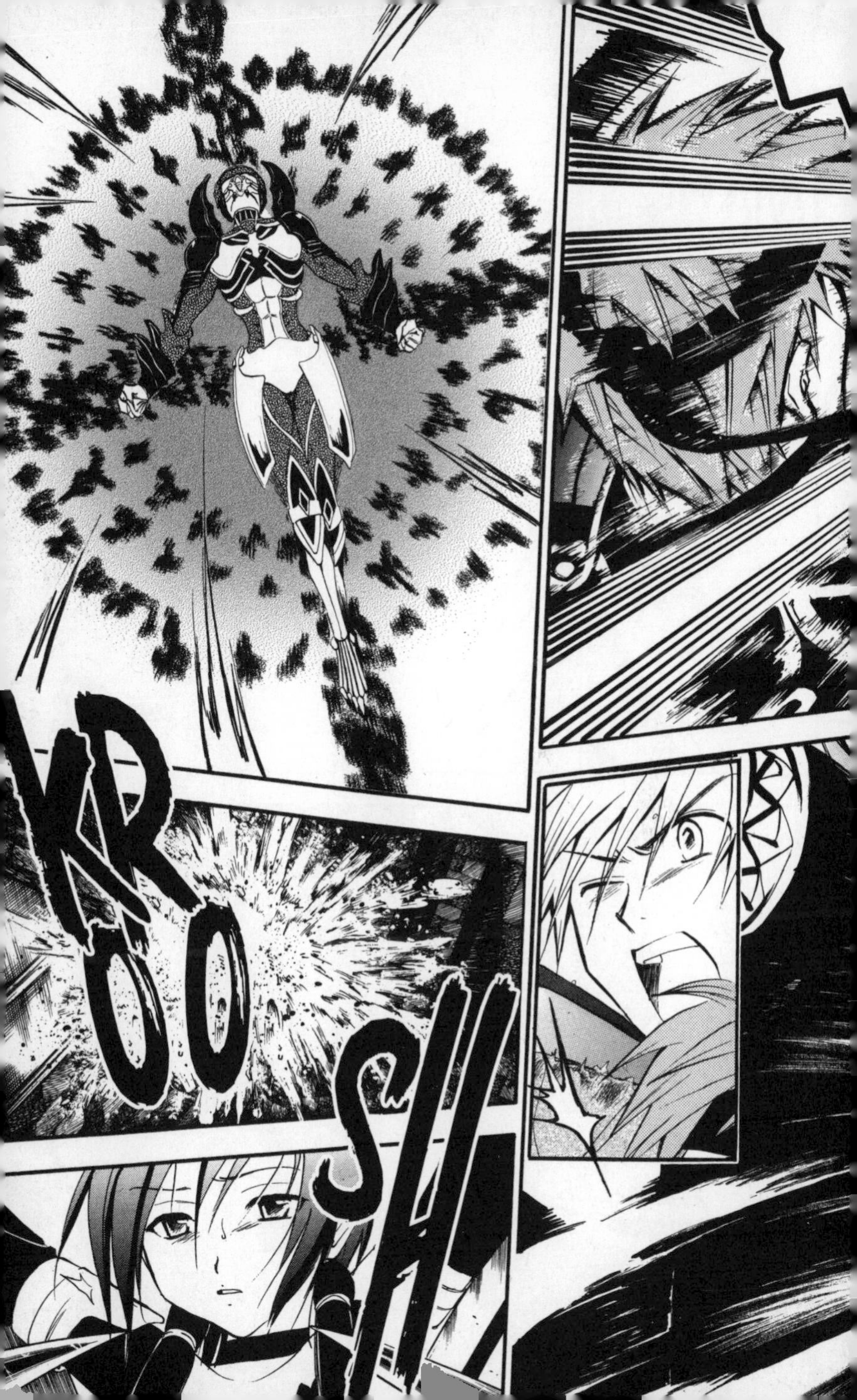
KRBOOSH

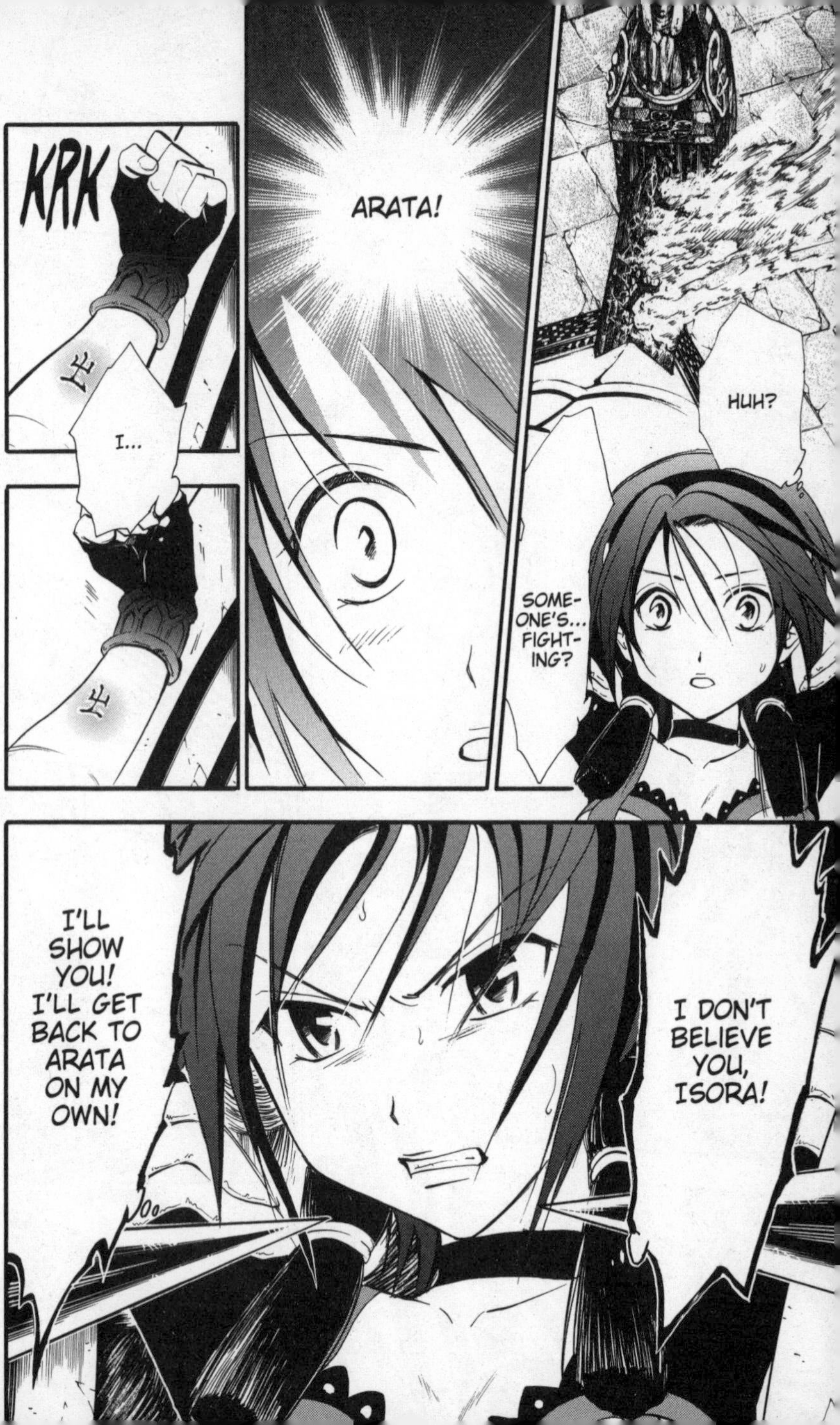
HUH?
SOME-ONE'S... FIGHT-ING?
ARATA!
KRK
I...
I DON'T BELIEVE YOU, ISORA!
I'LL SHOW YOU! I'LL GET BACK TO ARATA ON MY OWN!

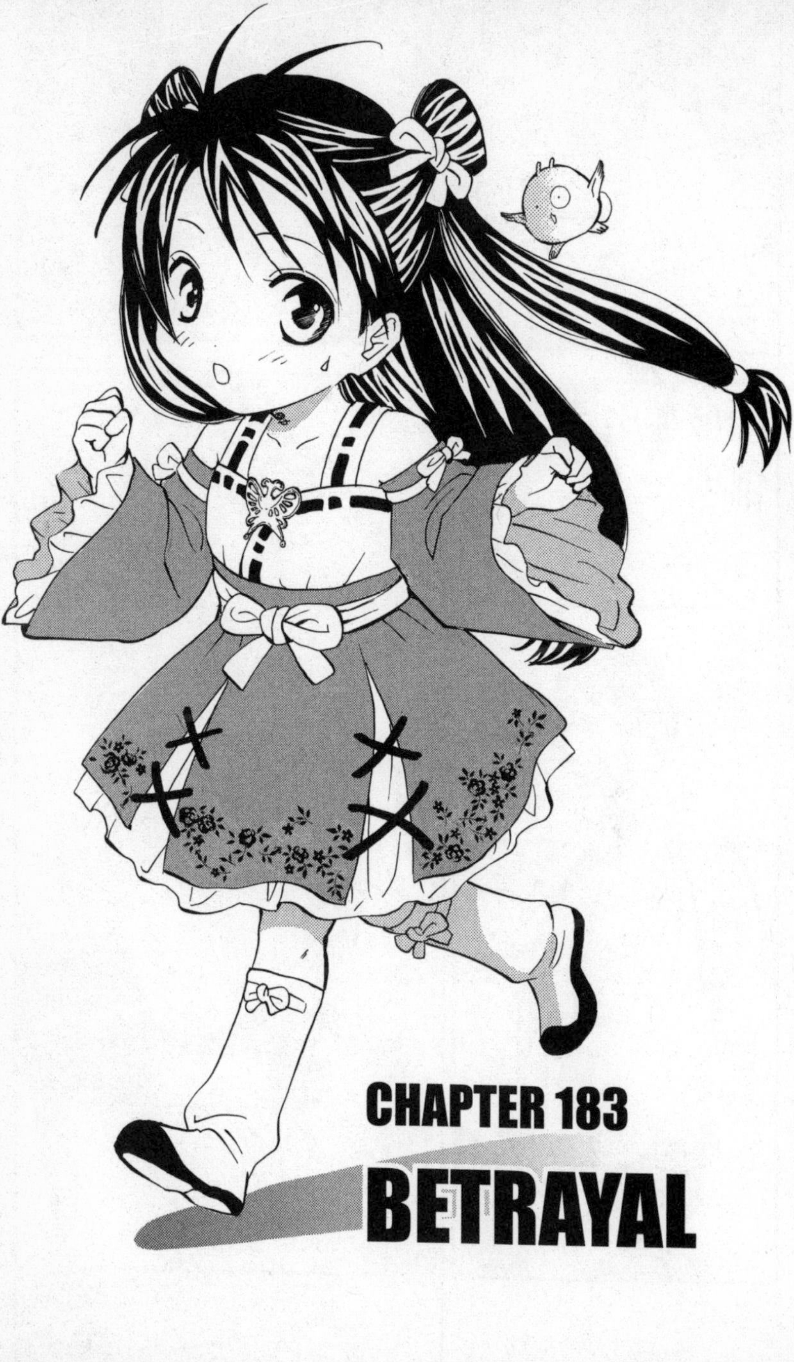

CHAPTER 183
BETRAYAL

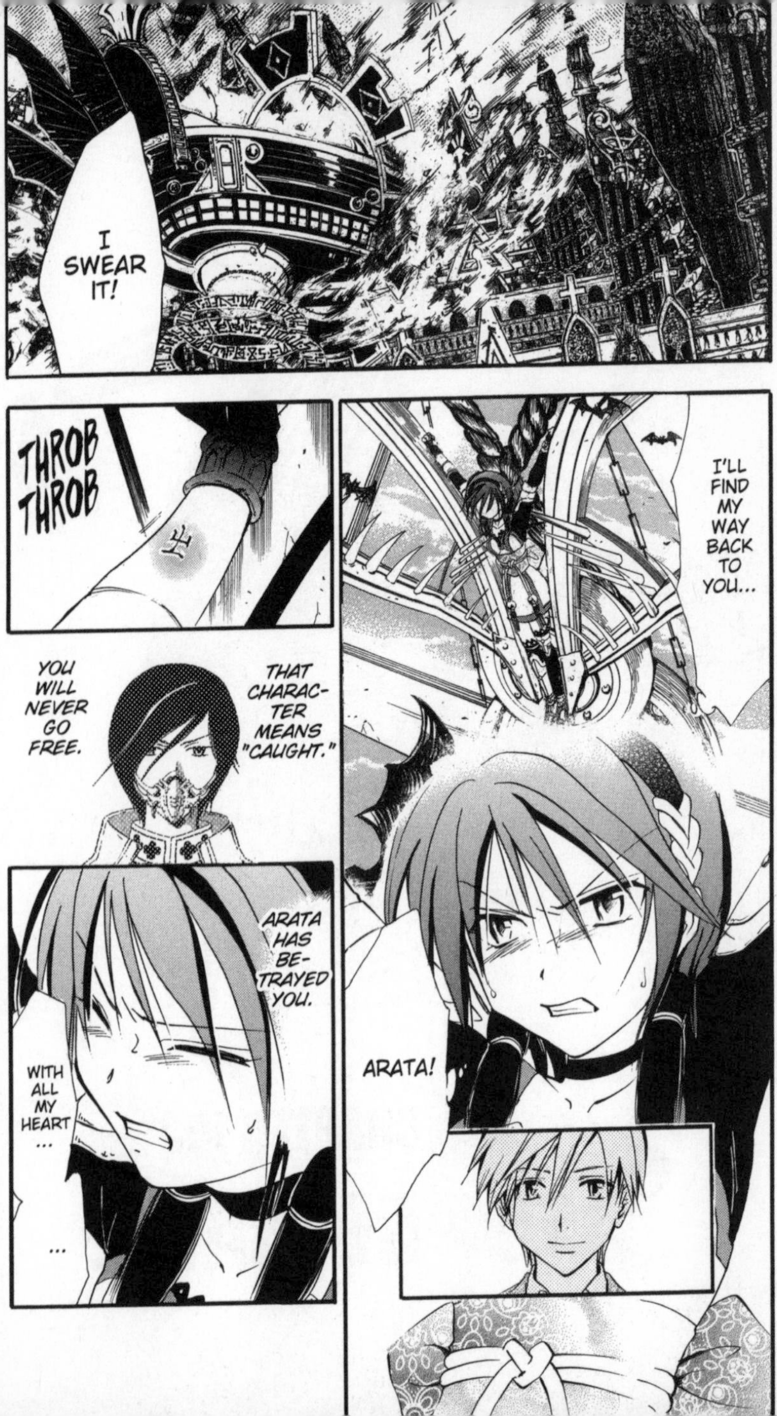
I SWEAR IT!
I'LL FIND MY WAY BACK TO YOU...
ARATA!
THROB THROB
THAT CHARACTER MEANS "CAUGHT."
YOU WILL NEVER GO FREE.
ARATA HAS BETRAYED YOU.
WITH ALL MY HEART...
...

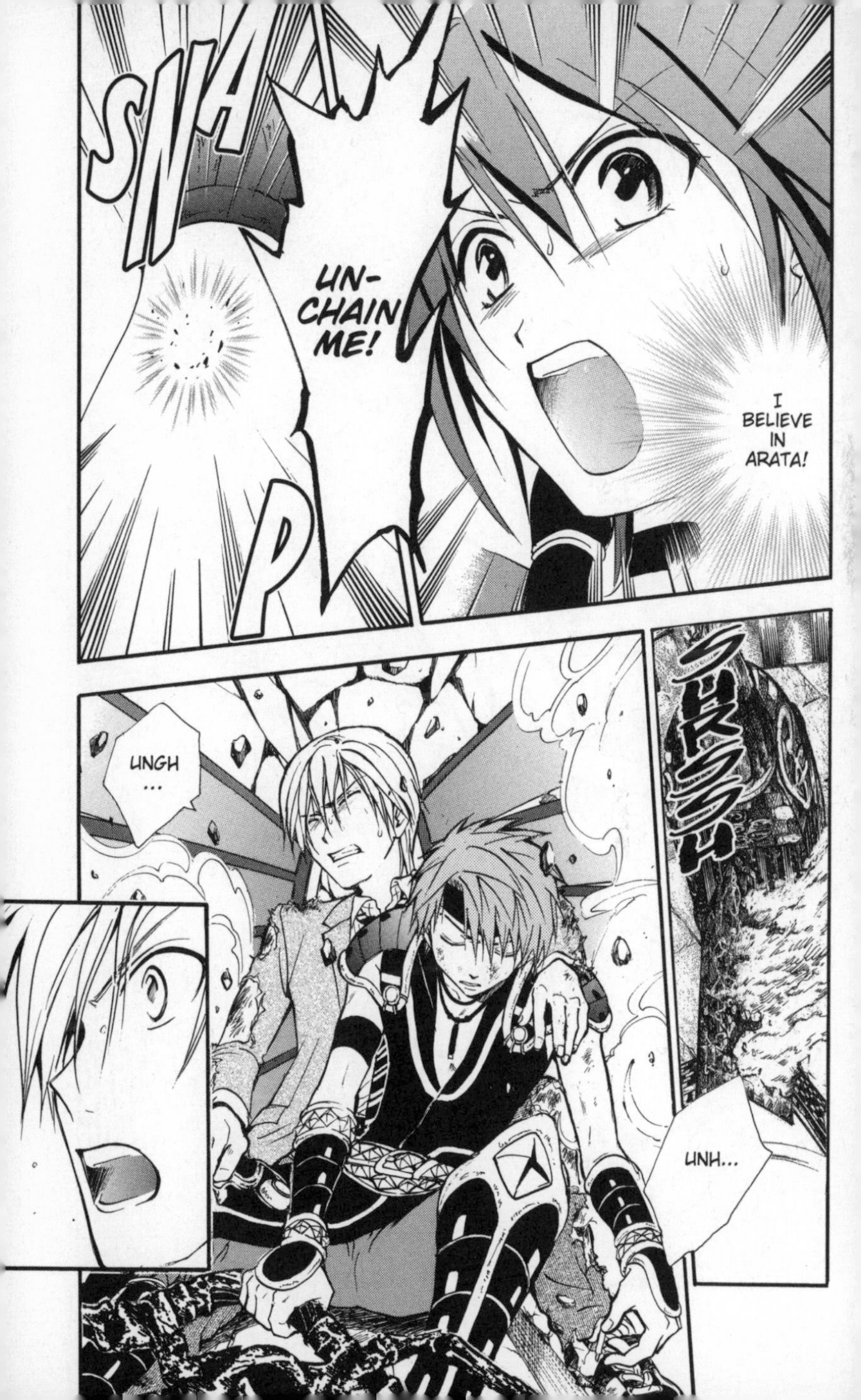
I BELIEVE IN ARATA!
UN-CHAIN ME!
SNAP
UNGH ...
UNH...

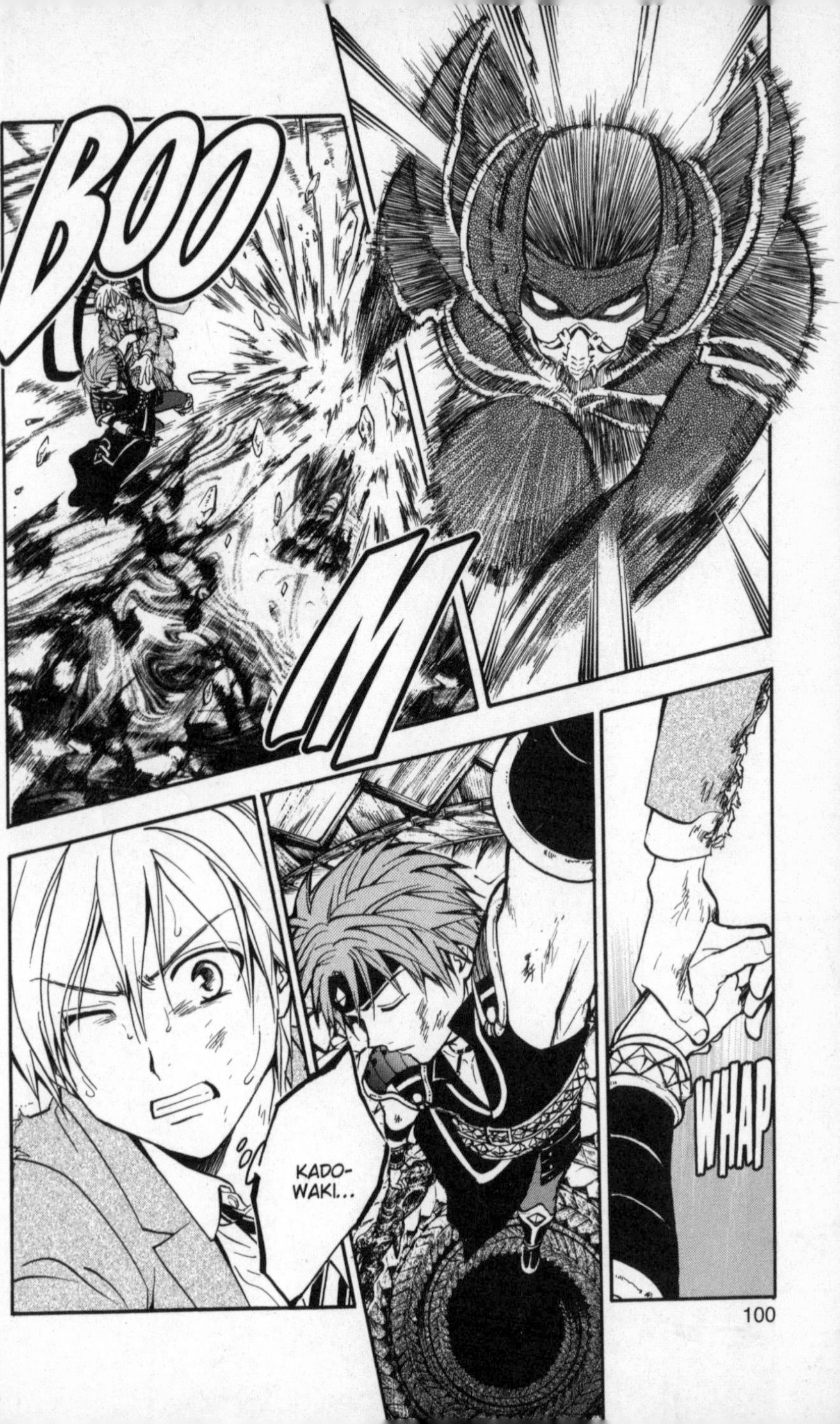
BOOM
WHAP
KADO-WAKI...

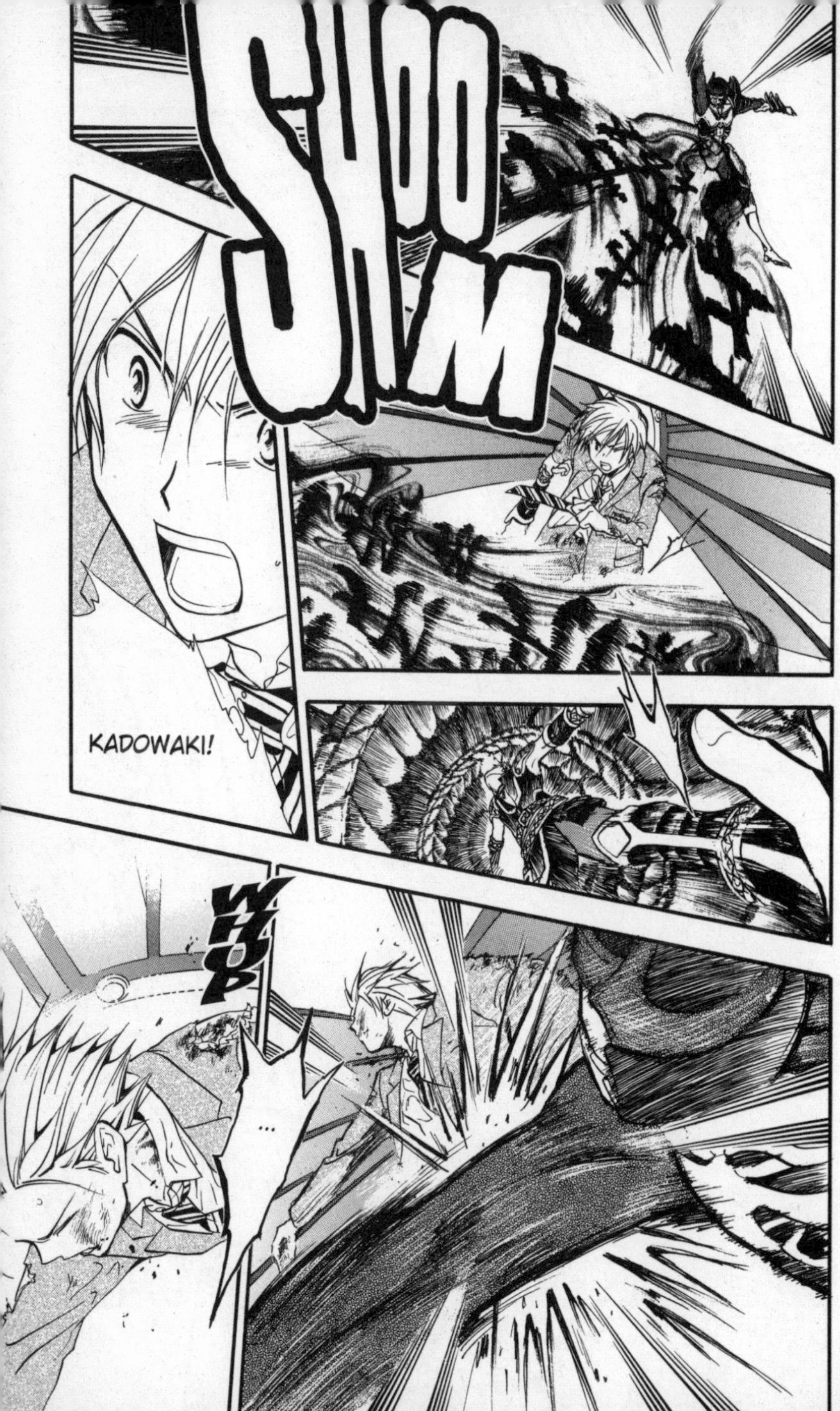
SHOOOM
KADOWAKI!
WHOP
...

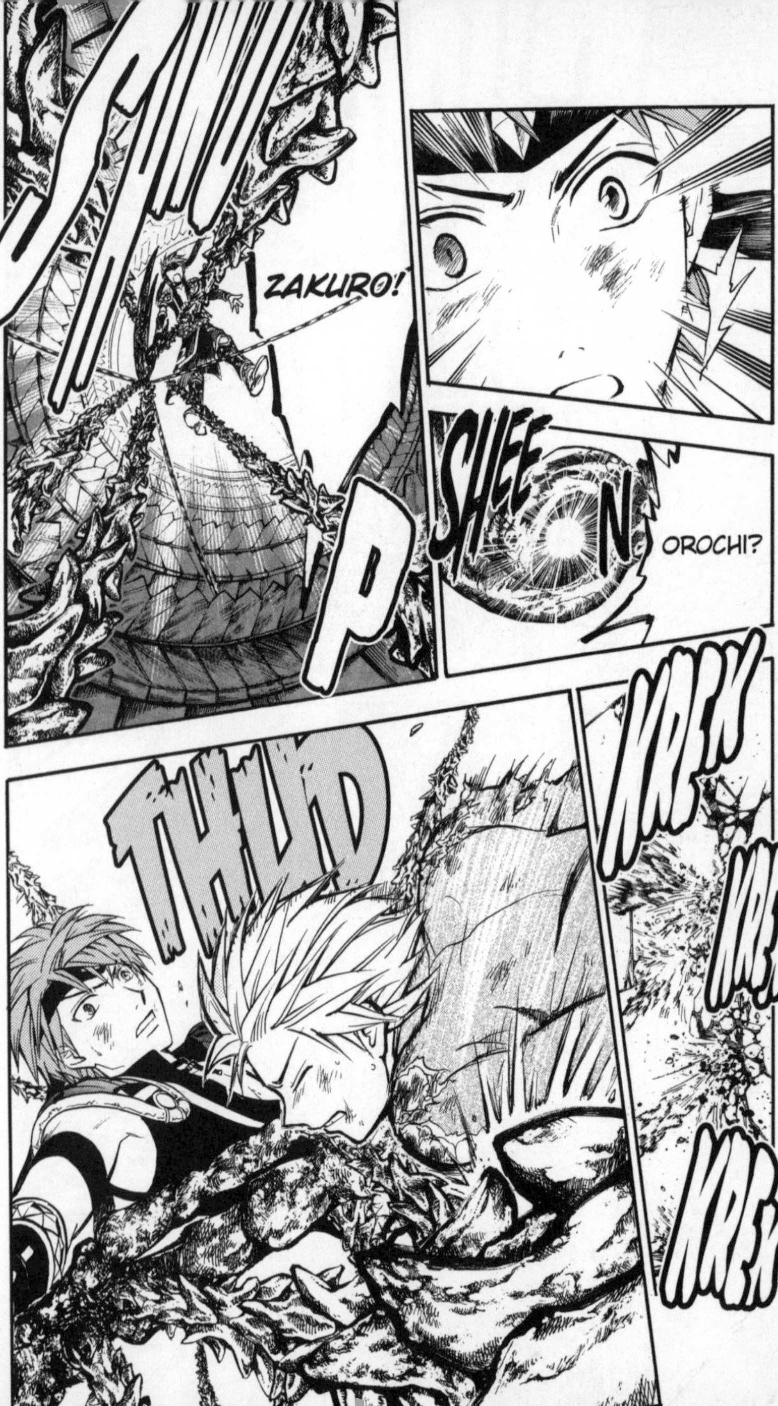
ZAKURO!
SHEEN
OROCHI?
KREK
KREK
KREK
THUD

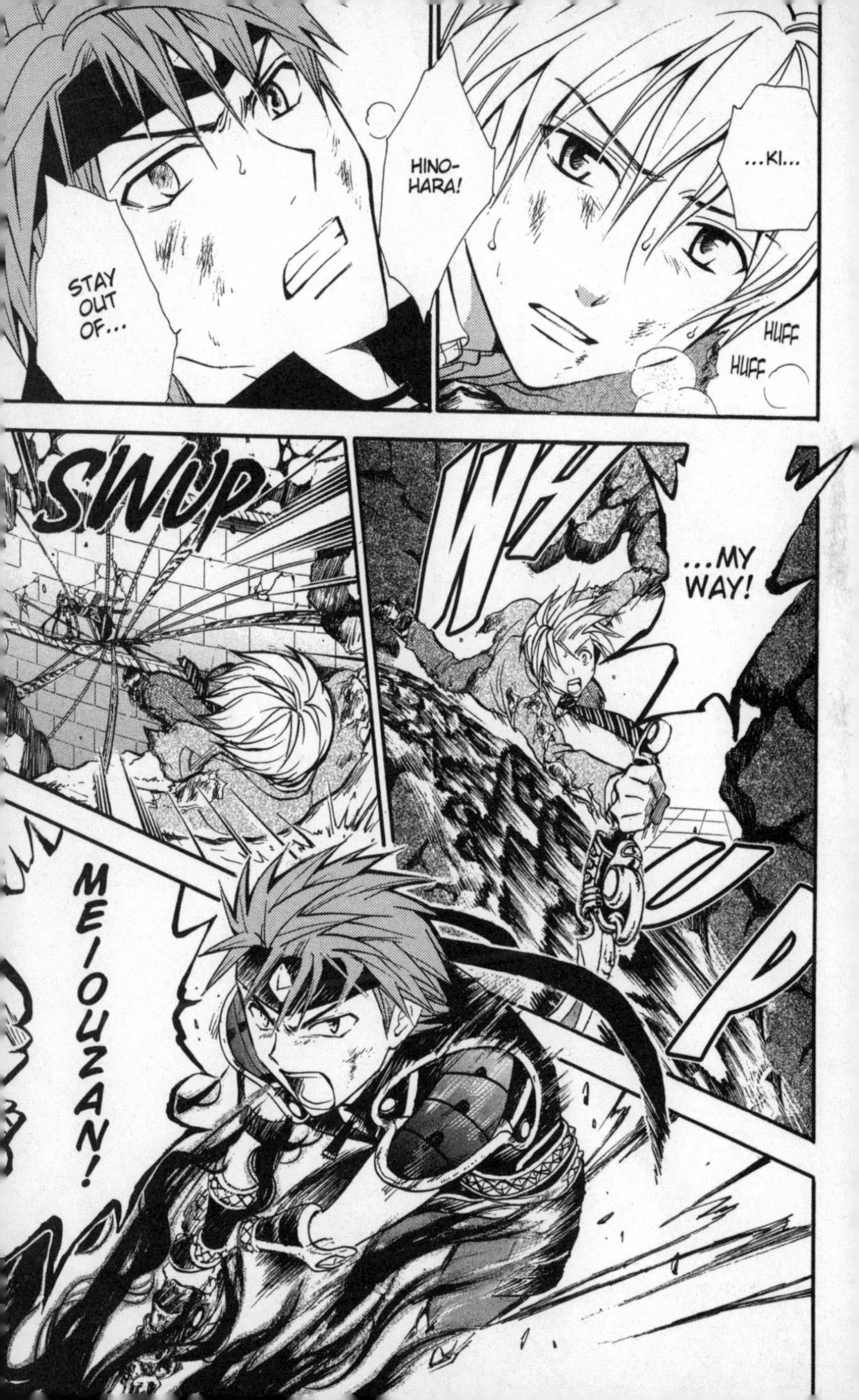
...KI...
HUFF
HUFF
HINO-HARA!
STAY OUT OF...
...MY WAY!
SWUP
MEIOUZAN!

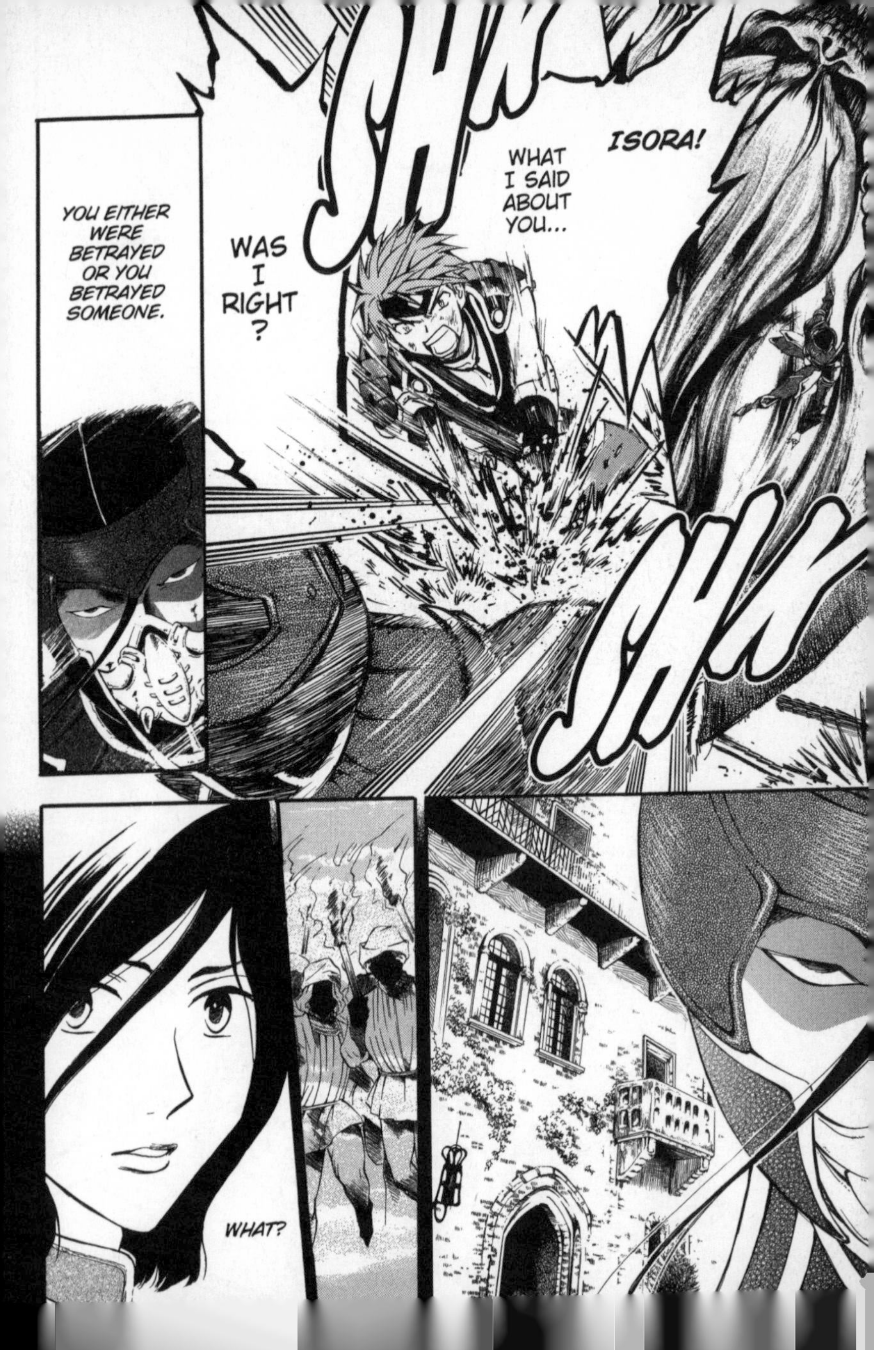
CHN
ISORA!
WHAT I SAID ABOUT YOU...
CHN
WAS I RIGHT?
YOU EITHER WERE BETRAYED OR YOU BETRAYED SOMEONE.
WHAT?

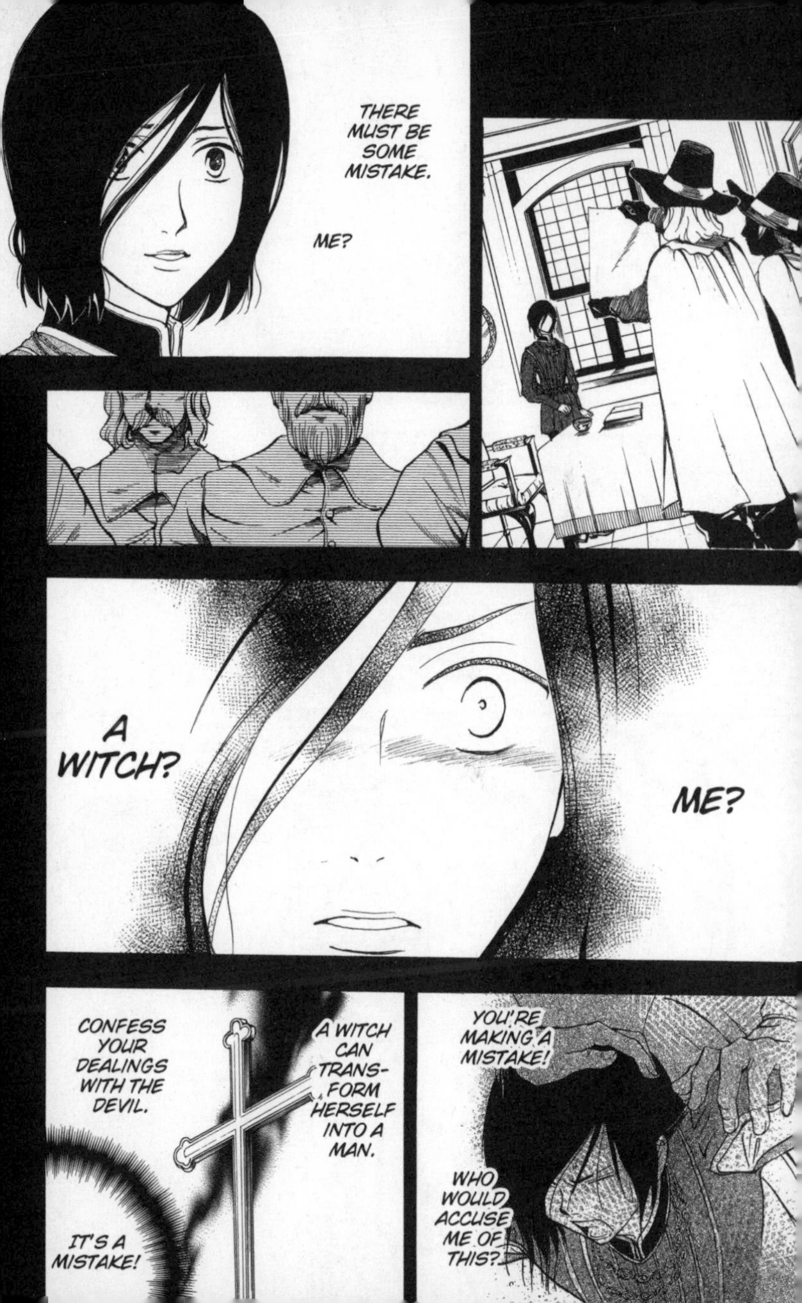
THERE MUST BE SOME MISTAKE.
ME?
A WITCH?
ME?
YOU'RE MAKING A MISTAKE!
WHO WOULD ACCUSE ME OF THIS?
A WITCH CAN TRANS-FORM HERSELF INTO A MAN.
CONFESS YOUR DEALINGS WITH THE DEVIL.
IT'S A MISTAKE!

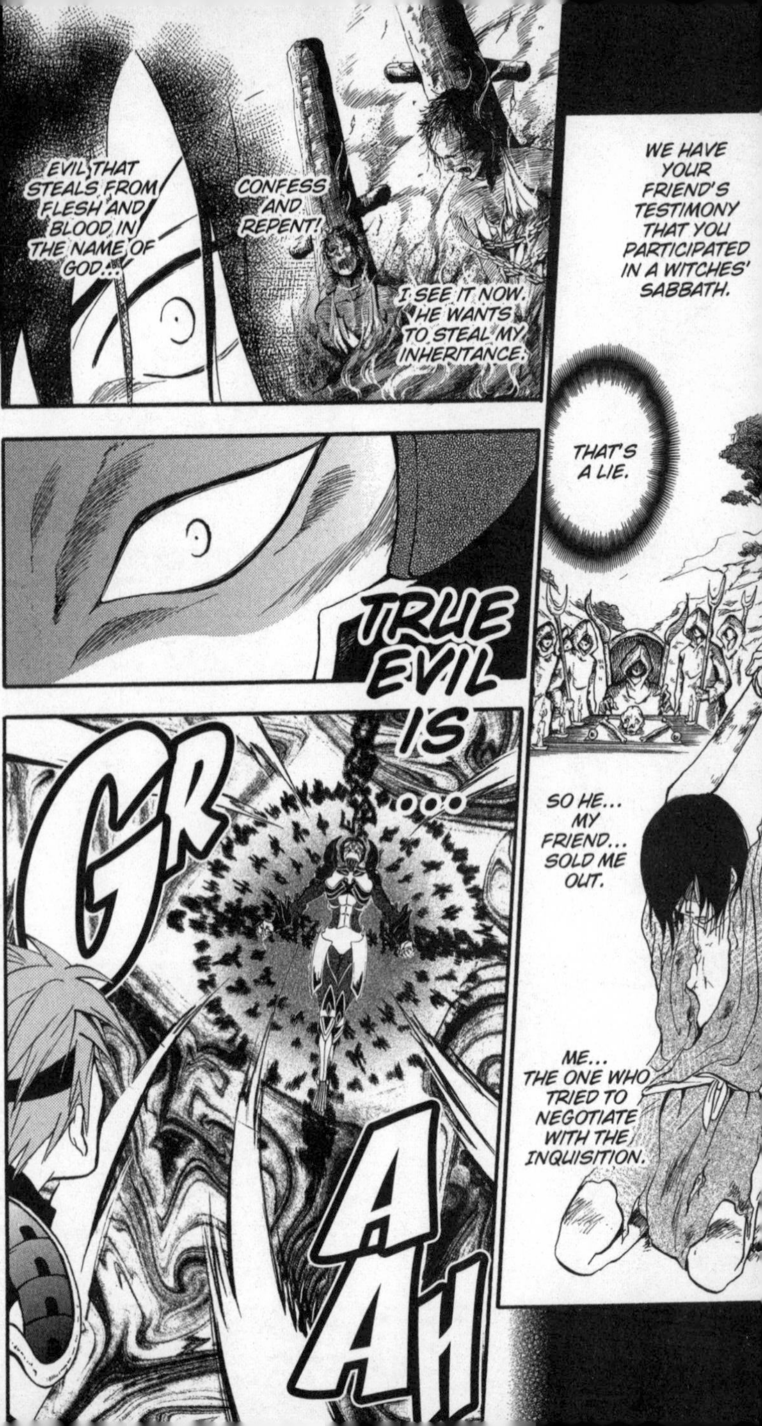
WE HAVE YOUR FRIEND'S TESTIMONY THAT YOU PARTICIPATED IN A WITCHES' SABBATH.
THAT'S A LIE.
SO HE... MY FRIEND... SOLD ME OUT.
ME... THE ONE WHO TRIED TO NEGOTIATE WITH THE INQUISITION.
CONFESS AND REPENT!
I SEE IT NOW. HE WANTS TO STEAL MY INHERITANCE.
EVIL THAT STEALS FROM FLESH AND BLOOD IN THE NAME OF GOD...
TRUE EVIL IS...
GR
AAH

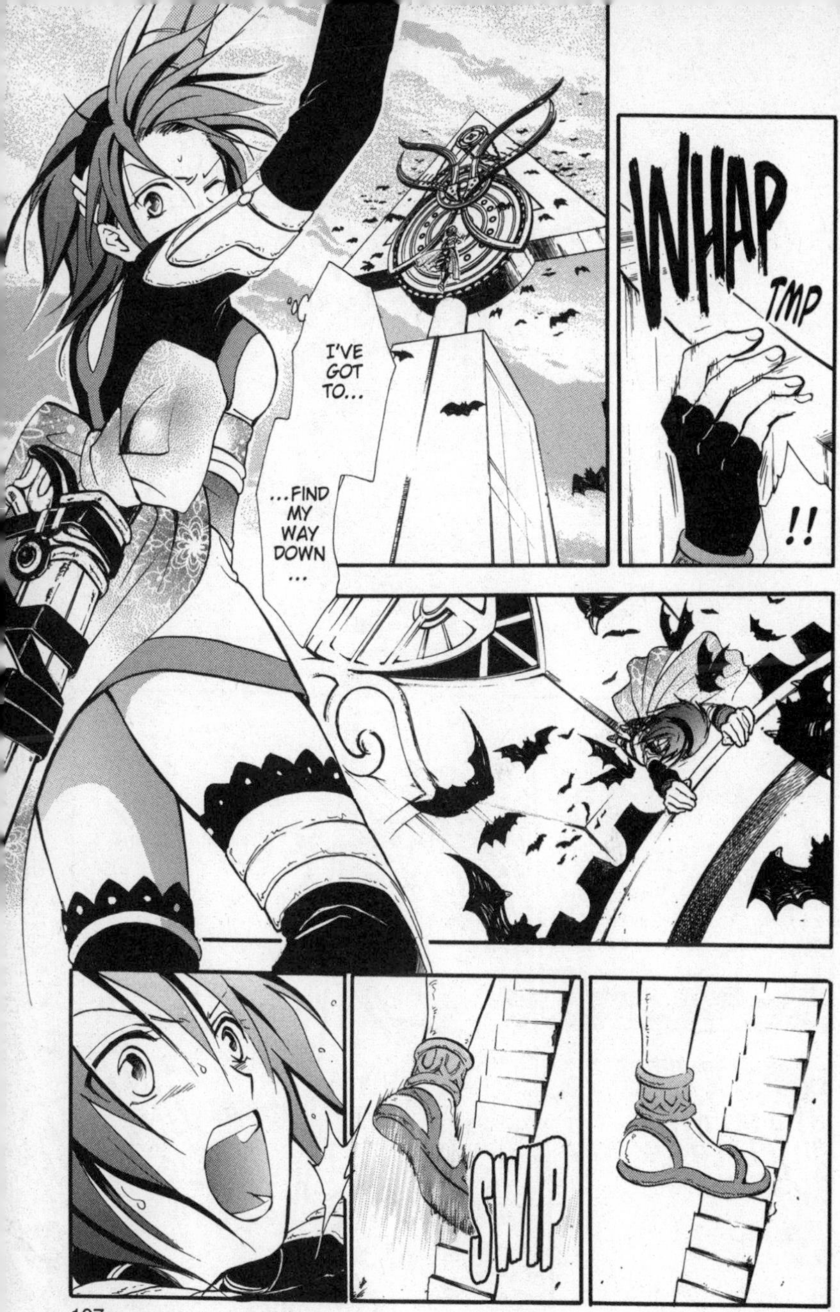
WHAP
TMP
!!
I'VE GOT TO...
...FIND MY WAY DOWN...
SWIP

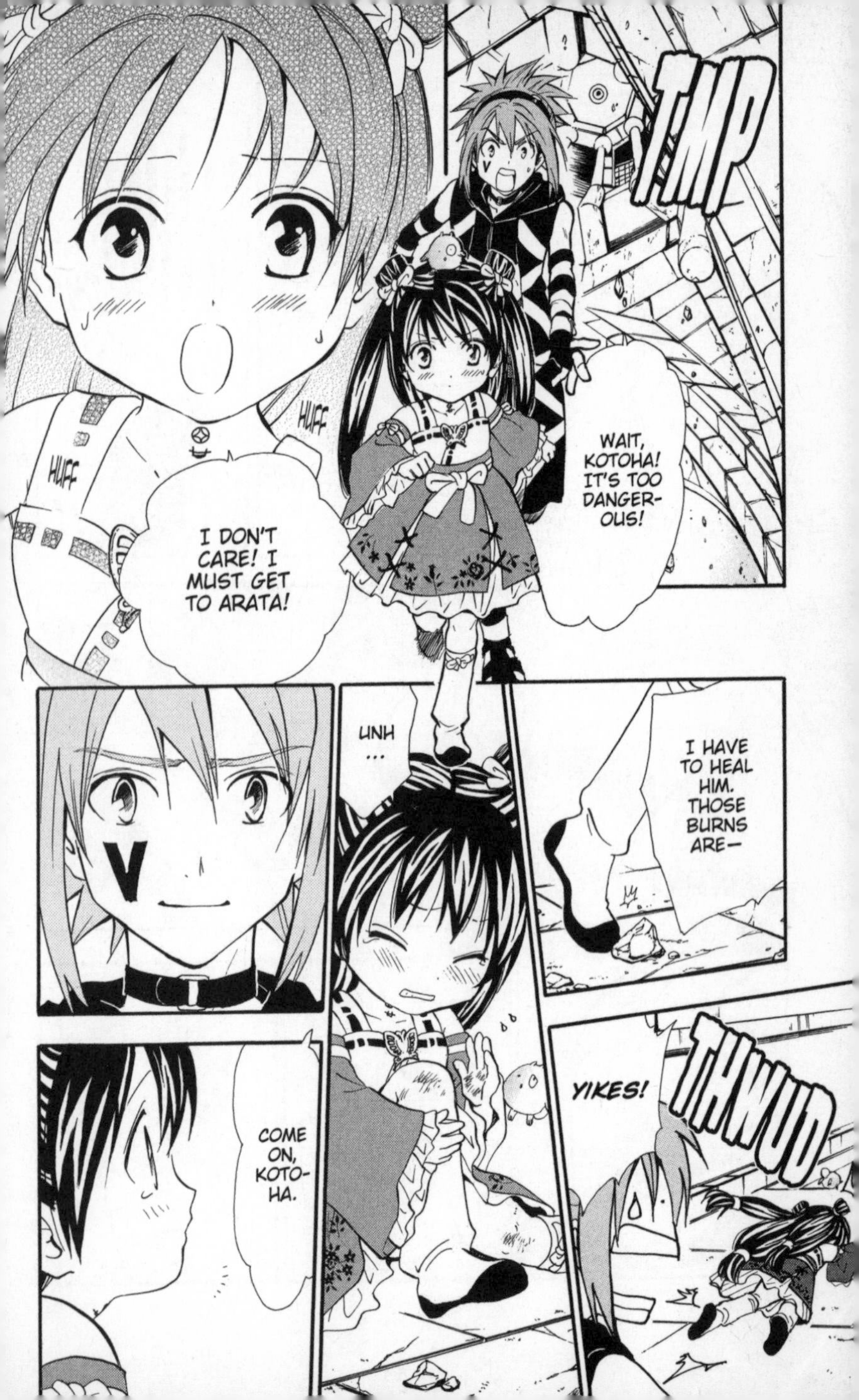
TMP
WAIT, KOTOHA! IT'S TOO DANGER-OUS!
HUFF
HUFF
I DON'T CARE! I MUST GET TO ARATA!
I HAVE TO HEAL HIM. THOSE BURNS ARE—
YIKES!
THWUD
UNH...
COME ON, KOTO-HA.

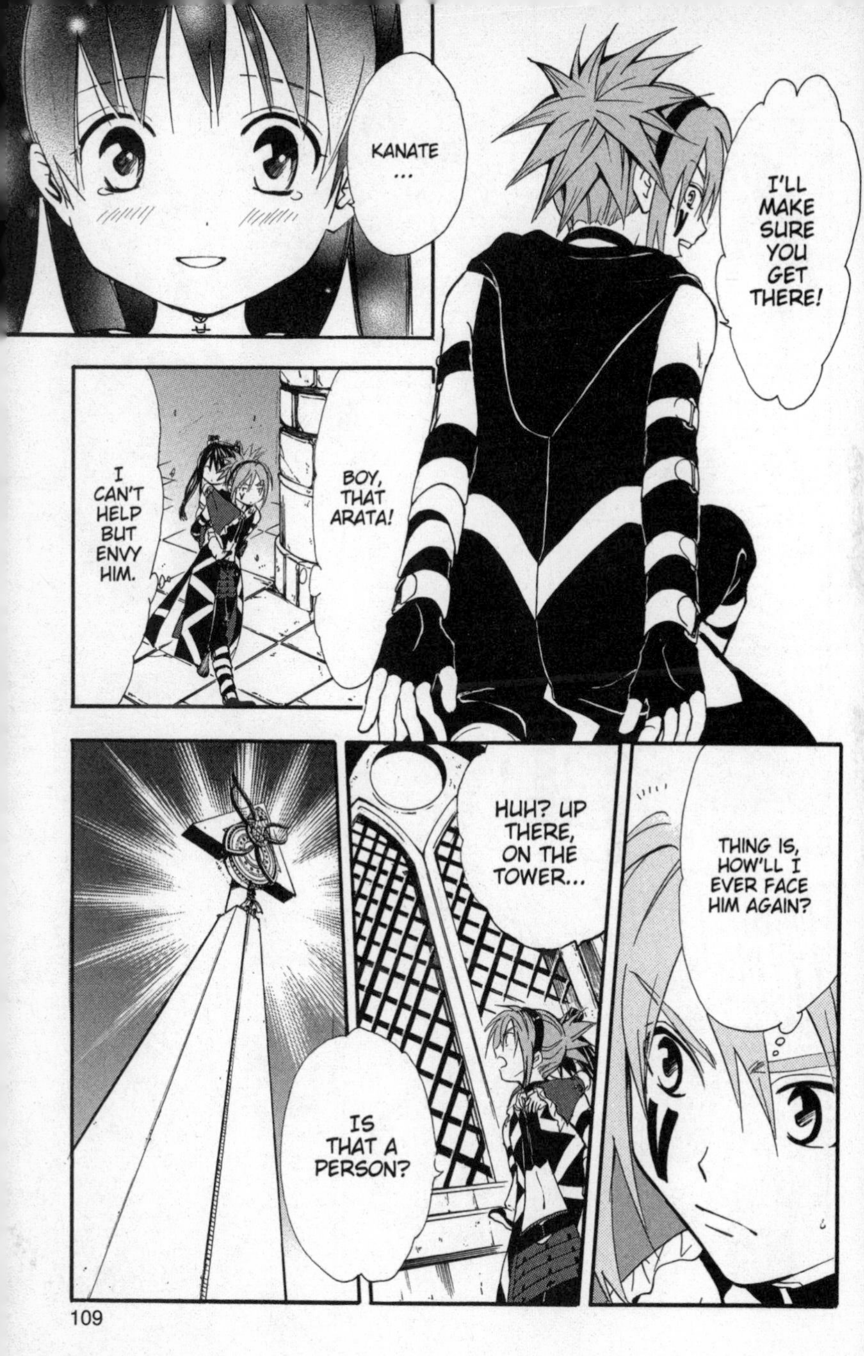
I'LL MAKE SURE YOU GET THERE!
KANATE ...
BOY, THAT ARATA!
I CAN'T HELP BUT ENVY HIM.
THING IS, HOW'LL I EVER FACE HIM AGAIN?
HUH? UP THERE, ON THE TOWER...
IS THAT A PERSON?

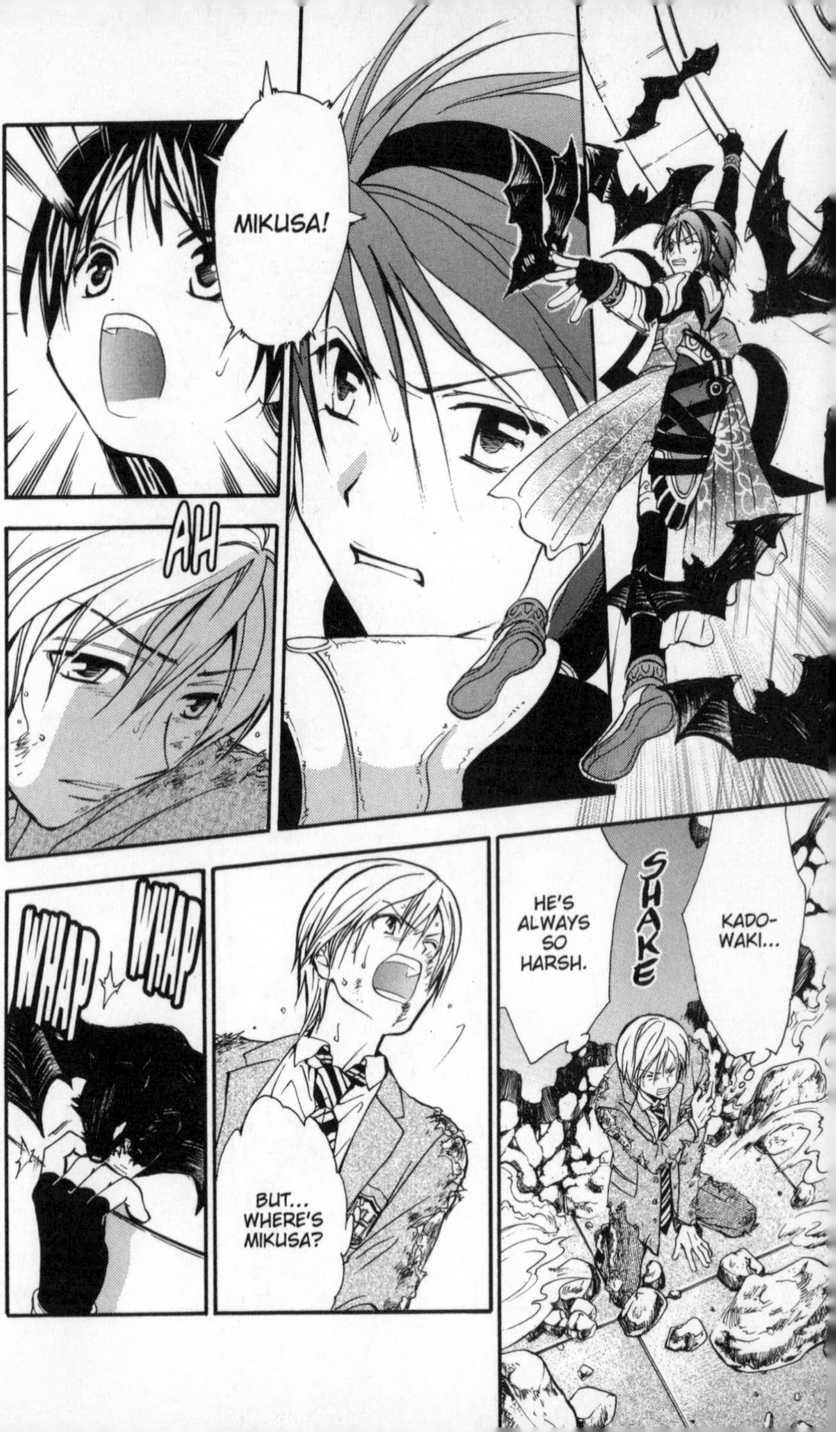
MIKUSA!
AH
KADO-WAKI...
SHAKE
HE'S ALWAYS SO HARSH.
BUT... WHERE'S MIKUSA?
WHAP
WHAP

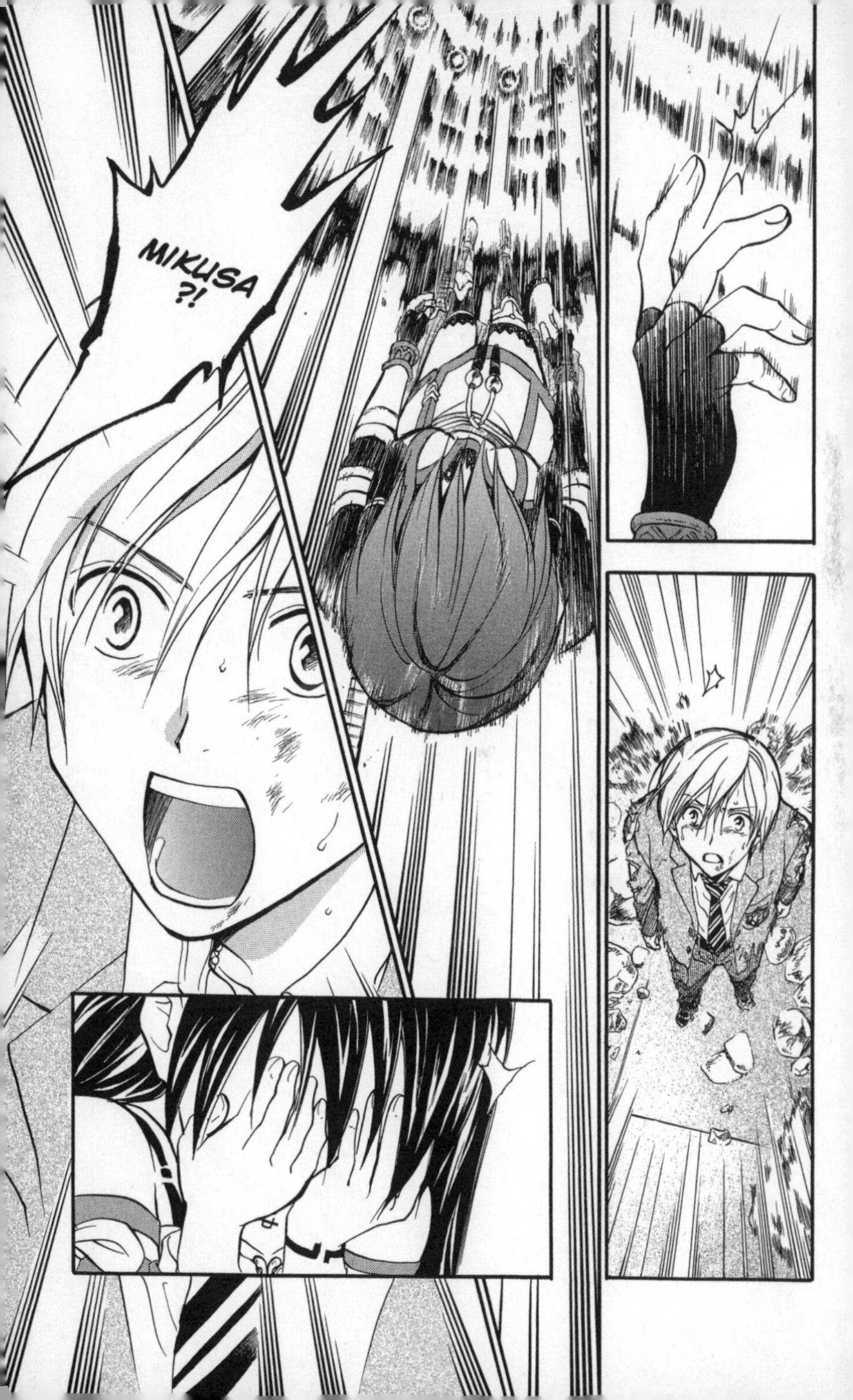
MIKUSA ?!

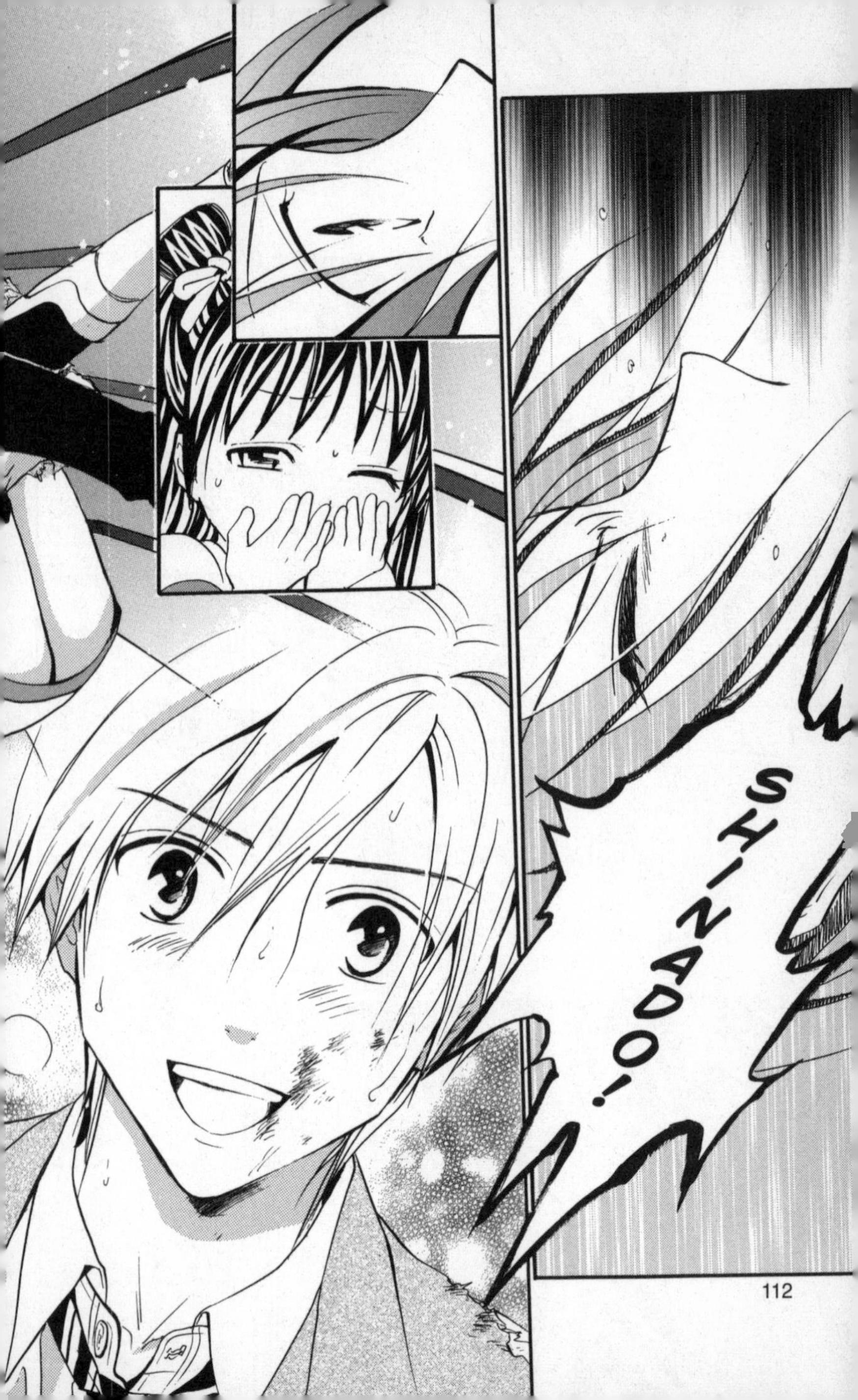
SHI-NADOO!

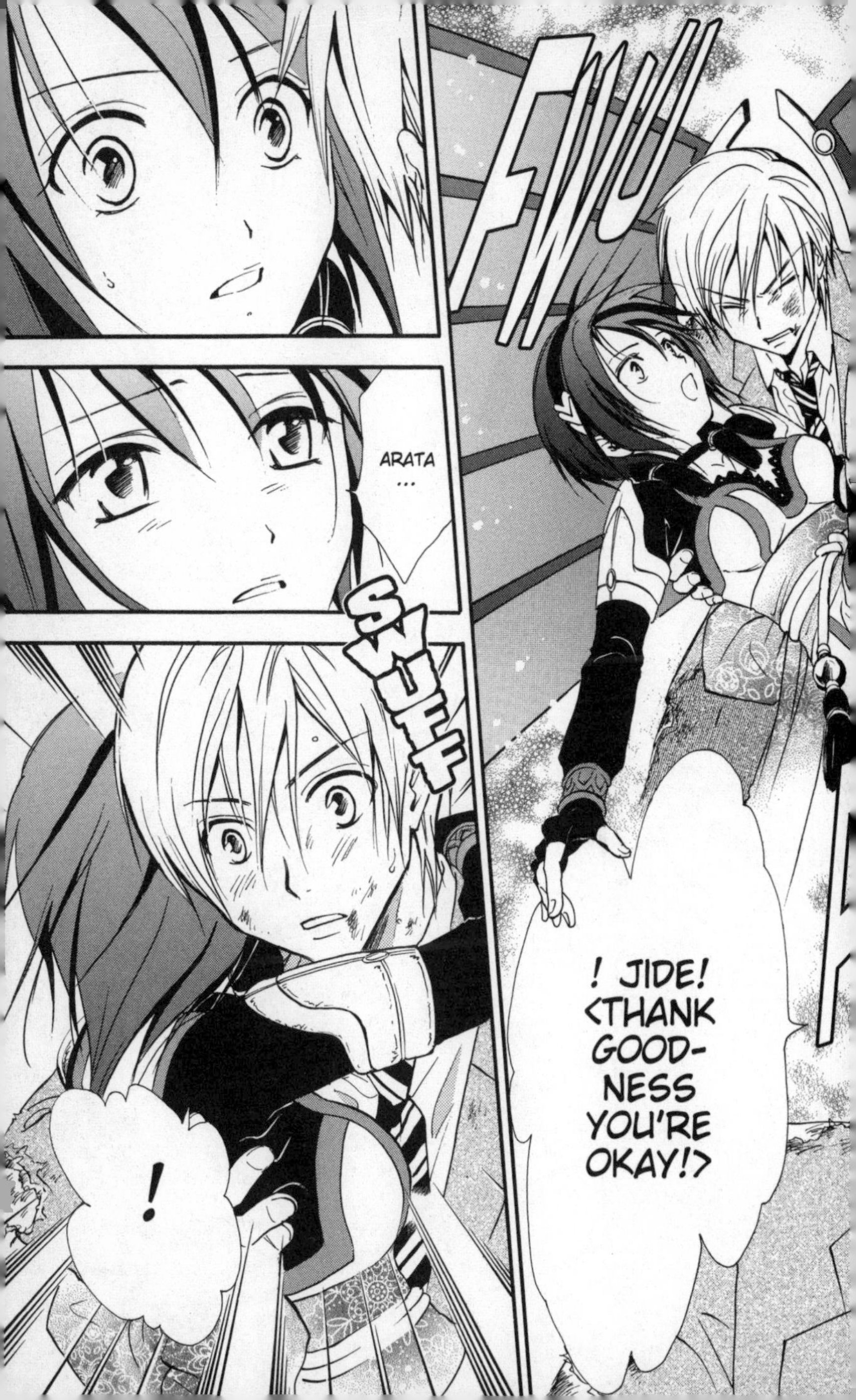

! JIDE! <THANK GOODNESS YOU'RE OKAY!>
ARATA ...
SWUFF
!

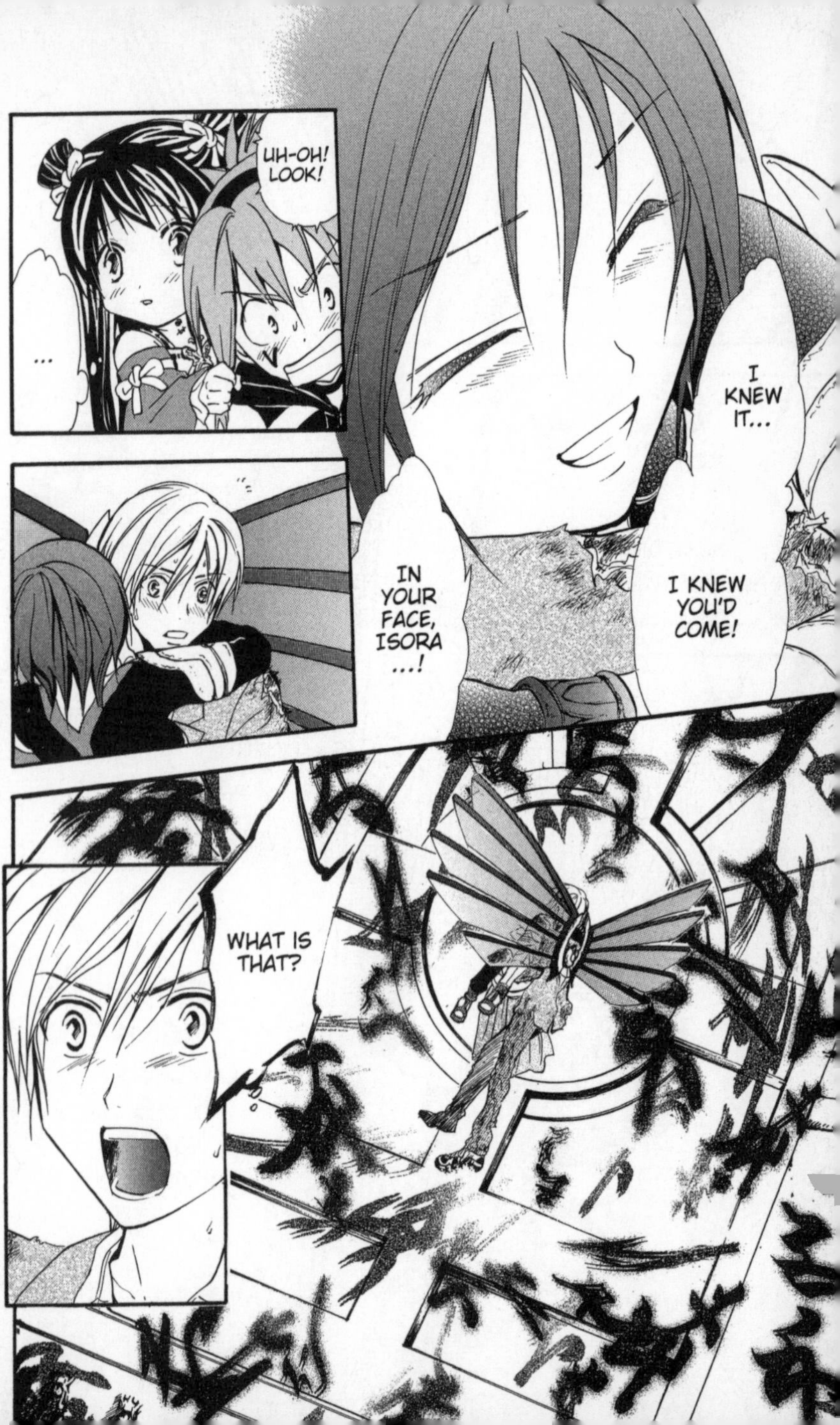
I KNEW IT...
I KNEW YOU'D COME!
IN YOUR FACE, ISORA...!
UH-OH! LOOK!
...
WHAT IS THAT?

CHAPTER 184
DEMON GOD

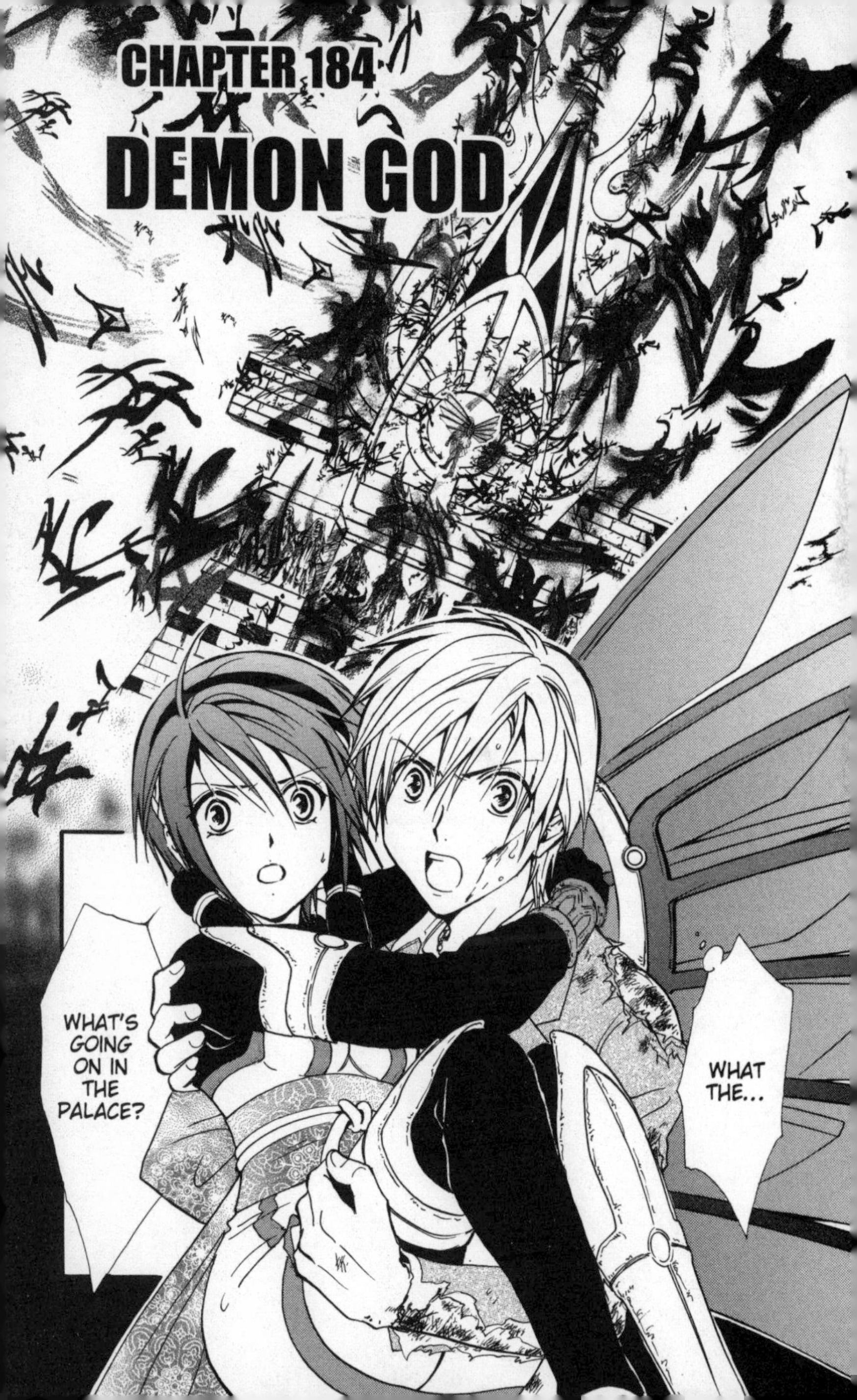
WHAT THE...
WHAT'S GOING ON IN THE PALACE?

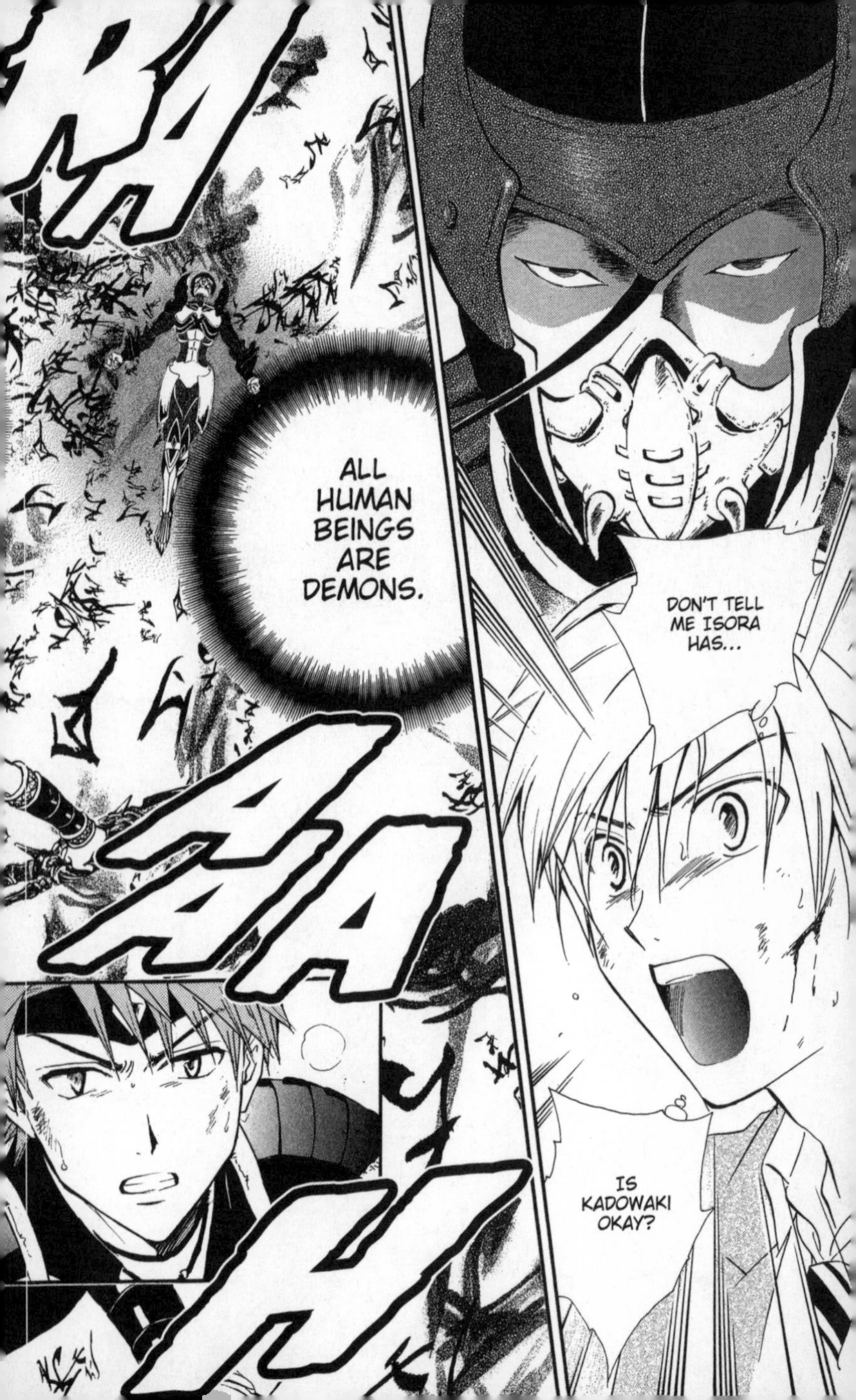
DON'T TELL ME ISORA HAS...
IS KADOWAKI OKAY?
ALL HUMAN BEINGS ARE DEMONS.

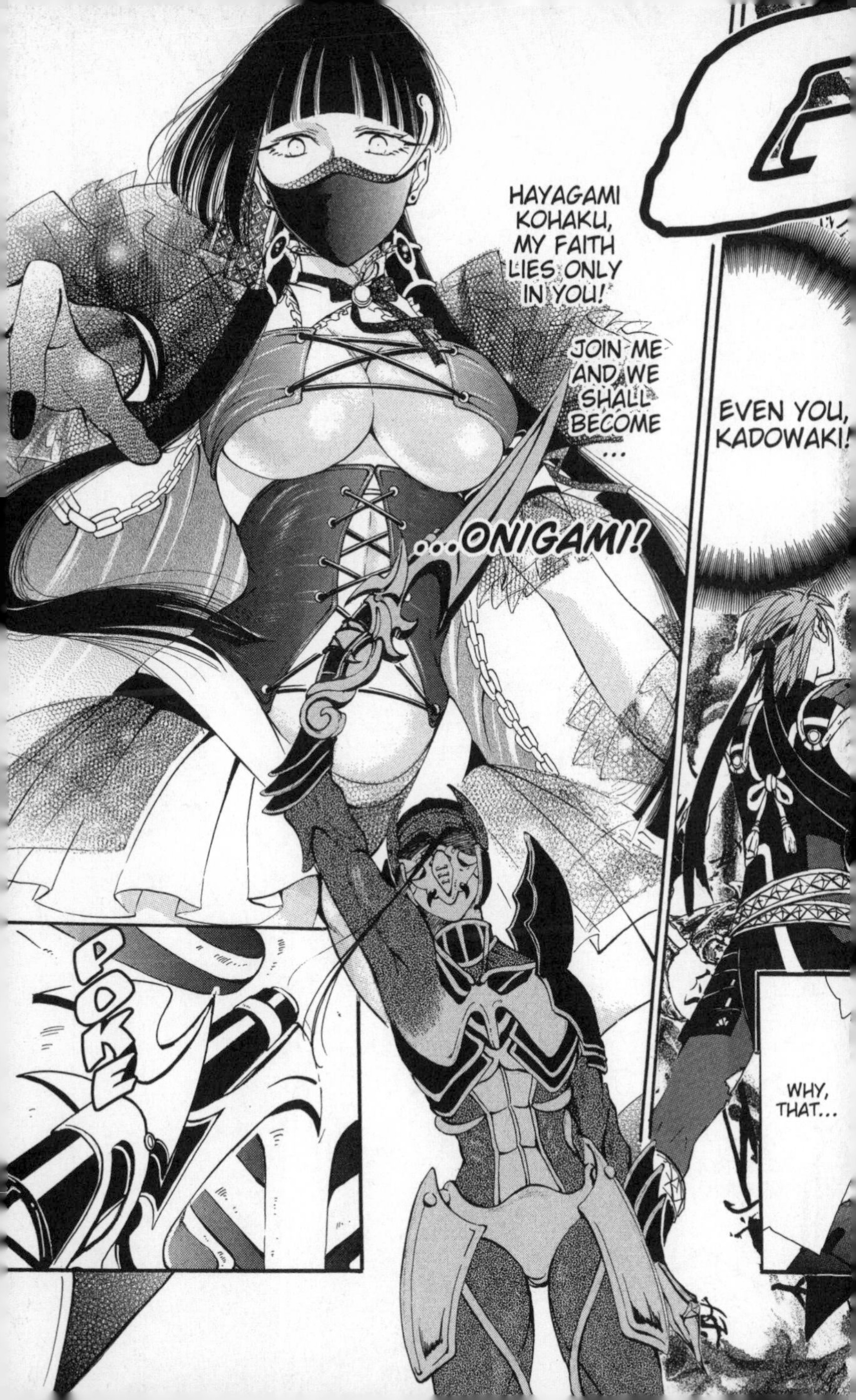
EVEN YOU, KADOWAKI!
HAYAGAMI KOHAKU, MY FAITH LIES ONLY IN YOU!
JOIN ME AND WE SHALL BECOME ...
...ONIGAMI!
WHY, THAT...
POKE

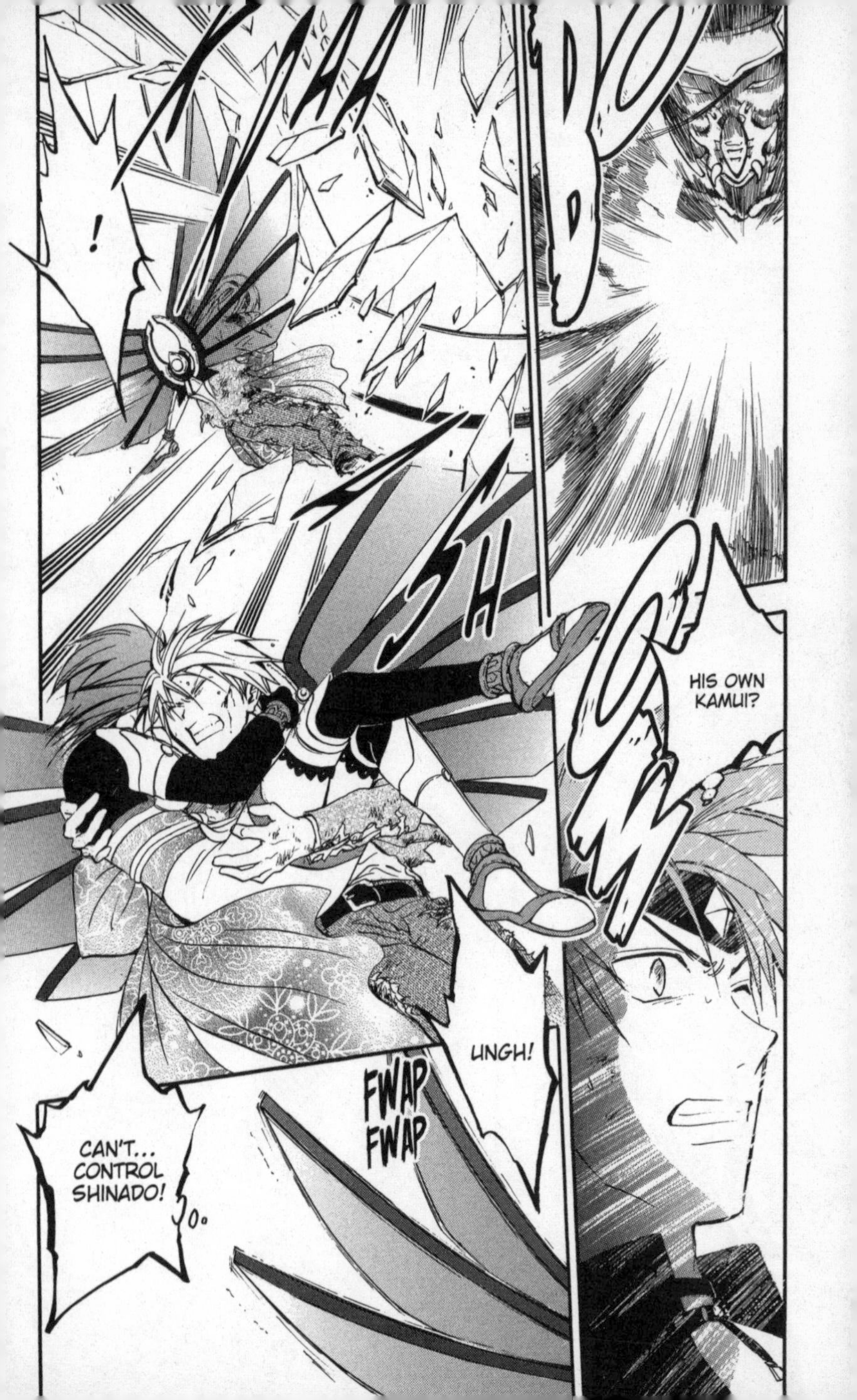
HIS OWN KAMUI?
KAHH
!
UNGH!
FWAP FWAP
CAN'T... CONTROL SHINADO!

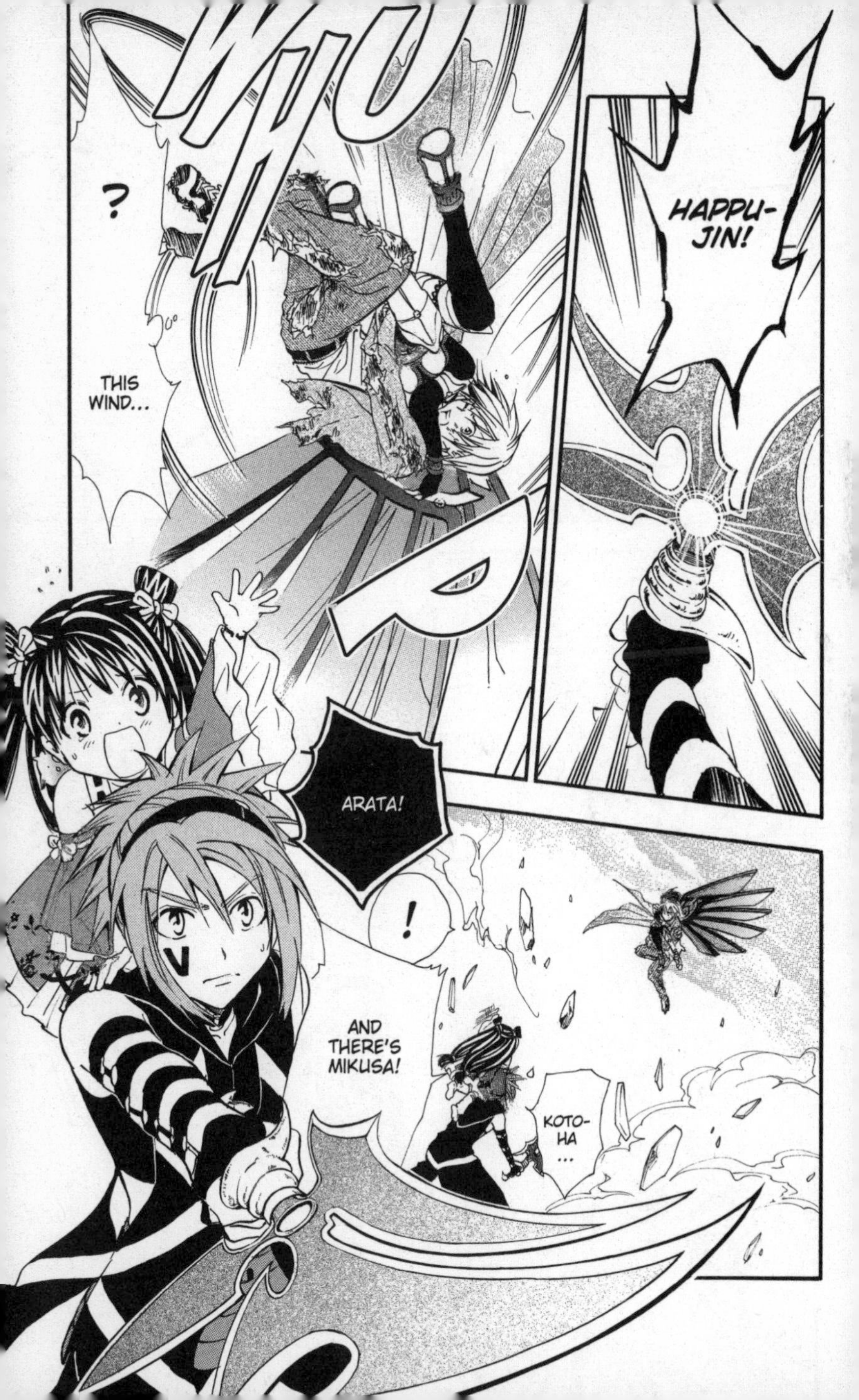
HAPPU-JIN!
?
THIS WIND...
ARATA!
!
KOTO-HA ...
AND THERE'S MIKUSA!

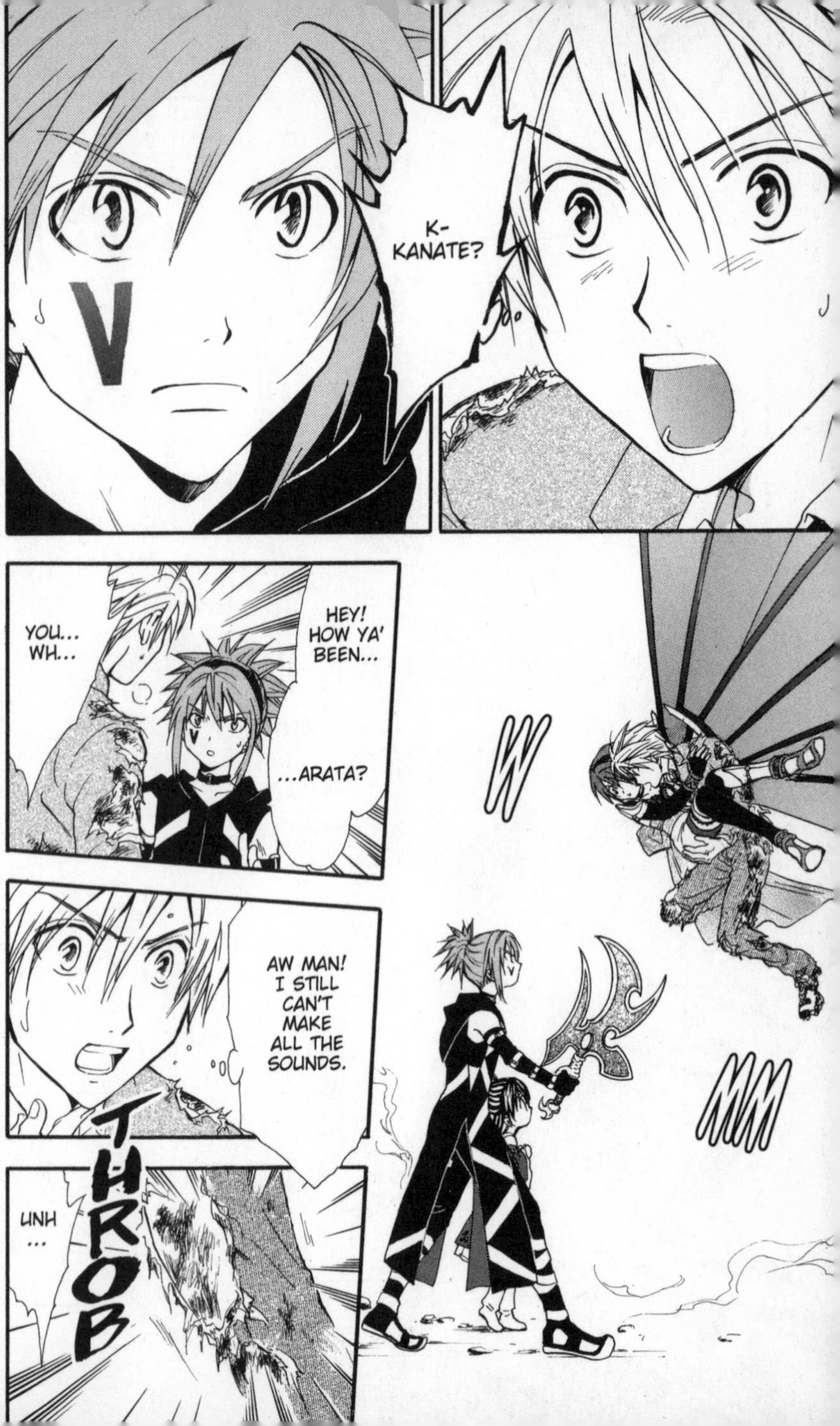
K-KANATE?
W
MM
HEY! HOW YA' BEEN...
...ARATA?
YOU... WH...
AW MAN! I STILL CAN'T MAKE ALL THE SOUNDS.
THROB
UNH ...

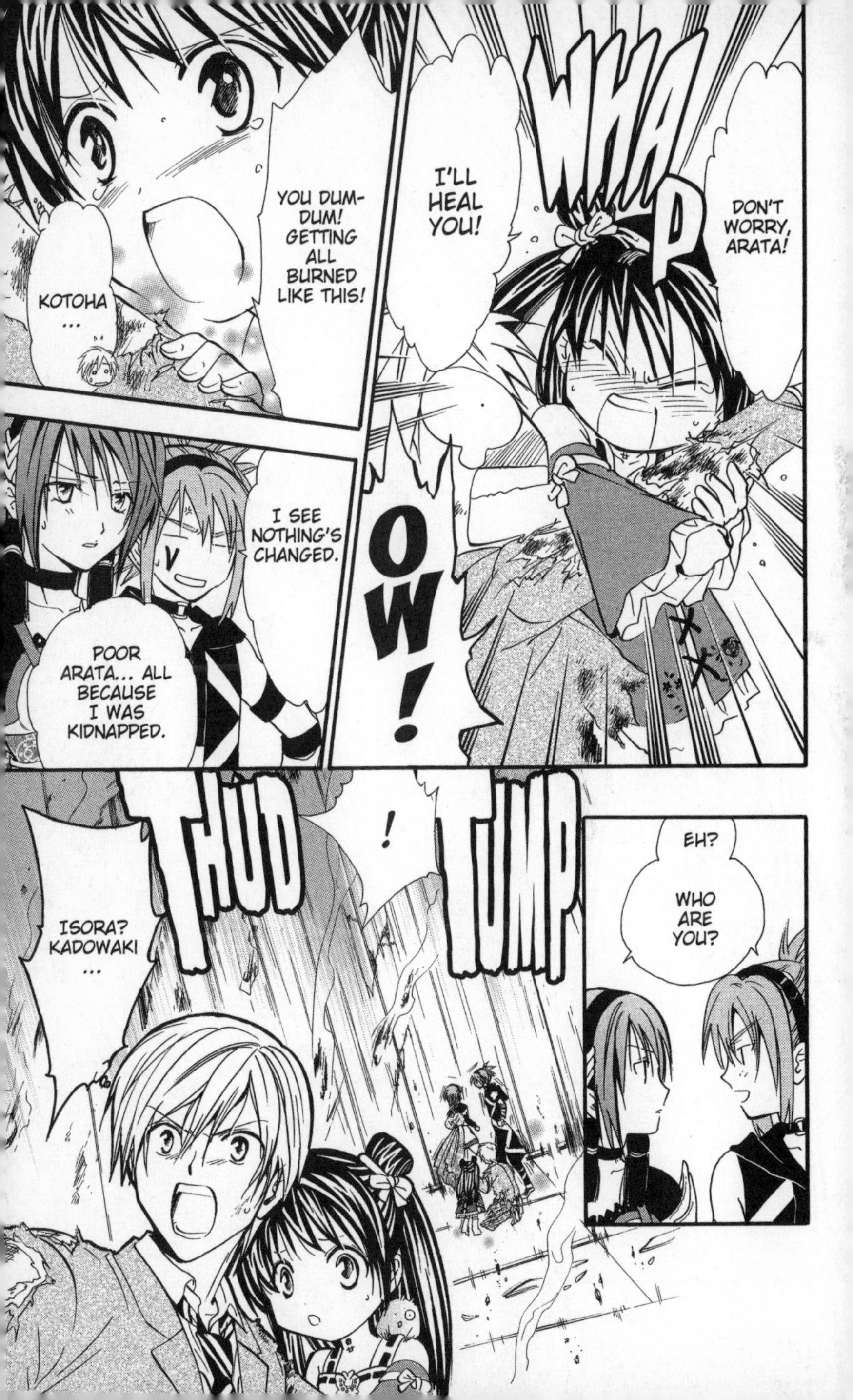
DON'T WORRY, ARATA!
WHAP
I'LL HEAL YOU!
OW!
YOU DUM-DUM! GETTING ALL BURNED LIKE THIS!
KOTOHA ...
I SEE NOTHING'S CHANGED.
POOR ARATA... ALL BECAUSE I WAS KIDNAPPED.
EH?
WHO ARE YOU?
TUMP
!
THUD
ISORA? KADOWAKI ...

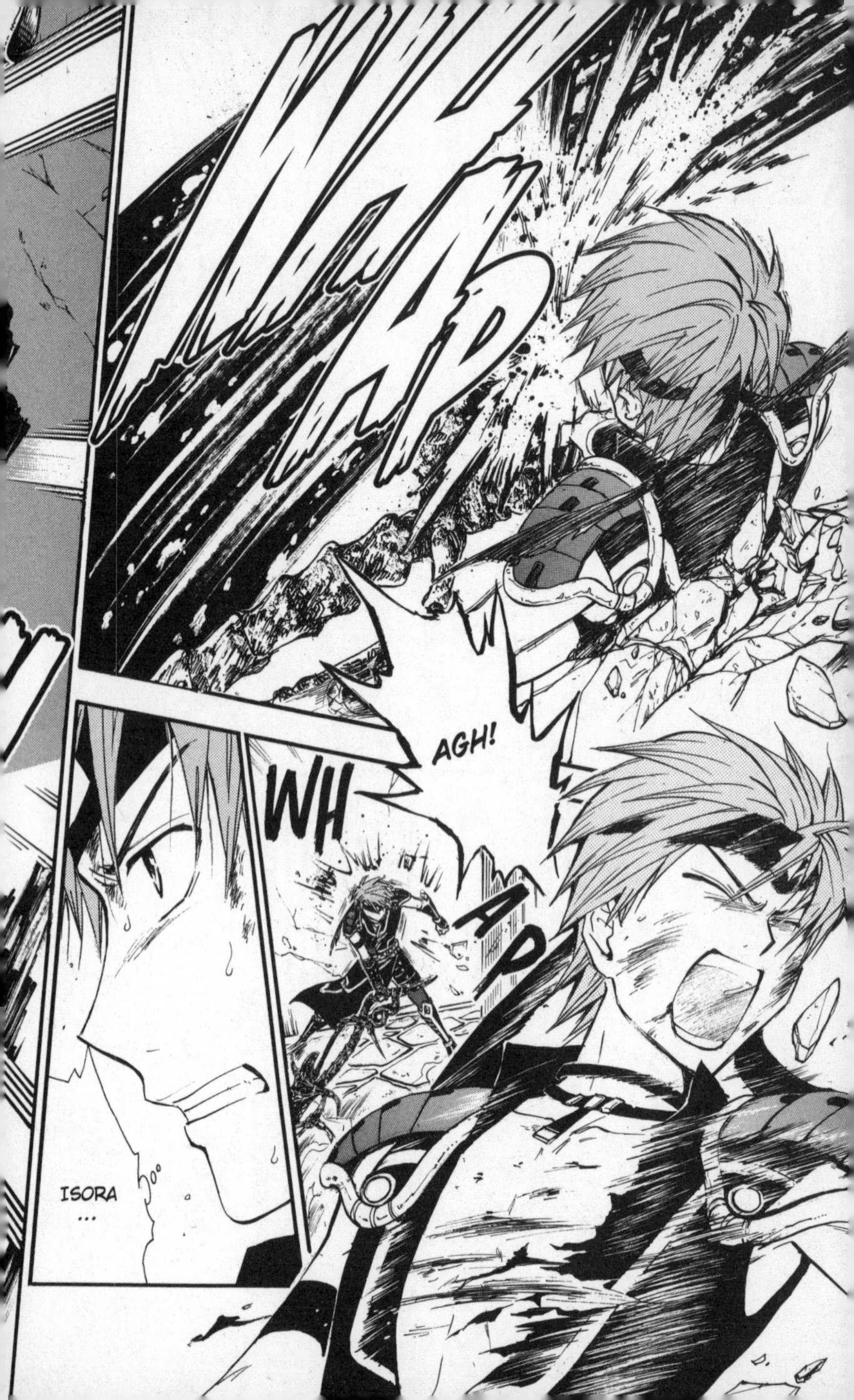
WHAP
AGH!
WHAP
ISORA
...

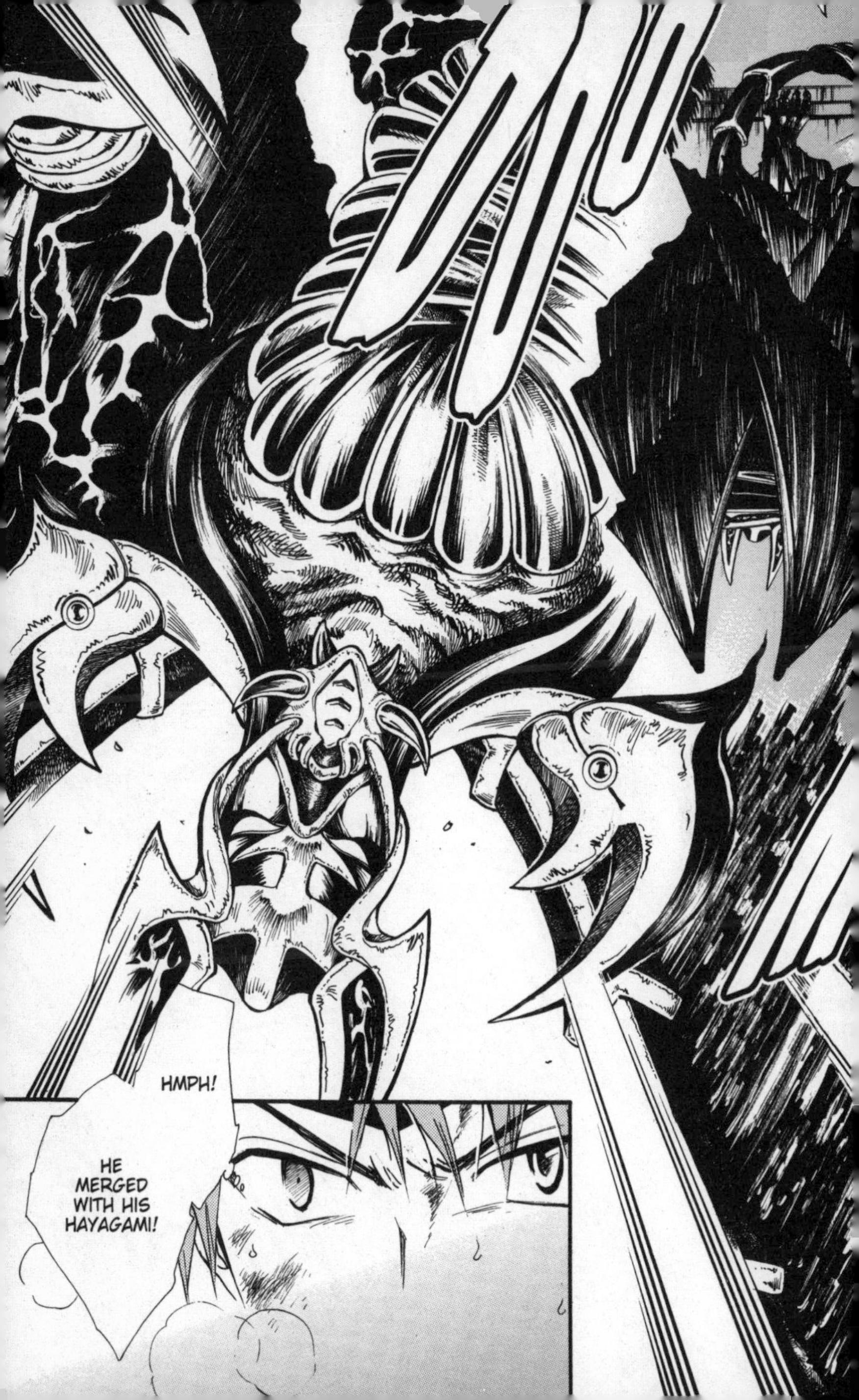
HMPH!
HE MERGED WITH HIS HAYAGAMI!

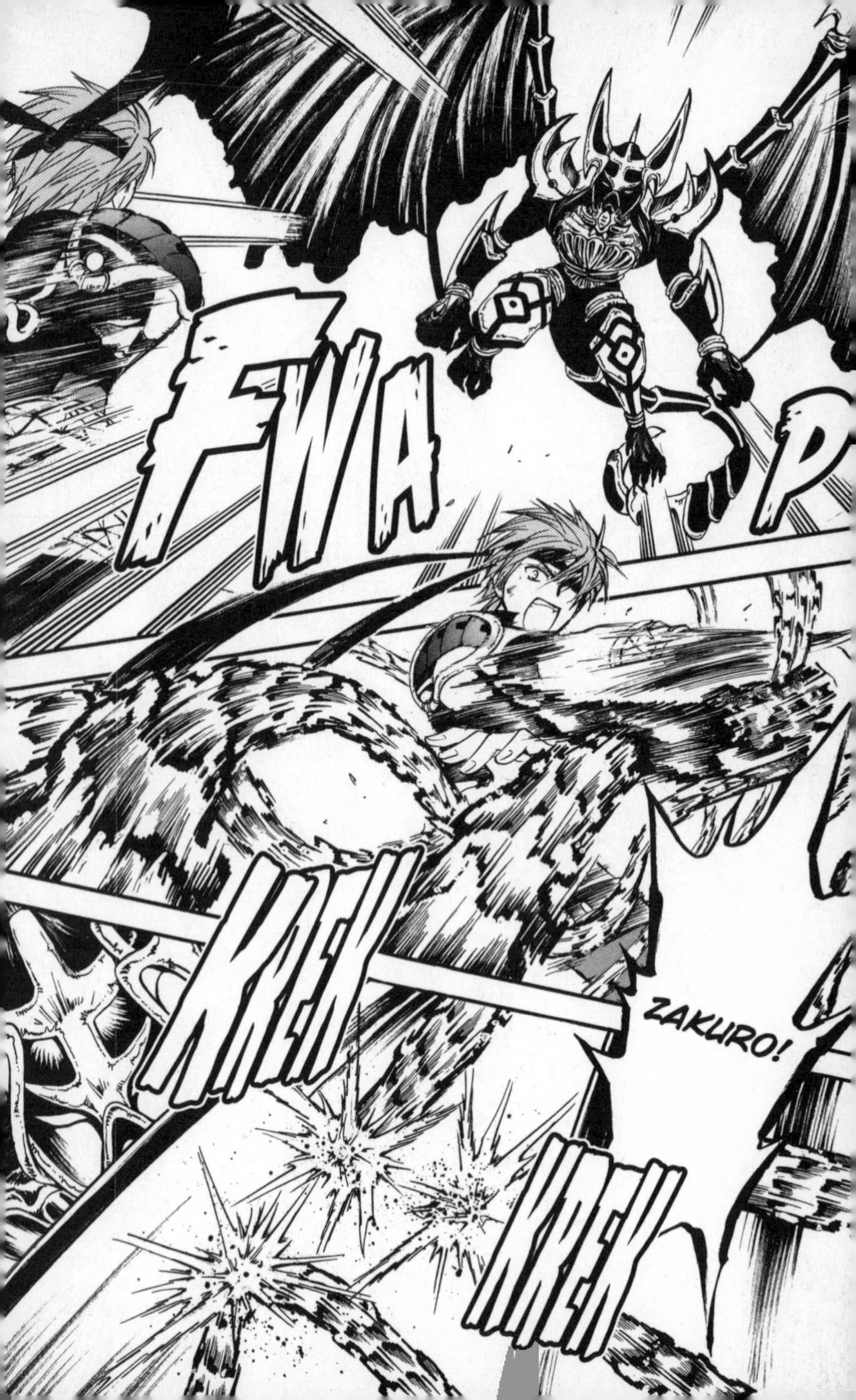
FWA
ZAKURO!
KREK
KREK

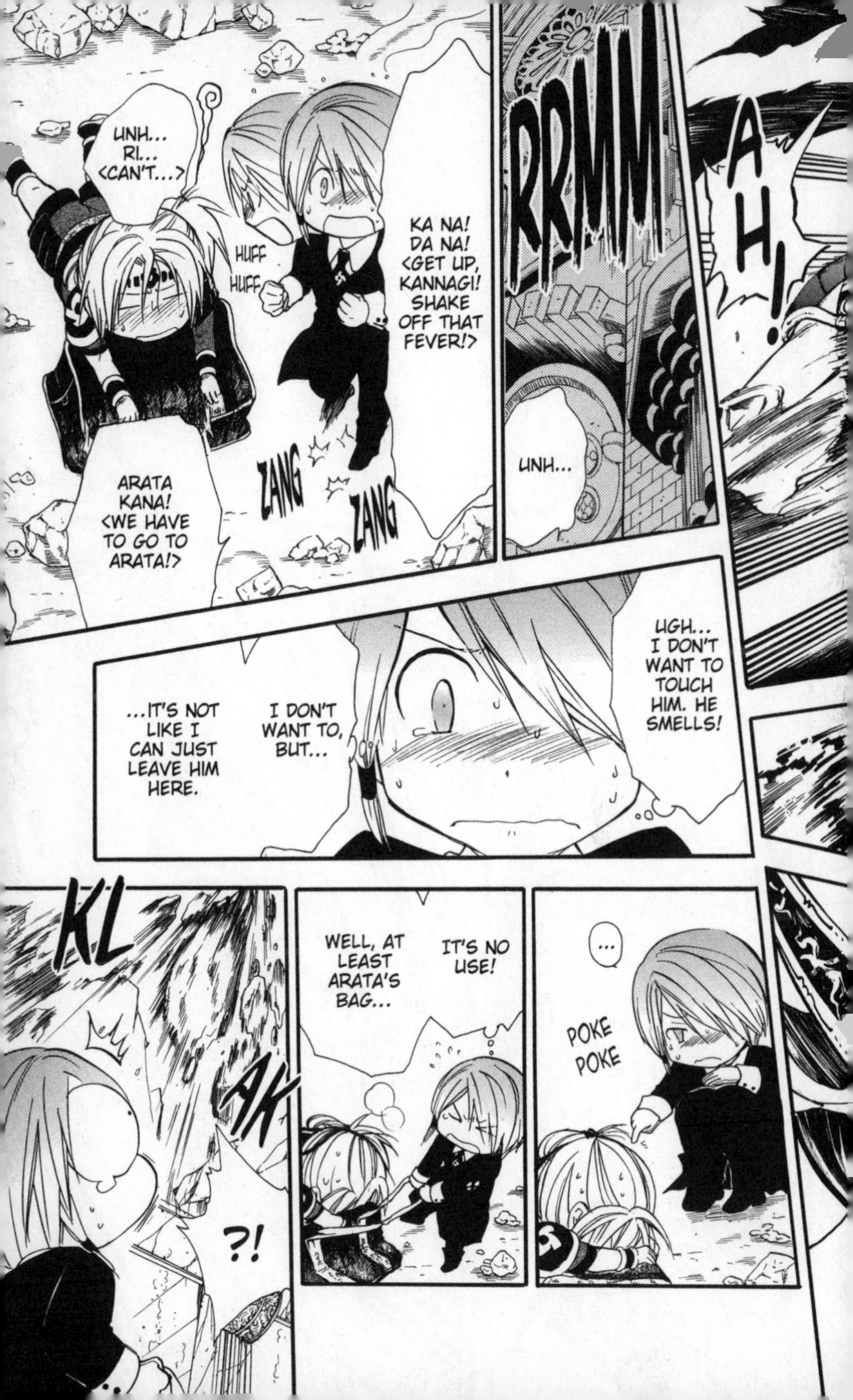
AH!
RRMM
UNH...
KA NA! DA NA! <GET UP, KANNAGI! SHAKE OFF THAT FEVER!>
UNH... RI... <CAN'T...>
HUFF HUFF
ZANG ZANG
ARATA KANA! <WE HAVE TO GO TO ARATA!>
UGH... I DON'T WANT TO TOUCH HIM. HE SMELLS!
I DON'T WANT TO, BUT...
...IT'S NOT LIKE I CAN JUST LEAVE HIM HERE.
...
POKE POKE
IT'S NO USE!
WELL, AT LEAST ARATA'S BAG...
KLAK
?!

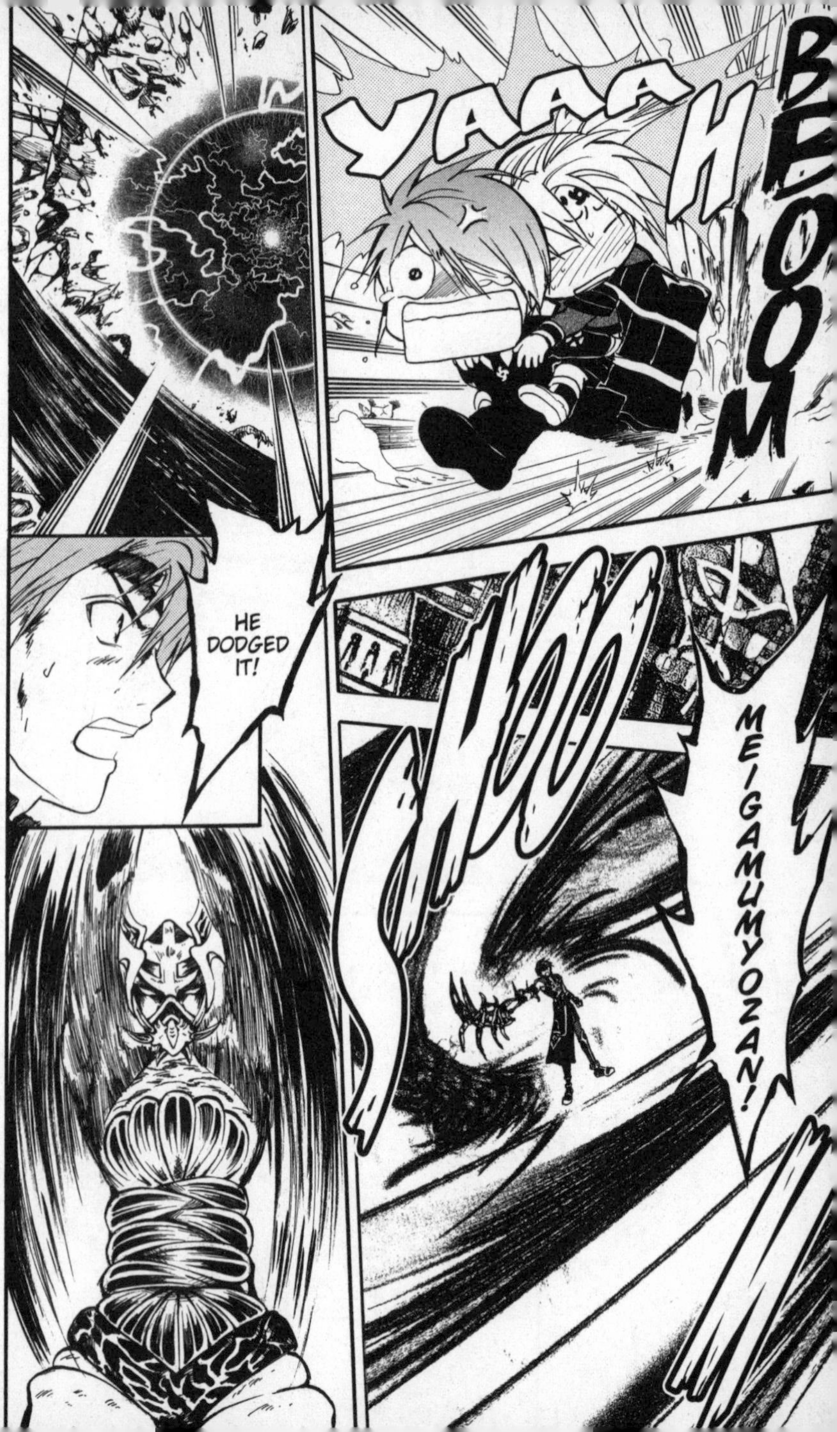
BEOOOM
YAAAH
HE DODGED IT!
MEIGAMUMYOZAN!

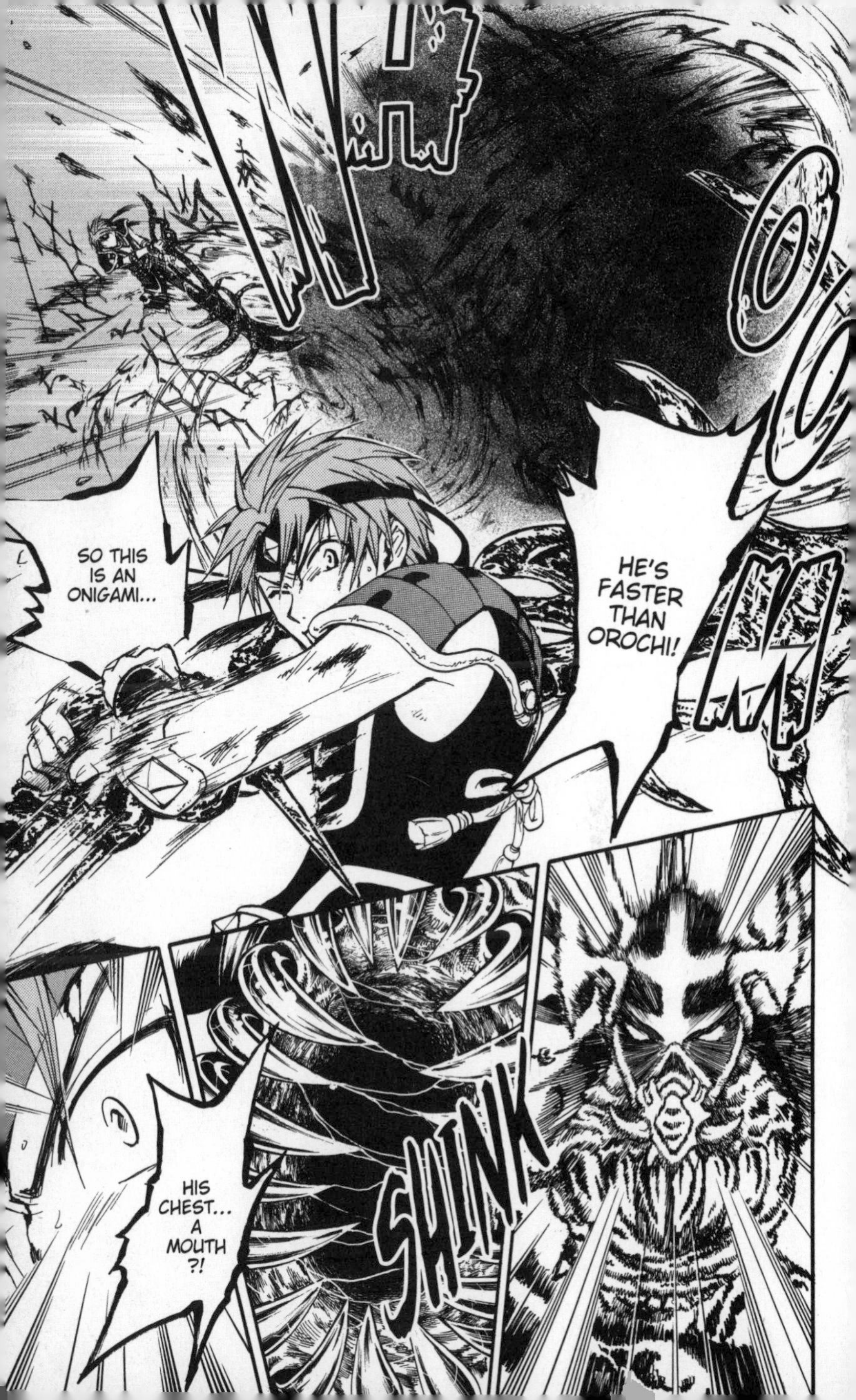
HE'S FASTER THAN OROCHI!
SO THIS IS AN ONIGAMI...
SHINK
HIS CHEST... A MOUTH?!

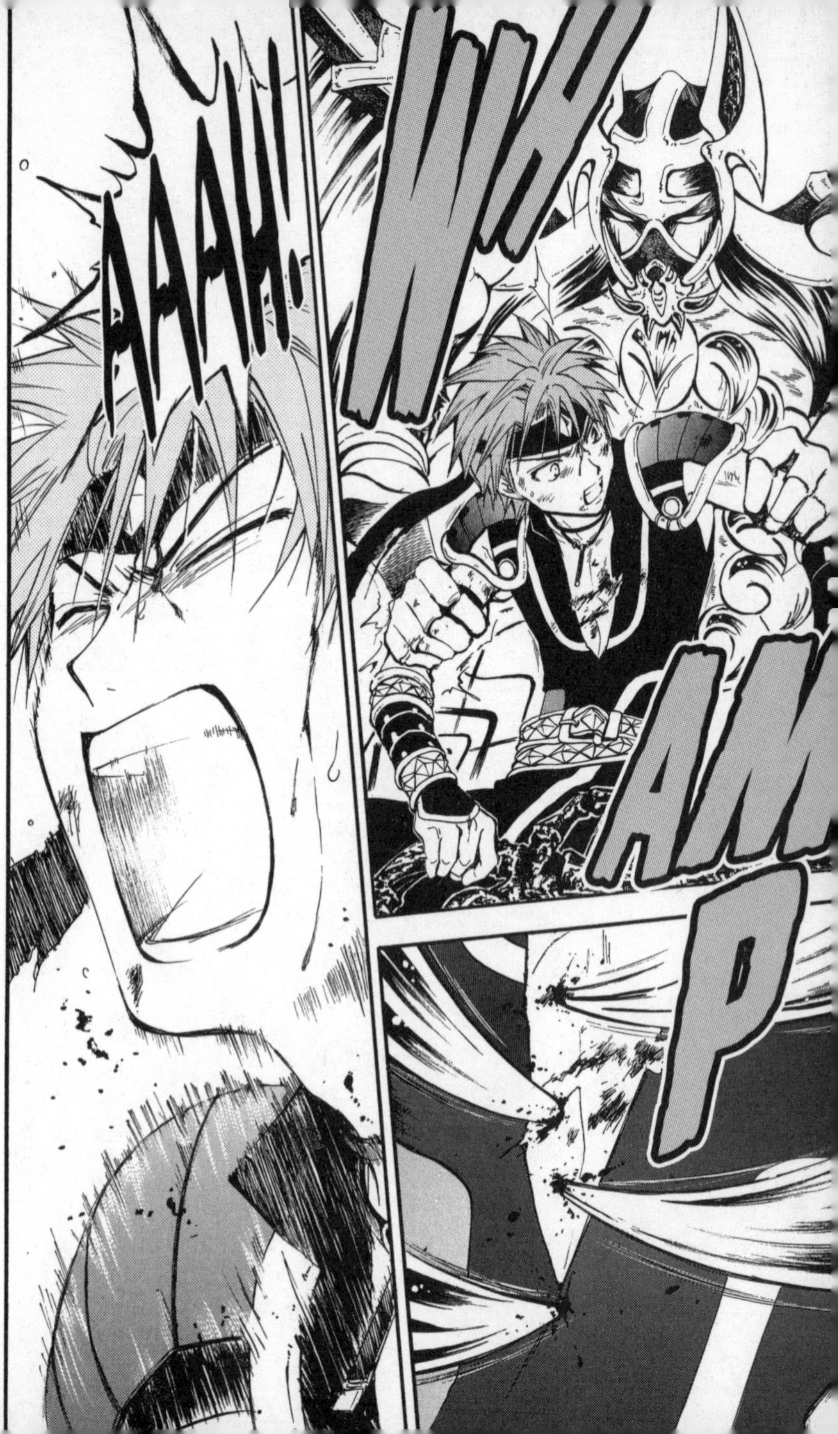
WH
AM
P
AAAH!!

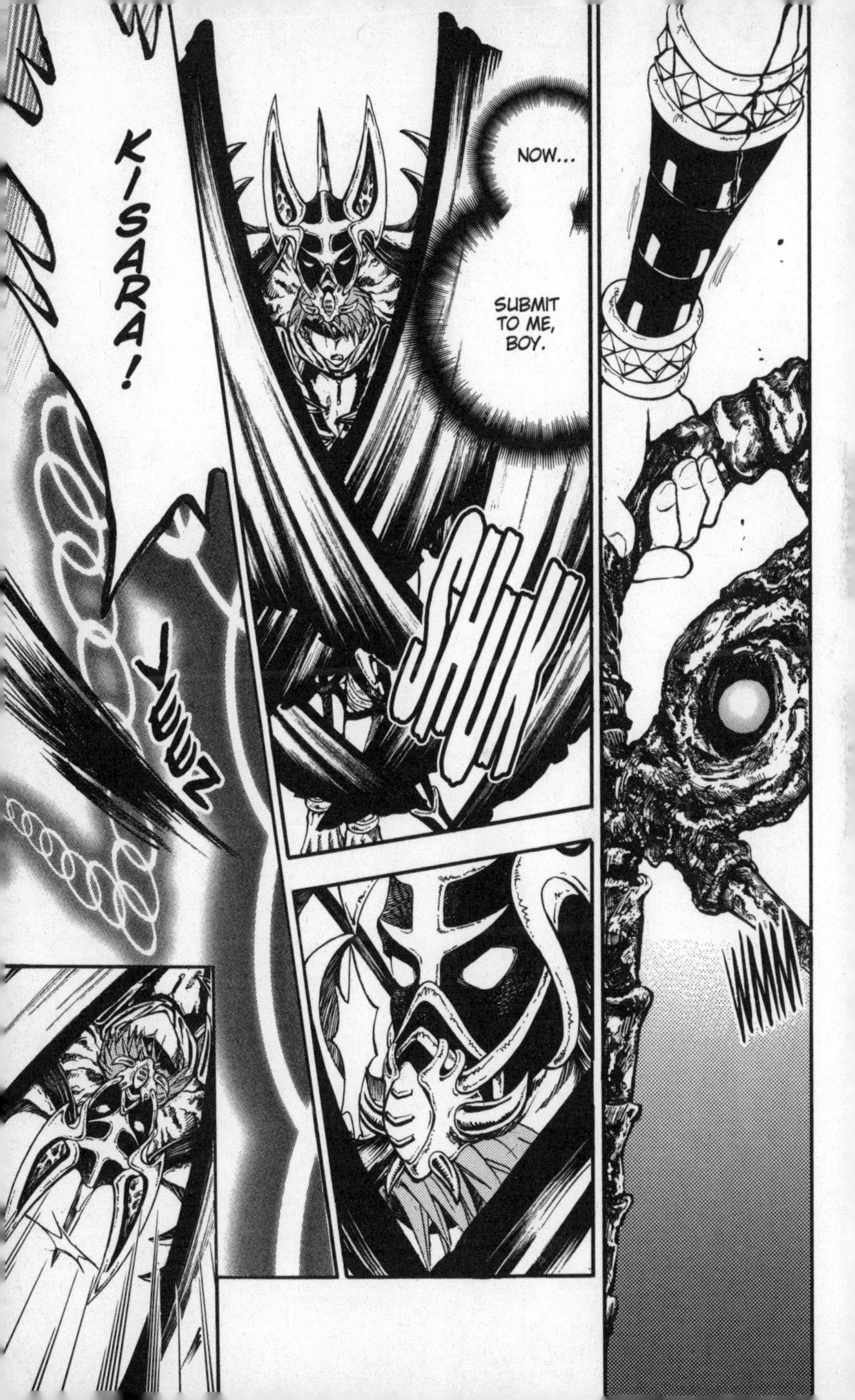
VMMM
NOW...
SUBMIT TO ME, BOY.
SHUNK
KISARA!
VUUZ

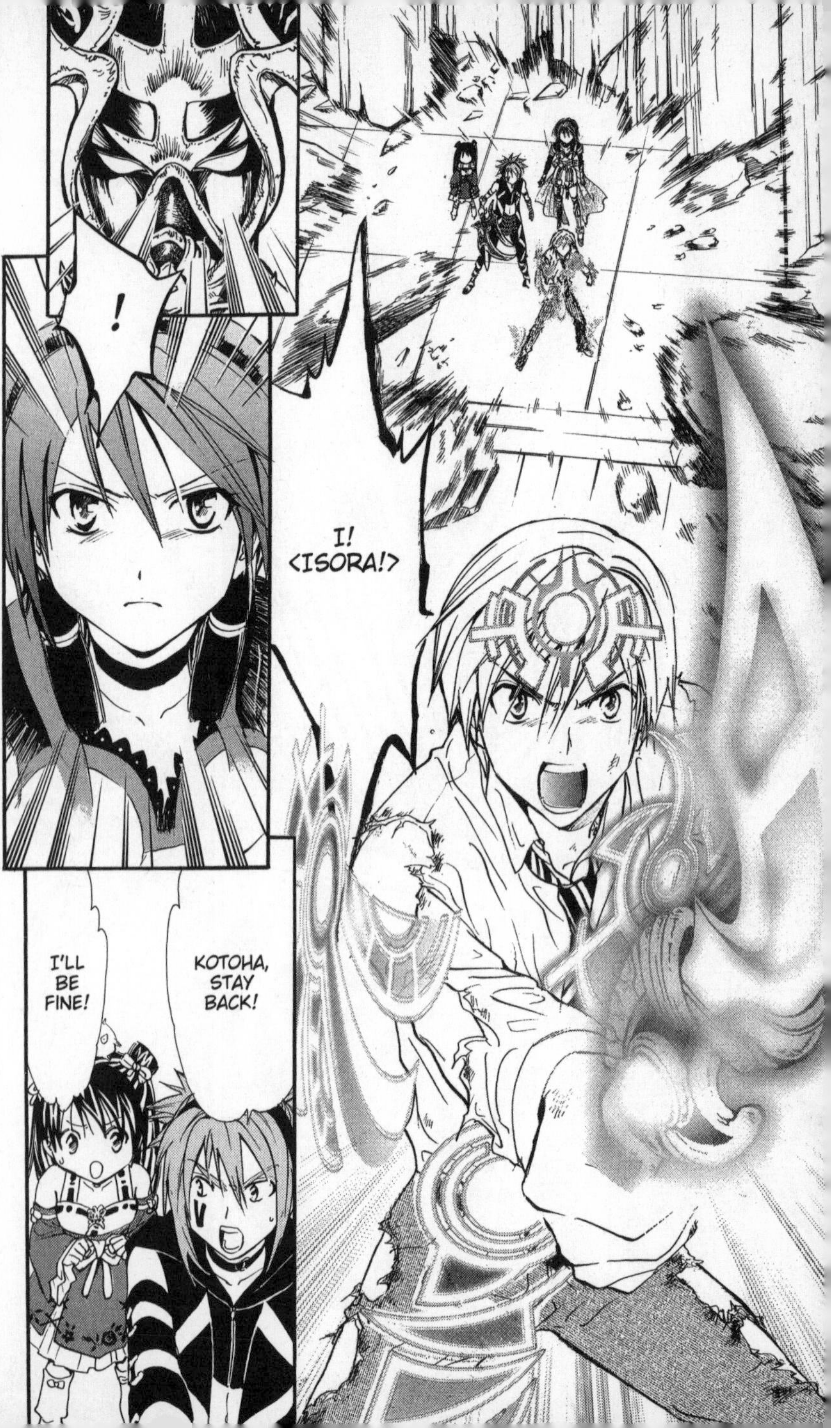
I!
<ISORA!>
!
KOTOHA, STAY BACK!
I'LL BE FINE!

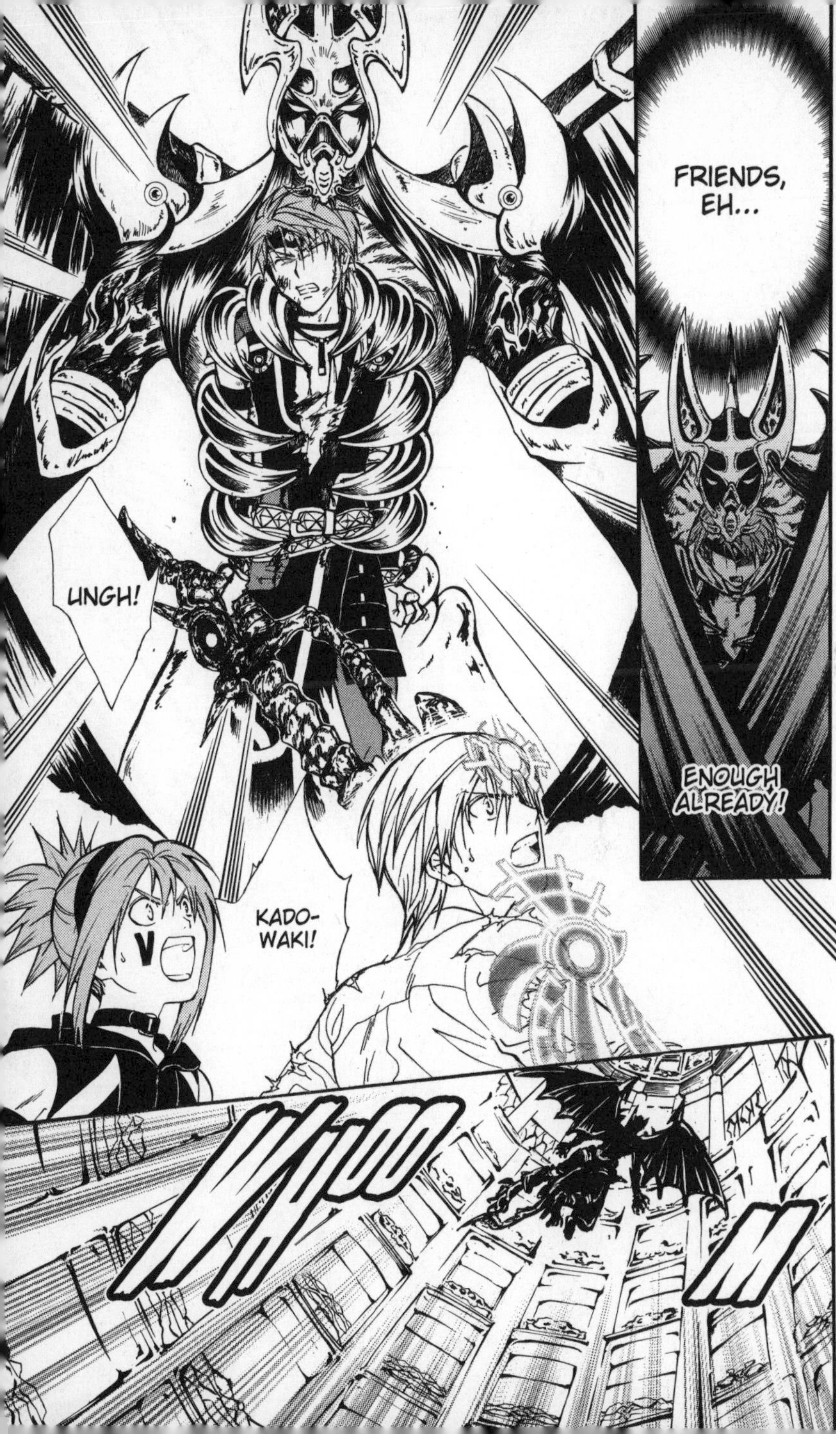
FRIENDS, EH...
ENOUGH ALREADY!
UNGH!
KADO-WAKI!

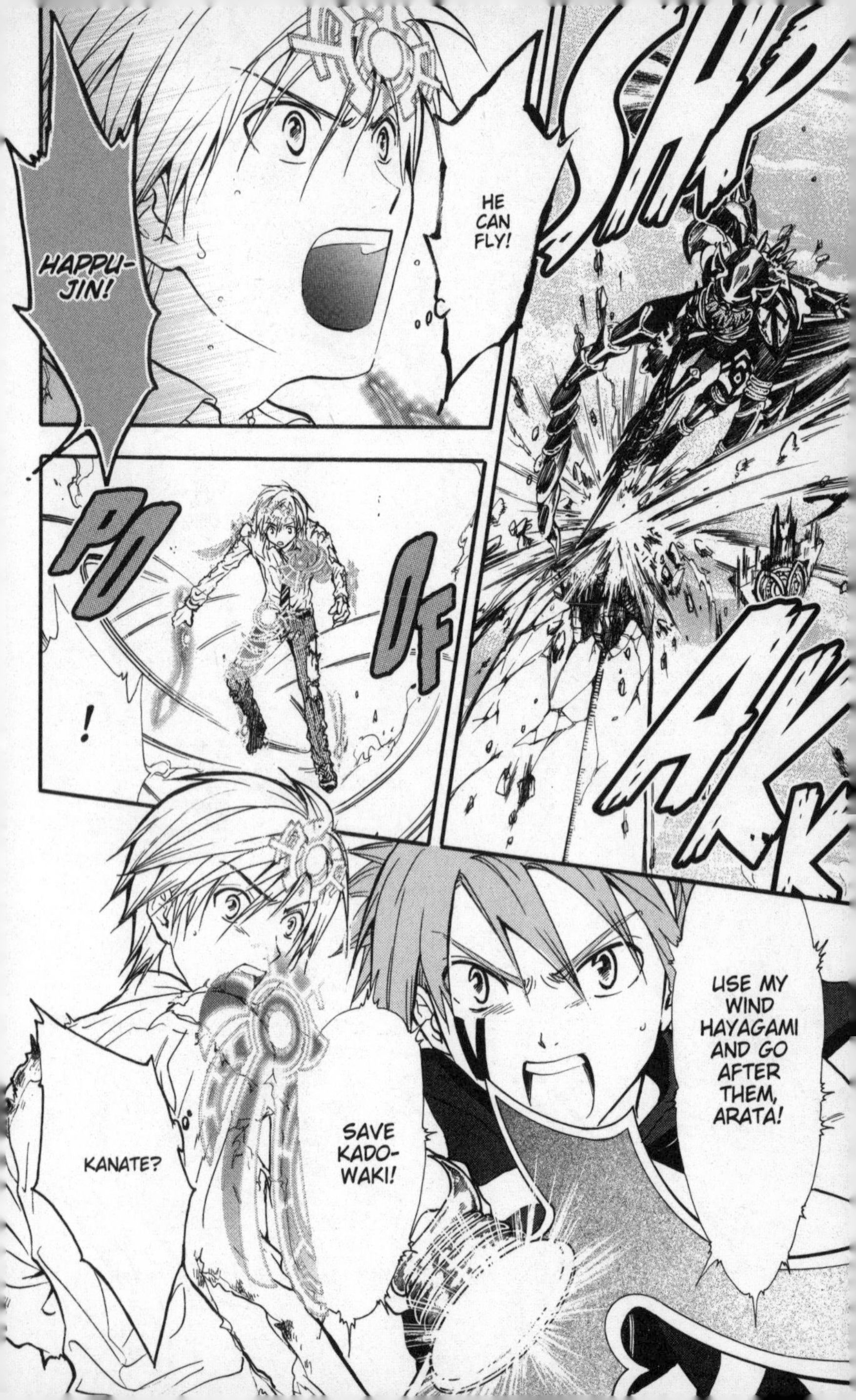
SHPAAK
HE CAN FLY!
HAPPU-JIN!
POOF
!
USE MY WIND HAYAGAMI AND GO AFTER THEM, ARATA!
SAVE KADO-WAKI!
KANATE?

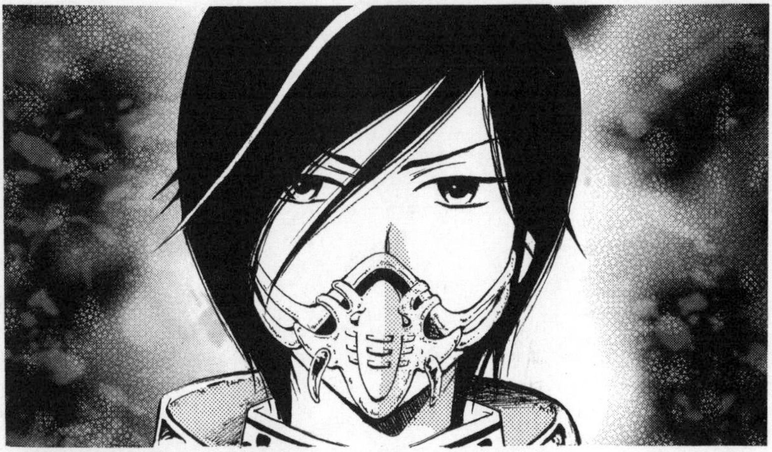

CHAPTER 185

JUST ONE FOE

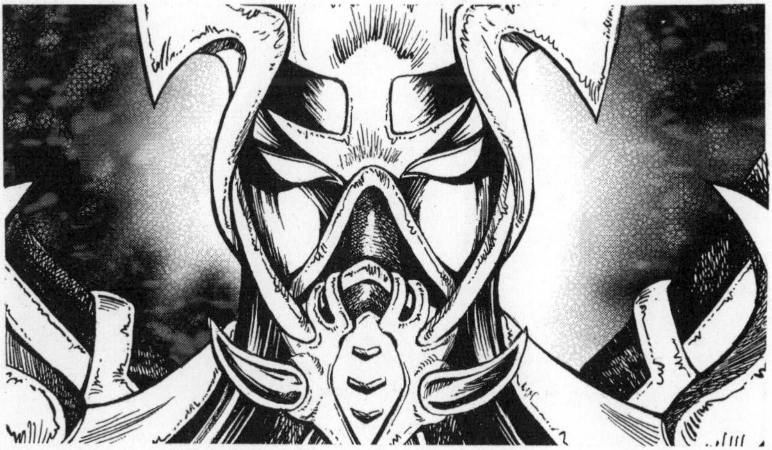

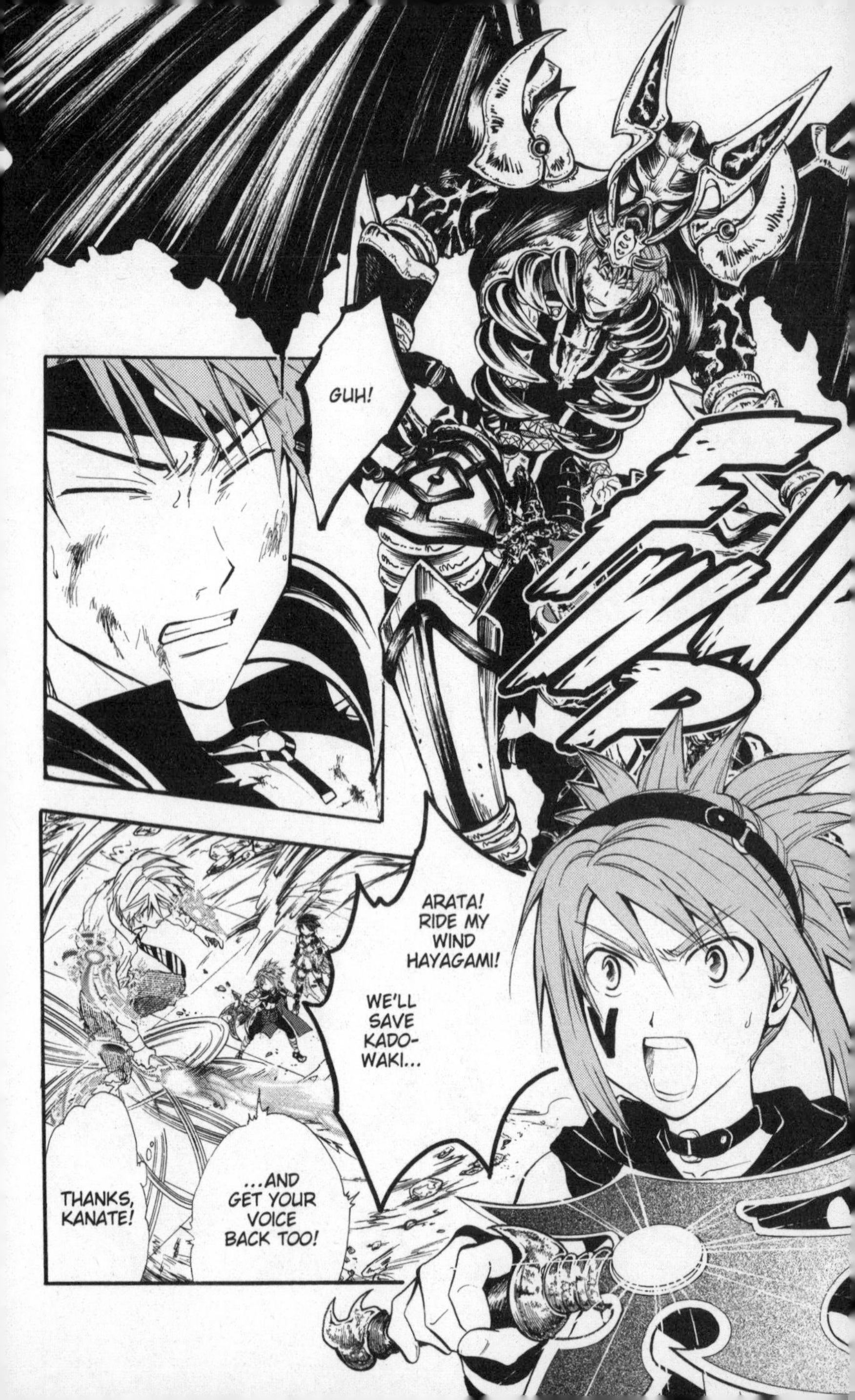
GUH!
ARATA! RIDE MY WIND HAYAGAMI!
WE'LL SAVE KADO-WAKI...
...AND GET YOUR VOICE BACK TOO!
THANKS, KANATE!

WHEN DID YOU JOIN UP WITH KADO-WAKI?

HE AND ARATA ARE BITTER RIVALS!

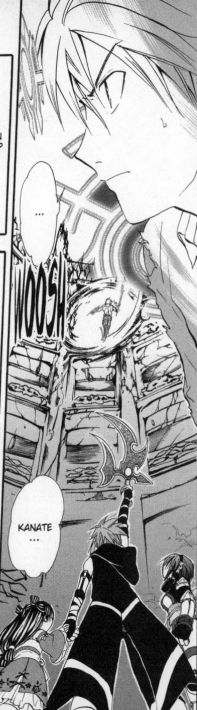

...

WOOSH

KANATE...

IT'S NOT LIKE WE'RE CHUMS, BUT I DON'T KNOW...

...HOW TO EX-PLAIN IT.

THERE'S A SPIRAL STAIR-CASE!

GRRR

MIGHT AS WELL USE IT!

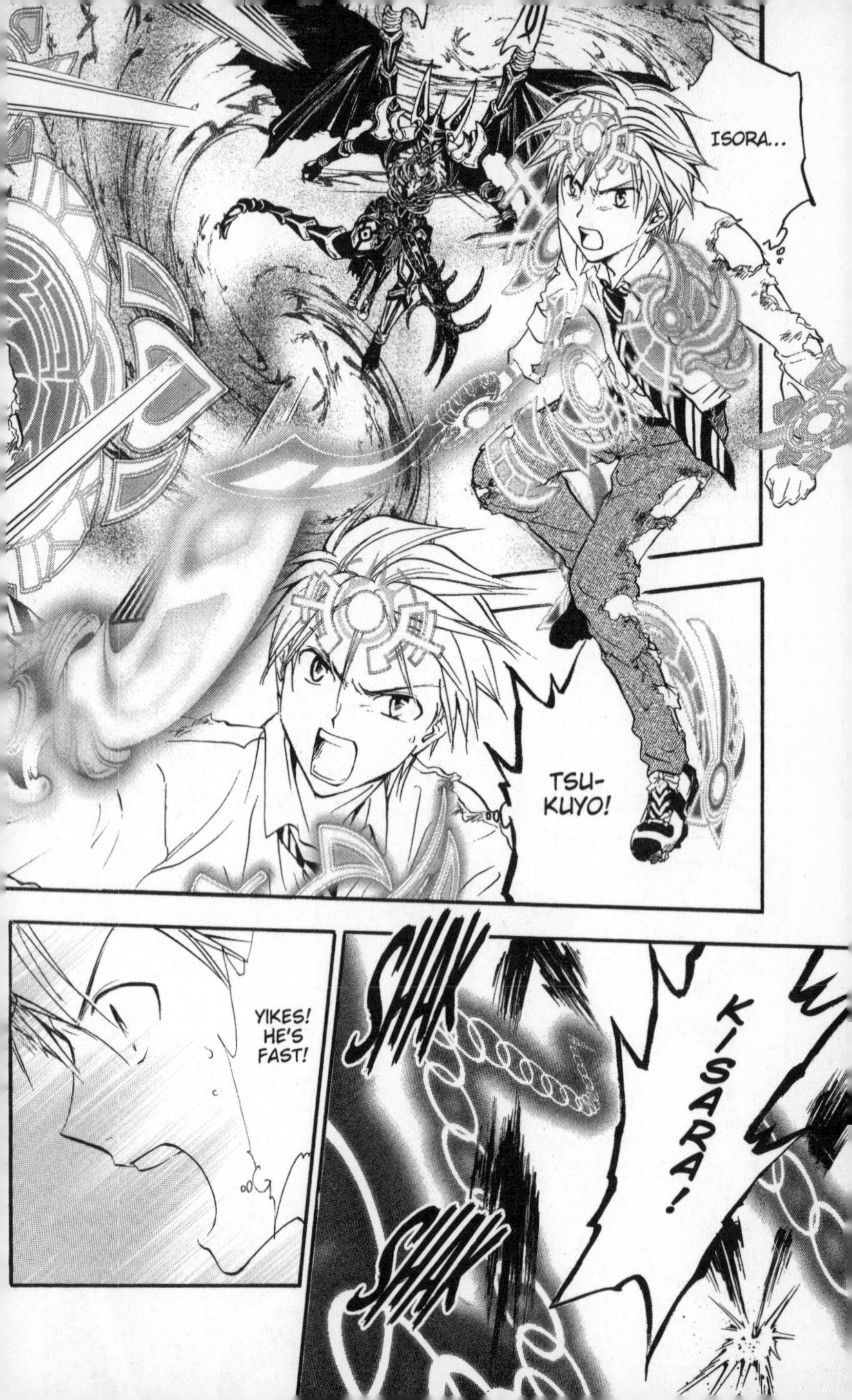
ISORA...
TSU-KUYO!
KISARA!
SHAK
SHAK
YIKES! HE'S FAST!

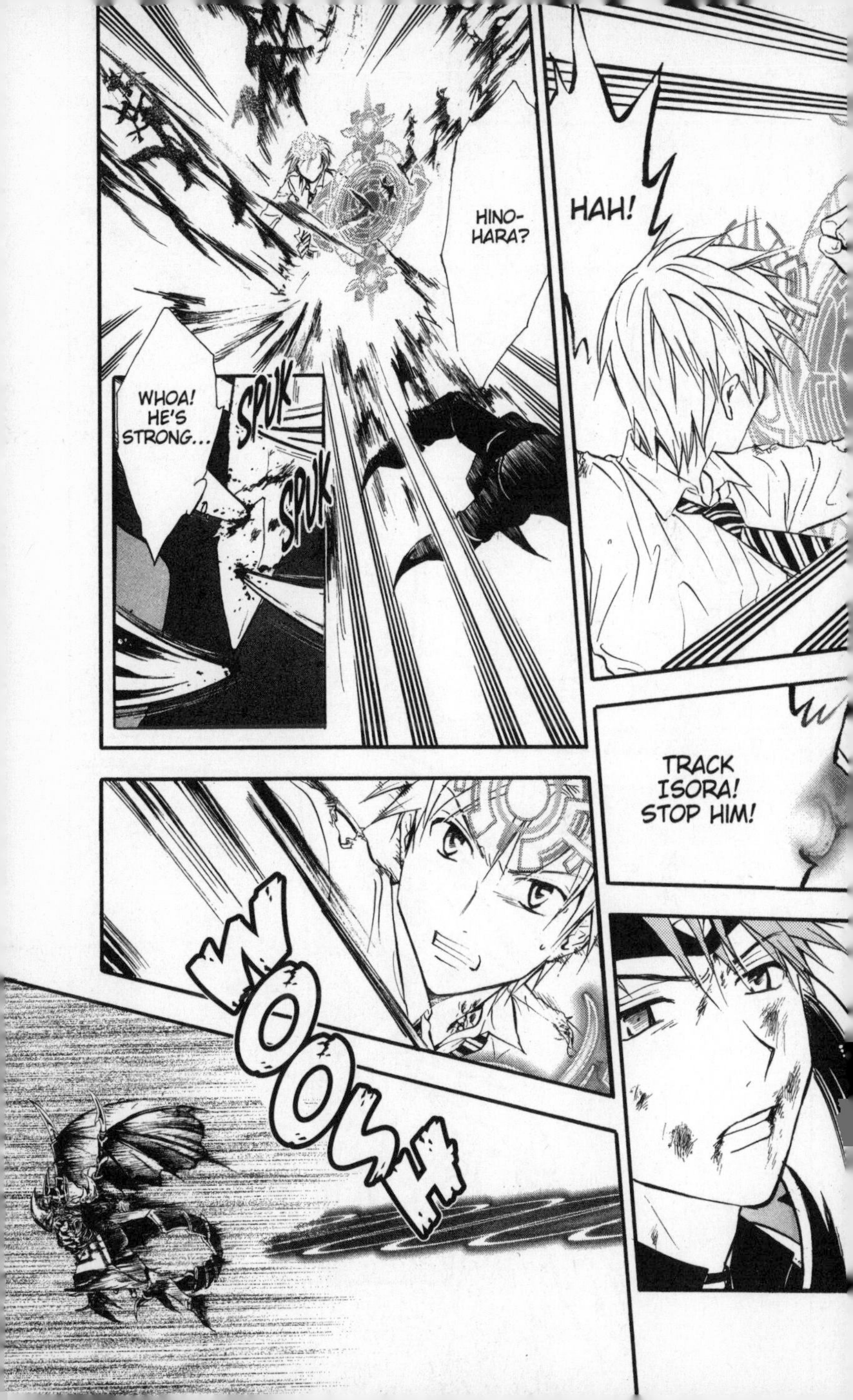
HAH!
HINO-HARA?
WHOA! HE'S STRONG...
SPUK
SPUK
TRACK ISORA! STOP HIM!
WOOOSH

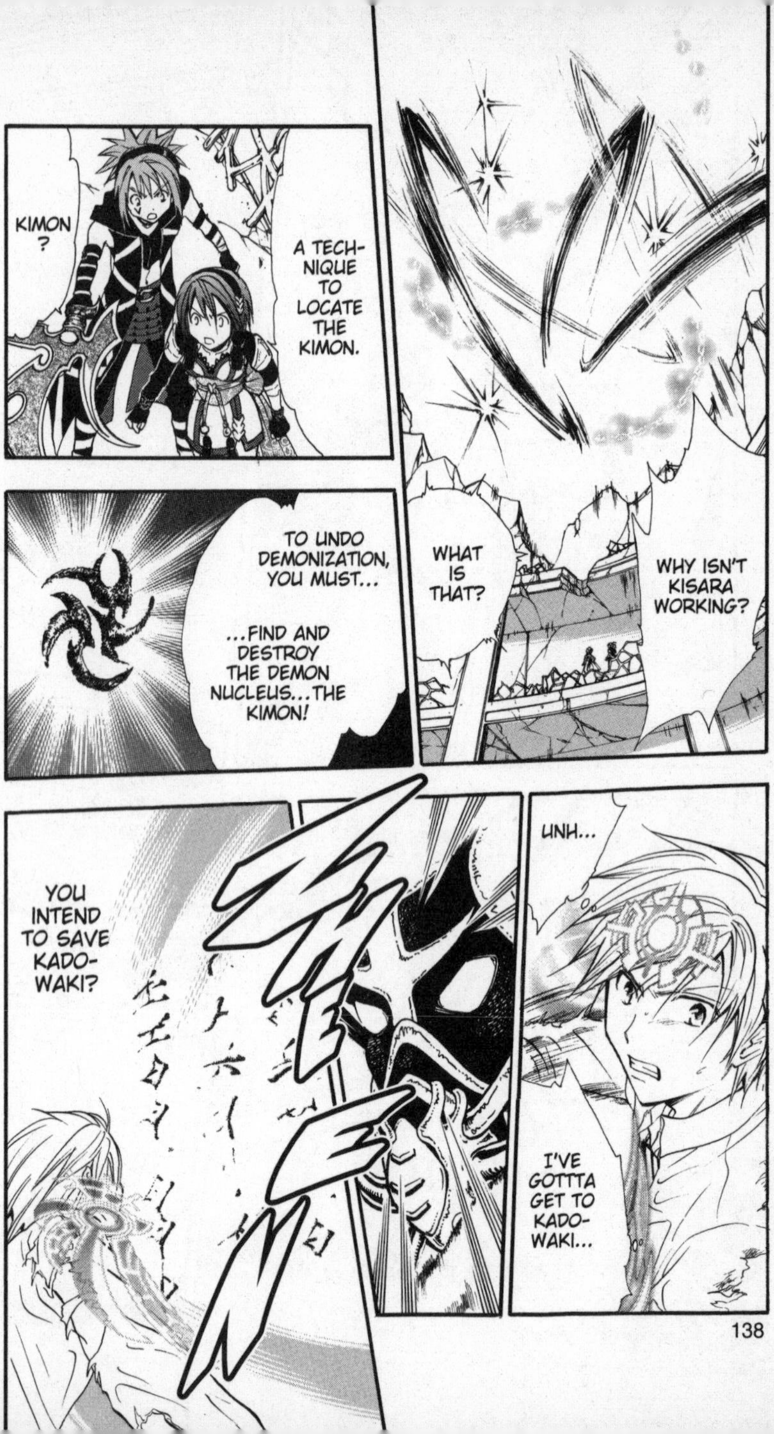
WHY ISN'T KISARA WORKING?
WHAT IS THAT?
A TECH-NIQUE TO LOCATE THE KIMON.
KIMON?
TO UNDO DEMONIZATION, YOU MUST...
...FIND AND DESTROY THE DEMON NUCLEUS...THE KIMON!
UNH...
I'VE GOTTTA GET TO KADO-WAKI...
YOU INTEND TO SAVE KADO-WAKI?

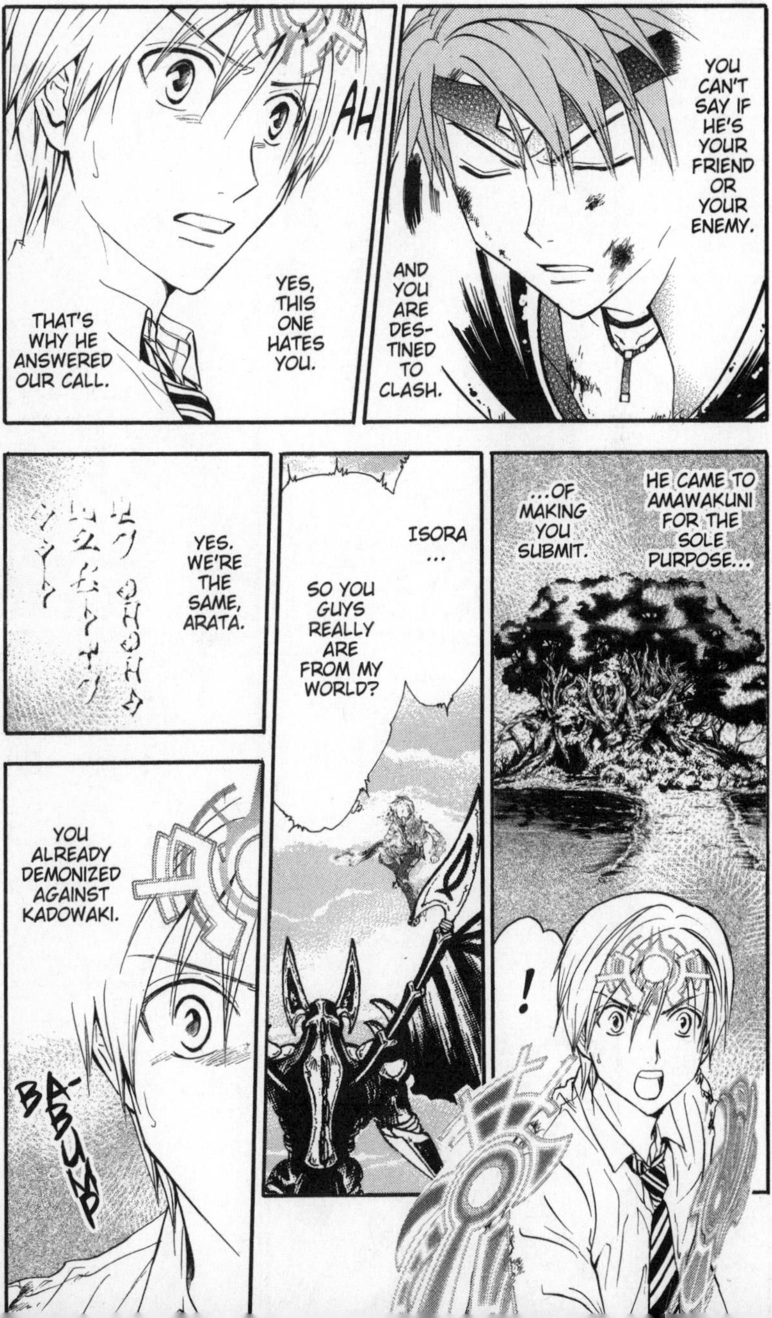
YOU CAN'T SAY IF HE'S YOUR FRIEND OR YOUR ENEMY.
AND YOU ARE DES-TINED TO CLASH.
AH
YES, THIS ONE HATES YOU.
THAT'S WHY HE ANSWERED OUR CALL.
HE CAME TO AMAWAKUNI FOR THE SOLE PURPOSE...
...OF MAKING YOU SUBMIT.
!
ISORA ...
SO YOU GUYS REALLY ARE FROM MY WORLD?
YES. WE'RE THE SAME, ARATA.
YOU ALREADY DEMONIZED AGAINST KADOWAKI.
BA-BUMP

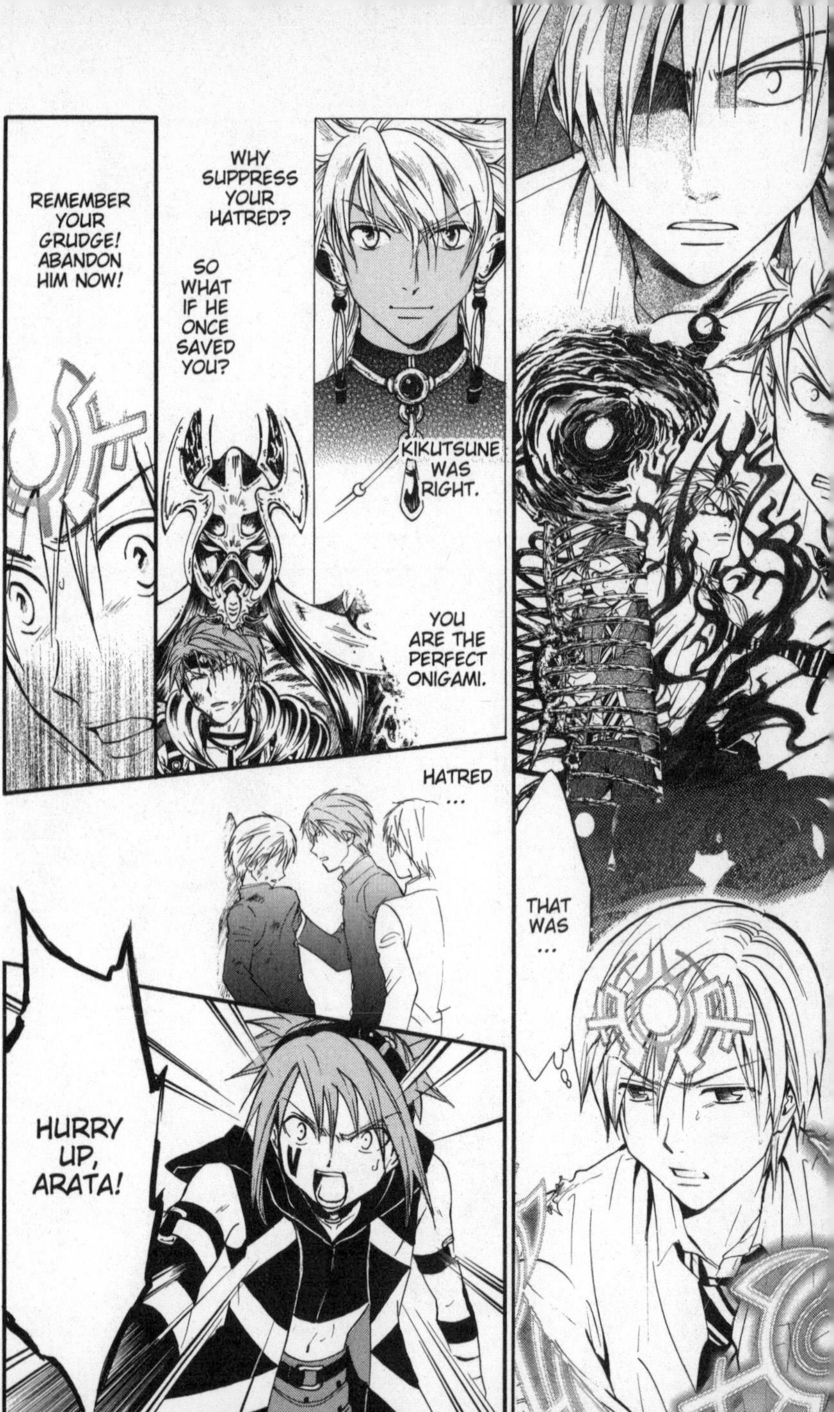
WHY SUPPRESS YOUR HATRED?
SO WHAT IF HE ONCE SAVED YOU?
KIKUTSUNE WAS RIGHT.
YOU ARE THE PERFECT ONIGAMI.
REMEMBER YOUR GRUDGE! ABANDON HIM NOW!
HATRED...
THAT WAS...
HURRY UP, ARATA!

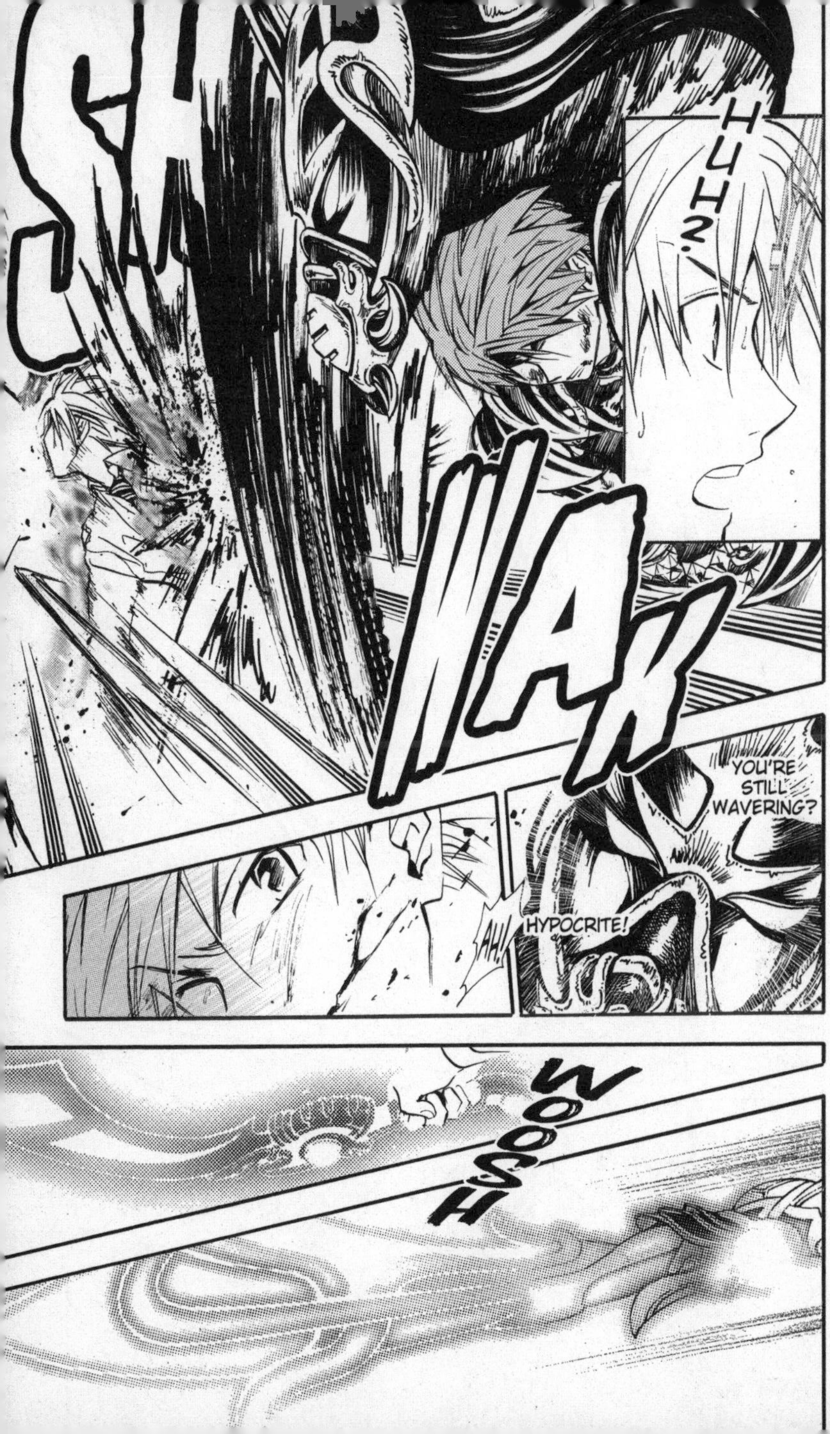
HUH?
WAK
YOU'RE STILL WAVERING?
HYPOCRITE!
AH!
WOOSH

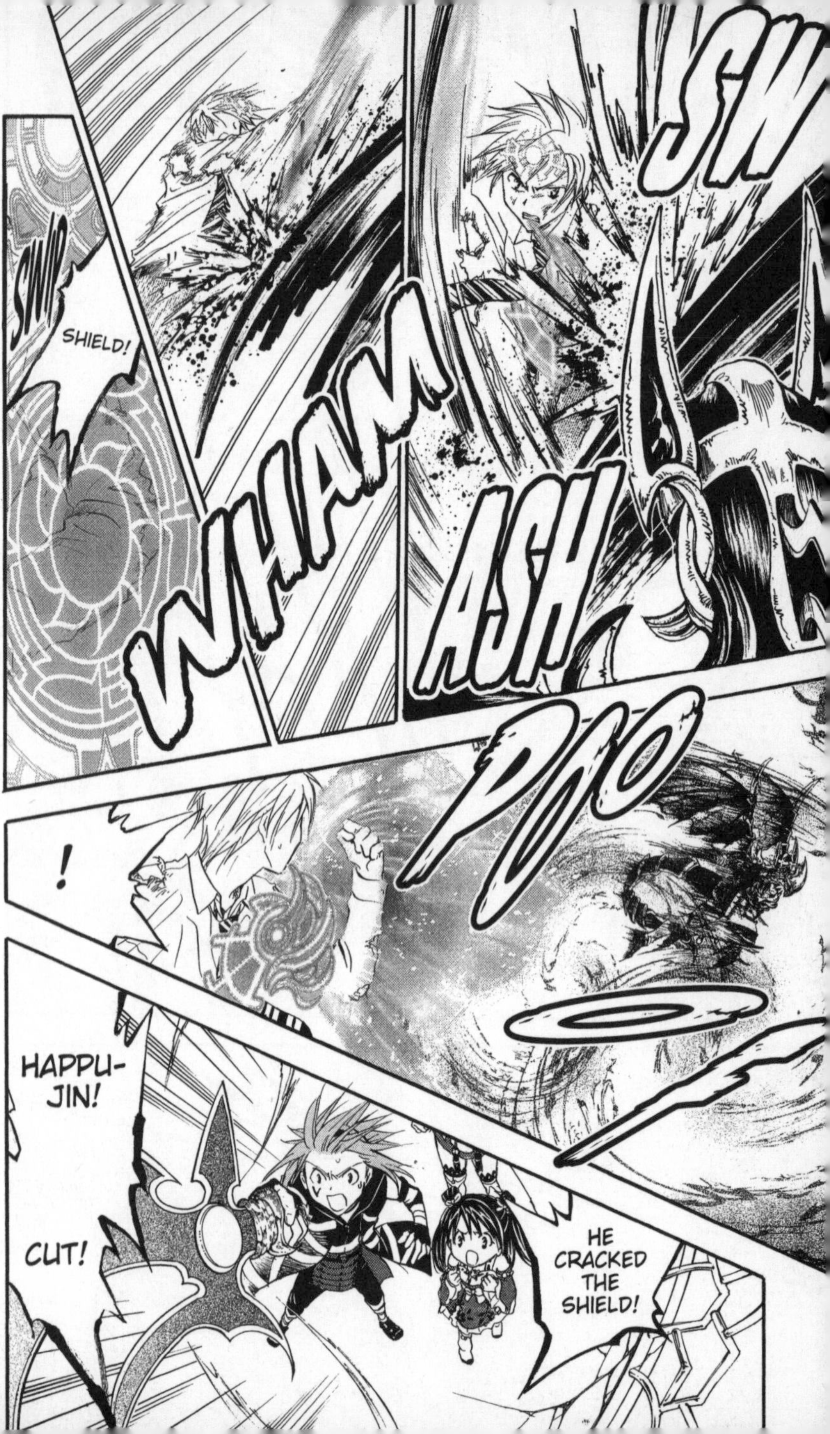
WHAM
SWIP
SHIELD!
!
HE CRACKED THE SHIELD!
HAPPU-JIN!
CUT!

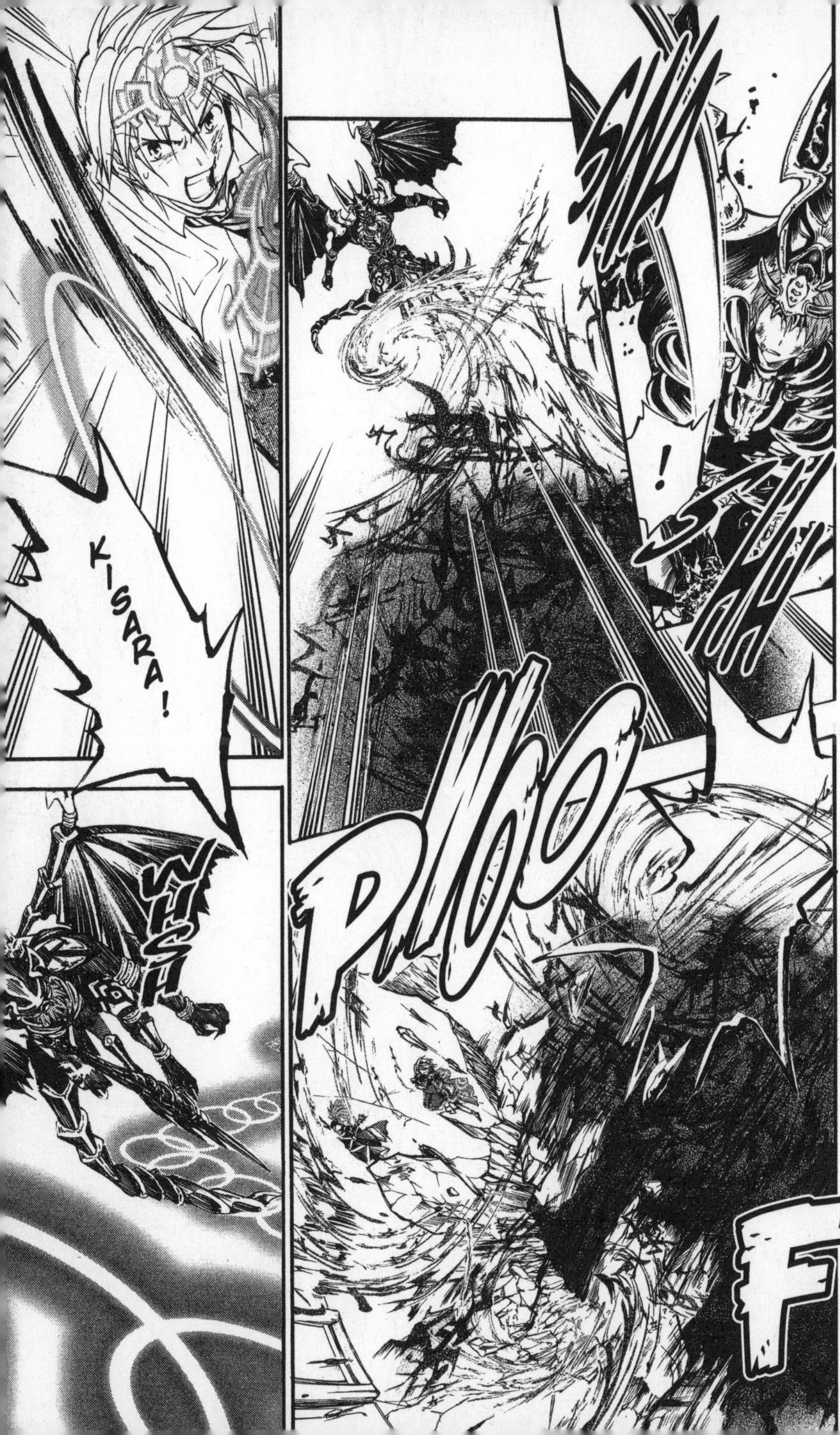
!
DHOOF
KISARA!
WHSH

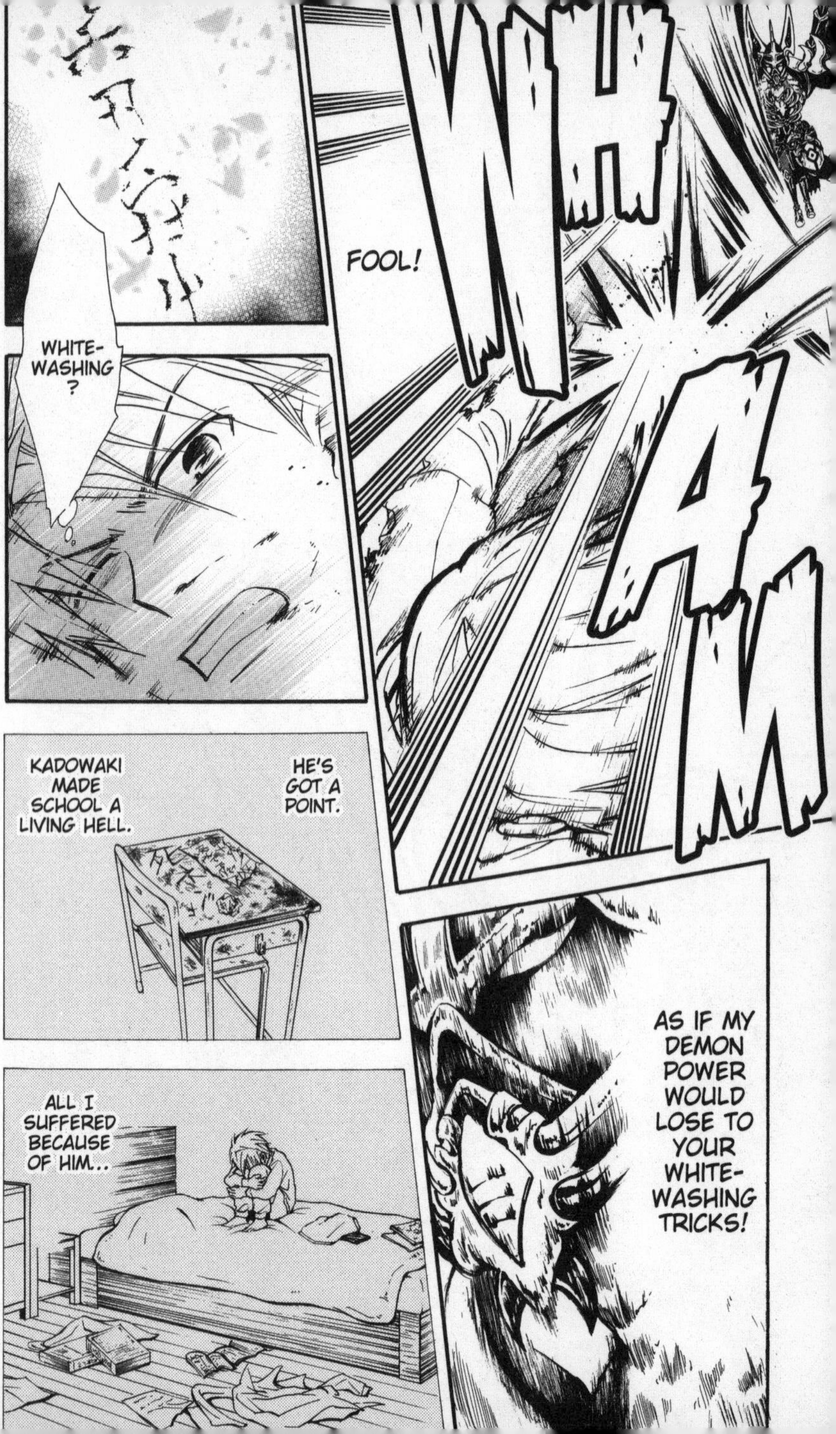
WHITE-WASHING?
FOOL!
WHAM
AS IF MY DEMON POWER WOULD LOSE TO YOUR WHITE-WASHING TRICKS!
HE'S GOT A POINT.
KADOWAKI MADE SCHOOL A LIVING HELL.
ALL I SUFFERED BECAUSE OF HIM...

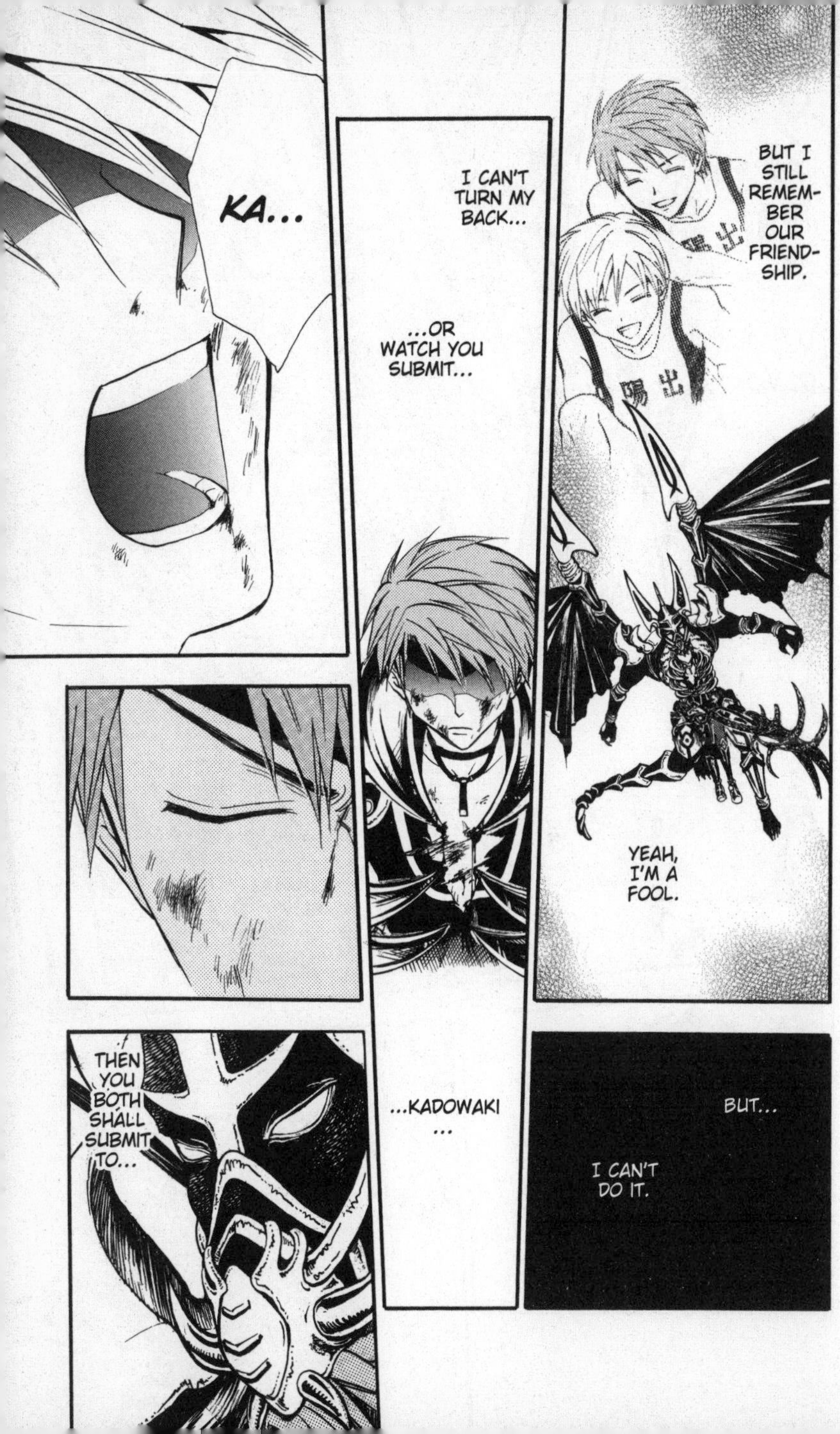
BUT I STILL REMEMBER OUR FRIENDSHIP.
YEAH, I'M A FOOL.
BUT...
I CAN'T DO IT.
I CAN'T TURN MY BACK...
...OR WATCH YOU SUBMIT...
...KADOWAKI ...
KA...
THEN YOU BOTH SHALL SUBMIT TO...

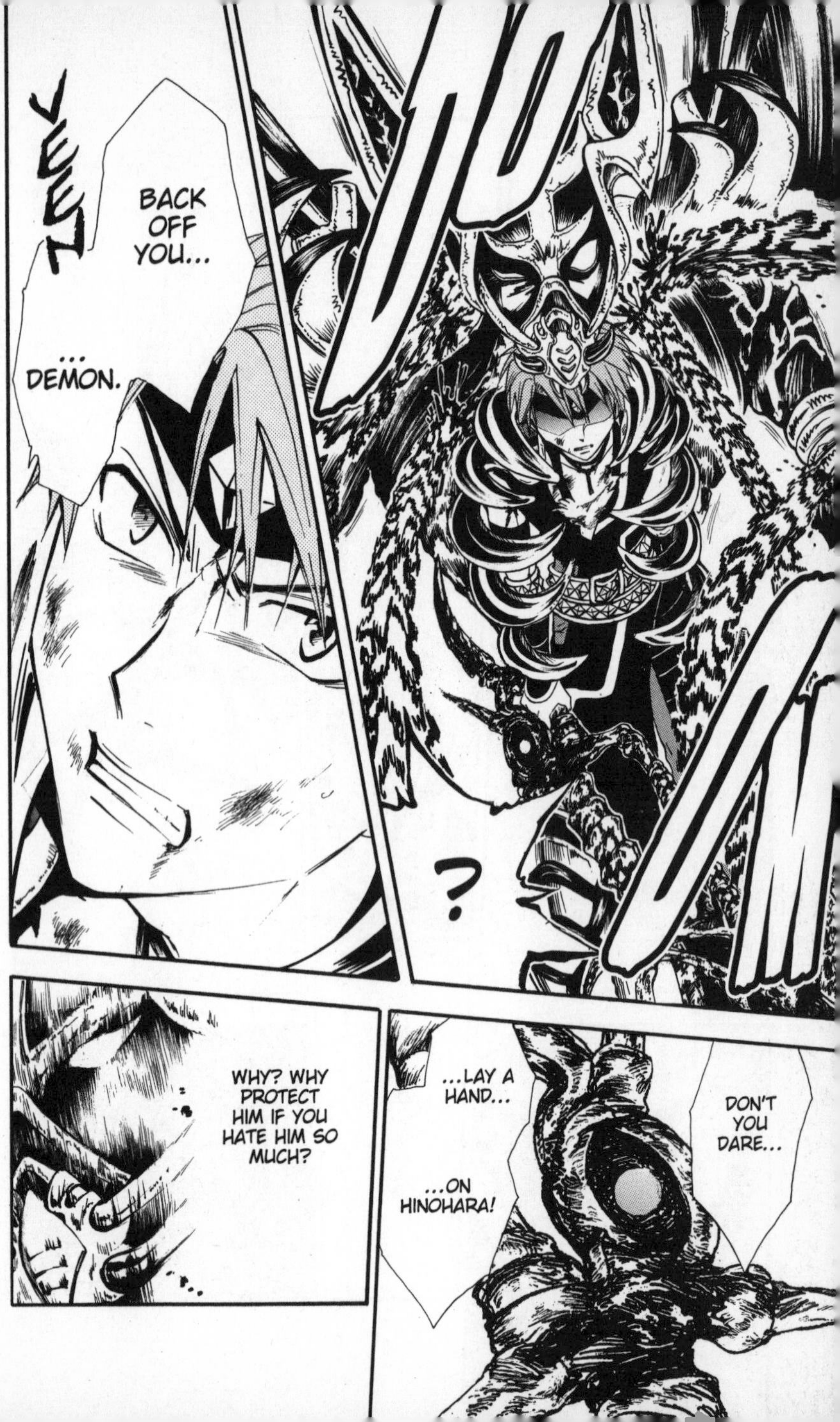
?
BACK OFF YOU...
...DEMON.
DON'T YOU DARE...
...LAY A HAND...
...ON HINOHARA!
WHY? WHY PROTECT HIM IF YOU HATE HIM SO MUCH?
...

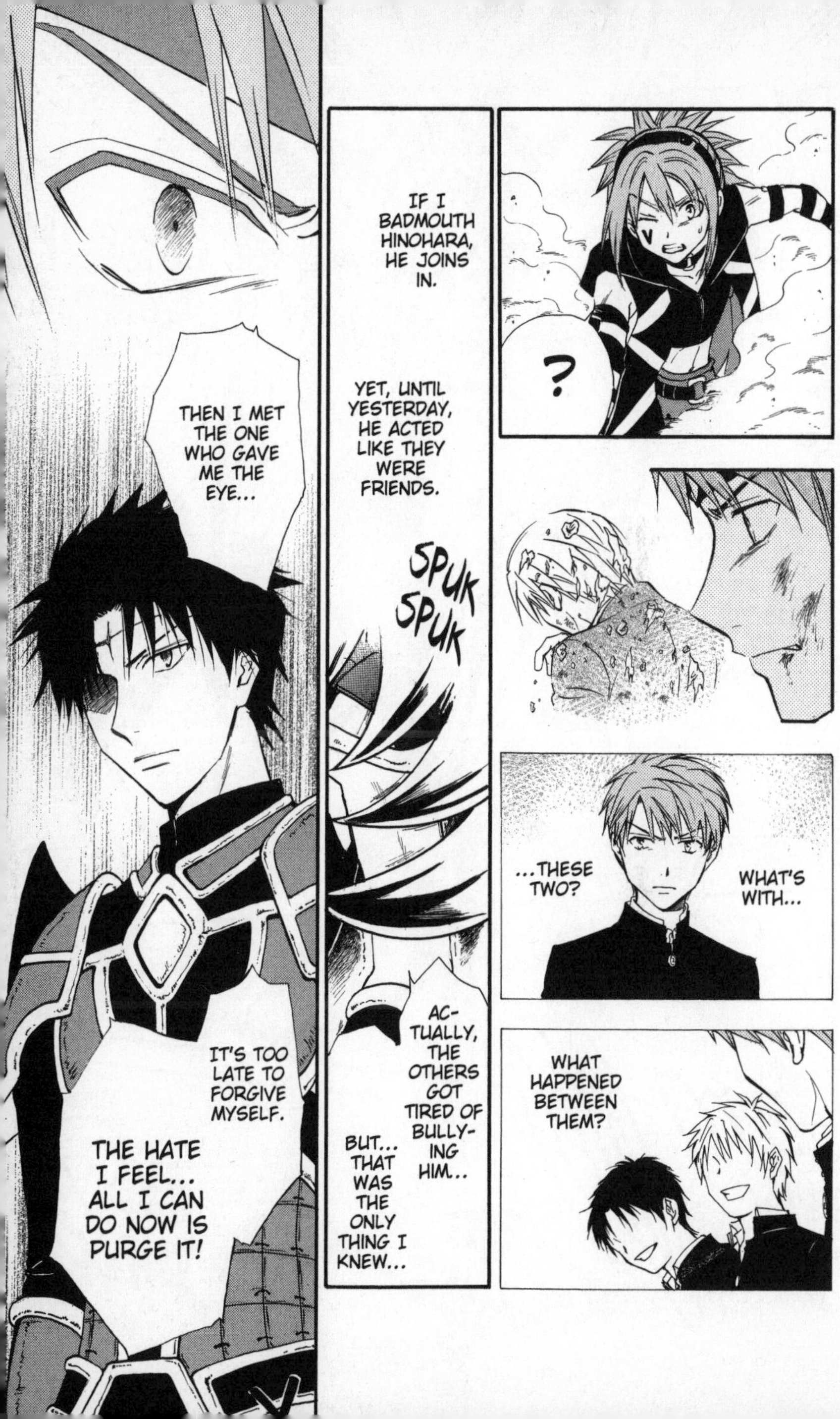
?
WHAT'S WITH...
...THESE TWO?
WHAT HAPPENED BETWEEN THEM?
IF I BADMOUTH HINOHARA, HE JOINS IN.
YET, UNTIL YESTERDAY, HE ACTED LIKE THEY WERE FRIENDS.
SPUK SPUK
ACTUALLY, THE OTHERS GOT TIRED OF BULLYING HIM...
BUT... THAT WAS THE ONLY THING I KNEW...
THEN I MET THE ONE WHO GAVE ME THE EYE...
IT'S TOO LATE TO FORGIVE MYSELF.
THE HATE I FEEL... ALL I CAN DO NOW IS PURGE IT!

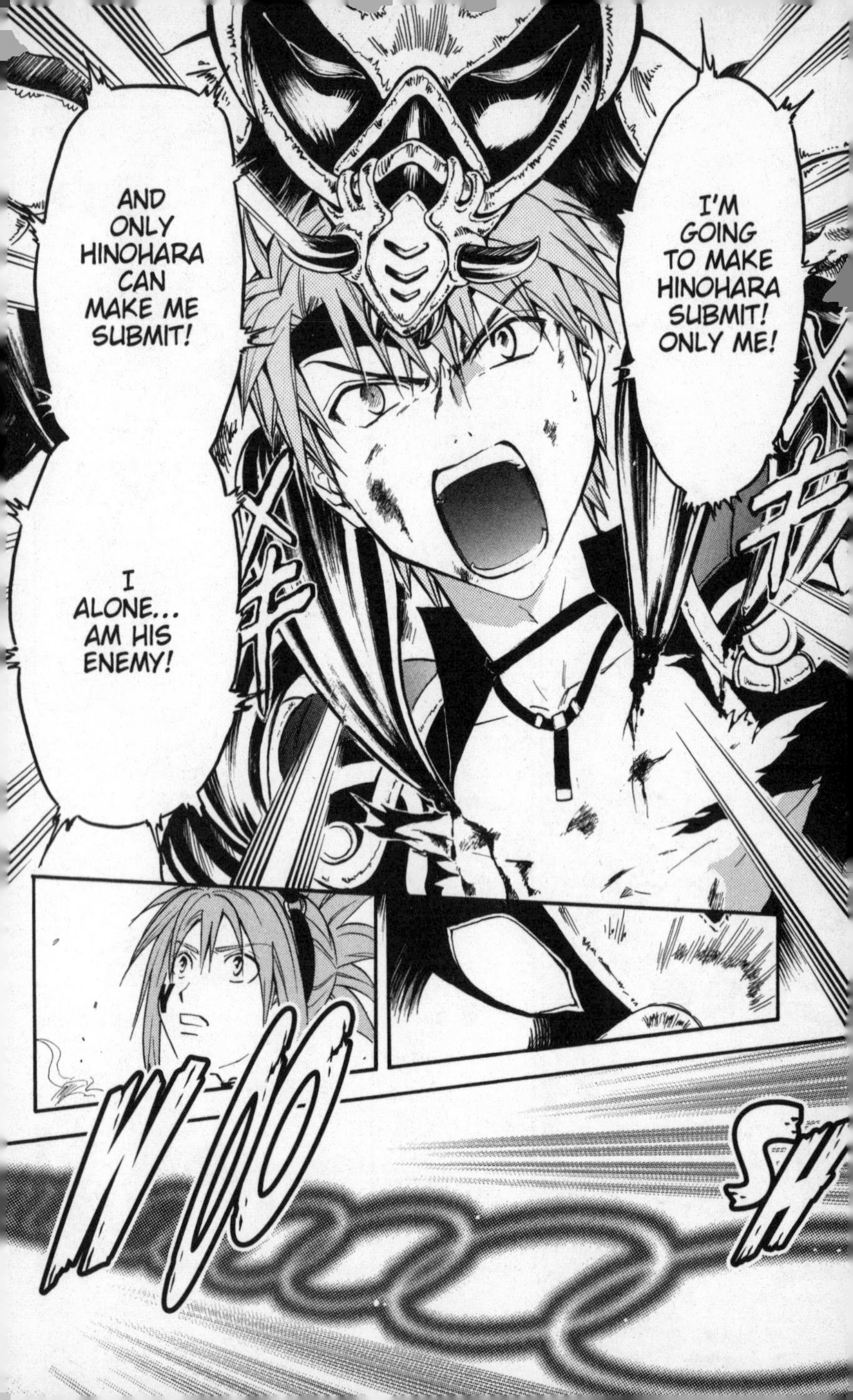
I'M GOING TO MAKE HINOHARA SUBMIT! ONLY ME!
AND ONLY HINOHARA CAN MAKE ME SUBMIT!
I ALONE... AM HIS ENEMY!
WHO
SH

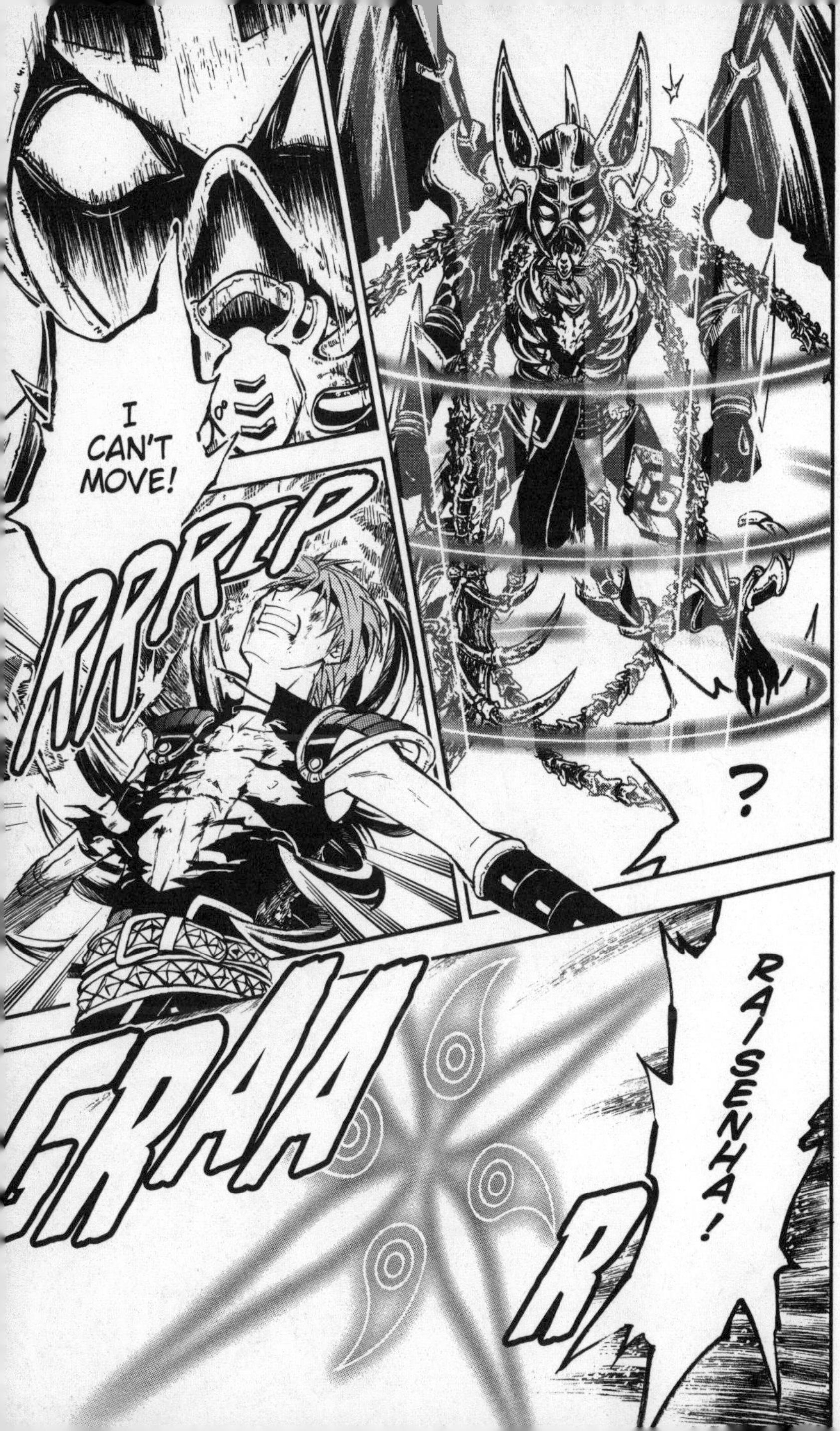
?
I CAN'T MOVE!
RRRIP
RAISENHA!
GRAHH
R

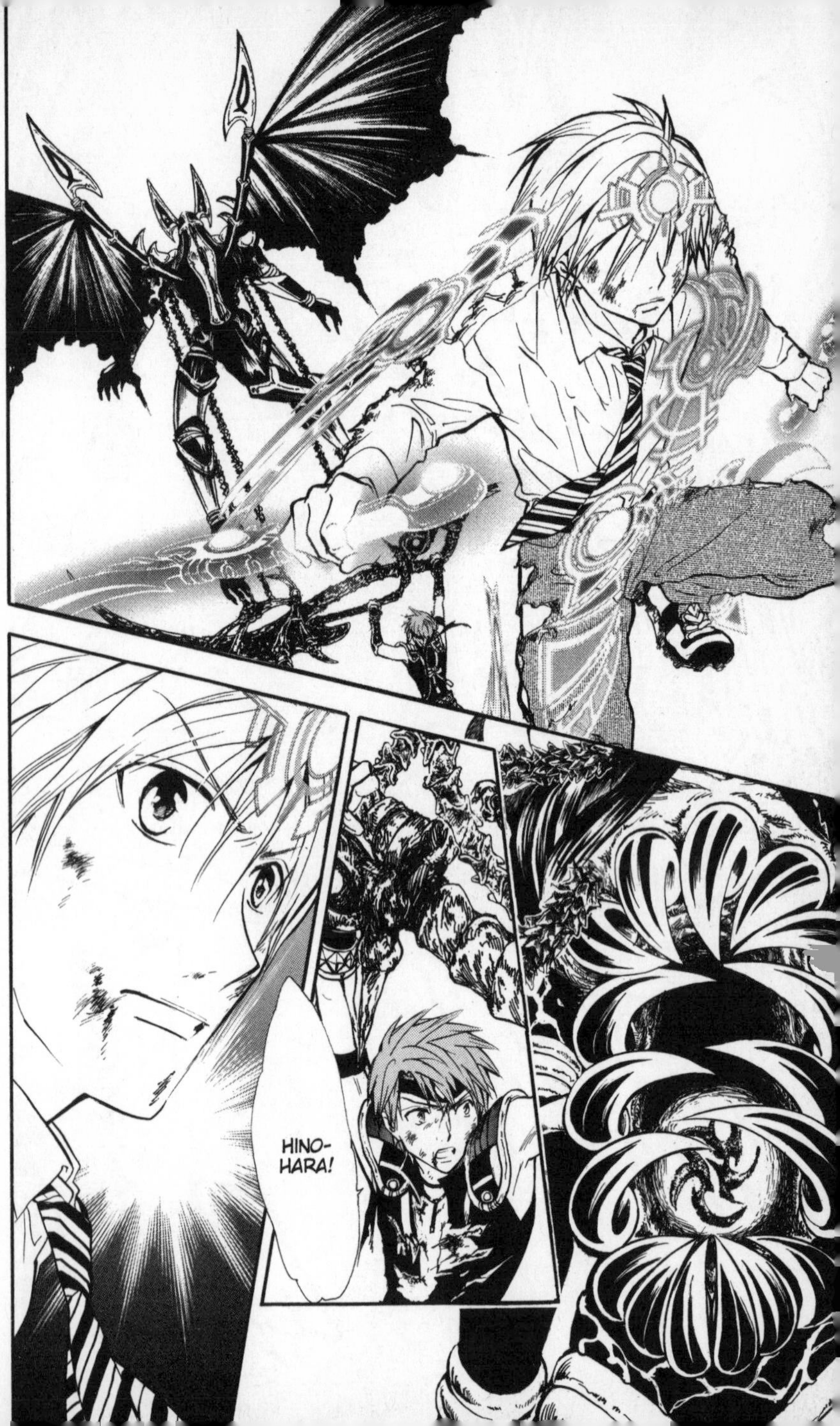
HINO-HARA!

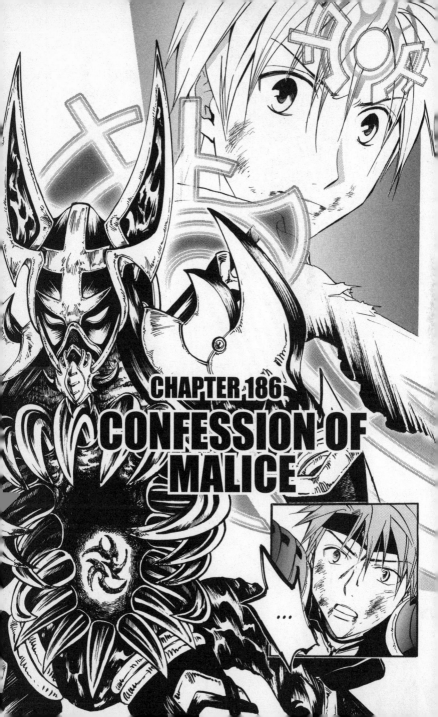

CHAPTER 186
CONFESSION OF MALICE

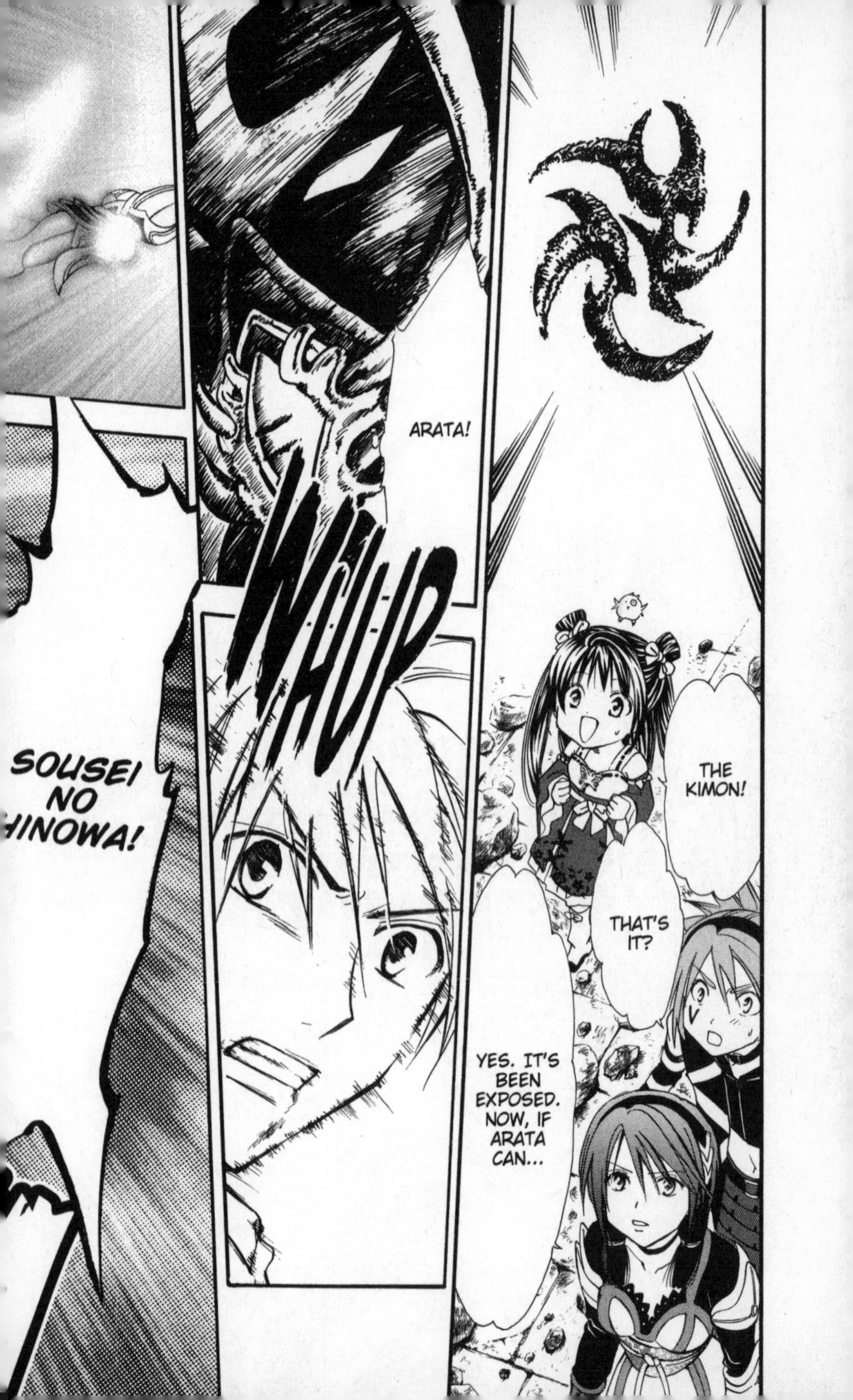
THE KIMON!
THAT'S IT?
YES. IT'S BEEN EXPOSED. NOW, IF ARATA CAN...
ARATA!
WHUD
SOUSEI NO HINOWA!

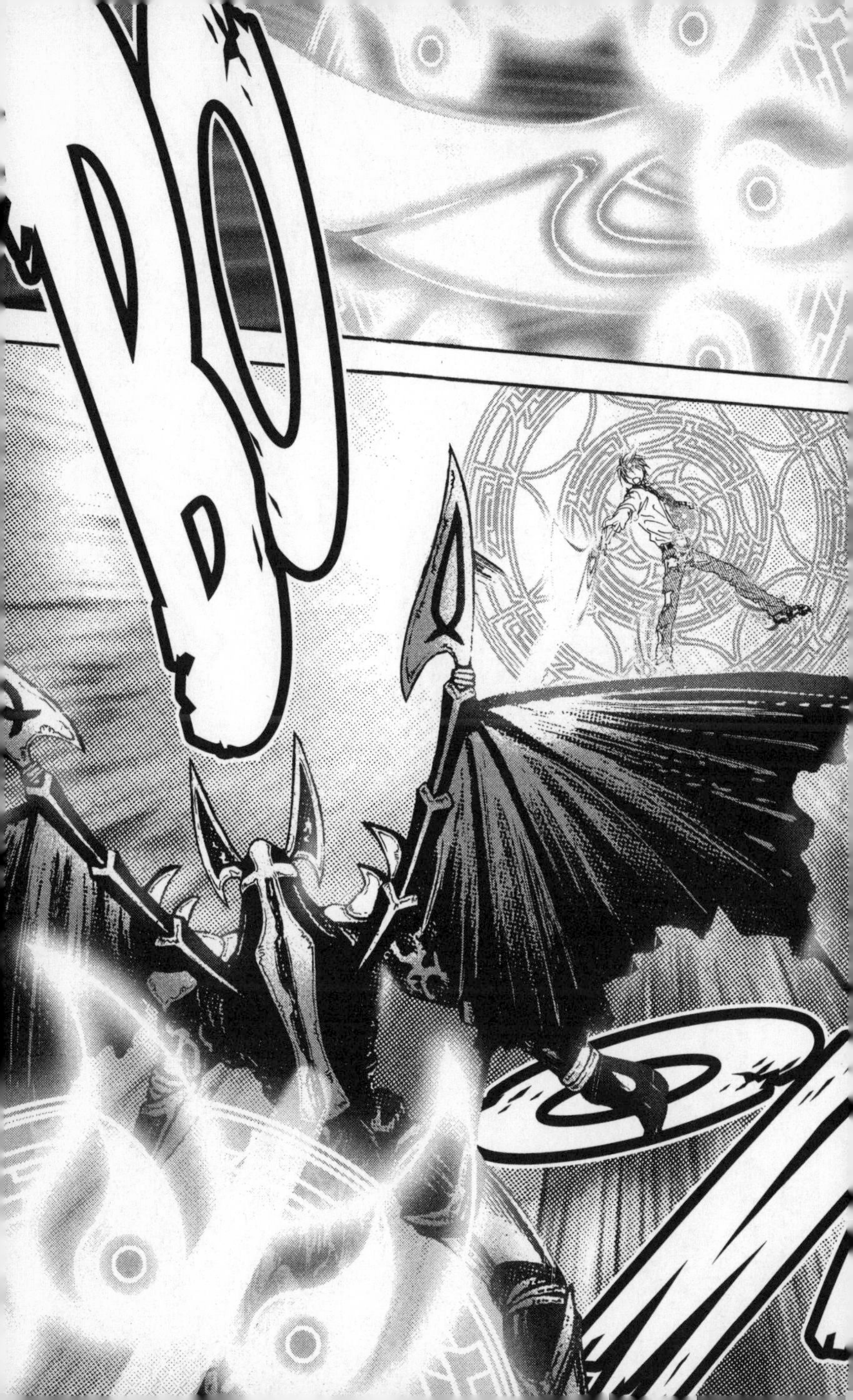

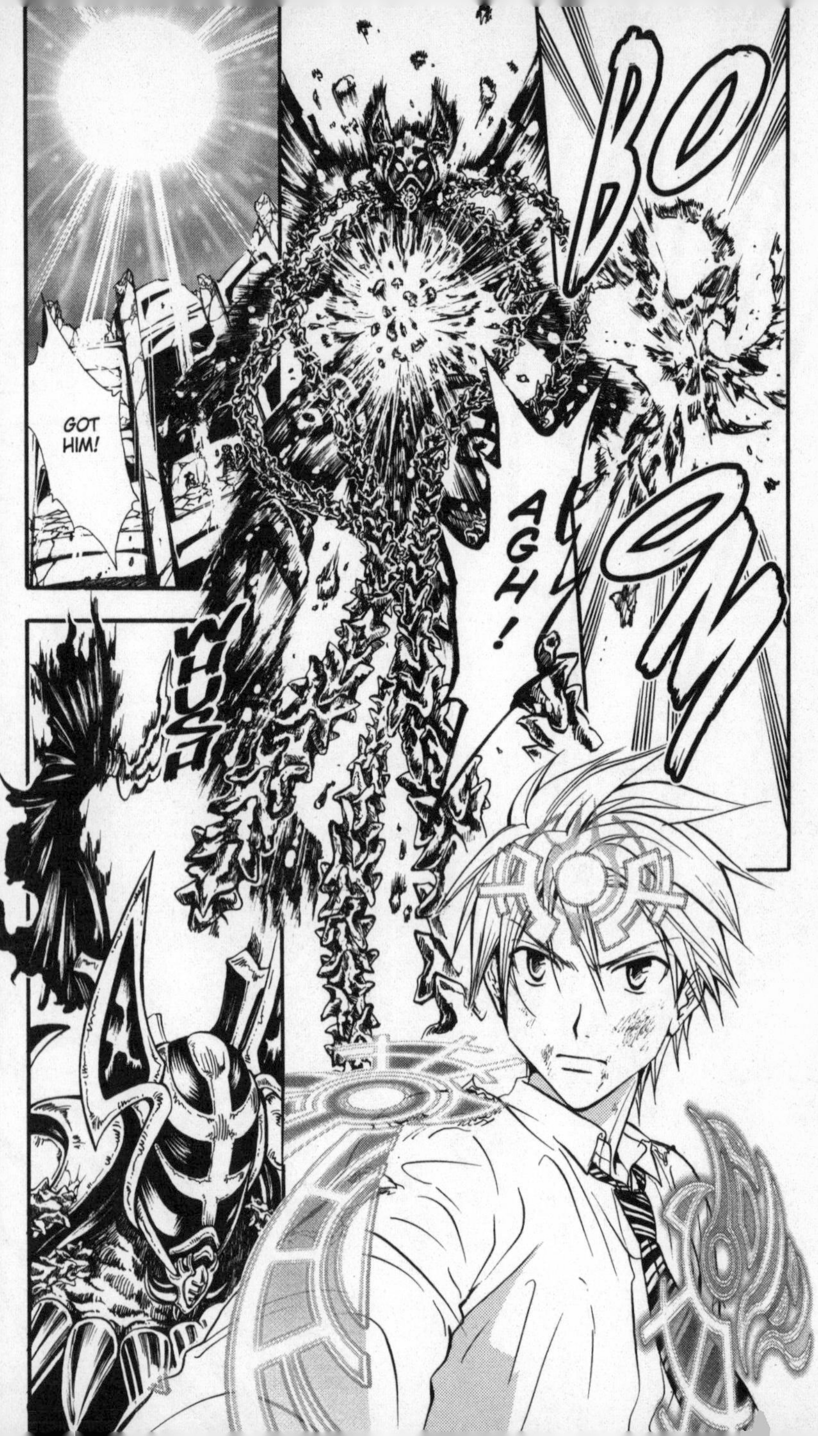
BOOOM
AGH!
GOT HIM!
WHOOSH

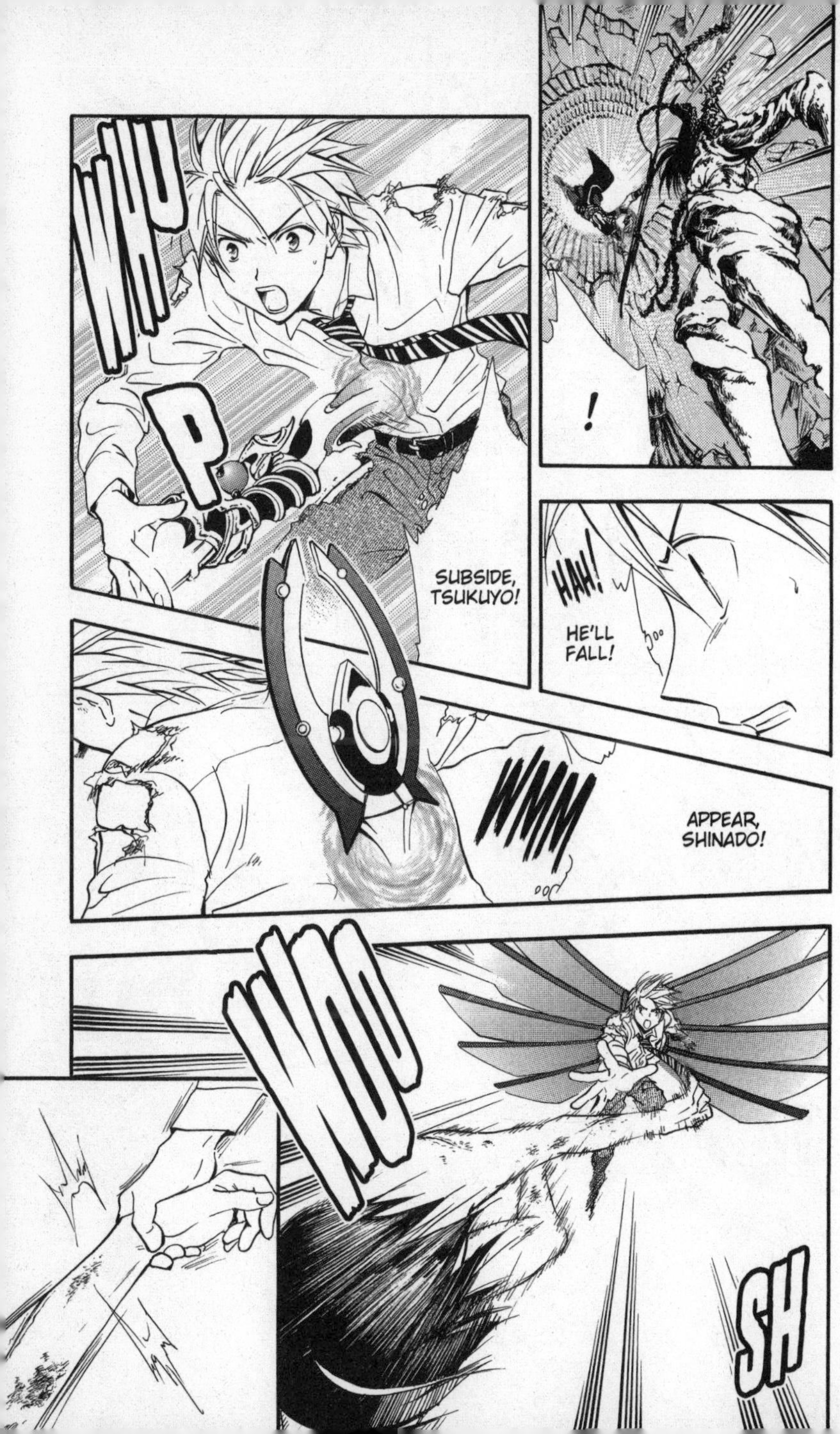
!
HAH!
HE'LL FALL!
WHU
P
SUBSIDE, TSUKUYO!
APPEAR, SHINADO!
WMM
WOO
SH

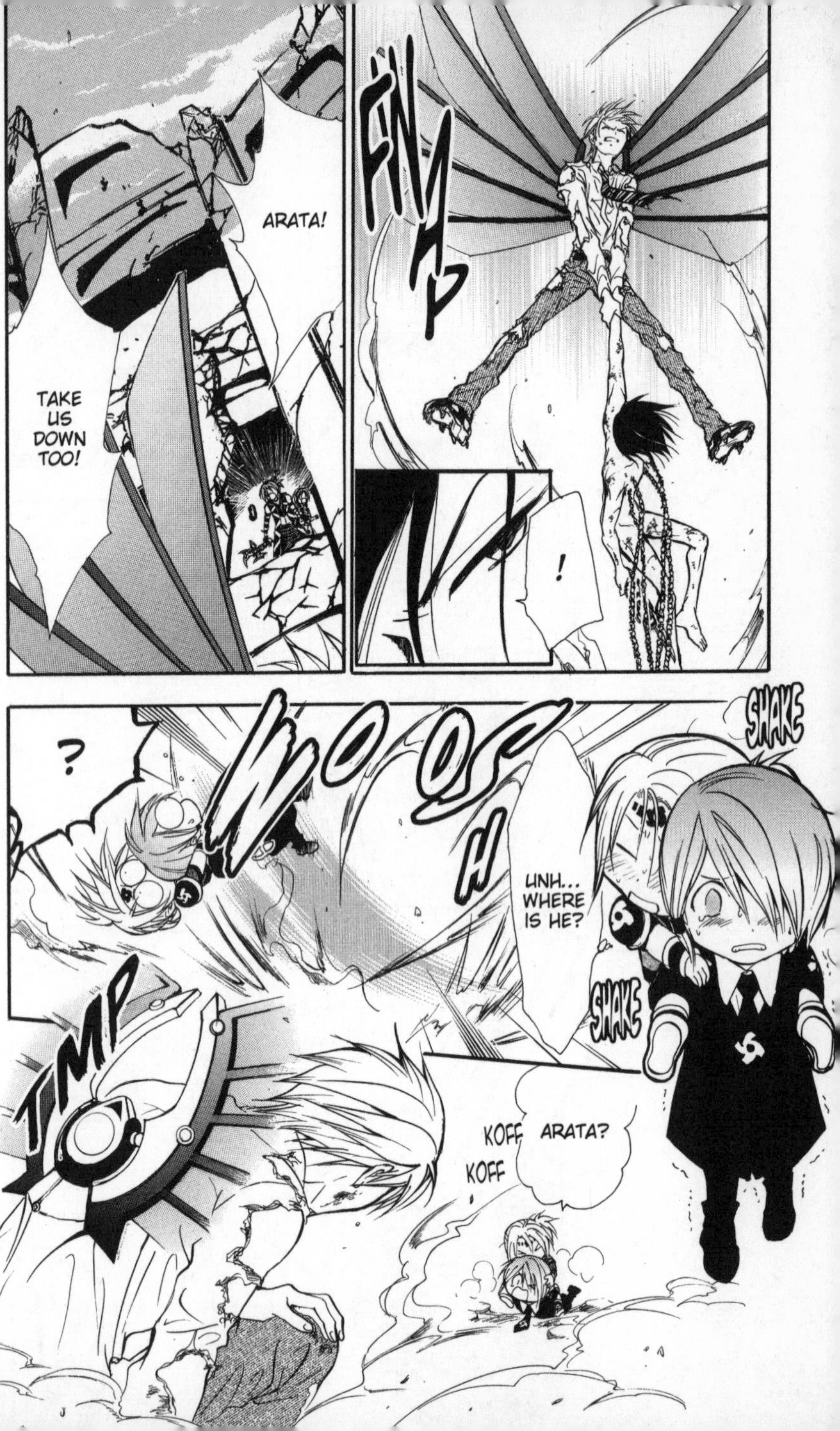
FWAP
!
ARATA!
TAKE US DOWN TOO!
SHAKE
UNH... WHERE IS HE?
SHAKE
WHOOSH
?
ARATA?
KOFF KOFF
TMP

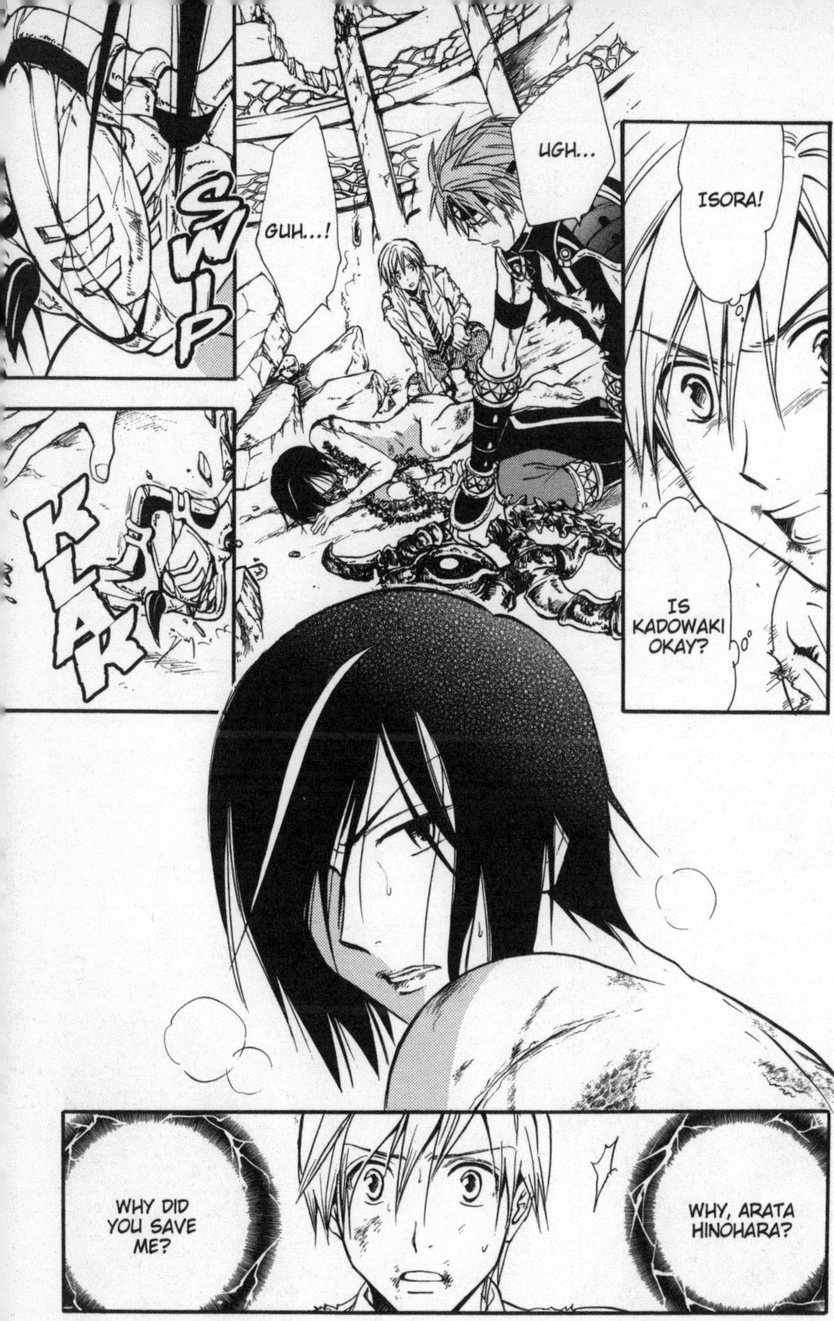
ISORA!
IS KADOWAKI OKAY?
UGH...
GUH...!
SWIP
KLAK
WHY, ARATA HINOHARA?
WHY DID YOU SAVE ME?

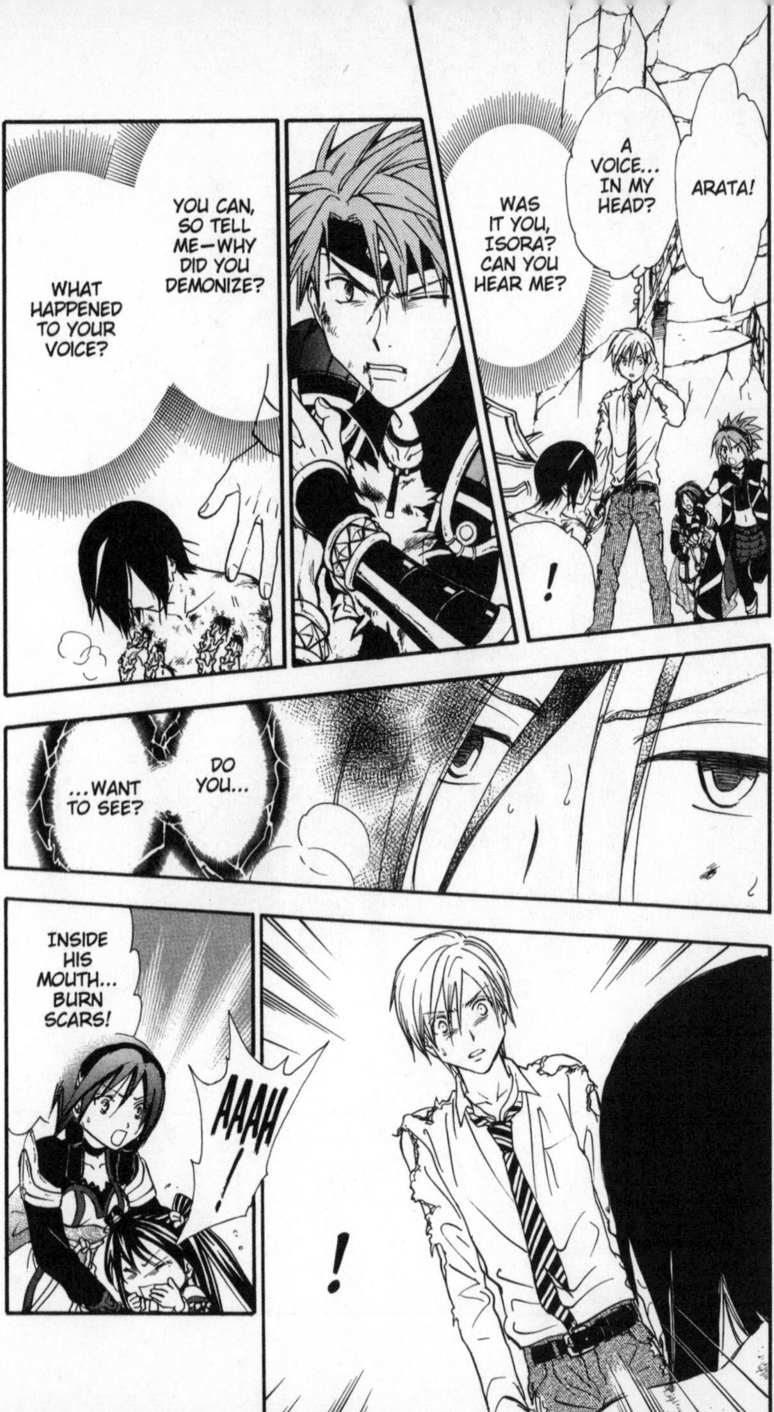
ARATA!
A VOICE... IN MY HEAD?
WAS IT YOU, ISORA? CAN YOU HEAR ME?
!
YOU CAN, SO TELL ME—WHY DID YOU DEMONIZE?
WHAT HAPPENED TO YOUR VOICE?
DO YOU...
...WANT TO SEE?
!
AAAH!
INSIDE HIS MOUTH... BURN SCARS!

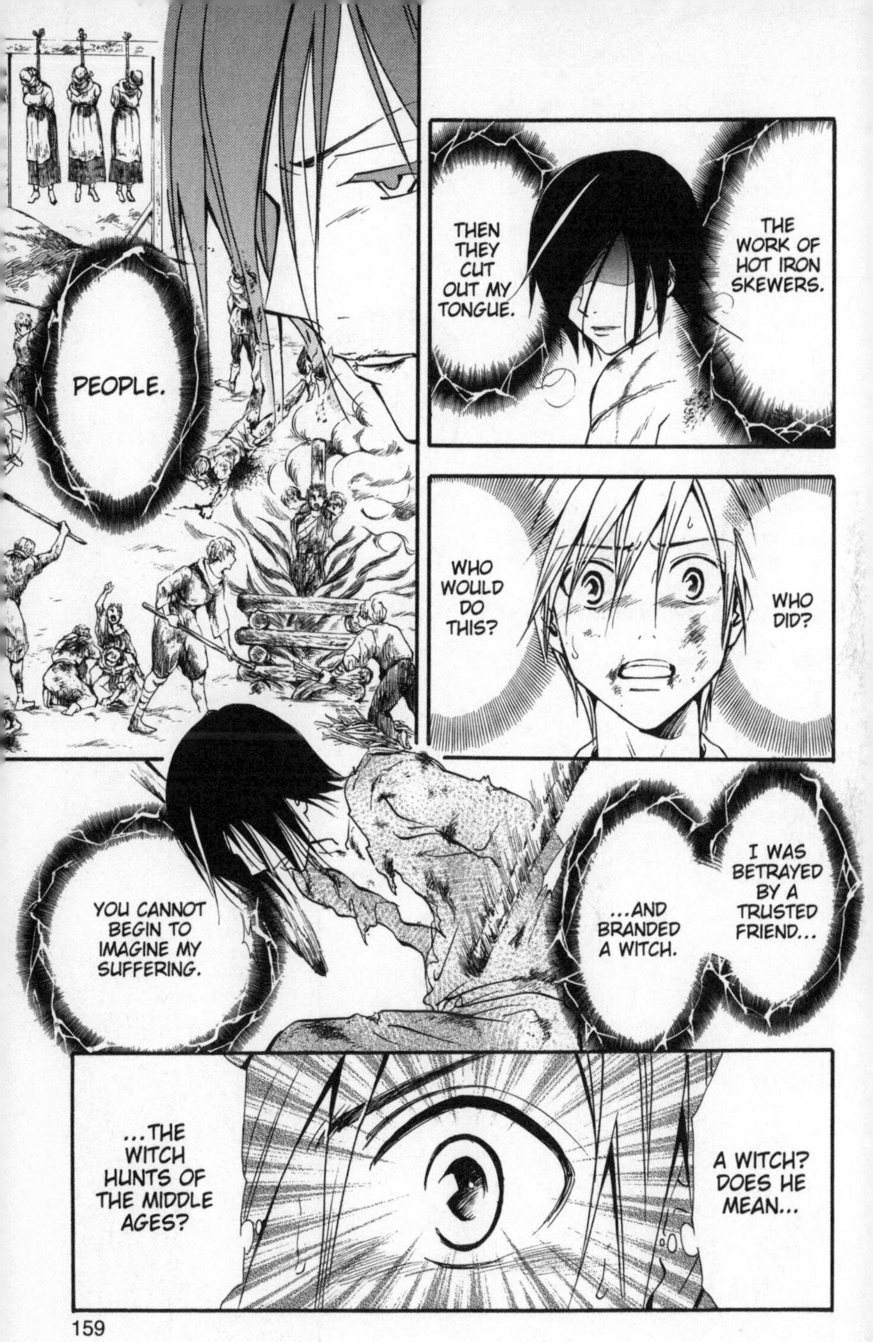
THE WORK OF HOT IRON SKEWERS.
THEN THEY CUT OUT MY TONGUE.
WHO DID?
WHO WOULD DO THIS?
PEOPLE.
I WAS BETRAYED BY A TRUSTED FRIEND...
...AND BRANDED A WITCH.
YOU CANNOT BEGIN TO IMAGINE MY SUFFERING.
A WITCH? DOES HE MEAN...
...THE WITCH HUNTS OF THE MIDDLE AGES?

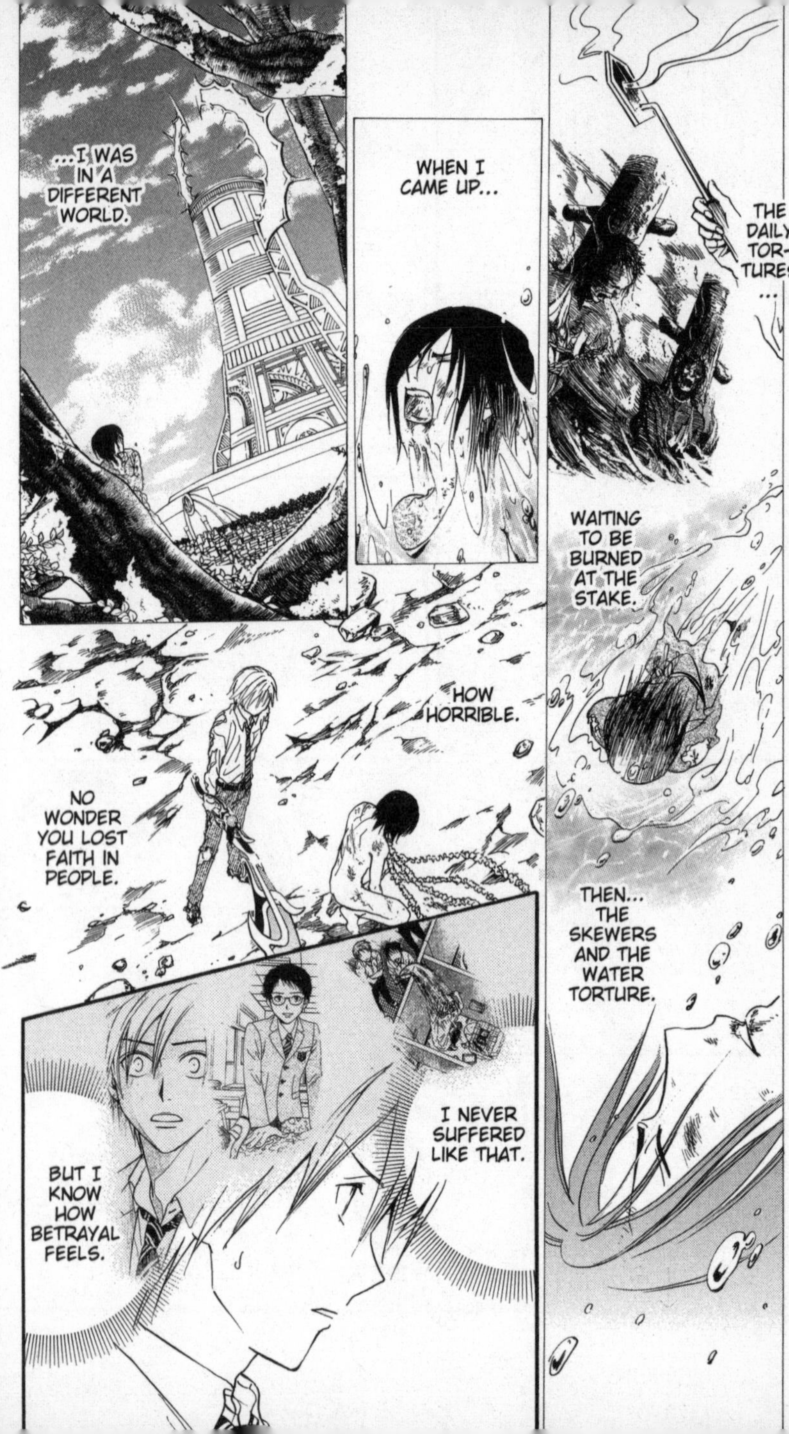
THE DAILY TOR-TURES...
WAITING TO BE BURNED AT THE STAKE.
THEN... THE SKEWERS AND THE WATER TORTURE.
WHEN I CAME UP...
...I WAS IN A DIFFERENT WORLD.
HOW HORRIBLE.
NO WONDER YOU LOST FAITH IN PEOPLE.
I NEVER SUFFERED LIKE THAT.
BUT I KNOW HOW BETRAYAL FEELS.

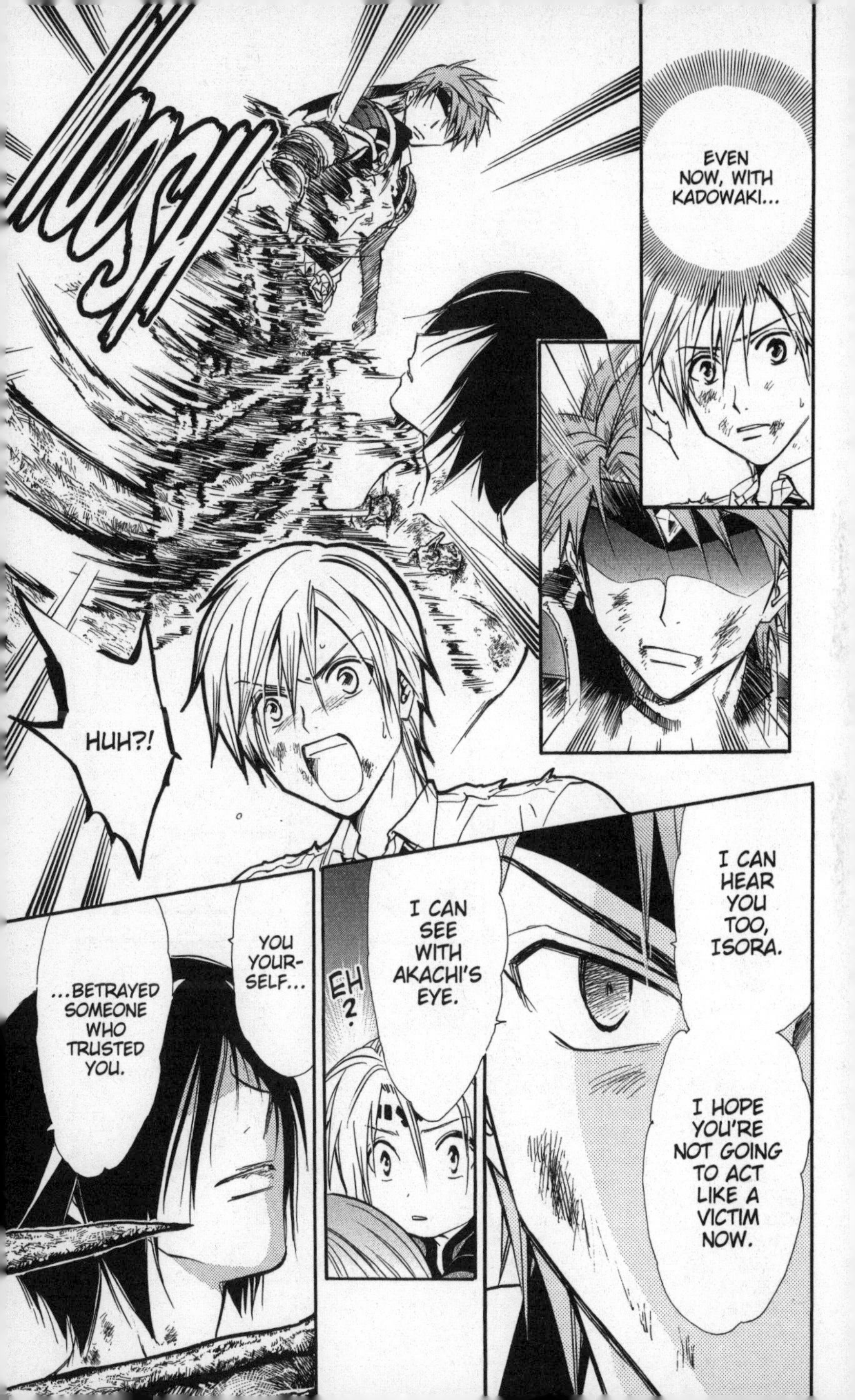
EVEN NOW, WITH KADOWAKI...
HUH?!
I CAN HEAR YOU TOO, ISORA.
I HOPE YOU'RE NOT GOING TO ACT LIKE A VICTIM NOW.
EH?
I CAN SEE WITH AKACHI'S EYE.
YOU YOURSELF...
...BETRAYED SOMEONE WHO TRUSTED YOU.

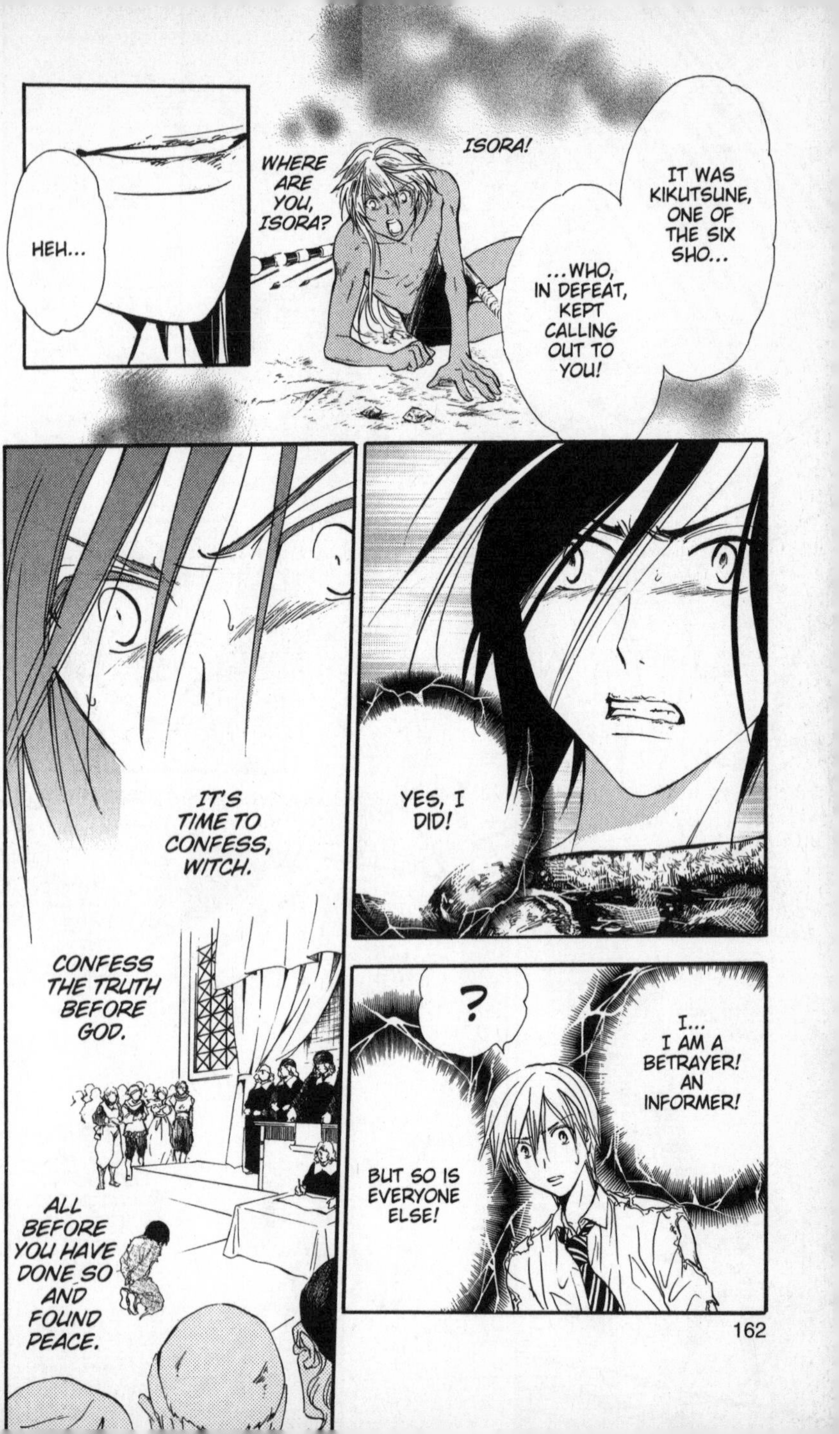
IT WAS KIKUTSUNE, ONE OF THE SIX SHO...
...WHO, IN DEFEAT, KEPT CALLING OUT TO YOU!
ISORA!
WHERE ARE YOU, ISORA?
HEH...
YES, I DID!
?
I... I AM A BETRAYER! AN INFORMER!
BUT SO IS EVERYONE ELSE!
IT'S TIME TO CONFESS, WITCH.
CONFESS THE TRUTH BEFORE GOD.
ALL BEFORE YOU HAVE DONE SO AND FOUND PEACE.

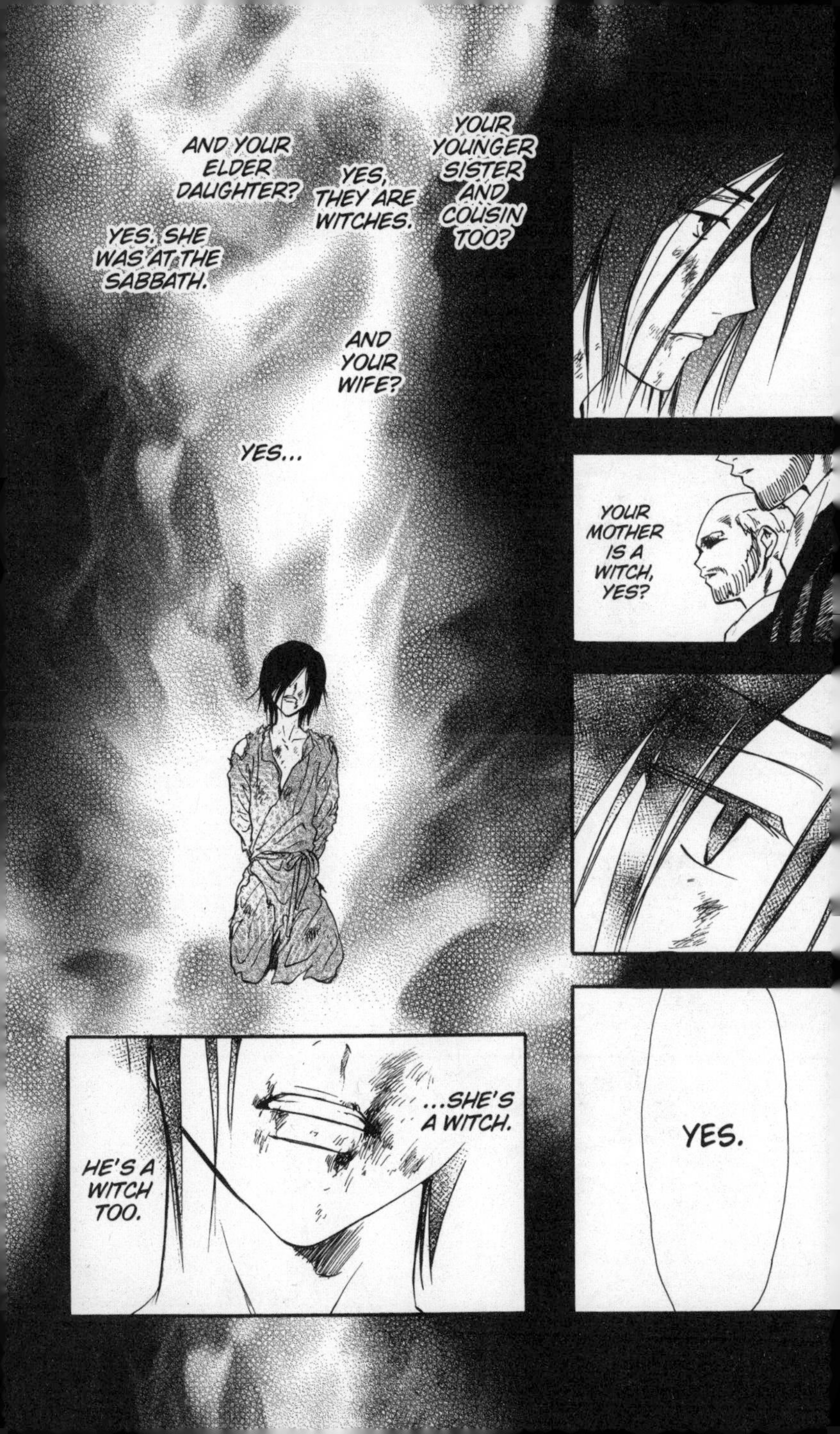
YOUR MOTHER IS A WITCH, YES?
YES.
YOUR YOUNGER SISTER AND COUSIN TOO?
YES, THEY ARE WITCHES.
AND YOUR ELDER DAUGHTER?
YES. SHE WAS AT THE SABBATH.
AND YOUR WIFE?
YES...
...SHE'S A WITCH.
HE'S A WITCH TOO.

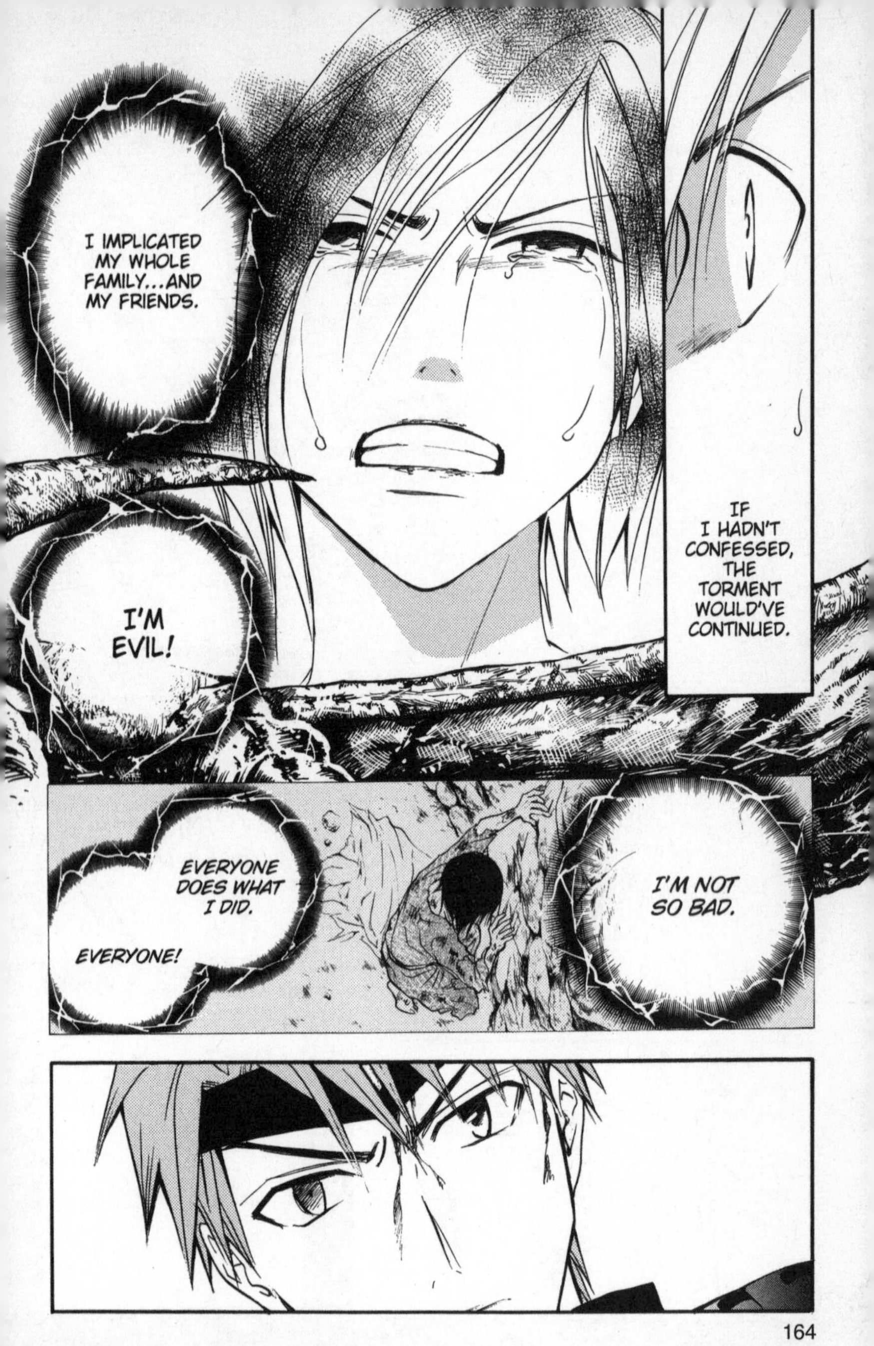
IF I HADN'T CONFESSED, THE TORMENT WOULD'VE CONTINUED.
I IMPLICATED MY WHOLE FAMILY...AND MY FRIENDS.
I'M EVIL!
I'M NOT SO BAD.
EVERYONE DOES WHAT I DID.
EVERYONE!

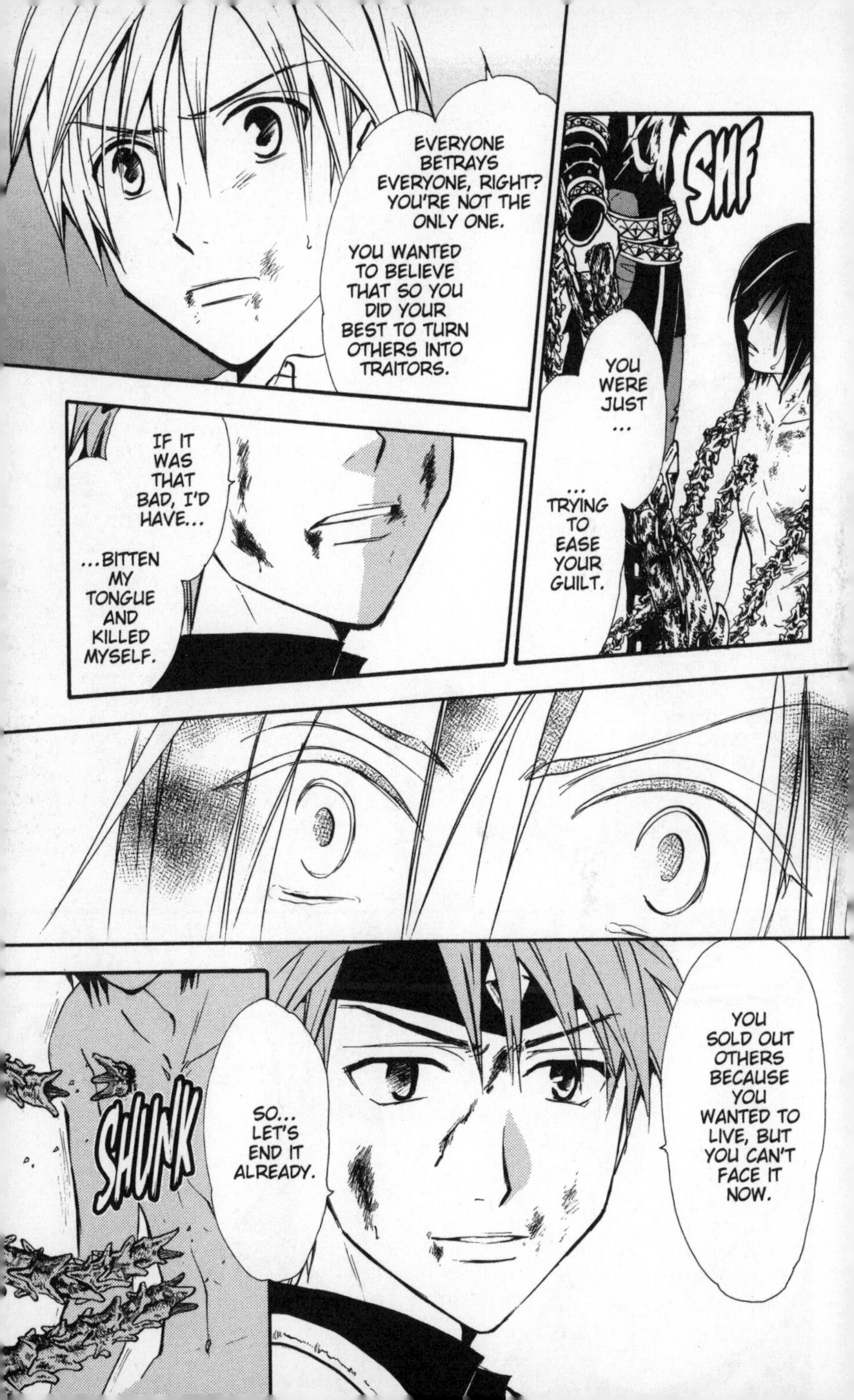
EVERYONE BETRAYS EVERYONE, RIGHT? YOU'RE NOT THE ONLY ONE.
YOU WANTED TO BELIEVE THAT SO YOU DID YOUR BEST TO TURN OTHERS INTO TRAITORS.
SHF
YOU WERE JUST ...
... TRYING TO EASE YOUR GUILT.
IF IT WAS THAT BAD, I'D HAVE...
...BITTEN MY TONGUE AND KILLED MYSELF.
YOU SOLD OUT OTHERS BECAUSE YOU WANTED TO LIVE, BUT YOU CAN'T FACE IT NOW.
SO... LET'S END IT ALREADY.
SHUNK

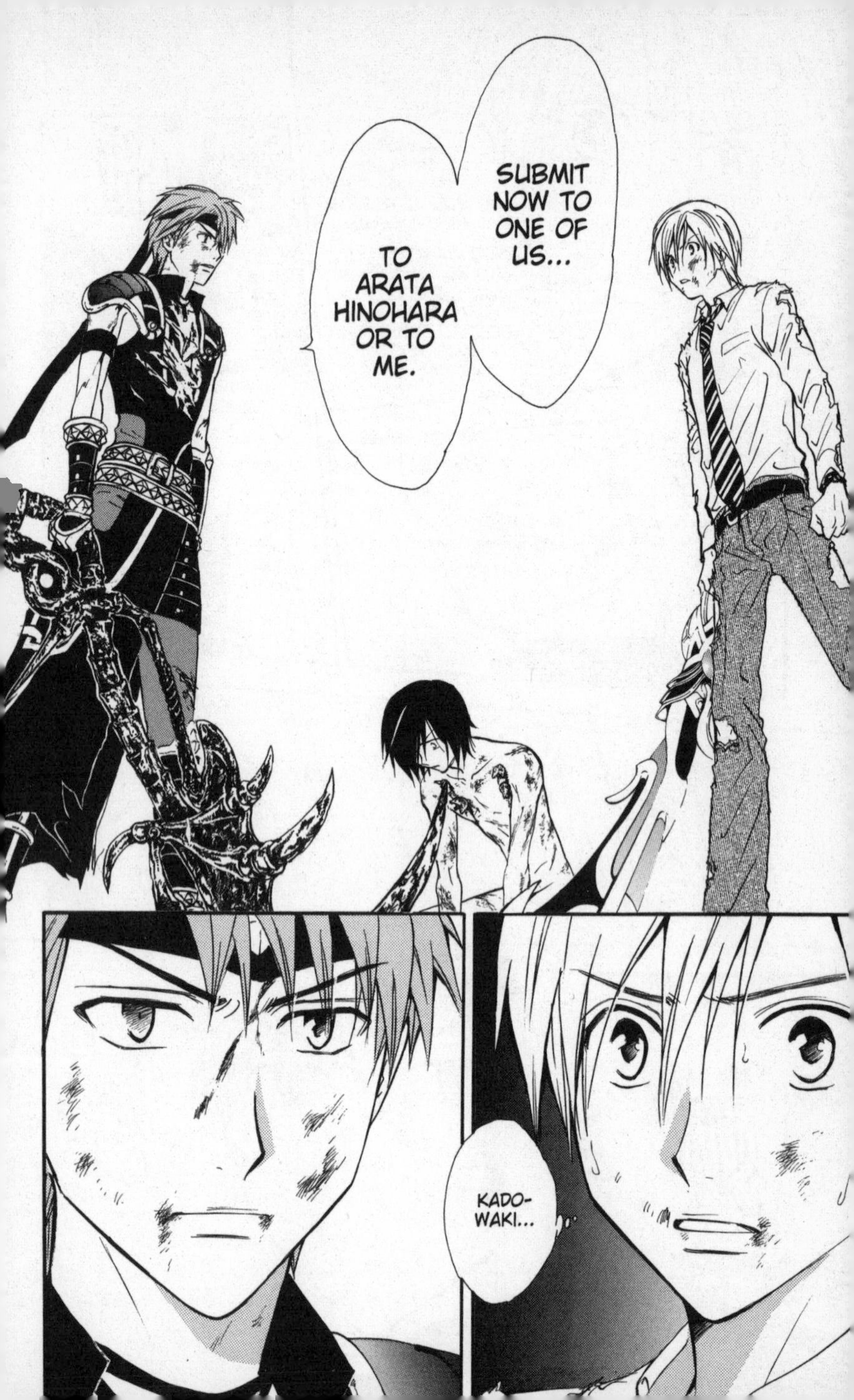
SUBMIT NOW TO ONE OF US...
TO ARATA HINOHARA OR TO ME.
KADO-WAKI...

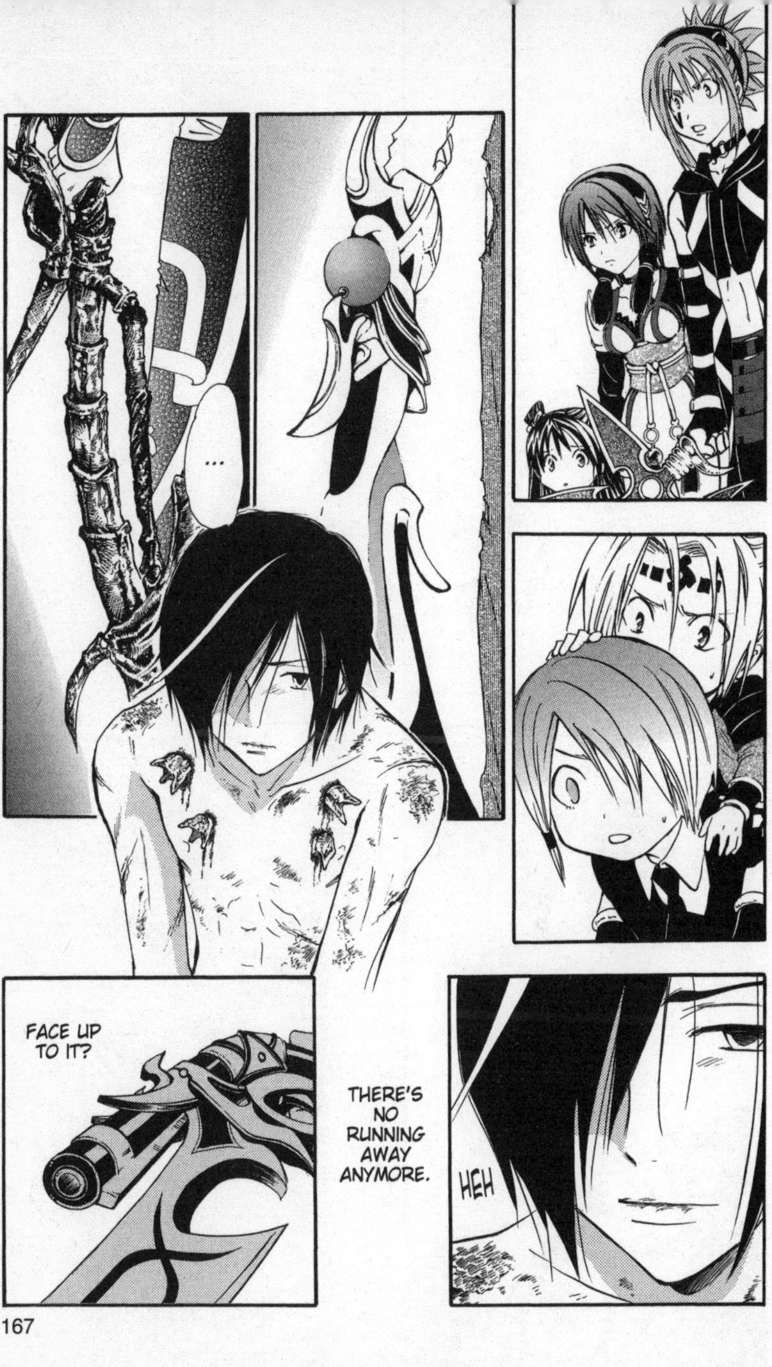
...
THERE'S NO RUNNING AWAY ANYMORE.
HEH
FACE UP TO IT?

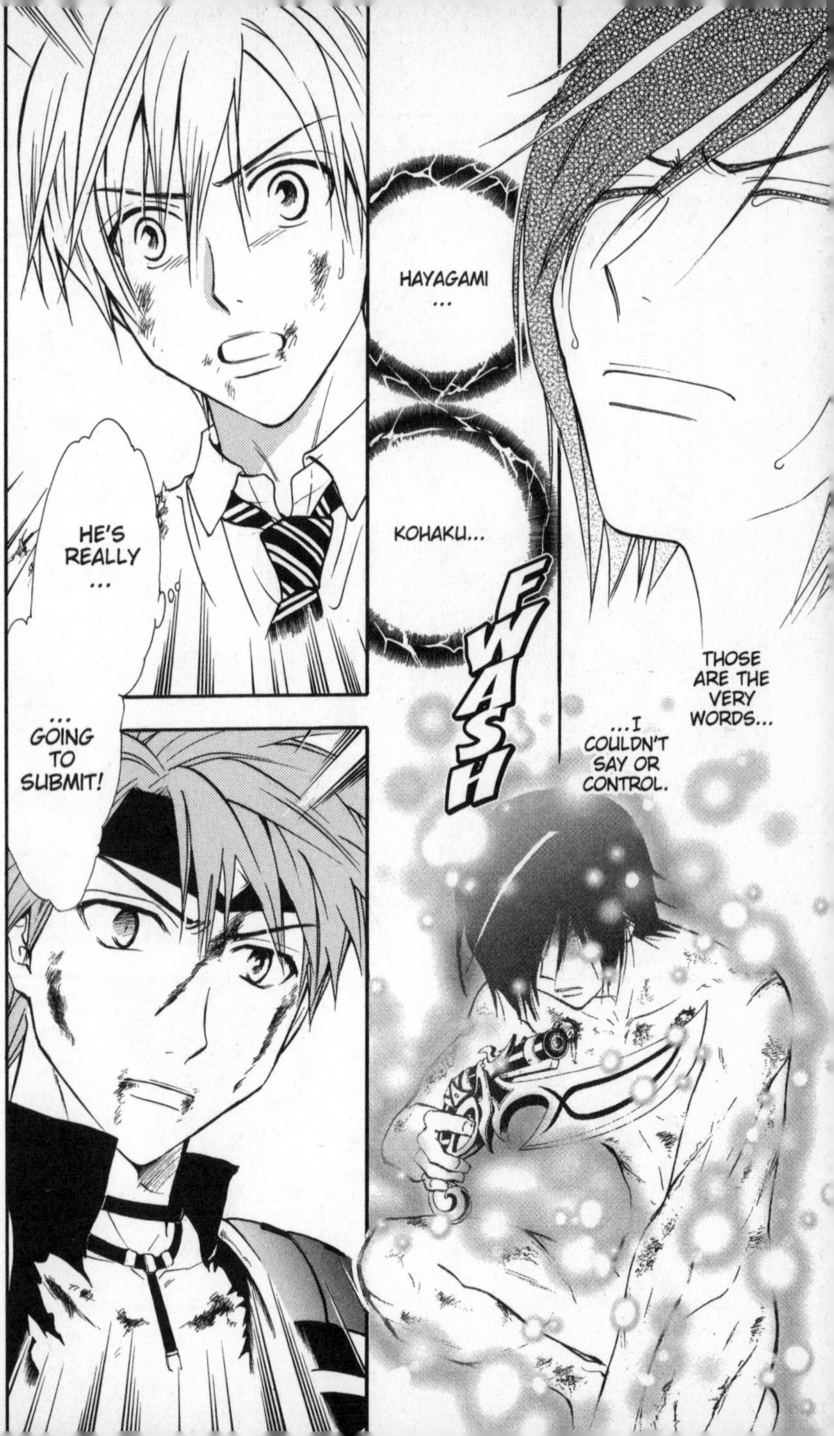
HAYAGAMI ...
KOHAKU...
FWASH
THOSE ARE THE VERY WORDS...
...I COULDN'T SAY OR CONTROL.
HE'S REALLY ...
... GOING TO SUBMIT!

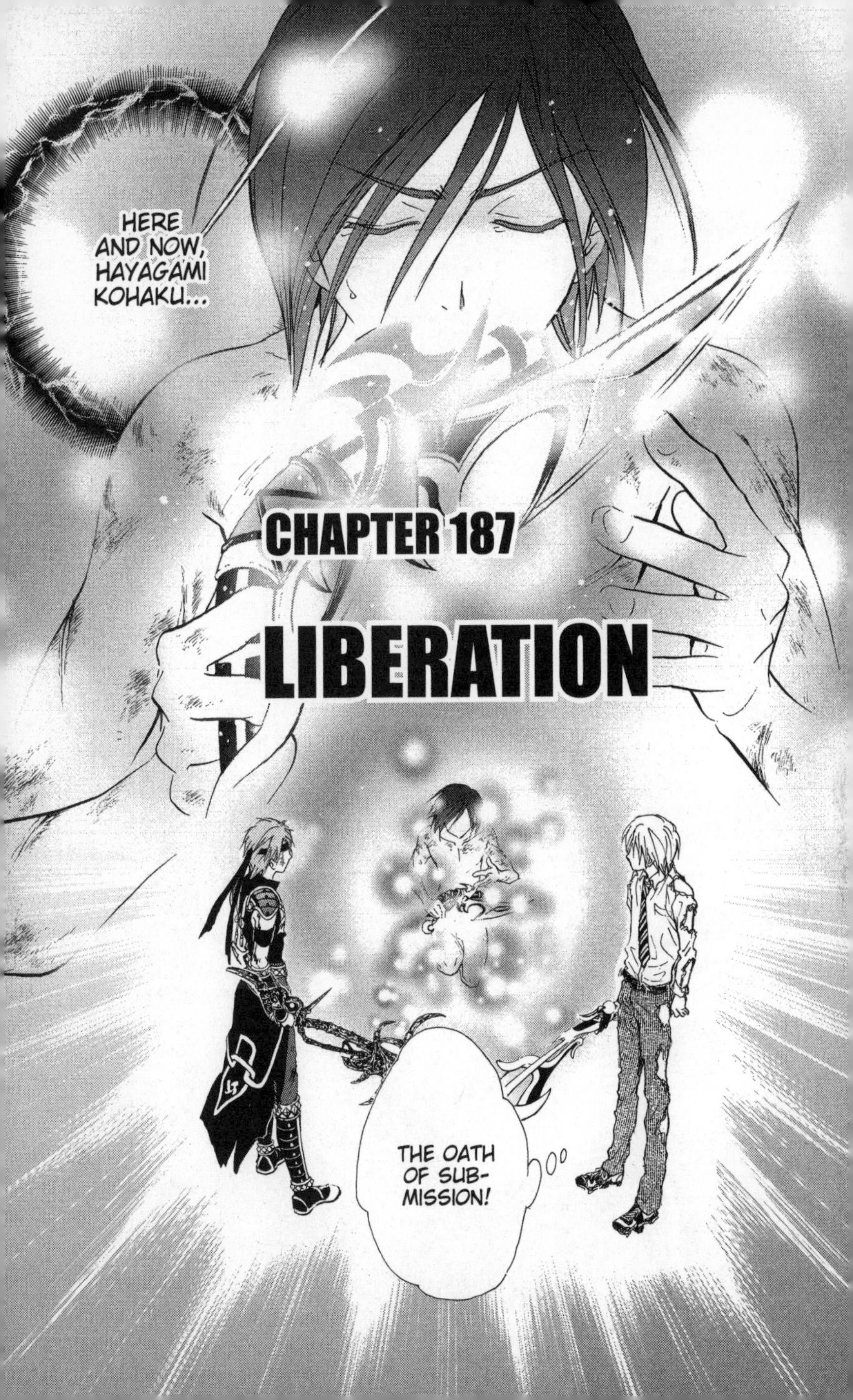
HERE AND NOW, HAYAGAMI KOHAKU...
CHAPTER 187
LIBERATION
THE OATH OF SUB-MISSION!

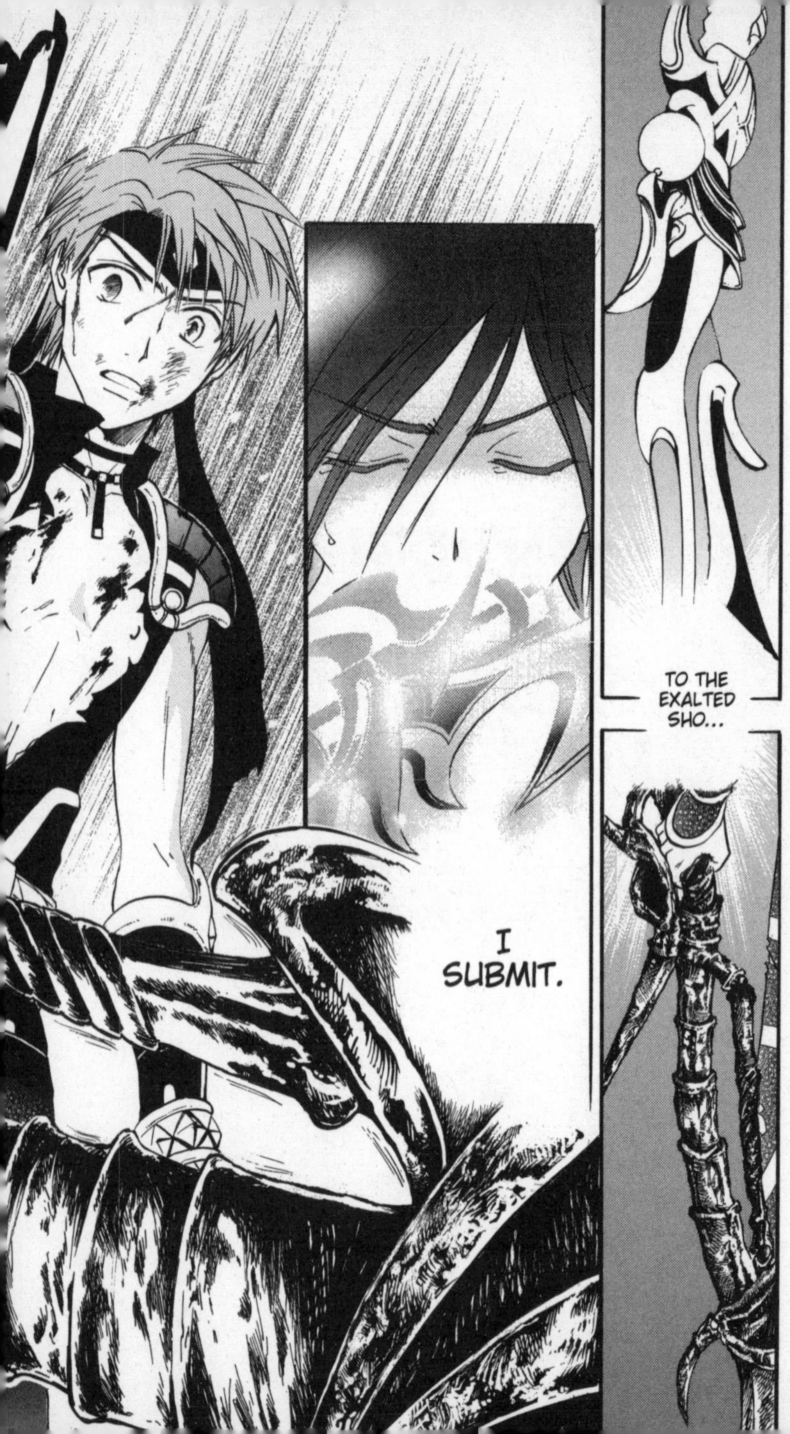
TO THE EXALTED SHO...
I SUBMIT.

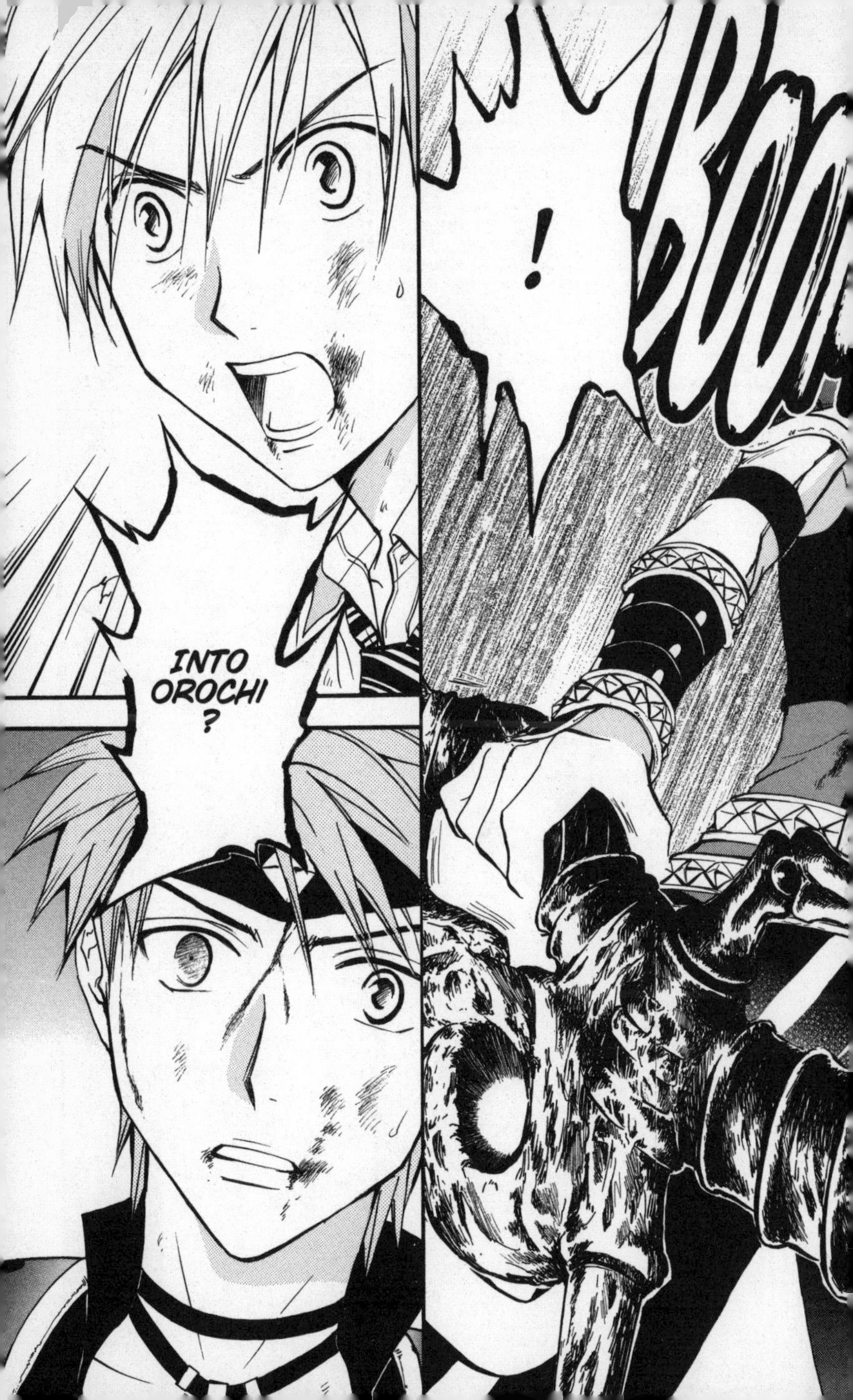
!
INTO OROCHI ?

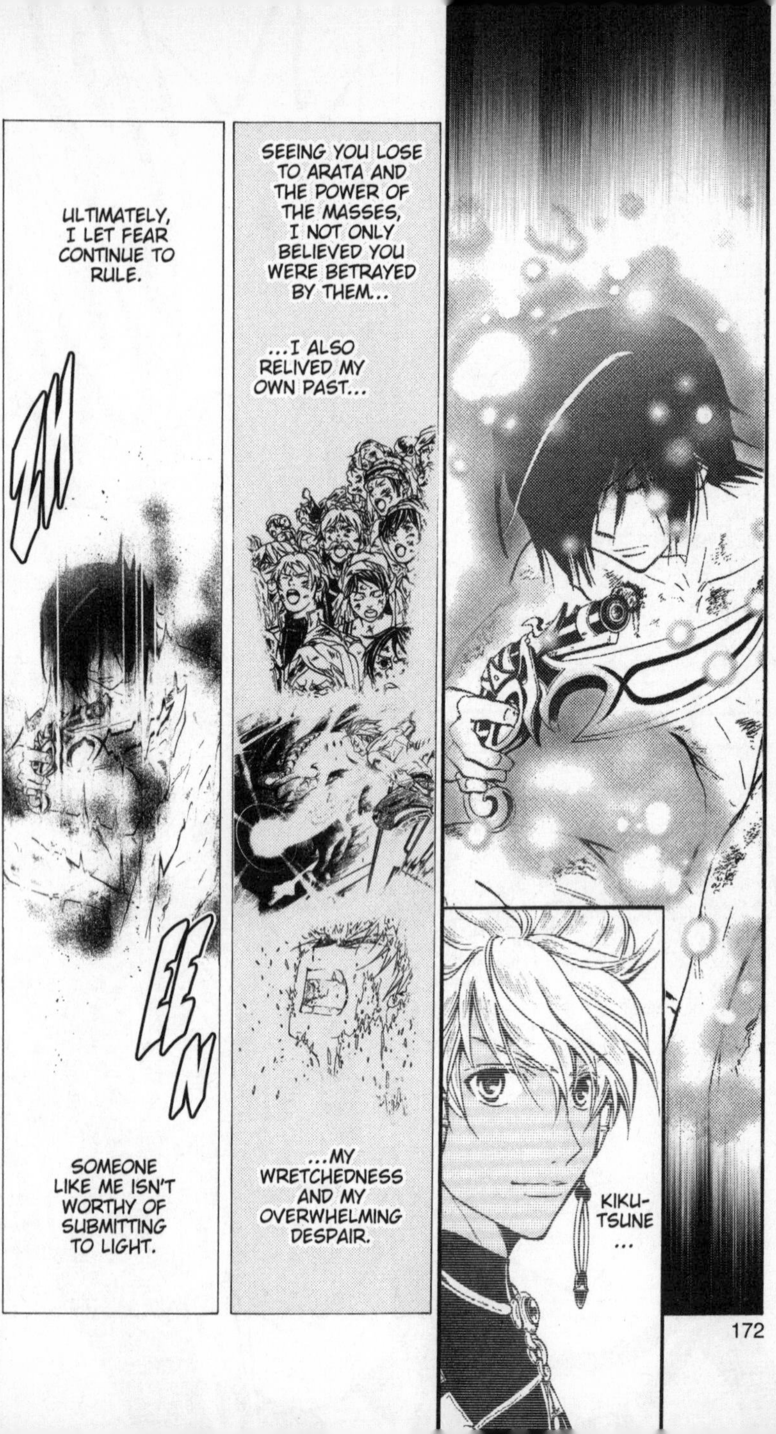
KIKU-TSUNE ...
SEEING YOU LOSE TO ARATA AND THE POWER OF THE MASSES, I NOT ONLY BELIEVED YOU WERE BETRAYED BY THEM...
...I ALSO RELIVED MY OWN PAST...
...MY WRETCHEDNESS AND MY OVERWHELMING DESPAIR.
ULTIMATELY, I LET FEAR CONTINUE TO RULE.
SOMEONE LIKE ME ISN'T WORTHY OF SUBMITTING TO LIGHT.

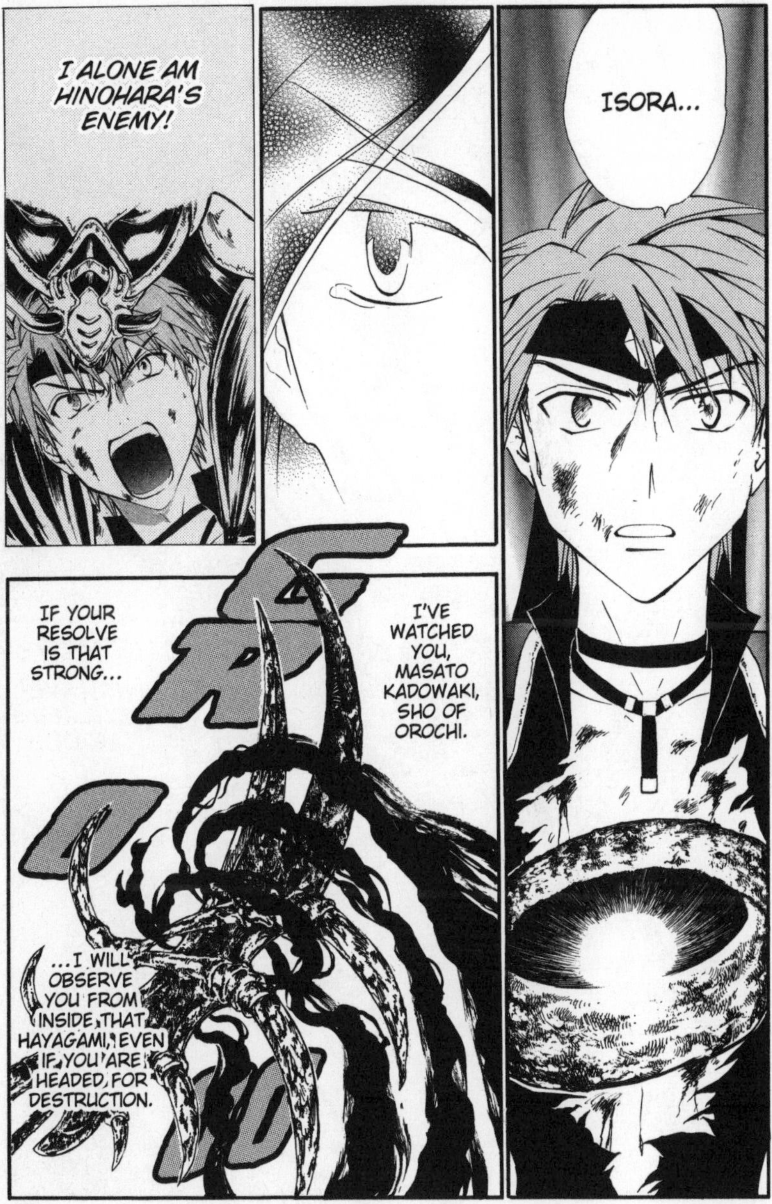
ISORA...
I ALONE AM HINOHARA'S ENEMY!
I'VE WATCHED YOU, MASATO KADOWAKI, SHO OF OROCHI.
IF YOUR RESOLVE IS THAT STRONG...
...I WILL OBSERVE YOU FROM INSIDE THAT HAYAGAMI, EVEN IF YOU ARE HEADED FOR DESTRUCTION.

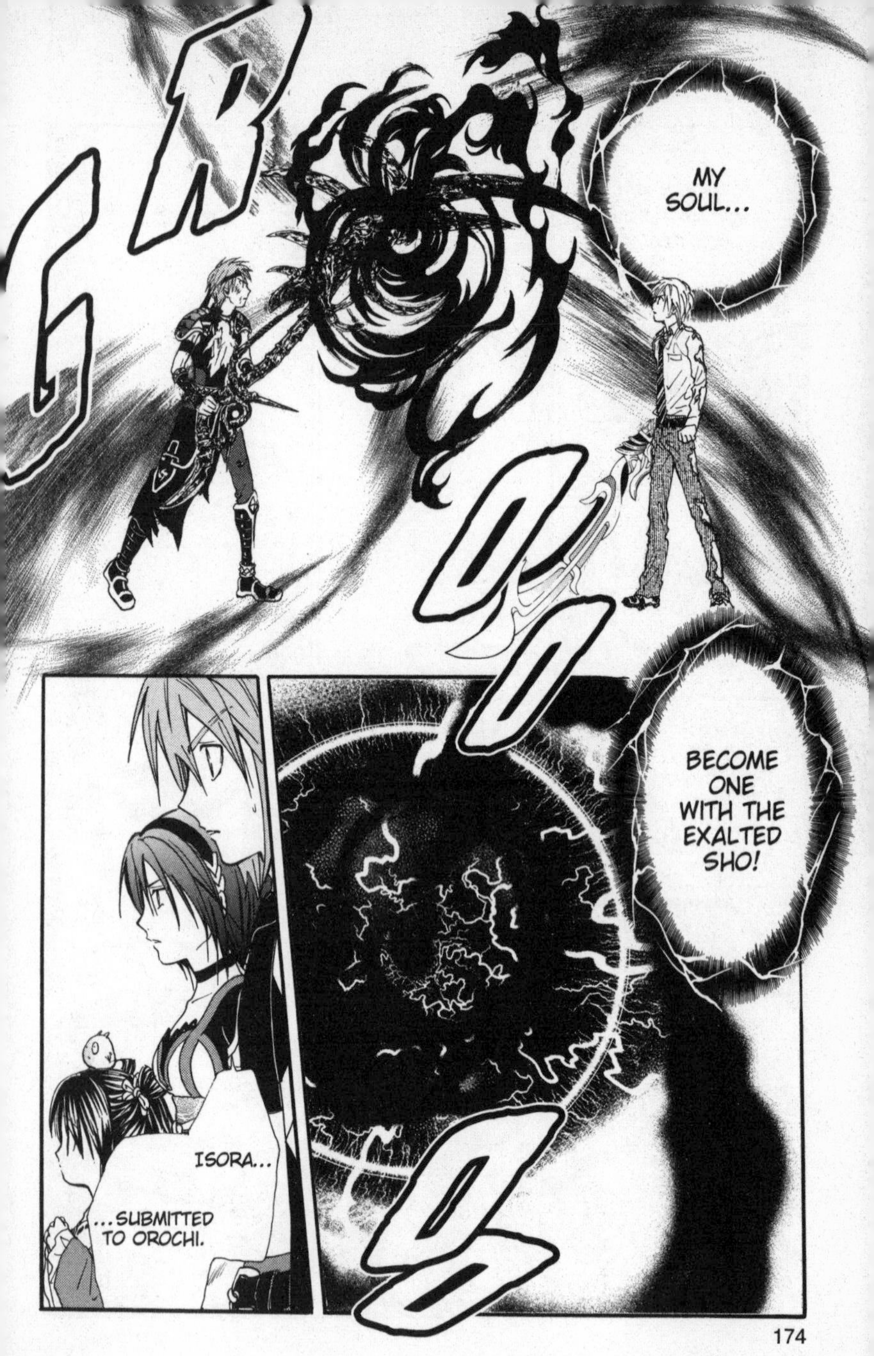
MY SOUL...
BECOME ONE WITH THE EXALTED SHO!
ISORA...
...SUBMITTED TO OROCHI.

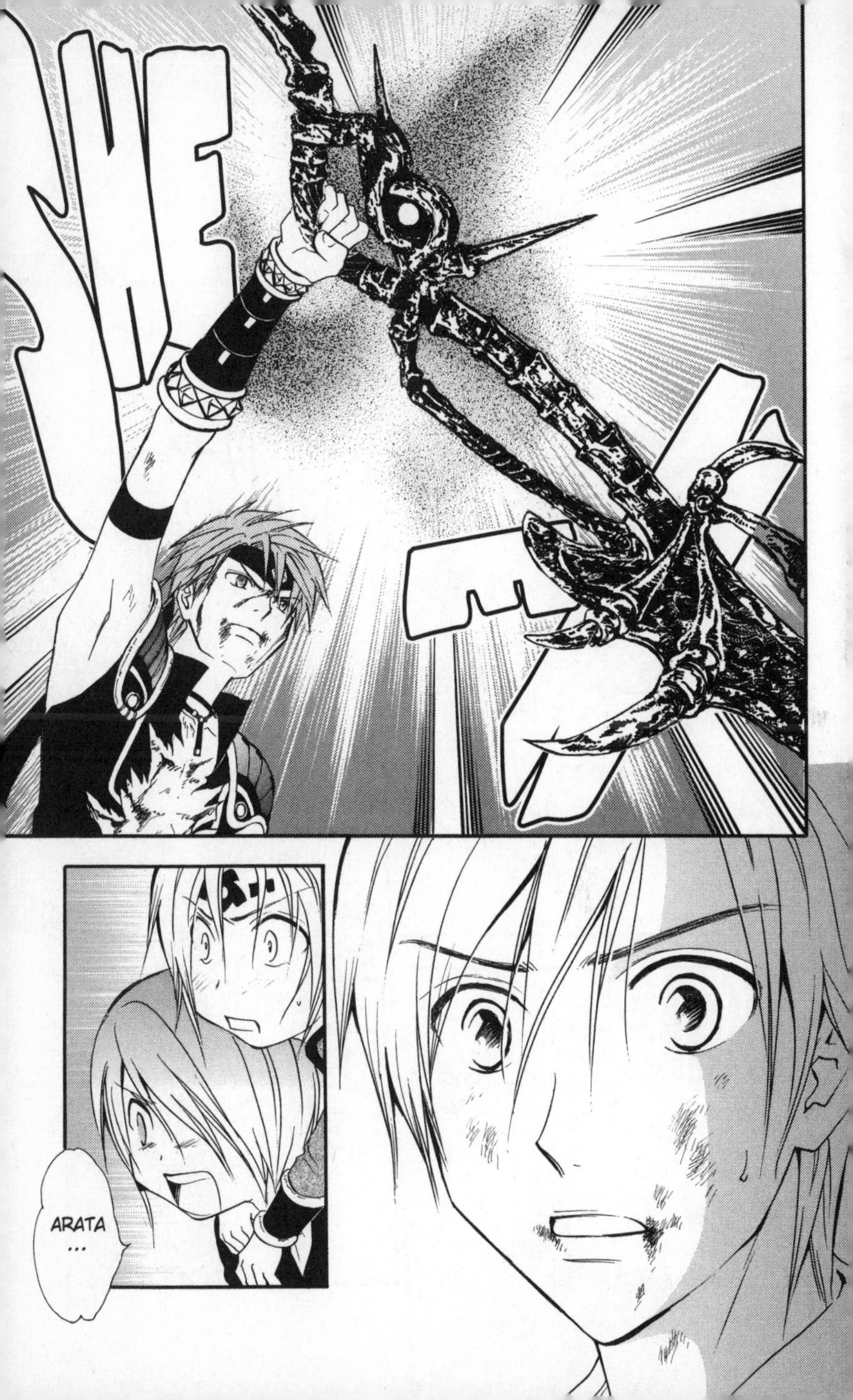
ARATA ...

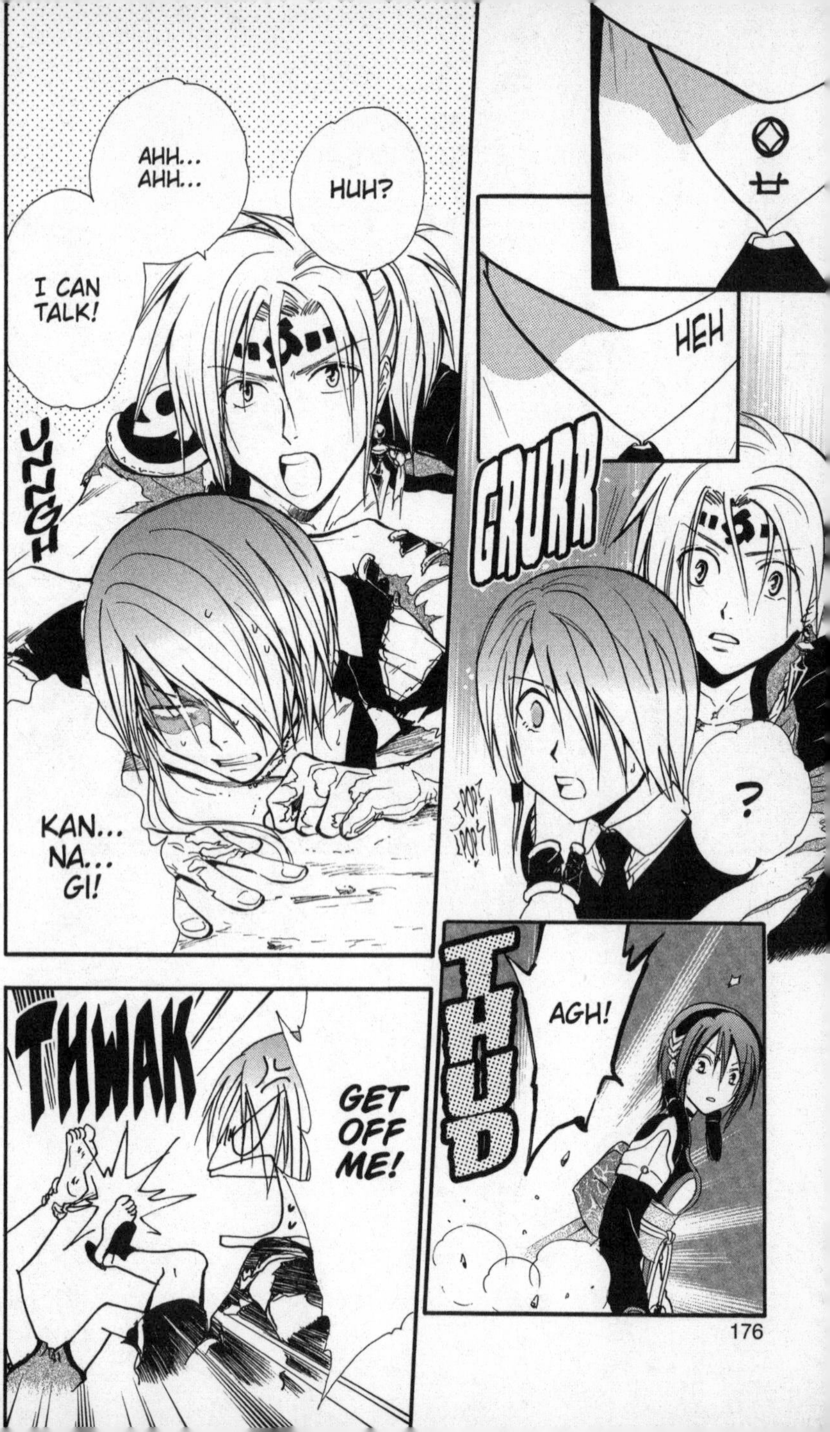
HEH
GRURR
POP POP POP
?
HUH?
AHH... AHH...
I CAN TALK!
UNNGH
KAN... NA... GI!
THUD
AGH!
THWAK
GET OFF ME!

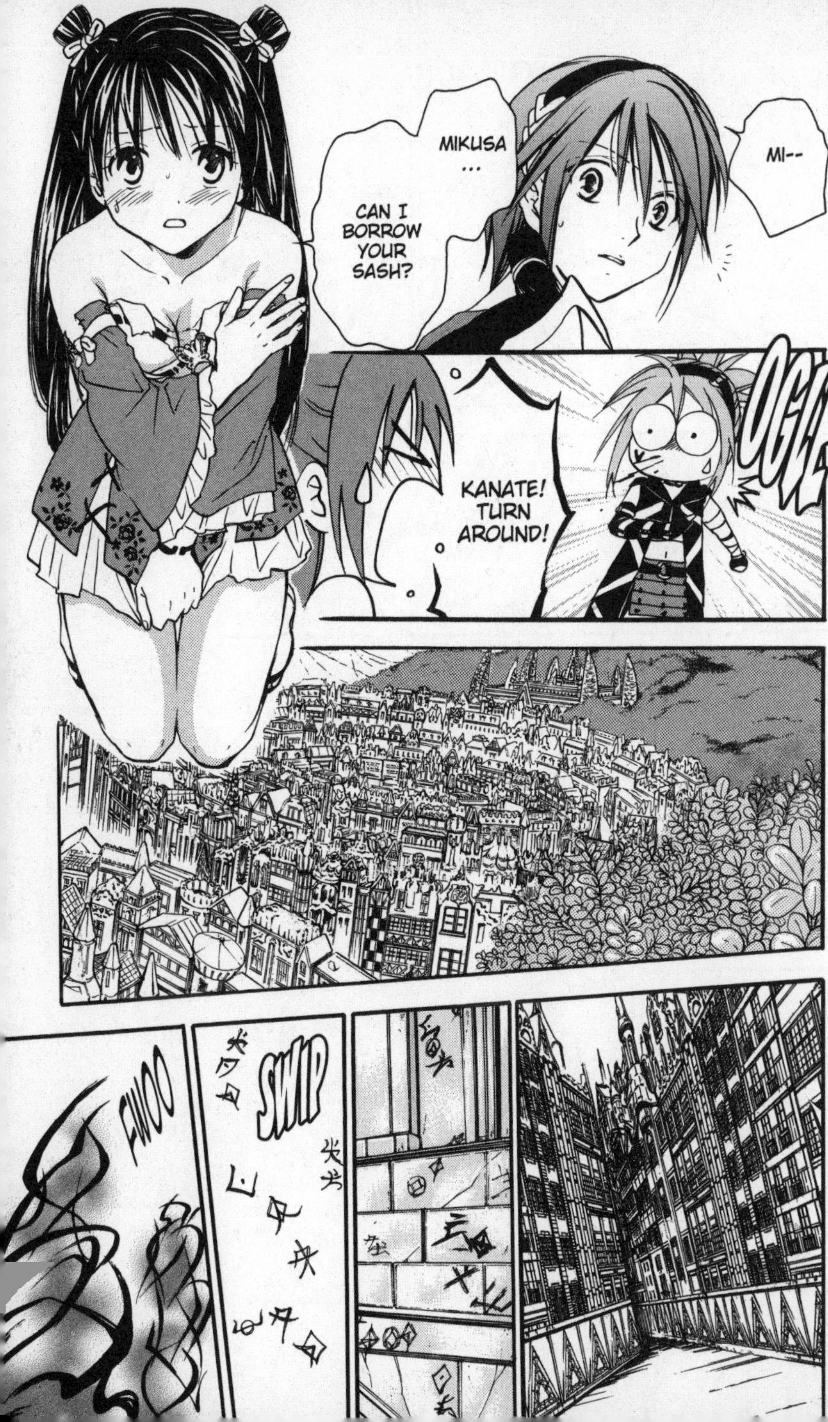
MI--
MIKUSA ...
CAN I BORROW YOUR SASH?
OGLE
KANATE! TURN AROUND!
SWIP
FWOO

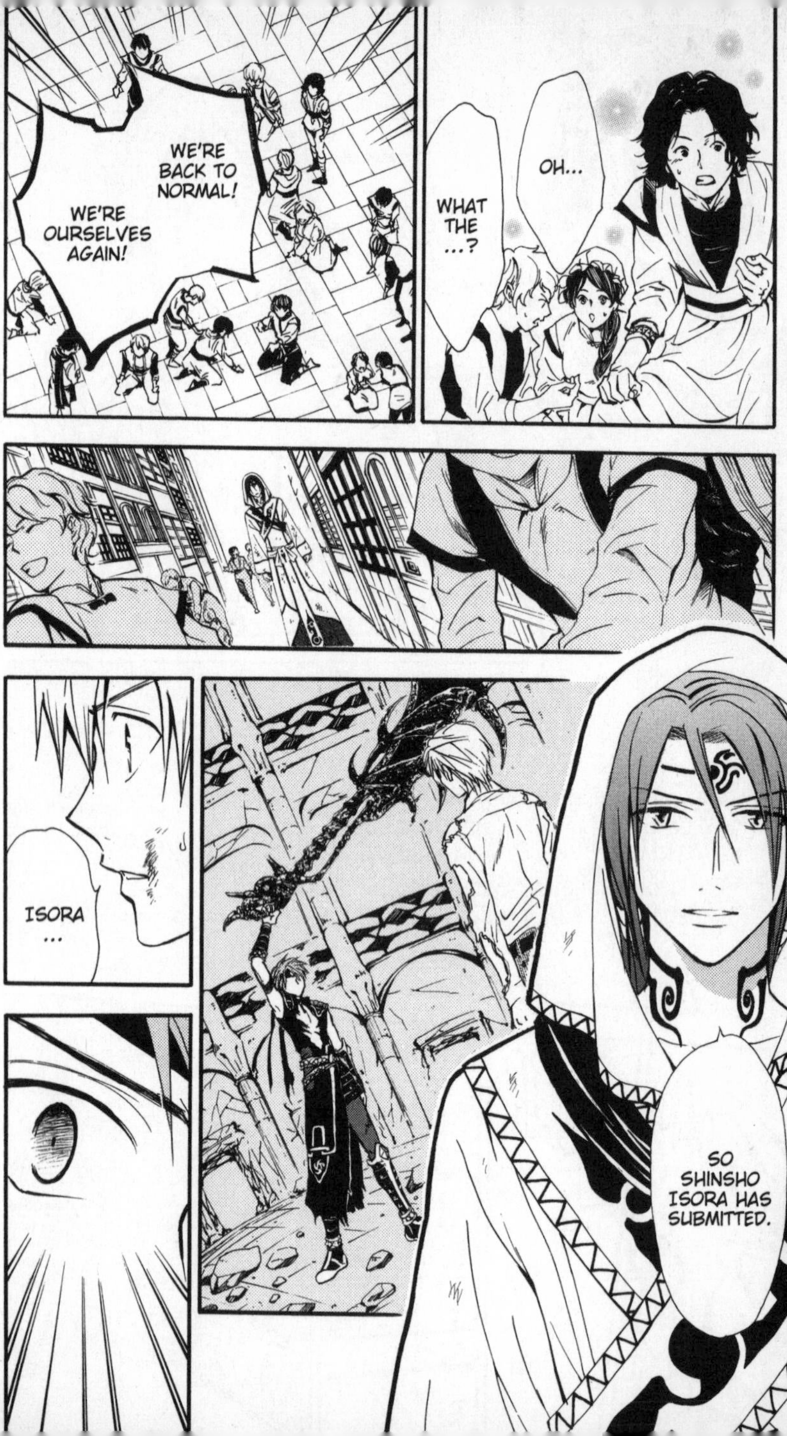
OH...
WHAT THE ...?
WE'RE BACK TO NORMAL!
WE'RE OURSELVES AGAIN!
SO SHINSHO ISORA HAS SUBMITTED.
ISORA ...

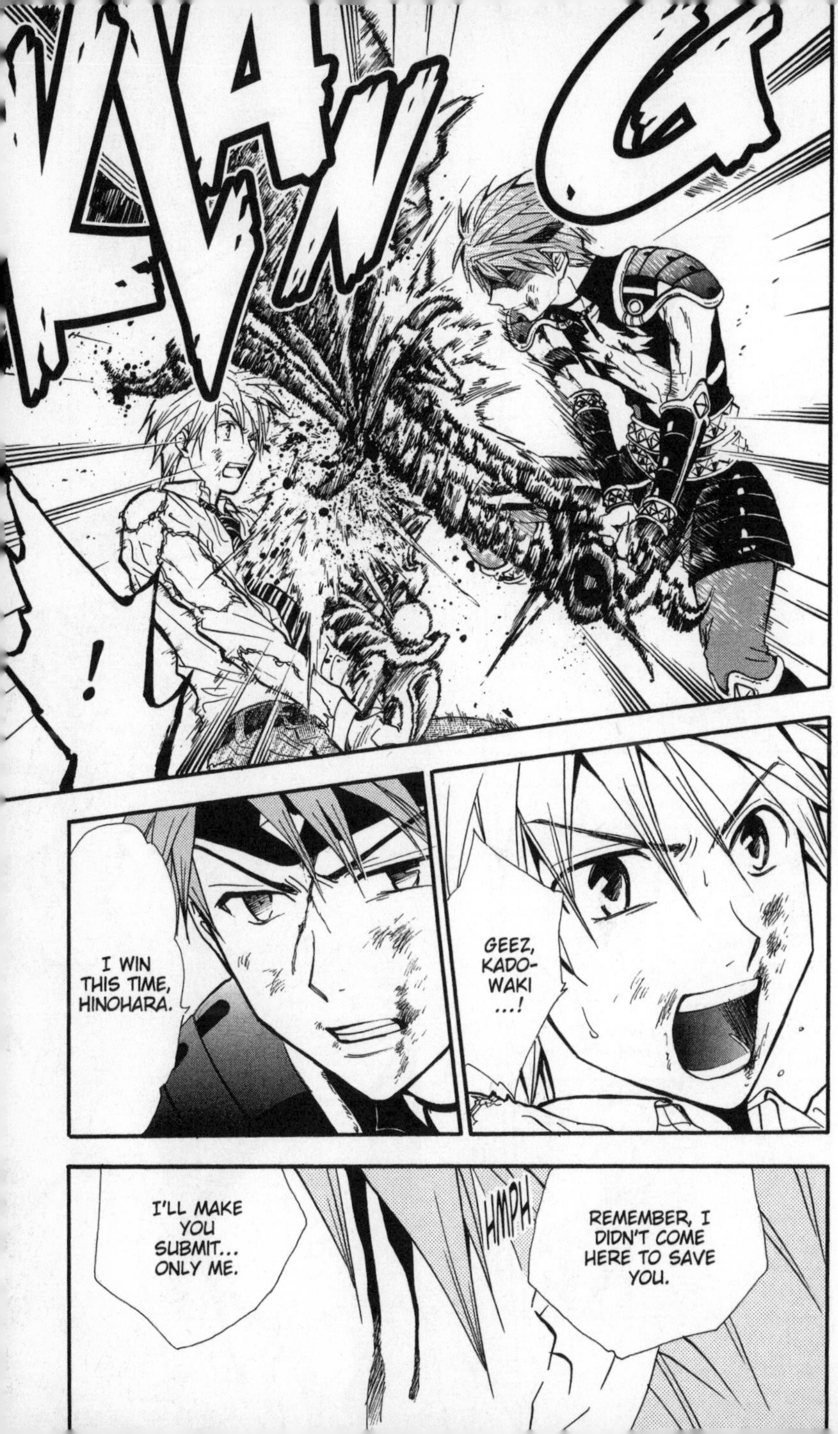
!
GEEZ, KADO-WAKI ...!
I WIN THIS TIME, HINOHARA.
REMEMBER, I DIDN'T COME HERE TO SAVE YOU.
HMPH
I'LL MAKE YOU SUBMIT... ONLY ME.

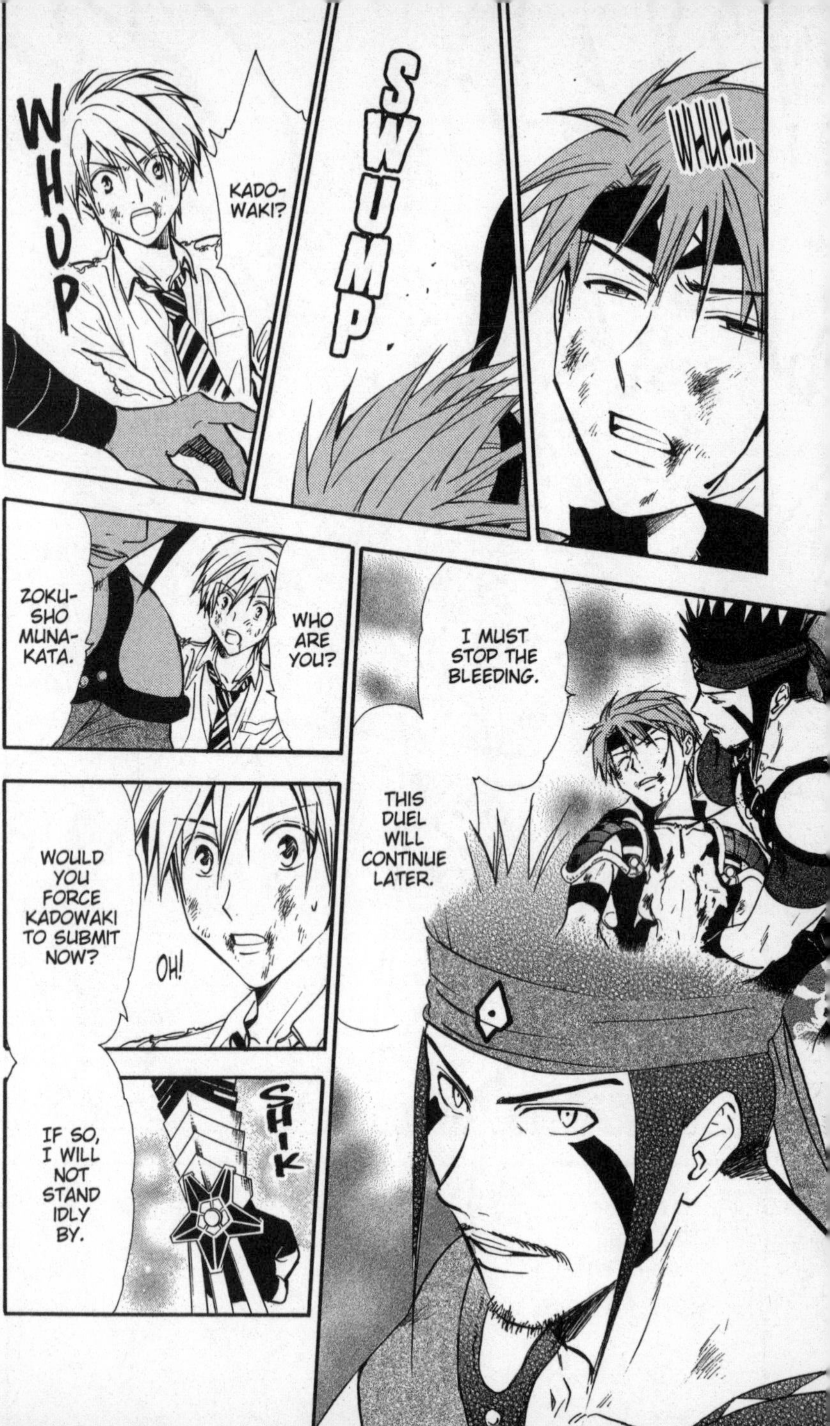
WHUH...
SWUMP
KADO-WAKI?
WHUP
I MUST STOP THE BLEEDING.
THIS DUEL WILL CONTINUE LATER.
WHO ARE YOU?
ZOKU-SHO MUNA-KATA.
WOULD YOU FORCE KADOWAKI TO SUBMIT NOW?
OH!
SHIK
IF SO, I WILL NOT STAND IDLY BY.

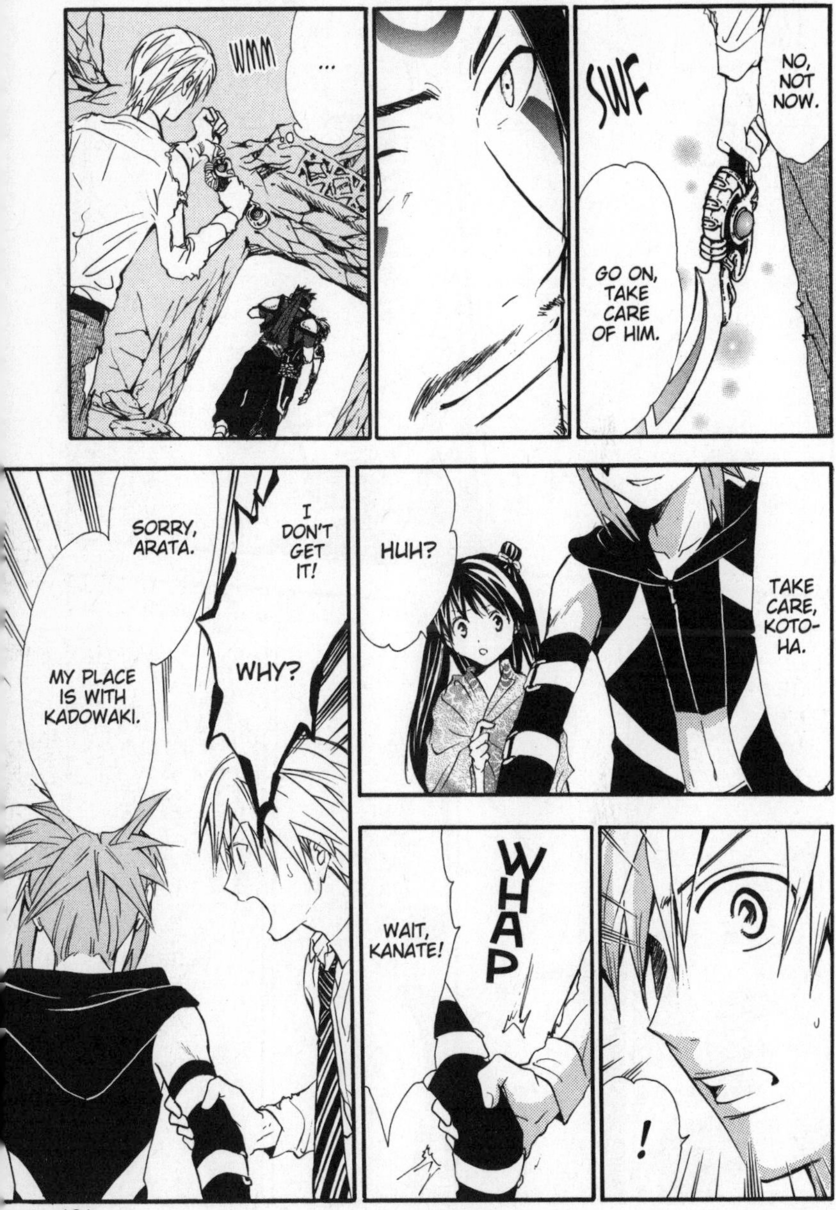
NO, NOT NOW.
SWF
GO ON, TAKE CARE OF HIM.
...
WMM
TAKE CARE, KOTO-HA.
HUH?
!
WHAP
WAIT, KANATE!
I DON'T GET IT!
SORRY, ARATA.
WHY?
MY PLACE IS WITH KADOWAKI.

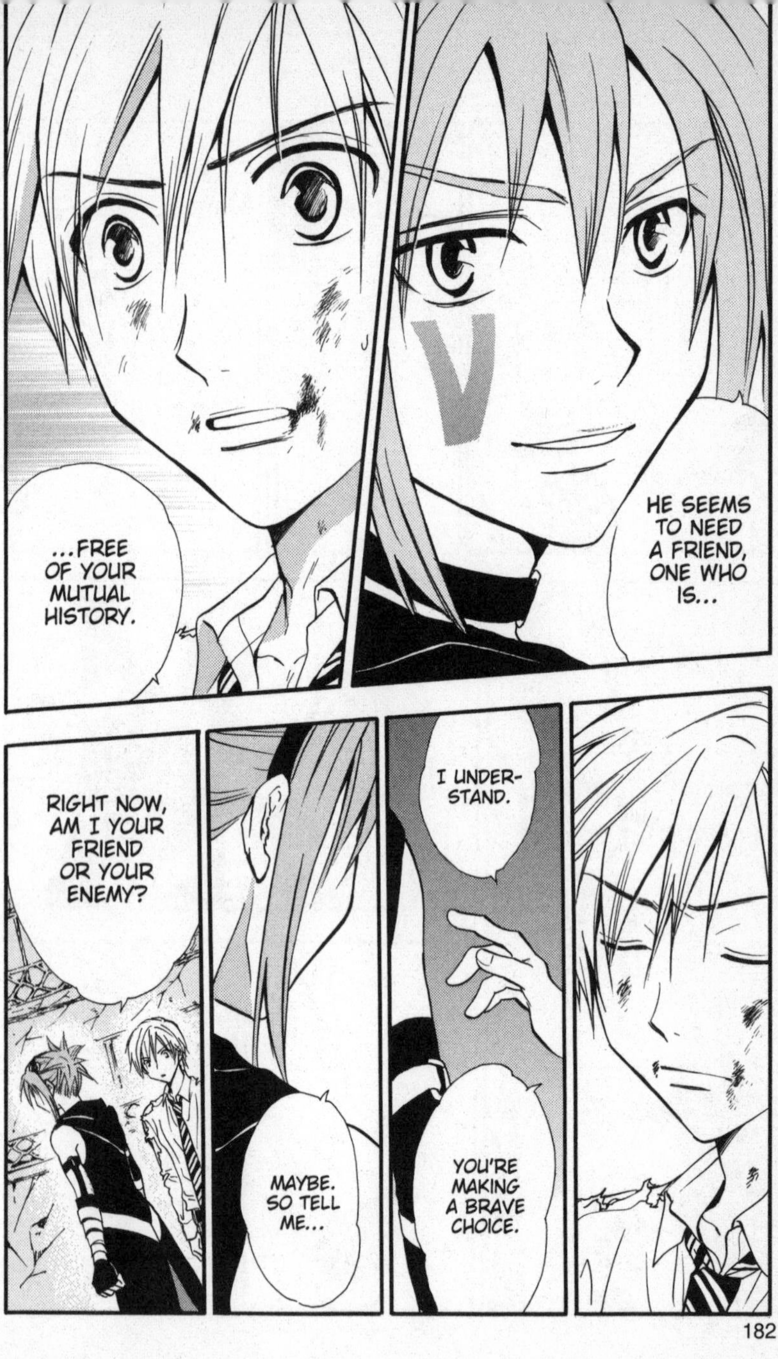
HE SEEMS TO NEED A FRIEND, ONE WHO IS...
...FREE OF YOUR MUTUAL HISTORY.
I UNDER-STAND.
YOU'RE MAKING A BRAVE CHOICE.
MAYBE. SO TELL ME...
RIGHT NOW, AM I YOUR FRIEND OR YOUR ENEMY?

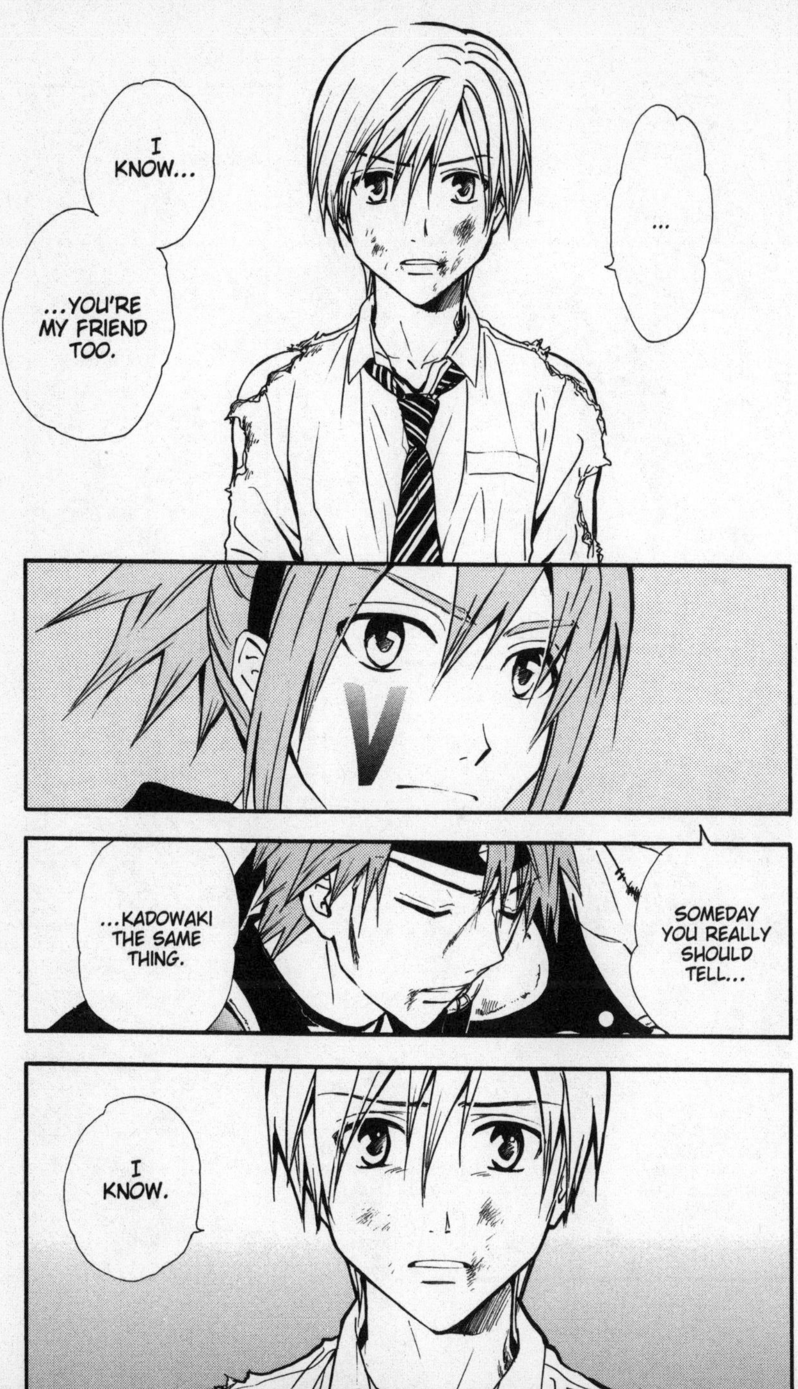
...
I KNOW...
...YOU'RE MY FRIEND TOO.
SOMEDAY YOU REALLY SHOULD TELL...
...KADOWAKI THE SAME THING.
I KNOW.

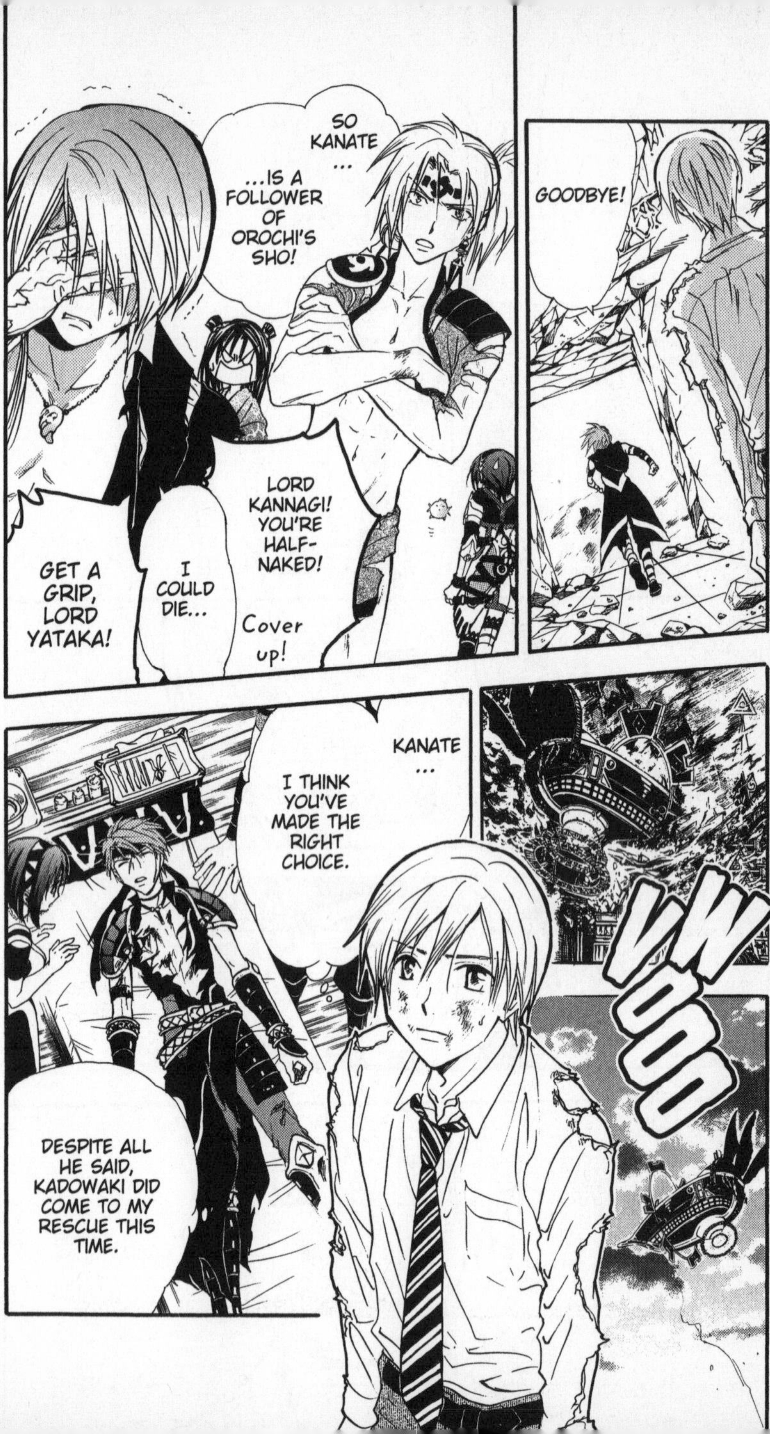
GOODBYE!
SO KANATE...
...IS A FOLLOWER OF OROCHI'S SHO!
LORD KANNAGI! YOU'RE HALF-NAKED!
Cover up!
I COULD DIE...
GET A GRIP, LORD YATAKA!
VWOOO
KANATE...
I THINK YOU'VE MADE THE RIGHT CHOICE.
DESPITE ALL HE SAID, KADOWAKI DID COME TO MY RESCUE THIS TIME.

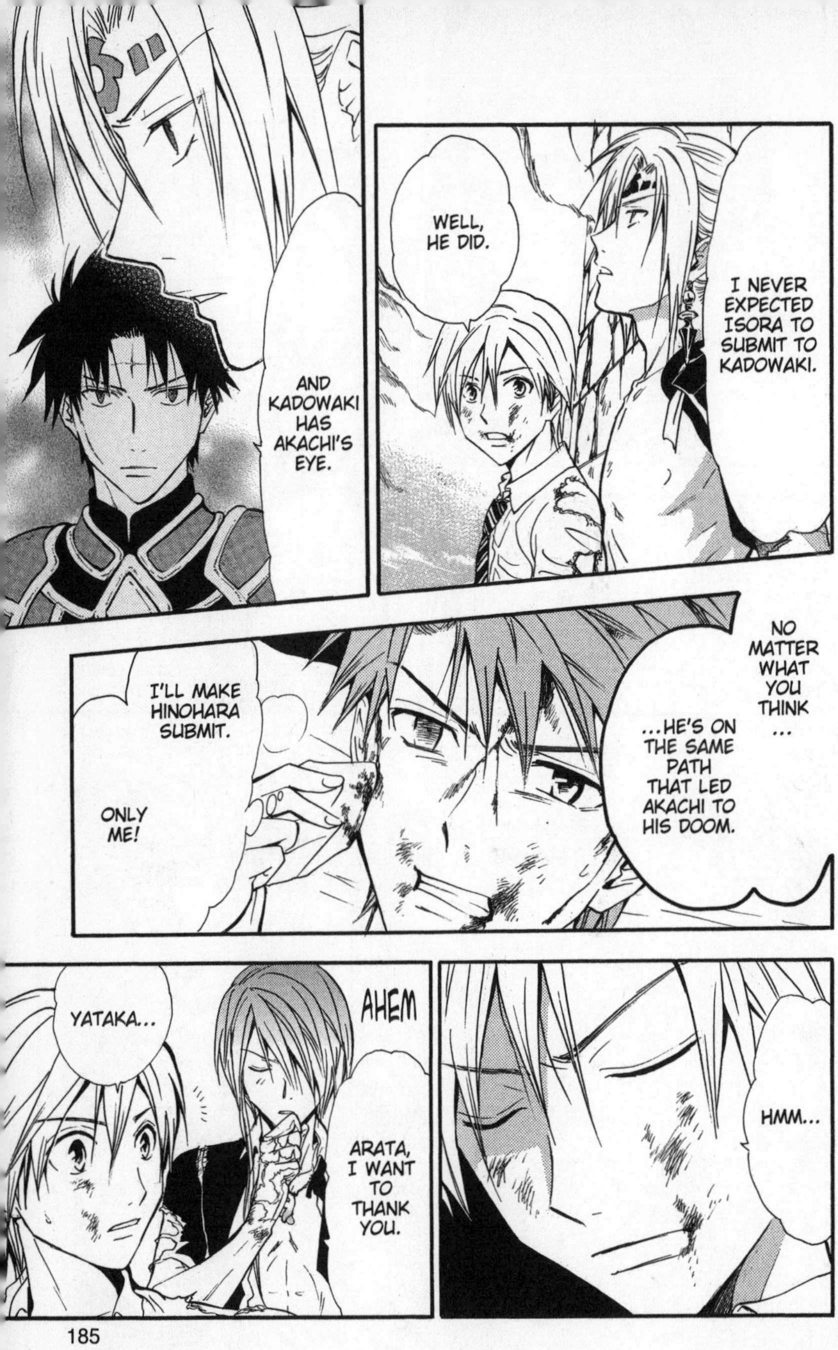

I NEVER EXPECTED ISORA TO SUBMIT TO KADOWAKI.
WELL, HE DID.
AND KADOWAKI HAS AKACHI'S EYE.
NO MATTER WHAT YOU THINK...
...HE'S ON THE SAME PATH THAT LED AKACHI TO HIS DOOM.
I'LL MAKE HINOHARA SUBMIT.
ONLY ME!
HMM...
AHEM
ARATA, I WANT TO THANK YOU.
YATAKA...

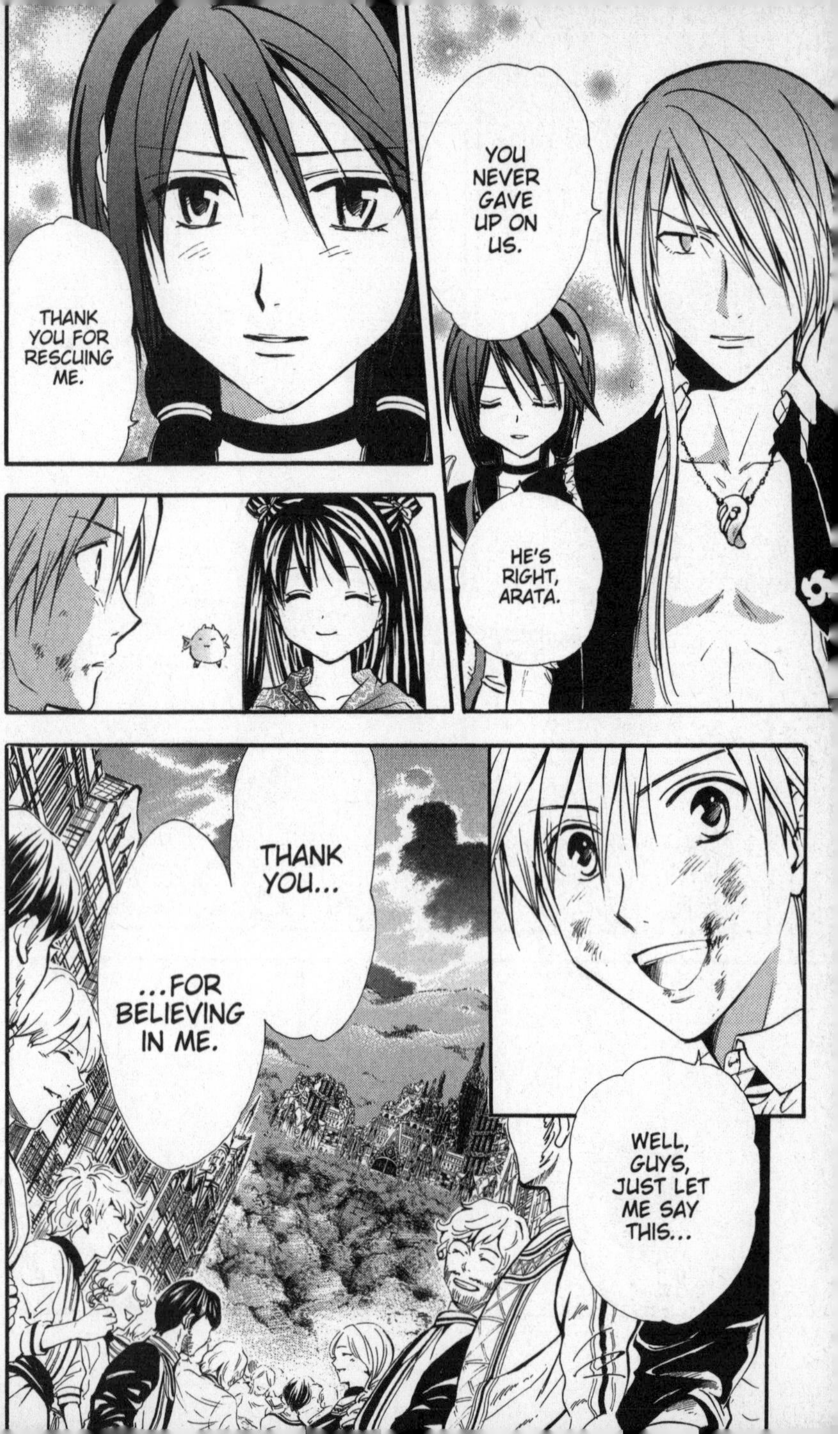
YOU NEVER GAVE UP ON US.
HE'S RIGHT, ARATA.
THANK YOU FOR RESCUING ME.
WELL, GUYS, JUST LET ME SAY THIS...
THANK YOU...
...FOR BELIEVING IN ME.

ARATA
KANGATARI

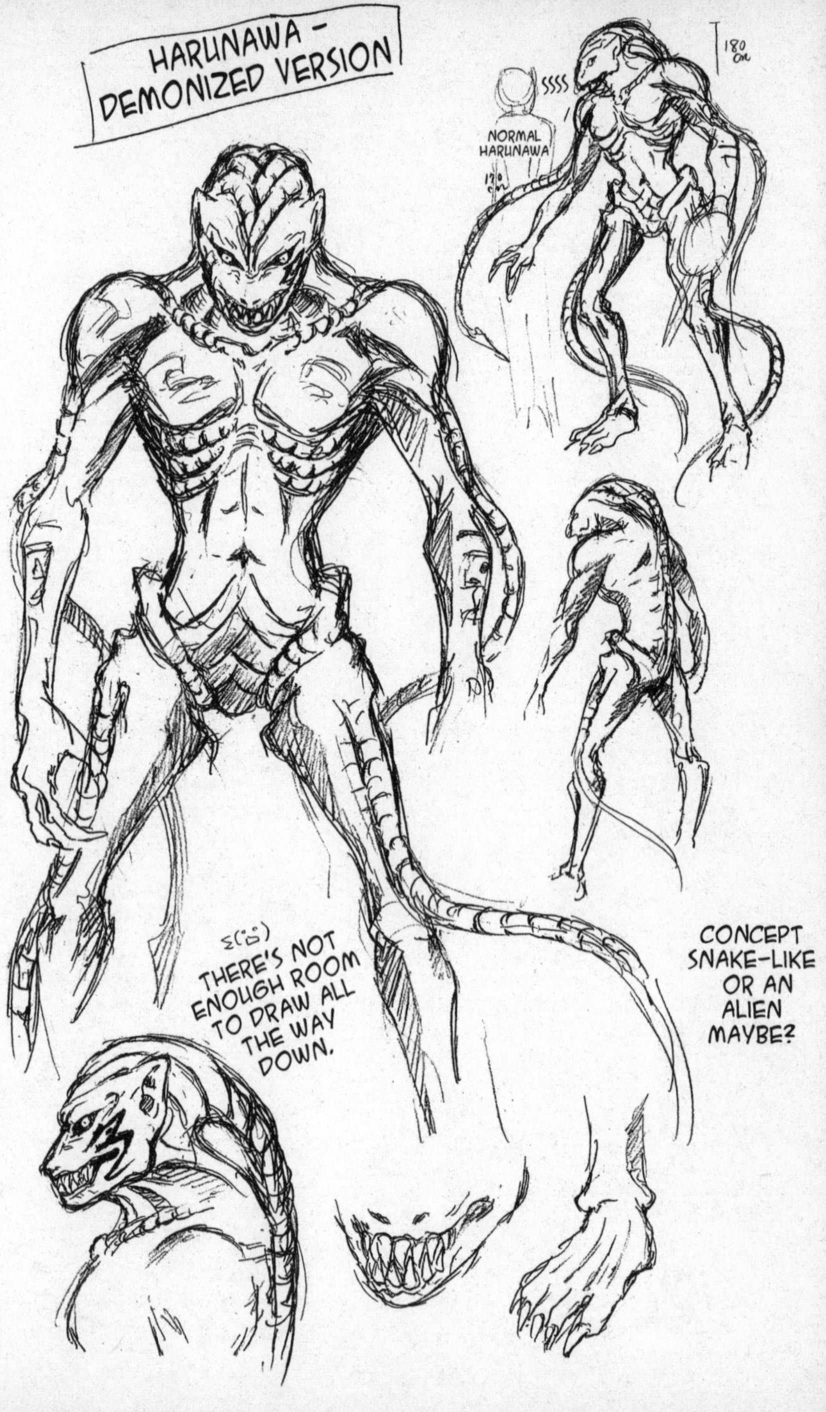
HARUNAWA - DEMONIZED VERSION
180 cm
SSSS
NORMAL HARUNAWA
170 cm
CONCEPT SNAKE-LIKE OR AN ALIEN MAYBE?
THERE'S NOT ENOUGH ROOM TO DRAW ALL THE WAY DOWN.

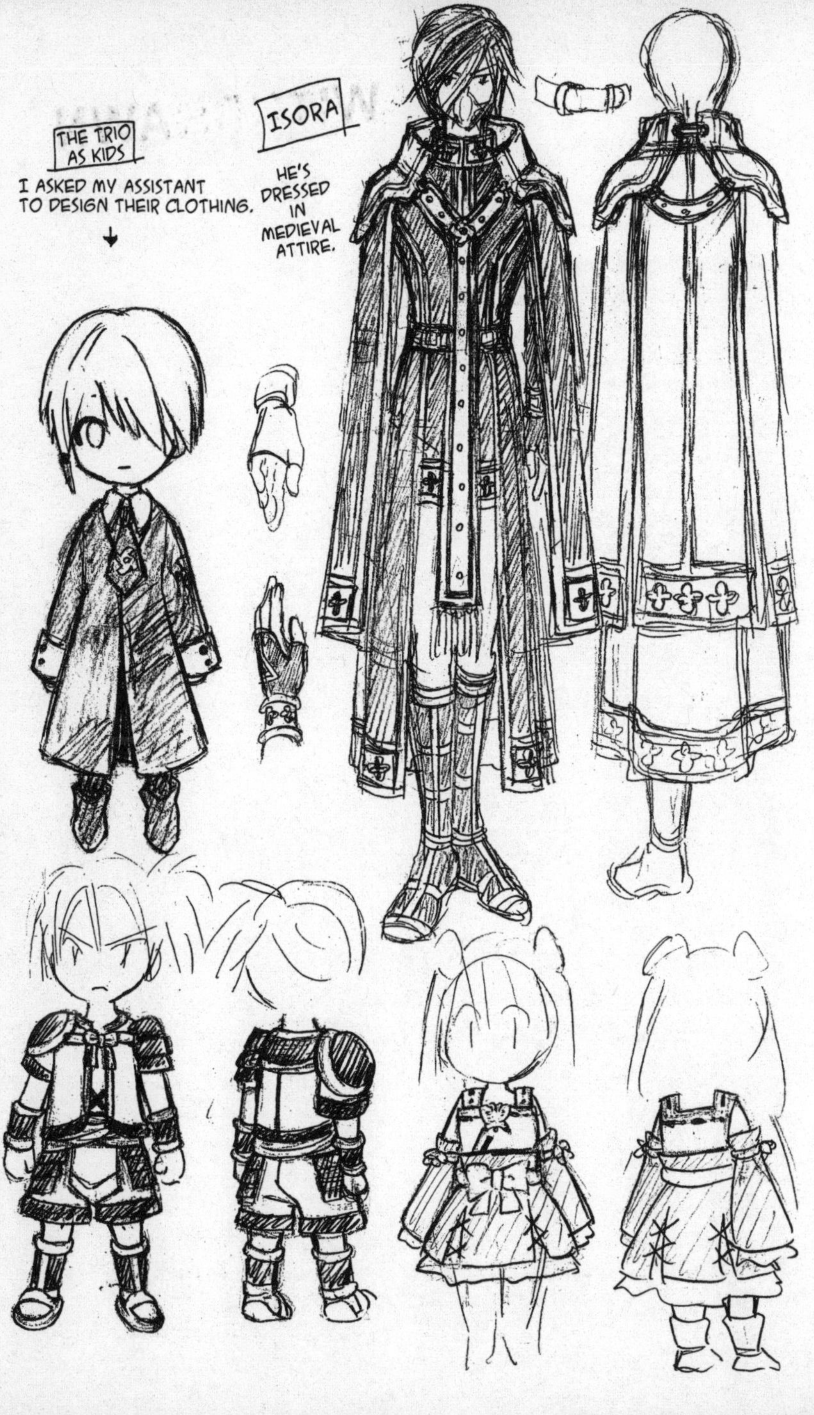
THE TRIO AS KIDS
I ASKED MY ASSISTANT TO DESIGN THEIR CLOTHING.
ISORA
HE'S DRESSED IN MEDIEVAL ATTIRE.

YA-GN
ARATA
432-2544

I love music.

I'm into all kinds of music, but I especially love trance-techno and dance music, folk songs, and symphonic music.

Music helps me with imagery during work, so I play music that matches that particular series.

Since I was a child, images suddenly pop up in my mind upon hearing different sounds. And I'm able to visualize scenes and events, so music is a critical tool in my creative process.

I've played several CDs over the years while working on *Arata* as well. But finally, with the anime series, musical compositions expressly for *Arata* were created! I have a data file and listen to them over and over again, and I never grow tired of listening to these wonderful tunes that give me great inspiration.

For those of you who watch the anime, please listen (be attuned?) to the background music too!

Of course, I highly recommend listening to the two theme songs as well. (^o^)

–YUU WATASE

AUTHOR BIO

Born March 5 in Osaka, Yuu Watase debuted in the *Shôjo Comic* manga anthology in 1989. She won the 43rd Shogakukan Manga Award with *Ceres: Celestial Legend*. One of her most famous works is *Fushigi Yûgi*, a series that has inspired the prequel *Fushi* in *Shôn*

FRANKLIN PARK PUBLIC LIBRARY
Franklin Park, Illinois
WITHDRAWN

ARATA: THE LEGEND

Volume 19
Shonen Sunday Edition

Story and Art by YUU WATASE

ARATA KANGATARI Vol. 19
by Yuu WATASE
© 2009 Yuu WATASE
All rights reserved.
Original Japanese edition published by SHOGAKUKAN.
English translation rights in the United States of America, Canada, the United Kingdom and Ireland arranged with SHOGAKUKAN.

English Adaptation: Lance Caselman
Translation: JN Productions
Touch-up Art & Lettering: Rina Mapa
Design: Veronica Casson
Editor: Gary Leach

The stories, characters and incidents mentioned in this publication are entirely fictional.

No portion of this book may be reproduced or transmitted in any form or by any means without written permission from the copyright holders.

Printed in the U.S.A.

Published by VIZ Media, LLC
P.O. Box 77010
San Francisco, CA 94107

10 9 8 7 6 5 4 3 2 1
First printing, September 2014

PARENTAL ADVISORY
ARATA: THE LEGEND is rated T for Teen and is recommended for ages 13 and up. This volume contains fantasy violence.
ratings.viz.com

www.viz.com

WWW.SHONENSUNDAY.COM

FRANKLIN PARK PUBLIC LIBRARY

31316 00432 2844

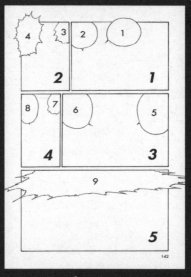

← Follow the action this way.

THIS IS THE LAST PAGE

Arata: The Legend has been printed in the original Japanese format in order to preserve the orientation of the original artwork.

Please turn it around and begin reading from right to left. Unlike English, Japanese is read right to left, so Japanese comics are read in reverse order from the way English comics are typically read. Have fun with it!